Let the People In

THE PUBLICATION OF THIS BOOK WAS SUPPORTED BY THE
GENEROSITY OF THE FOLLOWING PEOPLE IN HONOR OF
MARY MARGARET FARABEE, FOR HER INESTIMABLE
CONTRIBUTIONS TO THE UNIVERSITY OF TEXAS PRESS
AND TEXAS LETTERS.

Becky Beaver and John Duncan
Susan Block
Stephen L. Clark
Eleanor and Jim Cochran
Carolyn Curtis
Gabrielle de Kuyper Bekink
Jess Hay
Jane Hilfer
Joanna Hitchcock
Luci Baines Johnson
Cynthia Keever
Jeanne and Michael Klein
The Lebermann Foundation
Teresa Lozano Long

Alice Ann Lynch
Maline G. McCalla
The MFI Foundation
Brad and Michele Moore
Dr. Nona Niland
Rosalba Ojeda
Ellen and Ed Randall
Jean and Dan Rather
Edward Z. Safady
Jane Schweppe
Sander and Lottie Shapiro
Suzanne and Marc Winkelman
Mary and Howard Yancy

Let the People In

THE LIFE AND TIMES OF

UNIVERSITY OF TEXAS PRESS ❧ AUSTIN

Ann Richards

Jan Reid

RESEARCH ASSISTANCE BY SHAWN MORRIS

Requests for permission to reproduce material
from this work should be sent to:
    Permissions
    University of Texas Press
    P.O. Box 7819
    Austin, TX 78713-7819
    www.utexas.edu/utpress/about/bpermission.html

The paper used in this book meets the minimum requirements
of ANSI/NISO Z39.48-1992 (R1997) (Permanence of Paper). ∞

Design by Lindsay Starr

LIBRARY OF CONGRESS CATALOGING-IN-PUBLICATION DATA

Reid, Jan.
    Let the people in : the life and times of Ann Richards / by Jan Reid ;
research assistance by Shawn Morris. — 1st ed.
        p.   cm.
    Includes bibliographical references and index.
    ISBN 978-0-292-71964-4 (cloth : alk. paper)
1. Richards, Ann, 1933–2006. 2. Governors—Texas—Biography.
3. Politicians—United States—Biography. 4. Democratic Party (U.S.)—
Biography. 5. Texas—Politics and government—1951–   I. Title.
    F391.4.R53R45   2012
    976.4'063092—dc23
    [B]   2012016118

For Dorothy, Lila, and Isabelle

The future belongs to those who believe in the beauty of their dreams.
ELEANOR ROOSEVELT

Let me tell you, sisters, seeing dried eggs on a plate in the morning is a lot dirtier than anything I've had to deal with in politics.
ANN RICHARDS

Contents

Acknowledgments

THIS BOOK IS A BIOGRAPHY that contains a thread of memoir. I must thank Don Carleton, Evan Hocker, and their fellow archivists and librarians at the Dolph Briscoe Center for American History of the University of Texas in Austin; they have done a masterly job of sorting, arranging, and preserving a massive archive detailing Ann Richards's life and career. Joel Minor of the Wittliff Collections at Texas State University in San Marcos found and shared gems of the correspondence between Ann and Bud Shrake.

I am grateful to my wife, Dorothy Browne, who has been my best and most demanding source and reader, and Shawn Morris, my research assistant. The project drew thoughtful and enthusiastic input from the Richards family: David, Cecile, Dan, Clark, and Ellen. I am grateful to the late Bud Shrake and to Gary Cartwright for gentle and humorous pointers along the way.

I treasure memories of Ann, Bud, Phyllis Cartwright, Molly Ivins, Fletcher and Libby Boone, Lopez Smitham, Pat Cole, Bill Ramsey, Nancy Kohler, Wayne Oakes, Henry and Mary Holman, Marge Hershey, and Sam and Virginia Whitten.

Extremely helpful were professional associates of Ann, who include Mary Beth Rogers, Glenn Smith, Bill Cryer, George Shipley, Joe Holley, Joy Anderson, Marlene Saritzky, Rebecca Lightsey, Barbara Chapman, Richard Moya, Shelton Smith, Selden Hale, and Chris Hughes.

I am indebted to Suzanne Coleman, Monte Williams, Annette LoVoi, Margaret Justus, Ellen Halbert, John P. Moore, Chuck Bailey, Andy Sansom, Bob Beaudine, Jim Henson, Doug Zabel, Ronnie Earle, Carlton Carl, Harold Cook,

xiv   Joaquin Jackson, Dick DeGuerin, John Massey, John Keel, Nadine Eckhardt, Kaye Northcott, Jeanne Goka, Bill Head, Mark Strama, Gary and Tam Cartwright, Michael and Sue Sharlot, Doatsy Shrake, Ben Shrake, Alan Shrake, Jody Gent, Eddie Wilson, Bill and Sally Wittliff, Mark McKinnon, Jerry Jeff and Susan Walker, Ave Bonar, Wayne Slater, and Tad Hershorn. Some may not know how they helped, but they did. I learned much from the work of my fellow journalists and researchers Jan Jarboe Russell, Lou Dubose, Dave McNeely, Paul Burka, Mimi Swartz, R. G. Ratcliffe, Robert Draper, Skip Hollandsworth, and Brant Bingamon.

I thank Garry Mauro, John Hall, Richard Raymond, Bob Krueger, Peggy Garner, Judith Zaffirini, Bob Rosenbaum, Jim Phillips, Elliott Naishtat, Kirk Watson, David Braun, Christopher Cook, and Bill Young for the friendships and the achievements shared in Texas politics and government over the past forty years; Bill Broyles, Greg Curtis, Evan Smith, and Jake Silverstein, my editors at *Texas Monthly*; Clayton McClure Brooks, the anthology editor who planted one of the essential seeds; my friend and agent David McCormick; and Dave Hamrick, Allison Faust, Lynne Chapman, Lindsay Starr, Theresa May, Joanna Hitchcock, William Bishel, Casey Kittrell, and other friends and colleagues at the University of Texas Press, as well as freelance editor Kip Keller and fact checker Kate Hull.

Glimpses

THE FIRST TIME I SAW Ann Richards, she was playing gonzo bridge, as her Austin pals called their game, in the home of Fletcher and Libby Boone. The party was on a Sunday night in the late fall of 1980 or early winter of 1981. With children whooping in the bedrooms, foursomes of cardplayers going at each other across tables that filled up the living room, and much strong drink poured in the kitchen, I was parked on a sofa with no interest in learning to play bridge. I was there because I had begun to court Dorothy Browne, a friend of Ann who worked for the Texas chapter of the American Civil Liberties Union. (She later served as a senior aide on Ann's staff at the state treasury and in the governor's office. I was an adviser on environmental policy during Ann's 1990 race for governor, and during her administration, I wrote speeches and research papers for John Hall, her chief appointee in that realm. Full disclosure, or at least half the glass.)

I had been living out in the country fifty miles from Austin during the years when Ann emerged in Austin politics and government. I must have heard of her, but little more than that. The crowd in the Boones' house that night was full of characters who were hard to overshadow, but Ann filled up the room. She was forty-seven then. Despite premature lines in her face and throat, and a hairstyle that harked back to a time when "permanent" was used as a noun—some friends jokingly called the coiffure Hi Yo Silver—she was sexy as all get-out. Believe it; she sure did. Ann liked men, and when she turned on the charm, she was all blue eyes and dimples. As I watched her that night, she cocked an eyebrow at the dubious prospects of a hand she had been dealt, leaned back in her chair, and drawled

Ann looks over the crowd on the day of her inauguration as Texas governor, January 1991.

loudly, "I've just got to tell you all about *Club*. We have such a good time at Club. We just talk and talk. And when we get to the end, we vote on what'll be our next meeting's topic of discussion. I think I'm going to propose *vaginal itch*."

It was a while before I fully understood that joke. The bawdy and rowdy feminist was one of the familiar sides of Ann, but something else underlay her wisecrack about the stuffiness and pretensions of Texas social clubs. In a crowd that was well juiced and thought nothing of it, she was talking about the newness and rawness of her commitment to the twelve steps of Alcoholics Anonymous. A few Sundays earlier, her husband, David, her two oldest children, and nine of her closest friends had with great pain of their own reduced her to sobs in the ordeal of intervention. The ambush occurred in the home of her friends and neighbors Mike and Sue Sharlot. Mike was a law school professor, and Sue was then an administrative nurse who later got her own law degree. Sue called and made up some story about a parent who had fallen ill, and Ann rushed over to their house. Her two younger kids were away in school, and on seeing everyone, she responded with the instinctive fright of a mother: "Are the children all right?"

Hours later, she was on a plane to the St. Mary's Chemical Dependency Services facility at the Riverside Medical Center in Minneapolis. She said later that she had tried to fight off their pleas and their harsh testimony of what she was doing to herself, and to them. "I was terrified," she recalled in her subsequent memoir, *Straight from the Heart*. "I was a public person, there was no way I could survive it."

She feared that when she came home, she would have nothing in common with her friends. She feared that if she quit drinking, she would lose her gift for being funny.

———

THAT FALL SHE WAS REELECTED without opposition to the Travis County commissioner's court in Austin, and her monthlong absence from work never came up in the press. But her twenty-eight-year marriage to David had been strained for some time, and two months after she came back from Minnesota, he moved out. They made two attempts to reconcile, but by 1983 the parting of their ways was permanent. Ann said that accepting the divorce was the most difficult thing she had ever done. Dorothy Browne and I were married on Fletcher and Libby Boone's lawn in West Lake Hills on the Fourth of July 1982. We invited Ann, who was then waging a campaign for state treasurer, to join us that beautiful night. She sent us a nice gift, and I remember her note saying that she was having trouble with weddings right then. Dorothy recalled it as saying that "it would be like touching a warm burn."

Ann was wounded in spirit those first months I came to know her. By standards she held dear—as a wife, as a mother, as an elected official, as a responsible person—she had reason to feel like crawling under a rock. But that was not her way of doing things. With her wisecracks at that bridge party, she had been making a statement that she was not going to give up friendships and rituals that enriched her life. And those months at the start of the 1980s were the very time when she negotiated a leap upward in politics that would make her grin, drawl, and grit known and celebrated throughout the world.

Ann was one of those characters who seem to pop up everywhere all the time. When Ann lived in Dallas, she and her family were far too close for comfort to the John F. Kennedy assassination. A decade later, after moving to Austin, Ann and David became central figures in the most uproarious and bohemian years in the capital's history—anti–Vietnam War protests, a madcap bunch called Mad Dog, Inc., the coming of Willie Nelson, and the famous concert hall, Armadillo World Headquarters. In 1972, Ann managed the first state legislative race of Sarah Weddington, the young attorney who was preparing to deliver the winning Supreme Court arguments in *Roe v. Wade*, the landmark ruling that became the political and philosophical mainstay of American feminism. In her political coming-of-age, Ann experienced unpleasant face-to-face encounters with Lyndon Johnson and Jimmy Carter in the days of their overweening power. In 1982, taking advantage of a corruption scandal, she was elected state treasurer and became the first woman elected to statewide office in Texas in fifty years. Then came the opportunity that made her a sensation.

Most of the 1988 presidential race between Michael Dukakis and George Herbert Walker Bush has faded into obscurity. That race proved to be the most triumphant time in the elder George Bush's life. He emerged from the long shadow of Ronald Reagan, who had routed him in his first race for the presidency and then had largely ignored him during his eight years as vice president. Bush's landslide victory over the Massachusetts governor was a stinging rebuke of the Democrats. But at the start of the race, Dukakis led in many polls, and a telephone call initiated by his campaign changed Ann Richards's life. Paul Kirk, the chairman of the Democratic Party, tracked her down in the Austin airport one day and asked her to make the keynote speech at that summer's national convention in Atlanta. "I was standing there on the linoleum at a pay phone in the airport, and I was floored," she recalled in her book. "'You're kidding.'"

One of Ann's erstwhile allies in Texas Democratic politics, Attorney General Jim Mattox, responded with a huffy call to Kirk and bellowed that this wrong-headed scheme would be a grievous insult to his 1990 race for governor. But Ann was fifty-four when her call to the big time came; she was no unseasoned rookie. She ignored Mattox and sought advice from Mario Cuomo; Barbara Jordan; Liz Carpenter, Lady Bird Johnson's press secretary; and Ted Sorensen, JFK's famous speechwriter. Cuomo told her, "You have no idea how much your life is about to change."

Bob Strauss, a native of Texas, an associate of Lyndon Johnson, and a former chairman of the Democratic Party, recommended a veteran speechwriter in Washington, D.C. The writer faxed drafts to her tiny political office in Austin. Ann felt the speech was turning into a mishmash that sounded nothing like her. At the last moment, a computer crash destroyed the Washington speechwriter's files and morale. Ann and her party left for the convention in Atlanta with no speech. In her hotel suite, she went to work with a group of women who included the speechwriter she trusted to anticipate her thoughts and capture her voice. Suzanne Coleman was an affable former lecturer in political science at the University of Texas; for nearly twenty years, she had to be the most overworked speechwriter in the country, and though she was not widely known because Ann did not achieve national office, she was one of her generation's best.

The day of the speech, Walter Cronkite left a message at the hotel and asked Ann to come by and see him in the convention hall if she had time. The veteran CBS newsman had attended Houston public schools and the University of Texas; Ann had known him for years. She looked him up that afternoon and told him, "Walter, I want you to be prepared for what kind of speech you're going to hear from me tonight." Cronkite gave her a quizzical look. "I'm going to talk Texas," she announced.

With a snort of laughter he replied, "Oh. Well, that's great."

That night Ann wore a stunning blue dress—the color that is television's favorite—with her silver hair swept up and back. She began by criticizing her party. "Twelve years ago Barbara Jordan, another Texas woman, made the keynote address to this convention, and two women in a hundred sixty years is about par for the course. But if you give us a chance, we can perform. After all, Ginger Rogers did everything that Fred Astaire did. She just did it backward and in high heels!"

Ann and her team had anticipated that about fifteen lines in the speech would draw applause or laughter. She was interrupted more than forty times. Once during the applause she reached for her glass of water and realized her hand was shaking so badly that she very carefully set it back down. "She looked so small out there," recalled her son Dan, who sat with the family in the wings.

But viewers perceived none of Ann's anxiety. Her timing was exquisite, the material drawn from a populist upbringing that put her out in the world as a junior high schoolteacher when she was barely out of her teens. She was not impressed by class distinctions born of Connecticut wealth and privilege. "Poor George," she said, throwing her arms wide with a delighted grin, "he can't help it—he was born with a *silver foot* in his mouth." Though the *New York Times* and others quickly noted that the taunt was not original, Ann's delivery of that line made her famous.

Toward the end, she softened the tone and reflected on the promise and the challenges of this nation, which had come to mind while she was playing a game of ball on "a Baptist pallet" with her "nearly perfect grandchild, Lily." (She had one grandchild at the time, the daughter of Cecile.) "I spread that Baptist pallet out on the floor," she described the moment, "and Lily and I roll a ball back and forth." It was her metaphor of a politics that spanned generations and lived up to its obligation to make lives better.

Most political keynote speeches, and the speakers who deliver them, are forgotten in a few weeks or months. But now and then a few leave an aura of eloquence, reason, and passion that lingers on in the theater of democracy. When Ann walked offstage, she asked Wayne Slater, a reporter for the *Dallas Morning News*, "How'd I do?" He laughed and wondered whether she was serious. She had gone out into those lights a national unknown and come off a television superstar.

For several years, Ann had been a friend of the accomplished novelist, journalist, screenwriter, and dramatist Edwin "Bud" Shrake. After her divorce from David, Bud became the second great love of her life. The day after her speech, the avalanche of praise included a letter faxed from Bud.

> Dear Ann:
> Your speech was wonderful and your delivery was magnificent, and vice versa. You had me laughing, you had me crying. In short, you really got to me, kid.
> I am so proud of you it makes my eyes run. Ever since you caught me under your pool table in Dallas (or was it ping pong?) I've known you are an incredible person. Now the whole world knows it.

[He told her about a call he'd received from his literary agent in New York.]
She said, after much gushing of praise for your speech, "David Letterman's
people will be calling you today to see if they can get Ann on their show." This
is show biz thinking—call this one to get that one. . . .

You looked so beautiful on TV in your blue dress. The Belle of the Ball, for
sure. I saw one shot of Mattox, looking like a little boy trying to be brave in the
dentist's waiting room.

You realize what a huge leap you just took? A Hollywood guy might call it
"jumping over the shit."

Love, Bud

After that fall's election, Ann sent President Bush a telegram wishing him "the
very best" in his administration. He responded some days later with a note and a
small silver pendant in the shape of a foot. He wrote, "You've probably received a
hundred of these 'feet' but I wanted you to have this one from me—a peace offering." The gestures inferred that rough-and-tumble politics were just part of the
process and were all in good fun, as long as politicians kept their bearings and
remembered their purpose. But in the last debate with Dukakis, Bush had said, "I
don't want to be like the kid in the schoolyard—'he started it.'" Then he went on
to be just that kid in the schoolyard, arguing that the "ugly" and "nasty" tone of
the race had been set at the Democratic National Convention. Bush and his family were thoroughly annoyed by the impudence of that woman, and as time went
by, she made more sport of ridiculing the president. In tongue-lashing the elder
George Bush, Ann lit the fuse of a grudge match that may have altered the course
of American history.

Tiresome a throwback as televised political conventions seem today, huge numbers of Americans still watch them every four years, and like Barack Obama and
Sarah Palin in more recent memory, Ann Richards demonstrated that a powerful
and personality-enriched speech at either a Democratic or a Republican national
convention can be a politician's fastest climb up ambition's ladder. Late in life as
Ann got started in politics, and with the kind of base she possessed, it is almost
inconceivable that she could have gotten elected governor of Texas in 1990 or any
other year if she had not been handed that incredibly lucky break in 1988. Boosted
into contention by her celebrity and wit, she overcame long odds and brutal campaigns against two veteran Democrats and a rich, colorful Republican to become

the first ardent feminist elected to high office in this country. Hillary Clinton was her protégée, even when she was the nation's First Lady and then a U.S. senator from New York. Some of the cracks in the glass ceiling were put there by Ann.

The question remains, though—what did she accomplish with her high office? In a state that continued to be saddled with a sternly limited governmental structure devised when the South was just emerging from the bruising experience of the Civil War and Reconstruction, she also had to contend with the fact that national politics and changing demographics had left her swimming for her life as a liberal Democrat in an ocean of conservative Republicans. In a failed presidential campaign, Texas's Republican senator Phil Gramm once boasted that the best thing a politician can have is money. It helps, of course, and yet he was proved quite wrong: the biggest advantage a politician can have is that people *like* you.

Ann knew she had that going for her, and she shrewdly used it to her advantage. She knew that a governor or president elected with a slim majority or less had better push an agenda hard at the start of the term, before the sheer gravity of governing starts its ineluctable pull. Her greatest accomplishment was to bring to positions of responsibility and power in Texas the women, African Americans, Latinos, Asian Americans, gay men, lesbians, and disabled persons who had been so long denied. Because of that, the state government centered in Austin will never be the same. Whatever party wins the elections and controls the appointed boards that keep the bureaucratic agencies and institutions of higher education running, democracy in Texas is better because she won.

And yet like so many politicians who come into office promising reform and change, she found herself stymied and frustrated. As a philosophical leftist, she had to try to establish a footing at the center, and that was not so easy and comfortable as raising hell on the outside of power. Legislative majorities and courts enforcing lawsuits lost by the state forced her into unseemly compromises. She advanced some of the most progressive penal programs the country had ever seen, and yet she oversaw a massive prison buildup and did nothing to steer Texas away from being the nation's most prolific executioner.

Her ideology constrained her more than once, with damaging political results. Her rigid insistence on support for abortion rights as a litmus test for appointments helped cost her party a chance to retain one of its seats in the U.S. Senate—one that twenty years later appears lost for good. Like many politicians, she was loyal to a fault, sidling up to powerful men who acted as if they were friends and then tried to gut her the first chance they got. The feminist heroine was confounded by the fear, resentment, and obstacle of white males. On one matter of principle—the need to balance the Second Amendment and sporting and other legitimate uses of firearms against a paranoid and murderous rage of gunfire in the streets—she dug in her heels in a way that was counterproductive. She ridiculed men and women who disagreed with her on that issue, and in her mind, their rebellion against her governance cost her more years of opportunity to accomplish things that inspired her.

She far transcended being a mere regional politician, but her time in the spotlight proved fleeting. When the end came, she remarked that if she had known she was going to lose, she would have raised a little more hell. The fact was, she raised plenty of hell. But she found that her state and most likely the nation were not ready to be led by a smart-mouthed woman. She might have gone further and risen higher in politics if she could have adapted to the contemporary necessity of having a squeaky-clean background—or at least making it appear that way—and trying to be all things to all people. In that way, she never veered and remained fundamentally true to herself. One thing Ann Richards could never be was bland. She had a large share of flaws and failures; she could be one hell of a boss to work for. But young people who flocked to her grimy campaign office and worked in her administration described a euphoria and a sense of calling they had never before experienced in politics. In Texas, of all places, one fall night in 1990 a silver-haired fifty-seven-year-old woman climbed on a stage in an Austin hotel, pumped her fist in triumph, and set off scenes of unabashed joy.

But that's ranging far ahead of her story.

Let the People In

PART ONE

Gardens of Light

Portrait of Ann Willis as a Waco teenager, about 1950.

CHAPTER 1

Waco

THE STUDIO PHOTOGRAPH OF Ann Willis was probably taken in 1950, when she was seventeen. Born September 1, 1933, she answered to Dorothy or Dorothy Ann until her family moved into the small city of Waco from an outlying country town at the start of her high school years; she decided then that she liked her middle name more. A gangly teenager, Ann wasn't beautiful in all her pictures at that age. She printed a large, self-conscious "me" above her unflattering photo in her senior yearbook at Waco High, though elsewhere in the annual she was afforded a full-page airbrushed photo as the school's most popular girl. She had worked at gaining that popularity and being a model student. She and a partner won two state championships in girls' team debate, and as a delegate of a civics youth organization called Girls Nation, she got to go to Washington and shake President Harry Truman's hand in the White House Rose Garden.

But the best portrait of her that year was taken in the studio of her uncle Jimmie, a shutterbug and popular figure in Waco. He raced about town on a big motorcycle, wearing the style of cap popularized by Marlon Brando in the movie *The Wild One*. The awkward kid was now a lovely young woman. In the photo, she wears a light sweater over her blouse and a pair of short earrings. Her short brown hair is styled in a relaxed wave over her brow, curling over her temples and ears and nape of her neck as she looks back over her shoulder. The blink of the camera lens captured the beginning of a smile and an elegant pair of eyes—her prettiest feature—and a frank and mischievous glance. One could see the glint in those eyes already. One part of her was a born hell-raiser.

Ann may have inherited her affection for motorcycles from her uncle Jimmie Willis, a popular news shutterbug and studio photographer in Waco in the 1940s and early 1950s. Ann believed she received her first newspaper board endorsement in Austin in 1976 because of a newspaper editor's affection for her uncle.

Ann didn't exaggerate much when she said the people she came from were dirt poor. All four of her grandparents were raised on Central Texas tenant farms. Her father, Cecil Willis, came from a community called Bugtussle. In the version of events that Cecil passed along, Bugtussle got its name from a Baptist camp revival in which people from miles around circled up their wagons, built fires, put their children down after supper on piles of quilts and blankets—hence the evocative expression "a Baptist pallet"—and spent the evenings praising the Lord and singing hymns. When night fell on the camp revival, a fellow whose last name was most likely Bugg switched sleeping children from wagon to wagon as a practical joke that was not funny; it set off a panic and brawl. The farming hamlet of Bugtussle soon dwindled away. Cecil Willis had to quit school after he finished the eighth grade. He got a job delivering pharmaceuticals to drugstores for a salary of $100 a month.

Iona Warren was born near another farming hamlet, also now extinct, called Hogjaw, but she and two sisters grew up in the community of Hico. Iona, who finished the eighth-grade schooling available to her, found work in Waco as a sales clerk in a dry-goods store. On a blind date, Cecil took Iona to a picture show; when the projector broke down, they were given a rain check, which guaranteed another date. They soon married. They paid $700 for an acre of land and built a little house in the burg of Lakeview. The town's name must have referred to the summer's heat mirage; there was no lake close around.

Ann's parents were poor enough that at times they feared hunger. Cecil's family had once come into possession of a field of tomatoes, and his mother canned them all. For the rest of his life, Cecil couldn't stomach stewed tomatoes. Chickens, a major source of their protein, were just that to Iona—food that walked around. Dorothy Ann was born in a bedroom of their house in the hardest year of the Depression, following labor protracted enough that the attending doctor sighed and made himself a pallet on the front porch. The baby arrived at six in the morning. Iona had asked a neighbor woman to cook Cecil's supper the evening after Ann was born, but the neighbor couldn't stand to kill a chicken, so Iona had to wring the chicken's neck and watch it flop and bleed all over the floor because she did not have the strength to rise from the birthing bed.

Cecil got his World War II draft notice at the age of thirty-five. Ann was nine years old; it was the first time she could remember seeing her strapping daddy cry. He went through navy boot camp and pharmaceutical school in San Diego, where he was stationed the rest of the war. The company that had employed Cecil gave Iona a job, but after a few months she decided to take their daughter and

Studio portrait of the infant Dorothy Ann Willis, Waco, 1934.

join him. Before taking off on the long highways across the southwestern desert, Iona wrung the necks of every chicken they owned, plucked them in stinking hot water, then cut them up, stewed them, and preserved them in quart jars. She assumed they were going to be hungry and short of money. Cecil later said that when they drove up, they looked like characters in *The Grapes of Wrath*.

Housing was so scarce in San Diego that for a while they all slept in a cramped basement room. Iona lost a baby in a traumatic pregnancy during the less than two years they were in California. But for Ann, it was a thrilling time of riding a bus and streetcar to a large junior high school in the center of the city. There were verdant hills and palm trees. Shifts in the ocean breeze carried songs of the nation's warriors as they put in their miles doing double time; giant warships in the harbor moved across the horizon. San Diego had a powerful effect on the skinny girl from Texas. She reminisced in her book, "This was my first exposure to kids who were Italian and Greek and black and Hispanic." Yet she didn't get to make the kind of friendships that would have allowed her to roam the neighborhoods and spend the night at other girls' homes. Her parents feared having an eleven-year-old girl out on streets that were full of sailors and marines.

When the war ended, they moved back to the house in Lakeview. They had hunting dogs, some years they fattened and slaughtered a pig, and Dorothy Ann's daddy took her fishing all the time. She loved to tell a story about a junior high school basketball game against Abbott, a rival school where Willie Nelson was one grade behind her. As she prepared to shoot a free throw one night, an Abbott boy hollered, "Make that basket, birdlegs!"

Iona and Cecil had made up their minds that their daughter would get the best education possible, and they wanted her exposed to more prosperous and sophisticated people in high school. Cecil had risen from driver to sales representative for the pharmaceutical company. He and Iona worked hard and saved well, and on the north side of Waco they managed to build a home that had a den and a living room with a fireplace, bedrooms situated at each end of the house, and that feature of postwar middle-class status—a picture window.

For Ann, Waco proved to be one of those hometowns that declined to let go. Founded in 1849, the town got its name from a band of Indians who were part of the Wichita confederation and camped along the Brazos, the most Texas of rivers. Long after the Huecos (Wacos) were expelled to cultural oblivion in Oklahoma, the town had a genuine cowboy element: forty-five miles upriver, the Chisholm Trail crossed the Brazos at a low-water spot called Kimball Bend. The river carved a tortuous horseshoe bend of more than a dozen miles to come back within a mile of that ford. Once the drovers got the cattle across the Brazos, they had to herd them hard to keep them from falling off tall cliffs at a place called Broke Rock, taking horses and riders with them.

As Waco grew, its most distinctive attribute became Baylor University. Originally opened in Independence, Texas, in 1846, Baylor was consolidated with Waco University and moved to its present location in 1886; it became the largest institution of higher learning supported by the Southern Baptist Church. Not everyone in Waco subscribed to those beliefs, and perhaps the most durable aspect

6   of Waco's lore—the story that everyone raised there has heard told again and again—concerned Baylor's role in a gunfight that erupted downtown in broad daylight in 1898. Waco was the adopted home of a famous newspaperman, William Cowper Brann. Following the death of his mother in 1857, Brann, the son of a Presbyterian minister, was placed in the care of a farm couple named Hawkins in Coles County, Illinois. After running away at thirteen, and with only three years of schooling, he learned the journalistic craft in half a dozen American cities. At one point, he sold his newspaper, the *Iconoclast*, to Austin's William Sydney Porter, the short-story writer, embezzler, and ex-convict who took the pen name O. Henry. Brann bought the paper back and in Waco wrote screeds about Baptists, Episcopalians, Englishmen, Negroes, and New York City elites: "Sartorial kings and pseudo-queens . . . [who] have strutted their brief hour upon the mimic stage, disappearing at daybreak like foul night-birds or an unclean dream—have come and gone like the rank eructation of some crapulous Sodom . . . a breath blown from the festering lips of half-forgotten harlots."

Even by the yellow-journalism standards of the day, Brann's prose was sure to make its targets furious. His attacks on Baptists and Baylor University reached fever pitch in the last years of the nineteenth century. In an 1898 exposé, Brann claimed that Baptist missionaries were smuggling South American children into the country and making them house servants—tacit slaves—of Baylor officials. He alleged that a relative of the university's president had gotten a Brazilian student pregnant, that professors seduced female students as a matter of course, and that any father who sent a daughter to Baylor was risking her disgrace or rape. The college, he wrote, was nothing but a "factory for the manufacture of ministers and magdalenes." The slur was drawn from the centuries-old character attack on Jesus Christ's follower Mary Magdalene—magdalenes were reformed prostitutes.

Tom Davis, a prominent Baylor supporter and the father of a Baylor coed, was so enraged that he and another man fired on Brann as he walked on a downtown street. Brann the Iconoclast, as he was known, also carried a gun. He drew his pistol and flung off several shots, mortally wounding Davis and putting him down in the doorway of a cigar store. But a bullet fired by one of the assailants tore through Brann's lung. Waco police made him walk to the city jail, though friends were later allowed to carry him to his home. He died the next morning at the age of forty-three.

For many years, the town run by Baptists had a thriving red-light district. In 1916, a black teenager named Jesse Washington was convicted of murdering a white woman in Waco; a mob tortured, mutilated, and burned him to death as police withdrew and a crowd of 15,000 watched the lynching, which was condemned around the world as the Waco Horror. When Cecil Willis and Iona Warren found their first jobs there, members of the Ku Klux Klan dominated local politics and law enforcement. But the town's reputation and legacy were not all hypocrisy and violence. In 1885, a pharmacist named Charles Alderton, who was employed by Morrison's Old Corner Drug Store, had started fiddling with the recipe of a sweet syrup that the soda jerks mixed with carbonated water—the secret ingredient was rumored to be prune juice. The name "Dr Pepper" grew out of an ad pitch that the drink would pep you up during the day if you refreshed yourself with one at ten, two, and four o'clock. But when people were drinking their favorite beverage fresh made at Old Morrison's Corner Drug Store, they simply said, "Let me have a Waco."

Rich people lived on Waco's west side. One of those families had arrived in Central Texas in uncommon fashion. In 1926, Dick "Cul" Richards was a World War I navy veteran whose roots were in Iowa, but he got an offer to become the freshman football coach at storied Clemson University. A fellow coach assured Richards that would be a very good offer to accept. Dick Richards's wife, Eleanor, was tall, broad-shouldered, and assertive. She came from an Iowa family that owned a major seed company and, in the misfortune of those times, some banks that had failed. She had a degree from Grinnell College in Iowa and had started graduate work at Radcliffe before the collapse of her family's finances. The couple moved to South Carolina, and in the spring of '26, Cul coached the Tiger baseball team to a record of eight wins and eleven losses. When training for the football season began in August, he was the coach of the freshmen and an assistant with the varsity, but in October the head coach abruptly quit. Richards and another coach were charged with keeping the team together and salvaging the season. The regime lasted two weeks. According to his wife, Richards became so overwrought during his coaching finale that alarmed trainers and doctors packed him in ice, fearing he might die. Dick Richards recovered from the coaching experience and got a sensible degree at Clemson in construction engineering. He was helping build a highway in Texas when the large company that employed him went broke. He and Eleanor were literally stranded in Waco. Their only son, David, was born there in 1933.

Papa Dick, as he came to be known in the family, first found work with a small hardware store and then managed to buy it. Despite his age, he talked his way

8   back into the navy in World War II, and when he came back home, the fruits
of victory and the clout of Texas's congressional leaders had bestowed on the
small city an army flying school and the Blackland Army Air Field, and nearby is
the army's vast Fort Hood. Using his knowledge and experience as an engineer,
he made the hardware store into Richards Equipment Company, which supplied
machinery and parts used in road building and other heavy construction. Papa
Dick won bids for a sizeable number of military construction projects.

He built the family a large house near the golf course—golf became his athletic obsession after his ill-starred coaching career. The house had leaded glass
windows, a brass fireplace, and antiques throughout. Eleanor Richards, nicknamed Mom El, did not adapt as well to life in Waco. Thinking she would finish her graduate degree, she applied at Baylor; the hierarchy of Baptist academics
informed her that Baylor would not recognize the credits she had accumulated at
Radcliffe. That institution, they ruled, was nothing more than an effete girls' finishing school, even if it was an affiliate of Harvard University. Contemptuous of
such provincialism, Eleanor founded the Waco League of Women Voters and was
later a president of the state organization. She expected her son to carry on the
family trait of self-reliance. David was terrified as a small boy when his mother
put him on a train to go visit relatives in Iowa. It was up to him to negotiate the
transfer in the sprawling train station in St. Louis.

Dissatisfied with the quality of public education in Waco, or at least with the
way her son took to it, Mom El dispatched him for his junior year to Andover, the
famous prep school in a 300-year-old community in the Boston area. One time
when David was home, his mother was reading the newspaper and saw a story
and photograph about Ann Willis's trip to Washington as a Texas delegate to
Girls Nation. The photo of the delegates showed Ann sitting next to a black girl.
In Waco, that probably aroused more comment than her shaking the hand of
Harry Truman. On that trip, Ann gained an enduring friend in the granddaughter
of Coke Stevenson, the Texas governor who lost the notorious 1948 Democratic
runoff for the U.S. Senate to Lyndon Johnson by a fortuitously discovered, and
probably fraudulent, eighty-seven votes. Eleanor wondered aloud why her son
could not get interested in a smart girl like that? David doubtless gave his mother
the silence or harrumph the remark deserved.

ANN SAID THE BEST PART of her high school experiences began the day in 1949
when she met the tall, handsome, and jocular young man who had spent a year
at Andover and had then come back for his senior year at Waco High. In her

memoir, *Straight from the Heart: My Life in Politics and Other Places*, written with the help of Peter Knobler, she reminisced, "The A&W Root Beer stand was the local summer hot spot. You'd pull up in your car and they would come out and put a tray on your window, and you'd sit and talk and kids would come over. David was sitting at the A&W when I met him. . . . I thought he was just the nuts."

He took her out to dinner on their first date following her performance in a school production of Noel Coward's *Blithe Spirit*. She had never been around people who ate shrimp; she doubted that she had been in a real restaurant more than half a dozen times in her life. She carefully ordered what he did. As their senior year wore on, they became inseparable. Ann loved the way conversation just took off when she was with him. He had strongly held positions on social matters that most young people their age had not even considered. An English teacher at the high school remarked one day that he had the biggest vocabulary in her class. The praise won him endless razzing from their crowd of friends. "There he goes," they hooted when he embarked on some lofty statement of principle. Though he had little notion of where his beliefs might lead, David was an idealist. Inspired by his parents' reading of a story that never got old, he chose for his moral compass a rogue with a conscience and a sense of justice. Ann recalled, "Robin Hood, Little John, Friar Tuck, Maid Marian, Alan-a-Dale—the characters became personal friends of David's. Intimates. He lived in that world. . . . We would talk about it all the time; it was a recurring theme: 'What would Robin Hood have done?'"

Going steady with David ushered Ann into a milieu she had never known before. His family traveled, subscribed to magazines like the *New Yorker* and the *New Republic*, and talked about political events in the state and country. In her book, she conveyed how inspiring yet intimidating that was for her as an eighteen-year-old:

> I felt that I was not equipped, that I could not begin to keep up in this intellectual atmosphere. I'm sure I talked, and I'm sure I talked about things I knew nothing about. But if I did, the family was tolerant of me. A lot of the time, partly out of anxiety, I would retreat and do the dishes. Doing the dishes is a refuge, it's a place to go when you want to check out; you have an excuse for not being called upon to participate. So I listened and I absorbed everything I could of this very new, very different kind of conversation.

But most exciting were the times when David and Ann crossed a frontier into an entirely different culture. Waco was rigorously segregated then, but the teenagers became regulars at Scenic Wonderland, a dance hall that had been converted from

Snapshot of Ann, Waco, early 1950s.

an equipment warehouse on a murky road near the tire plant. Black promoters rented the dance hall on off nights and booked touring jazz and rhythm-and-blues bands. Ann and David and a few other kids who went over there were three years away from being of legal drinking age, but the owner sold them beer. They saw, heard, and danced to Fats Domino, Billy Eckstine, Ruth Brown, and their favorites, the Clovers, a rhythm-and-blues vocal group from Washington, D.C.

Ann said she liked the taste and buzz of beer, but the first time she got really drunk was at the all-night party for seniors just before their graduation. She won scholarship offers for debate from Baylor and Lindenwood, a liberal arts college in St. Charles, Missouri. "Ann really wanted to go to Lindenwood," David told me. "She had her heart set on it. But her mother just flat refused to let her go." The Baylor scholarship, her mother said, would cover tuition and allow her to continue living at home.

It was pretty clear to friends and parents where David and Ann were headed, and they were going there fast. Though Eleanor Richards later became a mentor and close friend of Ann, she took steps that slowed them down. "David and I graduated from high school in 1950," Ann reminisced. "His mother didn't feel he had received a sufficiently good education at Waco High and was sending him back to Andover for a post-graduate year, which didn't sit well with David or me. I also believe there must have been an ingredient in his mother's plans which served to separate us; we were very much in love and we were just children."

That first semester at Baylor, Ann lived at home. David came back for the Christmas holidays and flatly refused to go back to Andover. He enrolled at the University of Texas in Austin and pledged a fraternity with a big house at the end of the campus's South Mall. If separating David and Ann was Eleanor Richards's intent, for a few months it worked. At Baylor, Ann pledged a sorority. She liked the girls, but soon saw the ugly side of sorority rush: one girl was ridiculed and rejected because her father was a mere policeman, another slandered for allegedly whoring around in high school. Ann's parents let her move into a dorm the second half of her freshman year, and she was doing well on the debate team.

Another boy she dated was on the Baylor debate team and aspired to be a Baptist preacher. Though her parents had taken her to church at Lakeview's little Methodist church, where her dad was on the board of stewards, Ann did not really embrace religion until the night Billy Graham brought a crusade to the Baylor campus. Graham was as handsome and glamorous as a movie star, and when he finished his sermon and the invitation hymn began, Ann joined the throng streaming down the aisles to commit their souls to Christ. But when the passion of that moment waned, her doubts grew about angels and other tenets of the faith. Also, Iona Willis did not like the notion of this aspiring young minister who had turned her daughter's head. The life of a preacher's wife was hard and usually penurious. She knew that Ann would get her hackles up in defiance if told that she couldn't go out with him anymore, but she regained some control by making Ann move back home.

David had meanwhile identified the bars on the periphery of the University of Texas campus where a minor could buy a beer. He liked the university well enough, but at his fraternity house, he heard remarks that made him gnaw on his tongue. One time Ann got away from her mother for a weekend in Austin—David's fraternity was having a party—with the explanation that she would be staying with her friend, Coke Stevenson's granddaughter. "It was the only way we could have gotten Ann down there," David told me. The night of the party, an Austin outfit called Jack's Party Pictures took one of the best photos of Ann and David. Holding a beverage aloft, David is wearing a mock turtleneck sweater, the kind of jaunty short-billed cap that Hemingway often wore, and a confident, thoughtful expression. Playing the vamp, Ann is wearing a glossy scarlet cocktail dress with a mildly plunging neckline, lipstick of matching hue, and orchids in her hair. She was a knockout.

Soon David was driving to Waco all the time to go out with her, and she gave up her scholarship because the debate competitions were time consuming and scheduled on weekends. She wanted to spend that time with him. "Ann's dad was a big friendly guy, a lovely man," David said. "Ann loved her mother, but she fought to please and satisfy that woman as long as she lived. She'd been opening and reading my letters to Ann since my parents sent me back to Andover. A letter was what compelled us to go ahead and get married. I mean, we were going to do that eventually. But Ann pretty much laid it out—she wrote that we had to get her away from her mother and out of that house."

David had transferred to Baylor their junior year so they could see more of each other, and with much of their hometown in rubble from a horrific tornado, they got married in May 1953. Ann recalled: "Women were allowed to get married at eighteen, but in order to get the license David needed his daddy's signed permission and I teased him about that a whole lot." She also teased him about the matrimony: "The service was broadcast over the PA 'so the congregation could hear the vows.' Most of what they heard was David whispering, 'Which way do I go? Which way do I go?'" They honeymooned in New Orleans and on the beach in Biloxi, Mississippi. Back in Waco, they lived in a small apartment complex; that summer, he worked for his dad's equipment company and she worked in a dress shop. The next year they graduated from Baylor.

Later in life, David also wrote a memoir, *Once Upon a Time in Texas: A Liberal in the Lone Star State*, which is a revealing counterpoint to Ann's description of experiences and events they shared. David described a personal turning point that occurred one day when he was hanging out with cronies at Waco's country club. Suddenly, he blurted that he was going to vote for the liberal and populist lawyer Ralph Yarborough in his 1954 attempt to unseat the Texas governor, Allan Shivers. Political races in Texas were then decided by factions of conservative and liberal Democrats, with Republicans effectively a small third party. But Shivers, the conservative Democratic governor, had organized his forces to help the GOP war hero Dwight Eisenhower carry Texas in the 1952 presidential election against the urbane Illinois governor Adlai Stevenson. David thought Shivers was a bigoted scoundrel. But his friends at the country club reacted to his outburst in support of Yarborough by staring at him as if he had lost his mind.

David Richards and Ann Willis dressed up for a college party in Austin, about 1952.

Newlyweds David and Ann Richards, Waco, 1953.

My childhood as part of what passed for Waco society had certainly been privileged. I had been exposed to the dubious benefits of an eastern prep school and University of Texas fraternity life, both of which soured me on the values of the moneyed social order. More importantly, I suspect, I had been nourished on Robin Hood as a child and had discovered John Dos Passos' trilogy U.S.A. in my youth, which I may have read more for sexual titillation than for political content. In all events, somewhere along the line my disgust quota had overflowed, probably caused by a combination of racism, McCarthyism, and the smugness of the pooh-bahs who ran things, and I slipped my moorings.

David and Ann graduated from Baylor in 1954. The Soviet Union had the atomic bomb, the Korean War had ended in stalemate after intervention by the Communist Chinese, and David was going to be a conscript in the menacing Cold War if he didn't come up with a plan fast. He had majored in history, not the most financially useful degree. His parents urged him to consider going back east to pursue an MBA at Wharton, the business school at the University of Pennsylvania. But he won admittance to the University of Texas law school, which extended his student deferment, and Ann took graduate speech and education classes at the university that certified her as a public school teacher.

David thought law school was boring but politics was fun. In 1956, he was recruited to attempt a palace coup within the University of Texas Young Democrats, and he won the election. "The problem was," Ann wrote, "David had never run a meeting before. Here he was president with a full agenda and work to get done. I had taken a course in parliamentary procedure at Baylor, so I became the parliamentarian." These were not college students just playing at politics. Men who were well into their thirties jousted for power in the Young Democrats, for it was a major faction of the liberal wing of the party. Ann and David's first Democratic precinct convention, held at an Austin grade school, was attended by hundreds of contentious people. Hoping to quiet the insurgents down, the precinct party chief made David an alternate delegate to the Travis County convention in 1956. That was little more than a pat on the head, so he went to the state fairgrounds in Dallas, where he climbed through an open window in a restroom and crashed the party's state convention with a counterfeit ticket printed by Henry Holman, the president of the Austin carpenters union, and Jean Lee, a longtime conspirator among Austin liberals and the wife of the famous photographer Russell Lee.

The insurgents were thrilled and Lyndon Johnson was incensed when the liberals ousted the Shivers faction and sent to the national convention as Texas's

16 party chief Frankie Randolph, a Houston woman who inspired and helped fund many liberal causes and organizations, among them the muckraking *Texas Observer*. All this brought David and Ann into a hotbed of political dissent in Texas. Their faction of the liberal revolt met at the venerable Scholz Garten in Austin, where raconteurs on the shaded outdoor patio ignored the muffled clatter coming from the German Texan owners' adjoining private ninepin bowling alley. The Richardses' embrace of Democratic politics brought them into the lively circle of Henry Holman and his wife, Mary, a nurse who loved to dance drunk around campfires and roam off on spur-of-the-moment adventures in Mexico; Sam Houston Clinton, a cigar-smoking attorney who had once been David's Sunday-school teacher and basketball coach in Waco; Fletcher Boone, a talented but unprolific artist and an instinctive comic; and Wayne Oakes, a liberal scuffler and former junior college history teacher who loved to whack chords on his guitar and in a painful tenor sing cowboy laments like "Goodbye, Old Paint, I'm Leaving Cheyenne" and the Democrats' 1936 song of triumph, "We've Got Franklin Delano Roosevelt Back Again." Ann recalled that a lot of their politicking at Scholz's centered not on issues or strategy but on who was qualified to sit at the table reserved for the Horses Association, alias the Horses Asses, with Henry Holman its long-serving vice horse.

A man who had been Ann's principal at Waco High was now the superintendent of the Austin school district. Because of that, she believed, she got a job teaching social studies at Fulmore Junior High. She was not yet twenty-two. Her ninth graders were at least fifteen, some older because they had failed a couple of grades. She stood her ground and did her best, but did not believe she was a very good teacher. She had also been trying to get pregnant, and during that year she went to a gynecologist to find out whether something was wrong. Tests revealed she had a cyst on an ovary. She talked to her principal, a former coach, who said kindly, "Ann, take my advice and get that thing out. It's just like sleeping with a snake." Great. She had the operation and worked on through the spring semester. David was preparing to take the bar exam when he received his draft notice. But the day he went to take his physical, Ann found out that she was pregnant—he never had to worry again about the draft.

In 1956, Eisenhower easily carried Texas in his rematch with Adlai Stevenson, and in a Democratic race to succeed the retiring and scandal-tainted Allan Shivers, the junior U.S. senator from Texas, Price Daniel, beat Ralph Yarborough by 3,000 votes and became governor. But Yarborough and his revved-up organization kept right on running. To LBJ's dismay, Yarborough won the special election to fill Daniel's senate seat. Yarborough was the hero of Texas liberals for the rest of his long career.

While David was job-hunting, recruiters for the Central Intelligence Agency, of all people, briefly turned his head. But he took a job with a Dallas law firm, Mullinax, Wells, Morris & Mauzy. Not many law firms in Texas specialized in representing labor unions, but this one had a reputation as being among the best that did. Oscar Mauzy, the junior partner and a future Texas politician of note, let the tall new addition to the firm sleep on his sofa.

Iona Willis and Eleanor Richards agreed that Ann could not have a baby in a strange new city with no one to help but David. "I was so stupid I didn't argue," Ann recalled in her book. "I had been running my own household for more than three years now, I was independent, and it was no picnic living in my parents' house. I wanted to know what was going on with David, how our new life was progressing. Instead, he was starting a new career and I was in my old room. My mother scared up a tiny newborn rabbit in the yard and brought it to me. I nursed that little rabbit like it was a baby. Then the dog killed it and I had my first child the next day, July 15, 1957."

In the years to come, David admitted to having some long-standing contentious issues with his mother-in-law, but he frowned when I asked whether Ann's retreat to Waco was another instance of Iona Willis's overweening control of her daughter. "No, no," he told me. "That couldn't be blamed on her. That was, well, me."

Ann holds infant Cecile at home beneath her wedding portrait, Waco, 1957.

CHAPTER 2

New Frontiers

AFTER CECILE WAS BORN, Ann spent six more weeks at home in Waco being helped and schooled on how to be a mother. At last, she bundled up the infant and joined David in Dallas, where they lived in a small house with yellow rock siding that she thought was ugly. Every morning, David would put on his coat and tie and rush downtown while trying to quell his fears of being overwhelmed by the tasks at hand. For Ann, those first weeks and months in Dallas were stressful, monotonous, and lonely. She sewed baby clothes, cleaned the house, cooked, ironed David's shirts, and puzzled through the strenuous demands of motherhood. The highlight of many of her days was putting Cecile in her buggy and rolling it back and forth as she watched *American Bandstand* on television. Some nights their baby would go to sleep only if lulled by continual motion, so they would put her in the car and make aimless loops around the unfamiliar city.

"Thank God," Ann later wrote in her book, "little babies are pretty strong and resourceful and can usually survive no matter who they have landed with; I had no more idea how to take care of a baby than a man on the moon. David was sort of mystified by the whole deal. We had never discussed having children. It was a different era. You didn't think, 'Do I want to do this?' or 'Is it time?' or 'Are we mature enough?' None of these questions ever arose. We were typical of most Fifties couples: we got married; we had babies."

David later made his mark in the law as a litigator and an expert on the First Amendment, civil rights, and voting rights. But he spent the first twenty-five years of his career representing labor unions and workers in disputes with employers. He never gave up his belief that union organizers and activists were a driving force of American progressivism, that ideally they were like his Austin pal Henry Holman, the joking master carpenter, Democratic Party dissenter, and vice horse at the Scholz Garten. But victims of corporate greed were not always easily identified among the clients he encountered in his crash course in labor law. Nat Wells, one of the firm's senior partners, had been an attorney for the National Labor Relations Board and had successfully prosecuted Ford Motor Company strikebreakers during Franklin Roosevelt's administration. The Dallas firm now handled all the legal business of the International Brotherhood of Teamsters in the South—a major account. In 1957, just as David was breaking in, the Teamsters president, Dave Beck, was sentenced to prison on a bribery conviction, and Jimmy Hoffa took over. A federal judge in New York placed the union in trusteeship and appointed Nat Wells one of the trustees. The firm's senior partner was always traveling on business, and a continuing rain of strikes, injunctions, and grand jury investigations fell on the head of the rookie lawyer. "It seemed to me," David said in his memoir, "that every day for years was the same thing: I was constantly facing questions I could not fathom."

David and Ann were still deeply involved in the Young Democrats, which periodically gave them a reason to drive down to Austin and catch up with the Holmans, Fletcher Boone, Wayne Oakes, and the rest of the gang. But if liberal politics was going to be their ongoing passion and resolve, they had to accept the fact that they lived in hostile territory. "Who Is John Galt?" inquired countless bumper stickers on the cars of people enraptured by the conservative revolutionary in Ayn Rand's novel *Atlas Shrugged*. The editorial page of the *Dallas Morning News* was one of the most rabidly conservative in the country. A couple of blocks down Akard Street from Neiman-Marcus, the retail store that set the city's style for women's fashions and interior décor, the Adolphus and Baker hotels (the latter now demolished) presided over a spooky emptiness on the streets after the sun went down. Even bars were scarce. People came downtown to work and then hurried home. The nearest residents lived across a horseshoe-shaped clot of expressways and the floodplain of the Trinity River. The faces of people who lived east, south, and west of downtown were for the most part black or brown. The business oligarchy that controlled Dallas disposed of most of Deep Elm, pronounced "Ellum," the black district famous for its blues musicians and back-alley dice games, by condemning and tearing down boardinghouses, pool halls, and black mortuaries and then building Central Expressway through a broad swath of the area. Looming over commuter routes were billboards advertising the John Birch Society.

Public schools, public restrooms, and drinking fountains were rigidly seg-regated; in bus stations, people in need of a toilet chose among doors marked "Men," "Women," and "Colored." The Dallas school board simply ignored the di-rectives in *Brown v. Board of Education* (1954), the Topeka, Kansas, case in which the U.S. Supreme Court ruled that segregated schools violated the equal protection clause of the Fourteenth Amendment. In her book, Ann described the mundane cruelties imposed by segregation: "Black people were allowed to buy goods in department stores but they were not allowed to try them on; black women could buy hats but they couldn't put them on their heads."

Ann was frustrated, believing she knew no one of another race or culture. One night in 1958, after asking David to stay with Cecile, she went to an old house in east Dallas that was the local NAACP headquarters, where she stuffed envelopes for the insurgent campaign for governor of Henry González, a state senator from San Antonio who lost that race but went on to a long and distinguished career in Congress. To Ann's pleasure and surprise, she did know someone there. The man who welcomed her and introduced her to his small children was Pancho Medrano, a United Auto Workers activist who had worked with David on some of his union's legal business. During that time, Ann and David moved to another rental house, this one near Love Field airport. The neighborhood was integrated in the sense that many whites were moving out to suburbs, and black families were moving in. Ann put Cecile in her stroller and walked the blocks, knocking on doors and trying to get strangers to vote and participate in the Democratic precinct convention. She came away with the realization that these African Americans were afraid to do anything overtly political. She tried to assure them that law enforcement would protect their right to peacefully assemble. They con-sidered her with gazes that said: "You talking about the *cops*?"

———

ANN WAS PREGNANT IN 1959 with their second child, Dan. She convinced David that they had to have a bigger house, and on Coogan Drive they made their first real estate purchase. They began to host backyard parties for local and visiting liberals, and word got around about the convivial gatherings. But motherhood and the guidebook of Dr. Benjamin Spock dictated Ann's workaday routine. Dur-ing that period, a friend of David's mother introduced them to a couple that be-came as good a pair of friends as they ever had. Sam and Virginia Whitten, who had grown up in small towns in northeast Texas, first met while students at Paris Junior College. While serving in the navy in World War II, Sam had been thrilled to take part in some officer training at Harvard, but had little good to say about the long months spent on a supply ship. "It was like the movie *Mr. Roberts*, without Mr. Roberts."

After the war, they finished their educations as librarians at the University of Texas. Sam first worked for the Dallas Public Library, and then was head of the science library at Southern Methodist University. Virginia would make her career as a librarian in the public schools, but her calling in life then was like Ann's— she was a wife and mother. When Ann would start to get frantic, she would load Cecile and Dan in the car and drive to the house of her best friend. Virginia then had three children and was pregnant with a fourth. "I would charge through the door and there in the middle of this storm, with snotty-nosed children crawling, banging, screaming, Virginia would be placidly folding diapers," Ann wrote. "I had a diaper service, but Virginia washed her own, and she'd be sitting there folding them. 'Virginia,' I'd babble, 'I am just losing my mind.' 'I know,' she'd tell me. 'Why don't you sit down and have a cup of coffee?'"

The 1960 presidential election stirred liberal Democrats with a sense of uprising, if not confidence. The Richardses' first political volunteering effort that year was to work hard in support of the campaign of David's law firm colleague, Oscar Mauzy, for national president of the Young Democrats. Mauzy, who was then thirty-four, lost the race, but not before his friend David Richards got in a fistfight with one of their adversaries in the lobby of a hotel in Toledo, Ohio.

The Young Democrats believed that operatives of Lyndon Johnson, who was now a presidential candidate as well as the Senate majority leader, had tanked Mauzy's candidacy. The state Democratic convention took place soon afterward. The liberals descended on Austin and the Scholz Garten, growing more annoyed, as the night wore on, that a banner draped across Congress Avenue read "Lyndon Johnson: A Leader to Lead the Nation." After a while, they decided to sabotage the affront. David and Ann rode forth to battle in the convertible of their friend Bill Kilgarlin, who, like Mauzy, was a future justice on the Texas Supreme Court. The banner was tied up securely across the six lanes of Congress. The insurgents were about to cut it down when one of their comrades took a Tarzan-like ride on one of the ropes—and swung right into the arms of some Austin cops. The leaders of the plot vanished in the darkness, and later that night David sheepishly got the ones who had been arrested out of jail. The next day at the convention, the labor unions cut a deal with the Johnson forces, and the true liberals, as they perceived themselves, were left soaking their wounded spirits at Scholz's and singing "We Shall Overcome."

In April 1959, Johnson had pressured the Texas Legislature and Governor Daniel to pass and enact the so-called Lyndon Law, which removed a prohibition against a candidate being listed for two separate offices in the same election. Democrats of all stripes perked up in January 1960 when President Eisenhower declined to endorse Richard Nixon, just two days after his vice president had announced his candidacy—a stinging rebuke. As the year went on, Johnson led a "Stop Kennedy" alliance with fellow candidates Adlai Stevenson, Stuart Symington, and Hubert Humphrey. LBJ hoped to thwart JFK on the first ballot and take the prize away from those fellow aspirants on the second or later ballots. The Stop Kennedy forces did not come close to derailing him, though Johnson finished second in delegates. Participants and historians have not reached a consensus on why JFK offered the vice presidential nomination to Johnson, or why Johnson accepted, but there is no doubt that JFK's brother Robert "Bobby" Kennedy thought it was tantamount to a deal with the devil. It seems most plausible that after JFK looked at the field on which he had to engage Nixon, he took on Johnson as his running mate in hopes of carrying Texas and other states in the South and Southwest.

Kennedy repeatedly used the slogan "New Frontier" in his acceptance speech at the Democratic National Convention: "We stand on the edge of a new frontier. The frontier of the 1960s, the frontier of unknown opportunities and perils, the frontier of unfilled hopes and unfilled threats." Those words were prophetic in a chilling way—and they were also borrowed. Henry Wallace, the leftist secretary of agriculture and unhappy one-term vice president of Franklin Roosevelt, had written a book titled *The New Frontier* in 1934, and in 1936 the slogan was tested in a speech by Alf Landon, the Kansas governor and GOP presidential candidate whom FDR crushed that year.

Inspired by the charisma and apparent idealism of Kennedy, Ann did everything she could to contribute to the campaign. Babysitters enabled her to go to the local precinct headquarters one or two days a week and work the desk, handing out bumper stickers and arranging the distribution of yard signs. She lived with the fact that her assignments were menial, that she was the help. And in Dallas, it was hard to believe Kennedy had much chance of beating Nixon. On November 4, four days before the election, a crowd estimated at a million and a half cheered Kennedy in Chicago; that day in Dallas, Lyndon and Lady Bird Johnson were mobbed, jeered, and swatted with a protest sign in the lobby of the Adolphus Hotel.

But the alliance of convenience between JFK and LBJ delivered. Kennedy carried Texas by 46,000 votes, which he could not have done without Johnson.

24   Republicans alleged brazen fraud in places like Fannin County, the home of Sam Rayburn, the powerful Speaker of the House. That county on the Oklahoma border had 4,895 registered voters, but 6,138 ballots were reported cast and counted, and three-fourths of them went for Kennedy. The Nixon camp raised howls about similar irregularities in Chicago, where the totals helped Kennedy come from behind and claim Illinois. The electoral votes of Illinois and Texas made JFK president.

Although David was doing well in his law practice by 1961, on track to making partner, he and Ann were uplifted by Kennedy's election and worn out by Dallas. With the help of Johnson's aide Harry McPherson, who had been a good friend in law school, David got a job as a staff lawyer with the U.S. Commission on Civil Rights. He gave up his position at the law firm, they sold their house, and within a month of the inauguration, they moved into a house on Capitol Hill. Ann loved Washington at first. During the day, she bundled up Cecile and Dan and explored the matchless art in the National Gallery. They watched a parade honoring Alan Shepard, America's first astronaut to soar above the earth's atmosphere. A babysitter came once a week, and on many of those days, Ann went to the Senate gallery and listened in fascination to the debates. She was particularly taken by the Minnesota Democrat Hubert Humphrey because he seemed passionate about everything that came to mind, and by the Illinois Republican Everett Dirksen, who one day made a long speech about how the noble marigold ought to be named the national flower. (The rose was awarded that honor during the Reagan administration.)

At the Civil Rights Commission, David was happy enough at first. His office looked out over Lafayette Square. But Eisenhower had created the commission as a fact-finding entity, not one invested with real power. A major push on civil rights was not a bear that Kennedy and his New Frontiersmen longed to wrestle in the first months of the administration. But Bobby Kennedy, the attorney general, was keen on taking down corrupt union officials. In one investigation, David was assigned the task of going to Atlanta to survey any evidence there of racial discrimination in organized labor. On that assignment, he relearned a primary rule in the legal profession—never ask a question whose answer you are not prepared for. "While interviewing the business manager of the electricians local in Atlanta," he recalled, "I asked why there were no Negro electricians in the union. The answer was straightforward: 'All niggers are afraid of electricity.'"

One night, Ann and David were invited to the birthday party of a woman named Mary Margaret Wiley, who worked on the vice president's staff. A friend from their Austin days, she invited a few Texans over to celebrate. "We were sitting around drinking and telling stories when Vice President Johnson himself arrived," Ann wrote. "We were all dumbfounded. Mary Margaret worked with the vice president all day, but the rest of us had no access to him at all." The young adults fell silent, and David tried to offer some reasonably informed conversation. He mentioned an article in the *Texas Observer* that he thought had been complimentary to Johnson. LBJ knew that the *Observer*'s editor, Ronnie Dugger, despised him, and David had forgotten another article in that issue in which their San Antonio friend Maury Maverick, Jr., questioned LBJ's backbone for how he responded to the McCarthy hysteria of the 1950s. LBJ launched into a tirade about the disrespect shown him by the *Observer* and pipsqueaks like Maury Maverick, Jr. Why, he alone among Texans had the courage to stand on the Senate floor and condemn McCarthy!

"On it went for what seemed an eternity," David recalled. "None of my comrades stepped up to defend me; they left me as the sole target of this withering assault."

That encounter was one of the few times Ann ever admitted to being cowed. "Johnson was a large man with a powerful voice. He spoke with authority and cut a large wake. Standing in Mary Margaret's living room he was like an ocean liner in a small harbor. He was not a man you wanted to have an argument with about anything."

During David and Ann's sojourn in Washington, they conceived their third child, Clark. David grew disenchanted with writing legal opinions that were edited into mush and bore no resemblance to the arguments and passages he had crafted. Ann described her own unhappiness at that time in her book:

The entire time I was there the only thing asked of me was to bake cookies for the Capitol Hill house tour. The politics of Washington is the work of Washington. It's not an avocation. We had looked forward to meeting and being involved with the best and the brightest, and we would go to some social events, but after the first six months we began to tire of the eternal speculation about which senator was sleeping with which other woman. We pretty quickly came to the conclusion that when we had moved to Washington we had left the New Frontier. In February 1962, a year after we had arrived, we went back to Dallas.

Ann parodies John Connally in her last appearance in the "Political Paranoia" follies of the North Dallas Democratic Women, 1968.

CHAPTER 3

Lovers Lane

THE LAW FIRM WELCOMED DAVID BACK, and the Richardses bought a home on
the corner of Athens Avenue and Lovers Lane. By and large, David enjoyed his
work with union workers and organizers, whom he described in his memoir as "a
wonderfully irreverent, bawdy, and hard-boozing bunch who truly believed that
working people deserved a better shot." In his spare time, he ran for chairman of
their Democratic Party precinct, and largely thanks to SMU faculty members and
students who lived in the neighborhood, he won. Liberals prevailed in several
Dallas precincts in 1962, but it got them nowhere. The county chairman refused
to convene them unless a statute required him to do so.

The Richardses continued to battle the entrenched powers from their base in
Dallas, but the fight was no longer just against conservative Democrats and the
Johnson machine—the Lyndon Law had backfired. In Wichita Falls, John Tower,
a government professor at Midwestern University (now Midwestern State University), had offered himself as a Republican sacrificial lamb in the 1960 election
for U.S. senator, yet he ran surprisingly well against Johnson—perhaps because
of the perceived ham-handed arrogance of the latter's role in passing the bill
nicknamed for him—in any case pulling 41 percent and nearly a million votes.
Governor Price Daniel appointed a conservative from Dallas, William Blakley,
to fill Johnson's seat until the special election scheduled for May 1961. The Fort
Worth congressman Jim Wright ran for the Senate seat, as did the Richardses'
friend Maury Maverick, Jr., and San Antonio's Henry González—seventy-one
candidates in all. When the dust cleared in the runoff, by a little more than ten

thousand votes, Tower had eased past Blakley. It was the first time a Republican had been elected to statewide office in Texas since 1870.

But the biggest story in Texas politics in those months was the emergence of John Connally, who had managed five of LBJ's major campaigns (including the U.S. Senate primary in 1948, when the infamous box 13 in Jim Wells County gave him a victory margin of eighty-seven votes) and his presidential race against Kennedy. After a one-year resumé scrub as Kennedy's secretary of the navy, Connally had come home to run for governor. David distrusted the man's background as an oil baron's lawyer, but had to admire his deftness at bringing blacks and Hispanics into his organization. In that gubernatorial campaign, Connally positioned himself as a consummate centrist. He had battled the right-wingers of Allan Shivers but also had gotten into a nasty feud with the liberal senator Ralph Yarborough. Connally campaigned well, saying that he would emphasize education, improved race relations, and poverty reduction. He won a squeaker over the liberal Don Yarborough (who was not related to the senator) in the Democratic primary and then had to hustle to defeat Jack Cox, a Shivers-crowd Democrat turned Republican, by 131,901 votes. The improved race relations and poverty fighting evaporated from his agenda when he took office, but he delivered on public and higher education during his three two-year terms. He was a study in polish, finesse, and knowing how to get what he wanted from the legislature. By serving long enough to appoint all the leaders of powerful state agencies, he made the office of Texas governor, which the 1876 state constitution designed as a weak figurehead, into about as strong a power base as anyone ever had.

During her pregnancy and after the birth of Clark in May 1962, Ann joined with other politically dedicated women in a new organization called the North Dallas Democratic Women. Among these political-activist friends were Virginia Whitten; Claire Korioth, who later became a lawyer and one of Ann's most thoughtful and careful advisers; and a writer named Ruthe Winegarten, who, as a University of Texas student radical, had joined the Texas Communist Party and the Dallas Labor Zionist Party—since then her views had evolved into an earnest liberalism. Their outfit raised a little money and some hell by writing and performing an annual satirical skit called *Political Paranoia*. Ann was a star of the vaudeville-like revues. "The North Dallas Democratic Women was basically formed to allow us to have something substantive to do," she said. "The regular Democratic Party and its organizations were run by men who looked on women as little more than machine parts. It wasn't that I didn't like the men I worked with on campaigns; I did. It was just that we women did all the dumb work, were never allowed to make any decisions; basically didn't use our brains. No woman ever moved up in that organization."

During the same period, David and Ann took part in what they believed was a quiet and thoughtful group of activists called the Dallas Committee for Peaceful Integration. They were stunned one day to read in the newspapers that one of their fellow members was an undercover FBI agent. There was nothing to do but shrug—it was just Dallas. They gained another set of close friends in Mike and Betty McKool. Mike was an attorney specializing in condemnation law. Betty, like Ann, was a housewife, mother, and politically oriented ham. Ann and Betty sent out slickly produced, humorous Christmas cards, a tradition that they carried on for nine years for an ever-growing mailing list. In one of the cards, costumed as the magi, they are gawking at the manger and crying in the caption: "It's a girl!"

Betty McKool, left, and Ann pose for one of their popular Christmas cards from the 1960s and 1970s.

But while Ann was getting some pleasure out of all this, she couldn't kid herself that the environment she inhabited was any less hostile than it had ever been. Consider the prominence in Dallas of the Texas-born army general Edwin Walker. In April 1961, with Kennedy newly in office and trying to overcome the Bay of Pigs fiasco, a paper called the *Overseas Weekly* quoted Walker, the commanding general of an infantry division, as saying that Harry Truman, Eleanor Roosevelt, and Dean Acheson were "definitely pink," and reports came back to the Pentagon that Walker had hectored his troops to vote for archconservative Republicans. Kennedy's defense secretary, Robert McNamara, relieved him of his command and reassigned him. Walker instead resigned from the army. In September he organized protests against the enrollment of African American student James Meredith at the University of Mississippi, and the demonstrations there turned violent. Bobby Kennedy, the attorney general, issued a warrant for his arrest on charges of seditious conspiracy, insurrection, and rebellion.

Walker wound up jailed for five days, claiming that he was a "political prisoner" of the Kennedy administration. He moved to the posh Turtle Creek area of Dallas, and though he had the support of Barry Goldwater, he ran sixth and last as a gubernatorial candidate in the 1962 Democratic primary. He sang the praises of the John Birch Society and white Rhodesia and flew his American flag upside down, a signal of extreme distress. The Dallas press treated him as a serious figure, not a kook.

It was a schizophrenic time. One month after the Cuban Missile Crisis of October 1962, the preppy Kingston Trio hit the record stores and airwaves with the enormously popular folk LP *New Frontier* and its patriotic title track.

The following April, Lee Harvey Oswald told his Russian wife, Marina, that he was going to a typing class at Crozier Tech High School; instead, he carried a newly purchased rifle to the church parking lot next to Walker's house. One implausible but widespread account claimed he rode all the way across the city by bus, with no one noticing him or the rifle. But two teenagers indicated to the Dallas police and the FBI that they had noticed a man in a black and white Chevrolet parked beside Walker's property. In addition, one boy, who heard a rifle shot, said he saw a man jump in a black and white Chevrolet and speed away, and added that he saw a second man jump in a Ford and hurry off. Subsequent investigations indicated that a would-be CIA agent and anti-Castro insurgent in Florida may have been with Oswald and may even have fired the shot from Oswald's rifle. That man was never charged. Whether Oswald had an accomplice or not, the shooter narrowly missed killing the general, who was seated at his desk when the bullet ricocheted off a nearby window frame. Fragments of the shell's jacket were found in his shirtsleeve, and he was still removing slivers of shattered glass when reporters arrived. At that time police had no idea who the shooter might have been.

In June, Kennedy electrified 150,000 West Germans with his "Ich bin ein Berliner" speech beside the Berlin Wall. But back home, the president eyed polls that had him trailing Barry Goldwater in several states, including Texas. In Dallas, the animus against Kennedy reached fever pitch. One night in September 1963, David and Ann went to a municipal hall to hear a speech by Adlai Stevenson, now Kennedy's ambassador to the United Nations. The man had run two thoughtful and respectful campaigns for president against Eisenhower, and at the UN he delivered an exposé of Soviet behavior in Cuba; he deserved to be received with civility anywhere in America. David described the scene in his memoir.

> First, well-dressed young matrons began to jangle their arm bracelets, drowning out the speaker. As Stevenson appeared, the noise became overwhelming. The objectors had seated themselves in the center of the auditorium, and they began to rise and leave in unison, forcing those who wished to stay to stand to let them pass. In the midst of this bedlam, a long banner was unfurled behind Stevenson which proclaimed, "Get the U.S. Out of the U.N." . . . At this point, a man leaped up on the second row and began to shout through a battery-operated speaker about Yugoslavian pilots and communist conspiracies. Almost immediately, an old friend of mine, Pancho Medrano, a burly UAW staffer, got up and began to climb across the rows to grab the heckler. The last thing I remember is leaping up and screaming, 'Get him, Pancho!' When Ann and I finally got out of the hall, we faced a group of men dressed as Nazi storm troopers marching in the lobby. By this time my grip on my sanity was faltering, and I went head-to-head with one of the Nazis.

David said that in the mania that gripped the city as subsequent events unfolded, he convinced himself for a while that the storm trooper in the lobby had been Lee Harvey Oswald.

After that, Adlai Stevenson and the master Dallas retailer Stanley Marcus, the city's most influential Democrat, urged Johnson to talk the president out of coming to Texas that fall. Despite the polls, Kennedy hoped that in a year he would be running against Goldwater, not the moderate Nelson Rockefeller. But Kennedy was disgusted that LBJ could not put out the fire of animosity between Connally and Ralph Yarborough. It had been hard enough to carry Texas when the Democrats were united. So Kennedy scheduled a swing through the state just two months after the zealots spat on Stevenson and chased him to cover.

A ticket to the luncheon came Ann's way, and she got a babysitter and dressed up for the speech that the president was going to deliver on his arrival in Dallas. The John Birch Society took out a full-page ad in the *Morning News* with the mocking headline "Welcome Mr. Kennedy to Dallas." Bordered in black, it accused him of a dozen conspiracies with communists and fellow travelers. People downtown handed out leaflets accusing him of treason.

David rode the elevator down from his law office and strolled out at the lunch hour of what had become a bright fall day after rain that morning. From a sidewalk near his office building, he watched the Lincoln convertible glide past, bearing President Kennedy, Governor Connally, and their wives. "There appeared to be no security," David said. "I thought, my God, you could just reach out and touch them."

Meanwhile, at the Dallas Trade Mart, Ann poked at her food and listened to an announcement that the motorcade was delayed. A buzz of murmurs rose within the hall, and then the Dallas mayor came to the podium and told the crowd that the president had been shot. "I remember being terribly afraid," Ann said. "The only thing I could think of was that I had to get home. The escalator down was overwhelmed. More people were crowding on than could get off at the other end, and panic set in. People started raising their voices; there was a crush at your back and nowhere to go. The fear in the building was physical."

Both parents were desperate to reach the babysitter caring for their two small sons and get Cecile home from the University Park school where, they later learned with horror, older children had applauded on hearing the principal's announcement that Kennedy was dead. "In our office," David recalled, "immediate thoughts were of some right-wing putsch. Worrying about the welfare of my children, I fled home as quickly as I could to the sound of sirens wailing across the city. Cecile made it home from the first grade, and Ann eventually got through the crowds and back to the house. I was totally frantic until we were all safely together."

Then the news came that a suspect in the assassination had killed a police officer and had been arrested in a movie theater in the Oak Cliff section of town. Though a chilling Arctic norther blew through Dallas just after the assassination, Ann and David did what they often did to escape Dallas—they bundled up the kids, and with the family of their friends Sam and Virginia Whitten, they went on a freezing outing to the shore of Lewisville Lake, north of Dallas. "I had campaigned for John F. Kennedy," recalled Lynn Whitten. "I was seven years old—my mother made me go with her." In the middle of the chaos, the American Civil Liberties Union asked David's law firm colleague Otto Mullinax to get a message to Lee Harvey Oswald, offering legal representation; the answer flew back that Oswald wanted nothing to do with the ACLU. Meanwhile, David and Ann and the children made it back from their frigid outing. "Then, of course," David said, "before we could begin to reclaim our sanity, Oswald was shot on TV before our very eyes. . . . It felt like the whole place was just engulfed in madness."

In 1963, as Lyndon Johnson was preparing to put Barry Goldwater to rout, Ann had a complicated pregnancy and delivery of their fourth child, Ellen. Her blood pressure soared, and the delivery required a cesarean section. Days later, she started hemorrhaging, and for the first time in her life, she wondered how much she feared dying. She healed from that, but one day that spring, she and Virginia loaded up the kids and took them for a picnic. On the way home, Ann blacked out while driving—and stayed unconscious long enough that her head lolled. Virginia was able to grab the wheel, get a foot on the brake, and get them safely off the road. Ann had a second seizure a couple of months later when her mother was visiting them. That one put her in the hospital, and eventually her doctors told her she was having grand mal seizures. She started taking Dilantin, the powerful drug then widely prescribed for epilepsy.

A few months after that, she and David were staining a door in their house when she got a headache of such intensity that once more she wound up in the hospital. A doctor informed her that there was an encephalitis epidemic in Dallas and that that was what she had—a terrifying but ultimately incorrect diagnosis. "So there I was sitting in my hospital bed," she recalled, "in a fancy black nightgown that David had bought for me, David and I were playing cards, and this government man from the health department comes by to try to nail down the source of my disease. He was very respectful, making his rounds, and he asked me whether my house was on stilts and if we kept chickens under it. I guess the government health department had developed a standard set of encephalitis epidemic questions, and stilts and chickens were both on it, but the idea of having a house on stilts with chickens under it in University Park in Dallas struck me as pretty ridiculous, and I told him so."

Those episodes scared David and the children badly, but Ann carried on bravely. She described in *Straight from the Heart* their first adventure in challenging white-water rapids. Tony and Claire Korioth invited them to join a group that was going to run the Rio Grande through Boquillas Canyon in Big Bend National Park. The flotilla included the liberal legislators or ex-legislators Neil Caldwell, Joe Christie, Malcolm McGregor, and Bill Kugle; Willie Morris, on his way to becoming the editor of *Harper's*; and their Austin friend Henry Holman, the vice horse at the Scholz Garten. Ann had never gone canoeing, and she claimed that David's experience was then limited to his boyhood, at best. She also claimed that David was born with an unusual trait—nearsightedness in one eye, farsightedness in the other—and that he was too vain to wear glasses. She was not a strong swimmer, so her father-in-law, Papa Dick, had given her a pair of water wings that would inflate when she yanked straps on her wrists.

> We were perhaps ten minutes into our adventure when I said to David, "Which side of that rock do you want to go on?" David said, "What rock?" We hit it sideways. The rapid just dumped us right out, filled the canoe with water, and wrapped it clear around the rock. I was still fiddling with this damn thing on my wrist when David and some others drug me out of the river.
>
> When you get into river canyons, the only way out is down. . . . David got in with Joe Christie, who had been canoeing by himself, and I got in the center of Tony and Claire's. Our boat became known as Tony and his Oars. Much laughing and snickering about that.

Although the rude start to that trip proved they had much to learn as canoeists, it also demonstrated David's pluck as a lawyer. He decided they ought to be able to collect for their lost possessions on their homeowner's policy. The insurance company scoffed, retorting that their canoe was not a vehicle. David searched and found a precedent in which a judge had ruled that a vehicle is any form of conveyance, "including the patient mule or an ocean liner."

The insurance carrier threw up its hands and paid up. Of course, it might have been argued that the jurist who wrote that opinion knew very little about the patience of mules.

The Richardses' kids grew up steeped in politics, of course. "One time in Dallas," Cecile recalled, "the parents of some kid had taken me out to Fair Park, and the people there were giving away all sorts of stuff—emery boards and things like that. I came home with a bag supplied by HLH Enterprises. My dad blew a gasket. There were so many bad guys, and H. L. Hunt was the worst. And in fact you'd go in a store and gape at all the HLH products on the shelves.

"In Dallas we were kind of against everything. It made us the way we are. My dad was really into progressive labor politics, and we took part in the melon boycott, the lettuce boycott. I remember Mom taking us to the local supermarket, and she got the store manager out there and started demanding to see the boxes that the lettuce came in, so she could see if they were union or non-union. And it worked. Mom and Virginia agitated well enough that many grocers decided it was just easier to buy the union-picked produce."

David calculated that he and Ann and the three Dallas couples whom they saw the most had a total of sixteen children. That encouraged a family tradition of campouts where musicians played guitars and sang as sparks from the fires swirled toward the sky. Cecile said of the campouts, "They could put us in the station wagon and they could go out and put up the tents and drink a lot and stay up all night. Dallas didn't really lend itself to that." One of the campfire guitarists and raw-voiced singers was Stan Alexander, who had known and performed with Janis Joplin at Kenneth Threadgill's storied beer joint when he was a graduate student in Austin. Now he taught English in Denton at North Texas State University (now the University of North Texas), and at one of the parties, he brought along a student named Eddie Wilson, who became part of the gang. Though he was not a musician, Eddie belonged to a folk music club sponsored by Alexander; with members that included the future recording artists Michael Martin Murphey, Steven Fromholz, Ray Wylie Hubbard, and Spencer Perskin, the collegiate club played an essential role in the Texas music boom that soon exploded in Austin.

David met another new friend, Shel Hershorn, one night in 1964 while he was punching doorbells in their neighborhood and asking folks for support in his bid to be reelected the Democratic precinct chairman. Hershorn was a prominent photojournalist who worked on assignment for *Time*, *Life*, and *Sports Illustrated*, capturing images of Lee Harvey Oswald, catfish grabbers in Mississippi, the devastation of Hurricane Carla, and Red Adair putting out an oil-well fire. Hershorn at once dispatched David to post bail for a black man who had been arrested for demonstrating at a Piccadilly Cafeteria. The warm friendship with Shel and his family in turn brought into the Richardses' circle two sportswriters and authors of growing renown, Edwin "Bud" Shrake and Gary "Jap" Cartwright.

Bud spent the first part of his boyhood in the country town of Mansfield, but grew up on the outskirts of Fort Worth. Across the street from his home

"The halfback did what?" Fort Worth Press *sportswriter Gary Cartwright interviews a chimpanzee in a spoof promotion for the newspaper, late 1950s.*

was a golf course where Ben Hogan and Byron Nelson had once caddied for his dad. When he was a student at Texas Christian University in the early fifties, Bud began to find his voice while writing about crime, sports, and racial strife for the often-sensationalist *Fort Worth Press*. Bud persuaded Gary Cartwright, another young reporter, to come over from the *Fort Worth Star-Telegram*. Gary's dark, angular features were inherited from a grandmother who was a Comanche, but an old hand in the pressroom confused him with a past intern and complained about that useless Jap being back among them. Despite changing modes of political correctness, the nickname stuck; though he never used it in his byline, among his friends it was a term of endearment. Mentored by the editor Blackie Sherrod and running with other *Press* stalwarts, including the future best-selling novelist Dan Jenkins, Bud loped through his beats in stylish threads, sometimes sporting a Bogart-style fedora. He moved on to bigger papers and readerships, first at the *Dallas Times-Herald* and then the *Morning News*, where he was soon followed from Fort Worth by Jap.

In those newsrooms, the sportswriters were recognized and also resented as artists and stylists, the designated free spirits. Bud was the tall, handsome, twice-published novelist who would soon follow Jenkins to New York and *Sports Illustrated*. He was the *Morning News*'s star columnist, and for a while, he lent his local celebrity to an in-crowd bar called Bud Shrake West—until some bills didn't get paid and managers provoked the ire of hoodlums who had a monopoly on the jukebox and pinball-machine trade. Jap was abrupt, unpredictable, and mercilessly funny. A photo of him as a brash young reporter shows him squatting on his haunches and scribbling on a notepad as he interviews a chimpanzee in shoulder pads that appears to be having a good time, too.

Jap said that the first time they arrived at one of those parties on Lovers Lane, Ann and their friends were engaged in a contest to see who could talk the dirtiest. The crowd would improvise games of dirty-talk charades, offering lines such as "With My Thighs Wide Open I'm Creaming." On the scale of social wildness, the new arrivals must have found it pretty tame. Before the Kennedy assassination, Jap and Bud drank whiskeys on the house many nights at Jack Ruby's Carousel Club; Bud regularly shacked up with Ruby's star stripper, Jada. Jap later wrote in a 1975 *Texas Monthly* article that her act "consisted mainly of hunching a tiger-skin rug and making wild orgasmic sounds with her throat," adding that "as a grand climax Jada would spread her legs and pop her G-string." She loved to drive around Dallas in a gold Cadillac with "her orange hair piled high on her head, wearing high heels and a mink coat and nothing else."

Bud and Jap developed a mock-acrobatic act called the Flying Punzars. They pulled the stunt one night at a swank club as guests of Lamar Hunt, who owned the Dallas Texans, the American Football League team that was fighting a local tug-of-war with the Dallas Cowboys, the National Football League's expansion franchise. (Hunt later moved his Texans to Kansas City, where they became the Chiefs.) Bud and Jap liked the son of H. L. Hunt, and that night the Punzars wore not their costume tights and capes but red team blazers provided by members of the Texans' front office. Hunt's publicist took the mike and told members of the audience that the football team's distinguished guests were going to perform the death-defying triple. The drummer of the club's jazz combo contributed a slow roll of his sticks as they began. Cartwright described the performance in his book *HeartWiseGuy*.

> We had no idea what we were about to do, absolutely none. Shrake, who at six-feet-six is at least eight inches taller than me, crouched slightly to reduce the difference in our sizes, then clasped his fingers, making a foothold for me. I came running at him full-speed, leaping at the last second and attempting to engage my right foot in his clasped hands. Instead, my foot landed squarely against his chest, sending Shrake tumbling backward into the drummer. I fell across both of them, knocking over a set of cymbals, which crashed into more cymbals, creating a racket that sounded like the bombing of Dresden. As was our custom, we sprang to our feet and began to bow profusely and blow kisses to the audience, which sat stunned in an icy silence.

David Richards's days as an elected political official did not last long. Voters in their neighborhood turned him out as their precinct chairman in 1964 in favor of a dentist. At the polling station, he was puzzled by the hostility directed at him by neighbors and Democrats who had supported him before. He then found out that "all the voters in the precinct had received a mailing, over Governor Connally's signature, warning them that their precinct chairman—David Richards—was a lawyer for Jimmy Hoffa's Teamsters Union." That had not been anything close to the truth for several years. David was stung by his defeat but rather proud that Connally and his team knew who he was, and apparently thought he was important enough to carry their animus all the way down to the precinct level.

When David and Ann and the children had left Washington in 1962, he thought that someday he might like to try working there again. Ann was fed up with Dallas and no less eager to give D.C. another try. The opportunity came in

1967 when David and Ann's liberal hero, Ralph Yarborough, became chairman of   39
the Senate Labor Committee. With some lobbying, David got himself hired chief
counsel to the committee. In a festive mood, he and Ann flew up to the capital to
house-hunt. They had a fine reunion and dinner with their friends Harry and Clay
McPherson—he was by then counsel to President Johnson. The next morning,
David went to be sworn in and have his welcome-aboard meeting with Senator
Yarborough. Everything went well until David mentioned that he and Ann had
dined with Harry and his wife, Clay, the previous evening.

Yarborough threw a fit. He launched into a rage about the horrid people in the
White House, claiming that Johnson was determined to destroy him. As David
later put it, "He made it clear that no one on his staff could consort with any
Johnson people." David knew that LBJ had talked some conservative Democrats

*Original Flying Punzars, Dallas, mid-1960s. Bud Shrake, seated at left, compares notes with Gary
Cartwright, at right, as they prepare for a performance of their mock acrobatic group. Standing is
the duo's "catcher," famed Fort Worth and Dallas sports columnist and editor Blackie Sherrod. In the
group's Austin revival Sherrod's role was assumed by the singer Jerry Jeff Walker.*

out of running against Yarborough in the 1964 congressional elections. Johnson had not changed his mind about Yarborough, but he did not want any complications sprouting on his home turf as he geared up for his onslaught against Barry Goldwater. And on the subject of Johnson, Yarborough's paranoia and jealousy overmatched all logic. David knew himself well enough to know he would not put up with such tantrums. That night, he and Ann agreed that bad as Dallas was, they did not need to tackle Washington with David employed as an unhappy Senate staffer. The new job lasted twenty-four hours.

In a funk, they returned to Dallas, their house and children, and the law practice downtown. David salvaged morale with cases he took pro bono for the Texas chapter of the ACLU. One of those was a civil rights case that unfolded in federal courts for several months. David's client was Brent Stein, who wrote under the pen name Stoney Burns. He was a hippie journalist who had been kicked out of SMU and had started publishing an underground paper called *Dallas Notes*. One night the police raided his house with a search warrant for obscene material. Burns responded with an editorial in which he doubted that the forbidden words in his paper were making the Dallas police horny. "It may be possible, however, to visit the men's room of City Hall and find a pig holding a copy of *Notes* in his left hand and jacking off with his right." This time they really came down on him.

With a measure of delight, David took the case and honed an argument that writing about pornography was not pornography—it was an issue of free speech. A three-judge federal panel responded to the lawsuit by declaring the Texas obscenity statute unconstitutional. The state's attorneys appealed the ruling, and David argued the case before the Supreme Court in 1970. Though William O. Douglas dissented, with harsh words for the behavior of the Dallas police, the majority ruled it was not an issue in which federal courts should countermand the authority of the states. In a way, it was a victory for David because the case helped persuade the legislature to repeal the obscenity statute, and the charges against Burns were dropped.

Also, members of the Richards family came up to Washington for David's appearance in the big show. Ann described her experience in the hallowed gallery. "You cannot sleep in the Supreme Court. I know, because I had Dan and Cecile with me, and one particularly vigilant usher kept signaling me every time Dan's head hit my shoulder. Dan was all of ten years old at the time, but in the Supreme Court they are sticklers for the rules."

ANN CONTINUED TO ENTERTAIN herself with the Christmas cards she made
with Betty McKool and with the annual *Political Paranoia* shows of the North Dallas Democratic Women. In a 1968 takeoff on *The Wizard of Oz*, they cast George
Romney (Mitt's father) as the Scarecrow, Nelson Rockefeller as the Cowardly
Lion, and Richard Nixon as the Tin Man. Ronald Reagan had gotten elected governor of California in 1966 largely on the strength of an impassioned speech he
had made in favor of the presidential candidacy of Barry Goldwater. The Dallas
women wrote Reagan into the skit, singing:

Oh I know that I'm a cutie
Just a little Tootie-Fruitie
But I want to have my day
I can sing and dance and yo-yo
I'm a Hollywood-a-go-go
And I want to run and play

Of that time in their lives, Ann reminisced in her book about going to Mission,
Texas, with their children to attend the kickoff of a César Chávez–inspired farmworkers' march on Austin. "The night before," she wrote, "the farm workers held
a dance in a VFW hall or perhaps it was just some storage building for a Catholic
church. It was hot and dusty, but when we walked in the music was wonderful
and lively, and people were dancing, ranging around the whole floor to blaring
mariachi trumpets. Cecile was [nine] years old and she looked over with a big
smile on her face and said, 'You know, Mama, this is my first dance!'"

Near the end of the three-hundred-mile march, Governor Connally, other
elected officials, and a hefty contingent of Texas Rangers confronted the farmworkers and tried to intimidate them into turning back when they were just thirty
miles from the capital. David walked with the strikers the last ten miles of the
march.

But of that period Ann also wrote, "What was really going on from day to day
in my life, was birthday parties for little kids, Easter egg hunts, Indian Guide meetings, Campfire Girl meetings, Girl Scouts, ironing shirts, cooking large quantities
of food not only for a good-sized family but also for parties and meetings. This is
what went on at our house all the time. All the time."

As an adult, Cecile Richards told me her impression of her mother's state of
mind in those days: "We used to have the most elaborate Easter egg hunts at our
house. Hundreds of people with kids would come. We always had an enormous

42 Christmas, over the top. Mom was a woman with all this energy and talent, but there wasn't a way she could really express herself. Four kids, you don't have a lot of options. Twenty years of your life just raising kids must have been hard. I think there was a lot of intensity in how she lived, and a lot of resentment." One could not find any evidence that Ann had a notion she might one day run for public office—or find much fulfillment in who and where she was at that time. "I can't tell you how important it was that we finally got out of Dallas," David told me. "For Ann especially. I was so overwhelmed and isolated in my work, and she was at home coping with all those children. We were just so forlorn."

CHAPTER 4

Mad Dogs and First Fridays

BY 1969, ANN AND DAVID felt they could no longer stand living in Dallas. They looked at San Antonio and Corpus Christi as towns with more tolerable political and lifestyle climates and some possibilities for a new law practice, but from the beginning, Austin was the destination they longed for. Two years earlier, Sam Whitten had gotten a job teaching in the library school at the University of Texas, and the Whittens bought a two-story rock house near the campus that would soon become famous for its parties of hard-drinking liberals. During the time that the Whittens were away, David and Ann loaded up their children on weekends about once a month and drove down to visit their closest friends. The Richardses' chance to act on their wishes emerged at a political party in Austin one night—Sam Houston Clinton asked David (who by now was being called Dave by most of his friends and colleagues) whether he would care to join him in his practice. Though David had known the older man in Waco, their friendship had put down deep roots at gatherings of the Young Democrats and labor unions and during many nights at the Scholz Garten.

The Richardses were given pause by their forays to Washington, which had not gone well. They thought their children were old enough to have a voice in such an important matter. The parents called the family together one evening, took votes by shows of hands, and frankly told the kids that they had a plan to move to Austin, but that they really didn't know how it would work out. Cecile was eleven, Dan was nine, Clark was six, and Ellen was four. On hearing the prospect of moving to Austin, the kids raised a clamor as if they were about to go off

44 on one of their camping expeditions. Dan had one caveat and specific request—could they please find a house on a street where, if he had a dog, it would not always get run over?

The law office of Sam and David at first consisted of cubicles at the headquarters of the AFL-CIO. Ann meanwhile took over the housing search. Eddie Wilson, who had come into their lives in Dallas, was married to a woman named Genie, and after a year of teaching school in South Texas, they had returned to Austin, where Eddie grew up, and he renewed the friendship with Ann and David. Eddie had gotten a job as a lobbyist trainee for a beer distributor. "I happened to be riding around with Ann that day she saw that house up in the hills," Eddie said. "She made one walk-through and said, 'This is it,' and it was the one they bought."

West Lake Hills was then a scenic, sparsely populated enclave strung along the cliffs of the Balcones Fault and the winding course of the dammed-up Colorado River. It had been developed by a longtime criminal defense lawyer, Emmett Shelton, who acquired much land in the county by taking quitclaim deeds from cedar choppers who couldn't afford to pay their attorney bills when they got in trouble. The house that Ann discovered off Red Bud Trail was fairly large, sat on two acres, and had a grand view of the woods and river and the Austin skyline. "The house faced out over a canyon called Oracle Gorge," Ann recalled, "so named because if you stared down into it long enough, the answers would come." The family spent the first night on the floor in sleeping bags. As darkness gathered, the city spread out before them, glimmering, its skyline dominated by the Texas Capitol and the spire of the university tower.

"Mama," Clark said, "it's like a garden of lights."

After deciding to do some renovating, Ann had an architect draw up some preliminary plans, but then she found a carpenter named John Huber, who had known them in the political battles. He was also known for getting sauced and writing doggerel verse that the *Austin American-Statesman* sometimes printed on the editorial page. "I sat down with John, who had built a number of houses in his life, and showed him on a piece of paper what I wanted to do," Ann wrote. "He said, 'Oh, don't worry about it—we don't need an architect. We'll just build it.' I liked to hear that. It wasn't as brave as Mama going to town and getting day help, but it was close. John would arrive in the morning and say, 'Well, what do you think we ought to do today?' And I'd say, 'Well, I don't know, why don't we knock out the living room wall and start there.'"

Over the course of several months, Ann and her new chum worked on a large living and dining room built over the master bedroom suite. She clearly did not envision a cozy place where the family would watch television. The upper room had a vaulted ceiling, tiled floors, and artful windows framed in stained wood. Ann had a fine eye for rugs and original art and other interior décor. A screened-in porch warded off mosquitoes in the warm season, and there was a large patio and a swimming pool. "John was the most hilarious man," Cecile told me. "He and Mom were really working closely together. After the house was finished, he came back and built us a chicken coop, and so we had chickens, and then for Mom and Virginia the big deal got to be organic gardening, so he built her a greenhouse and the bin for composting."

Her younger brother Dan reminisced, "I thought we'd moved to the country. Back then there wasn't a lot out there in West Lake Hills. It was a great place for kids, though. We could camp out, hang out in the woods all the time, and there was not the concern about getting run over like there had been in Dallas. We'd build tree houses and do whatever we wanted to do. Emmett Shelton, the town marshal, lived right up the hill from us. His father, Emmett Sr., was the one who developed West Lake Hills. Emmett's son Ricky was my age. We became friends, and all the Shelton kids were troublemakers . . . So that was highly entertaining."

"What kind of trouble?" I asked.

"Oh, just out in the woods, setting things on fire, throwing rocks at cars, that kind of stuff. And the older Shelton boys had dune buggies; they all drove dune buggies. Constantly there was a mechanical repair operation going on in their driveway."

Ann volunteered at the small Eanes Elementary School, where she and Virginia Whitten, now its librarian, dreamed up and constructed elaborate bulletin boards for the kids of West Lake Hills to ponder. Through a small Episcopal church in the scattered suburb, Ann and David became friends with people associated with the university—among them Standish and Sarah Meacham. Standish was a scholar of American history and later a dean at the university, and Sarah joined the library faculty of West Lake's grade school; he was also an accomplished parlor piano player. David and Ann likewise grew close to Mike and Sue Sharlot. He was a professor at the law school, at one point its dean, and Sue was an administrative nurse. She later got her own law degree.

Virginia Whitten was the friend that Ann called "the rock." Reticent, practical, sometimes uproariously funny, she was the best friend Ann ever had. In their rock house on West 32nd Street, the Whittens started a tradition of several years' standing called First Friday. One night every month, they opened their home to

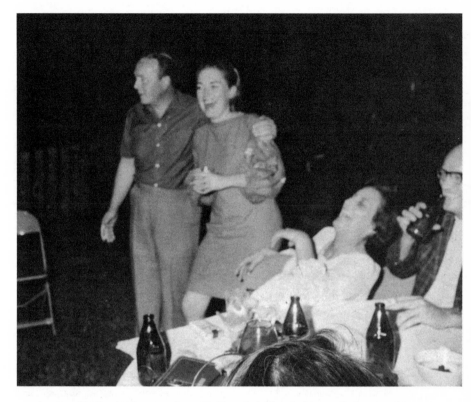

At a monthly First Friday party that spilled into the backyard of Sam and Virginia Whitten, Ann laughs at a joke told by John Henry Faulk, the radio humorist blacklisted during the McCarthy red-baiting episode, who won a landmark libel case and returned to his native Austin as an authority on civil liberties and the United States Constitution. The man at far right with glasses is Sam Whitten.

all who would bring booze and something to eat, and the parties went on for hours, a packed house of shouting, laughing, arguing people—it was home base for Austin liberals. At First Friday, you could find yourself talking to Russell Lee, the photographer who contributed sensational Farm Security Administration images while working with his peers Walker Evans and Dorothea Lange; or John Henry Faulk, the radio comedian who had been blacklisted during the McCarthy mania, but then had won a libel suit and become a resident sage in Austin and an authority on the Bill of Rights; and uproarious Molly Ivins and quiet Kaye North-cott, whom Ronnie Dugger hired as the new editors of the *Texas Observer*. After several months of First Fridays, Virginia threw up her hands and declared that everyone had to be out of her house by ten thirty. It seldom happened, of course. "The best stories," Lynn Whitten told me, "came the next morning, when we were cleaning up and everybody was reporting on who said what."

Ann wrote about the friendship that she and David shared with the Whittens: "Every weekend we would get together at someone's house, and after dinner David and Sam would argue. They would argue about anything you could name. They would argue with each other, and then if other people were around they would team up and argue with whoever was there."

Lynn Whitten said, "Most nights there wasn't a whole lot of shouting in our house. But David and Daddy would go on and on, and it got louder and louder. One time I ran downstairs and shouted at David, 'You quit yelling at my daddy!' Daddy let out a big laugh, caught me up in a hug, and assured me everything was all right. It was so ridiculous, because they agreed about everything."

WHEN EDDIE WILSON WASN'T LOBBYING for the beer association, he managed a psychedelic rock group called Shiva's Headband, which was one of the most popular groups in Austin as well as a house band of the Vulcan Gas Company, a club on Congress Avenue with fanciful poster art and strobe lights but no alcohol for sale. Steve Miller, Boz Scaggs, and Johnny and Edgar Winter were among the burgeoning talents who passed through the Vulcan scene. No less hopeful was Spencer Perskin, another alum of Stan Alexander's folk-music club at North Texas State, and now the leader of Shiva's Headband. He was a talented singer and player of lead guitar, the electric fiddle, the harmonica, and an electric jug. They landed a recording contract with a major label, and Eddie tried to enlist David in the management of the band. David couldn't understand what they wanted him to do.

Eddie also called on him to intercede in behalf of some avant-garde radio types. A local businessman had decided to redesign the format of his station to appeal to the youth culture, and the station had hired a group from San Francisco to remake the image. The second day on the air, the new regime aired a lengthy tape produced by the Pacifica station in San Francisco. It included an interview with a mysterious writer named M. D. Shafter. The owner happened to catch that part of the program and blew a gasket. He called the station, ordered "that filth" off the air, and promptly fired all the new arrivals. M. D. Shafter, it turned out, was the alias of one Gary Cartwright. David had to tell Eddie they really had no case.

Shiva's Headband could never fulfill its promise because Perskin kept getting busted on marijuana charges. (Later in life, Ann would regularly be called on to try to help him find an easier place to do his time.) By 1970, the Vulcan Gas Company was about to close. One night, Wilson said, he and some pals were riding around South Austin and drinking beer when they pulled off in an alley to relieve their bladders. He saw a dark hulk of a building, and he soon took Ann and David on a tour of his prized discovery. "It was just enormous—a great cavernous space," Ann recalled. "Most of the windows were up high and were broken out, and it was all cobwebby and had many years of filth and about a city block of junk stored in it. Eddie said, 'Look at this wonderful place. This is going to be the biggest and best music spot in Texas.' Well, Eddie was always given to exaggeration, and David and I looked at each other and thought, 'Lord help us, what is he off on now?'"

But their children got the idea at once. "For us," said Cecile, "this was really cool, this place where Armadillo World Headquarters came to be. I was in the sixth grade when we moved to Austin. Dad was defending the rights of these self-proclaimed anarchists to hand out an underground paper called *The Rag* on the University of Texas campus, and they were participating in all these protest marches. I remember Mom taking me to see Jane Fonda. And the counterculture overlaid everything in Austin. It was such a young person's place. Growing up in that period permeated our lives, and I think it was that way for Mom, too. In Dallas, I remember them having one record album—*This Is Sinatra*. Once we got to Austin, suddenly we were going out to see Willie Nelson and Jerry Jeff Walker, and now at home we were listening to the Jefferson Airplane."

In 1967, Bud Shrake had finished his novel *Blessed McGill*, an inspired western novel, and Jap Cartwright had gotten fired by the *Philadelphia Examiner* after a three-month stay. Cartwright rallied to write an acclaimed essay for Willie Morris and *Harper's* called "Confessions of a Washed-Up Sportswriter," which brought him many prestigious freelance assignments—work that later made him a founding contributor of the Austin-based magazine *Texas Monthly*.

Bud's reporting for *Sports Illustrated* took him to Thailand, Malaysia, Cambodia, Hong Kong, Japan, Algeria, and Lebanon; sent to Argentina to write about the boxing champion Carlos Monzon, he wound up jailed and incommunicado for several days as a suspected terrorist. The authorities had a habit of throwing people like that out of planes high over the Atlantic Ocean. Bud's first wife, Joyce, was an actress turned English professor. She was the mother of his two sons; they married and divorced each other twice. For a few years, he had a romance with Diane Dodd, a gorgeous girl he had met when she was a University of Texas student. She was the model for the character Dorothy in his novel staged around the Kennedy assassination, *Strange Peaches*. When they broke up, she boarded the now-legendary bus of Ken Kesey and the Merry Pranksters, and later died in her midtwenties from a brain tumor. After numerous adventures abroad, Bud convinced his New York editors that he could deliver on his assignments just as well while living in Austin. He arrived with his stunning new wife, Doatsy Sedlmayer, the daughter of a Long Island banker and an assistant editor at *Sports Illustrated*.

About the same time, Jap moved to Austin with his wife, Jo, and their children. He published a novel about pro football, *The Hundred Yard War* (1968), and then got busted for handing two joints to a couple of hippie strangers who knocked on his door and maneuvered inside their apartment by talking about friends they had in common; they were undercover narcotics agents. Jap and Jo were evicted, their Volkswagen van was repossessed, and he faced trial at a time when Texas judges and juries were still handing down decades-long prison sentences for marijuana possession. David Richards was a backup on the defense team when the case finally went to trial in February 1970. The lead attorney was Warren Burnett, of Odessa, the most masterly Texas trial lawyer of his generation. Burnett shredded the prosecution's probable cause for a search warrant of Jap's house, which prompted the irked judge to declare a mistrial. The district attorney dropped the charges, but that event did not get nearly as much press as the arrest had, and the episode did not help Jap's marriage. Toward the end of his life, Bud told Brant Bingamon in an interview, "My name was on the warrants they served the day in 1968 when they busted Cartwright, but an officer who knew me slightly and had read *Blessed McGill* scratched my name off the list."

On May 4, 1970, Ohio National Guardsmen fired into a crowd of antiwar protestors on the campus of Kent State University in Kent, Ohio, killing four students. The next day in Austin, a demonstration in protest of the Kent State violence spilled from the University of Texas campus into surrounding streets. The police responded with tear gas and force—a dozen injuries were reported. Leaders and allies of the students obtained a parade permit from the city, and on May 8, 25,000 people marched peacefully through downtown Austin. To the astonishment of many, the cadres of police lining the route kept their distance. That summer, the Armadillo World Headquarters opened, just as Eddie Wilson had said it would. Bud invested a thousand dollars in the venture, and David drew up incorporation papers for the club. Eddie and his principal partner, the entertainment lawyer Mike Tolleson, built on concerts by Willie Nelson, country-rock singer-songwriters like Michael Murphey and Steven Fromholz, and Nashville rebels Waylon Jennings, Billy Joe Shaver, and Guy Clark. The Armadillo soon hosted shows by the Pointer Sisters, the strange little Irish dynamo Van Morrison, and Bruce Springsteen when he was first becoming a star. Wilson recalled, "Ann liked being backstage, mingling with the bands and peeking at the crowds. The pleasures taken in the Armadillo were awful brazen. She'd ask me, 'How in the world do you keep from getting busted?' I'd laugh and say, 'I don't know, Ann. I don't know.'"

Those friendships and evenings led David and Ann to become charter members of an unruly crowd called Mad Dog, Inc. David drew up its articles of incorporation, too. Bud's generosity as an investor in the Armadillo won them an office in the big hall, which was adorned with surreal armadillo murals by the talented resident artist Jim Franklin, who lived upstairs with his pet boa constrictor. A widely distributed photo of the Mad Dog founders shows them standing and sitting around a large table. Toward the end of their time in Dallas, Ann had worn her dark hair long and straight, tied with a scarf in back. Now it was dyed blond in a heavily sprayed flip, like that of the actress Mary Tyler Moore. David was grinning and wearing the only coat and tie in the room (because, he said, "I was the only one with a goddamned job!") Smoking a cheroot, Bud was seated beside David, and next to Bud was a young woman naked from the waist up, except for a sign positioned above her lovely breasts that read "Jap." Though everyone remembered Julia, a promising academic and the companion for a time of the architect and raconteur Stanley Walker, no one could really say what her stunt was all about. The same could be said of Mad Dog, Inc.

The Mad Dogs' motto was "Doing Indefinable Services to Mankind," their credo "Everything that is not a mystery is guesswork." Their grandest hope was to buy their own town and write their own laws. In his book *Texas Literary Outlaws*, Steven Davis described their stab at buying Theon, a burg northeast of Austin. They were at a place called the Squirrel Inn discussing the plan when Bud wanted some water to dilute his Scotch, opened the joint's refrigerator, helped himself to a pitcher, and poured some of it into his glass. He downed it in one gulp.

> The "ice water," as it turned out, was kerosene. With Shrake ailing, the group rushed back to Austin but was stopped by the highway patrol. Cartwright got into an argument with the cop, and the Mad Dogs wound up spending the night in the Williamson County jail. A doctor friend was called to come check on Shrake. After a cursory exam, he gave Shrake a handful of pills and told him to swallow them all. Those turned out to be speed. "He thought that would make me feel a lot better," Shrake recalled. "And I guess it must have. My heart exploded about twenty-five times and I bounced around the walls of the cell for a while."

The involvement in the movie business of Bud and Jap brought into the Mad Dogs' company prominent actors, including Dennis Hopper and Peter Boyle. Those associations resulted in one wild film shoot in Durango, Mexico, and the resulting cult western starring Hopper and Boyle and written by Bud was called *Kid Blue*. Bud reminisced that on the *Kid Blue* shoot he discovered cocaine, developing a habit that lasted twelve or thirteen years. He also got a bit part as the town drunk. The veteran actor Ben Johnson, who played the sheriff, erupted one day and whacked him on the head with his gun because he was tired of looking at him. Bud was so tall that it seemed as if he fell for about two minutes. Flying Punzars were adept at that.

Mad Dog, Inc.: The board of directors of this group probably met just on this one occasion, according to David Richards, who filed the incorporation papers. David is the man wearing a coat and tie at the table, upper right. Across the table from him is Ann, whose hairstyle then resembled the flip of actress Mary Tyler Moore. Bud Shrake is seated on David's right. On Bud's right, topless but for the sign "JAP," is a young woman filling in for the absent Gary Cartwright. Austin, 1970.

Bud later commented on his addiction in e-mails to Brant Bingamon:

> With the money I spent on coke, I could have bought a suburb. I made some
> very poor decisions because of it, but it did lead me into some interesting
> places. You suddenly look around, and it's five o'clock in the morning and you
> realize you are in some stranger's house with a bunch of people you don't know
> and everybody is very loaded and it might be a surfer's house or an actor's
> house in the Hollywood hills or it might be a roomful of Mexican gangsters. . . .
> I have one piece of advice about cocaine—do not use it. It will make you stupid.

Bud and Jap also wrote a script about a bull rider, called *J. W. Coop*, which the actor
Cliff Robertson wished to star in. He had come to Texas and hung out with the
writers for a while. Don Meredith, the Dallas Cowboys' quarterback, watched the
man closely one night and murmured to his writer friends and David Richards,
"That's not Cliff Robertson. I've met Cliff Robertson." Another night Jap goaded
the vain actor by introducing him as Biff Richardson.

Later the actor sent them a letter of regret that he had been unable to get the
movie produced. They shrugged and moved on. Then, amazingly, the film pre-
miered, with a virtually unchanged script and all credits claimed by Robertson,
who was coming off an Oscar-winning performance in *Charly*. A lawsuit over the
writing credits ensued in an Austin state district court, with David representing
Bud and Jap. The matter might not have gotten so rancorous had Robertson not
claimed that he had gotten caught up in a Manson-type gang, he allegedly characterized Jap as an ex-convict hustler. Bud sent the actor's lawyer a letter on Mad
Dog, Inc., stationery that vilified Robertson, and he attached a clipping from the
Fort Worth Press: "Police Believe Frozen Dog Weapon in Beating Death." He signed
off, "Mad Dog on Prowl."

At trial, David said his plaintiffs "looked like street people, with coats and ties
that didn't fit and a distinct aura of seediness." The handsome and suave Robertson schmoozed with the gallery, prospective jurors, and the judge. After that
first day, David told his clients that they had to be back in court at eight o'clock
the next morning. On hearing that, they quickly caved in and agreed to a settlement giving them screenwriting credits and at least some of the money they had
coming. But on the screen in the revised print the Texans' names floated in yellow
against a field of wildflowers the same color.

Mad Dog, Inc., was mostly beer, whiskey, and marijuana talk, and the collective brainstorm quickly petered out. But before it did, the wild seeds proposed a magazine called *Mad Dog Ink*, which, in its first issue, would feature the prison poetry of Candy Barr, a famous stripper and porn movie star who had run afoul of Texas's antimarijuana laws. Another brainstorm was a publishing company named the Mad Doggerel Vanity Press. Jap, Bud, and others egged on an heiress to write a novel titled *Sweet Pussy*, which they proposed to publish. All this was extravagantly sexist, of course. Bud and Jap claimed that they could read fortunes by inspecting bare nipples, not mere lines in hands, and some young women peeled off their shirts to let them. Ann saw no humor in that, and she occasionally let them know it. But she did consent to be seated and photographed at a table with a young woman who was topless except for a sign across her chest.

She and David enjoyed going out on the town in costumes. She liked to make herself up like Dolly Parton, her face smeared with lipstick and padded boobs projecting from her shirt like a pair of howitzer shells. One night they went to a beer joint and honky-tonk called the Broken Spoke. "This one guy asked me to dance," Ann recalled his approach to the two-step. "If he had let me go, I would have flown through the walls. He was driving me around that dance hall like a truck, and he said, 'I don't care if you're Dolly or not. Come back to the Motel 6 with me and we'll have cotton all over that room.'"

Ann was a practiced flirt, but a part of her was quite conventional about sex and fidelity. She and David had a good friend named Bill Kugle. He had won election to the legislature from Galveston, where he played a role in the dismantling of the long-established but illegal gambling empire of the Maceo family, and the backlash in Galveston was so harsh that he abandoned his House seat and moved away to the East Texas town of Athens, where he set up a practice with the esteemed William Wayne Justice for a while. Kugle was thoroughly delightful but randy as a goat. "Ann was really shocked one time when Bill made a pass at her," David said. "She couldn't believe he was so direct and explicit." But another night at First Friday, an academic who considered himself a Don Juan hit on Ann in a particularly obnoxious manner. The man's daughter, who witnessed the incident, later told me, "I've never seen a woman take down a man like that. She sent him out of there like a dog with his tail between his legs."

David and Ann were considered the straightest Mad Dogs, but they held their own in the frolics. Their home, said Jap, "became a sort of Mad Dog sanctuary." The *New York Times* editor Abe Rosenthal appeared one night and was greeted at the door by Ann, who was costumed as a giant tampon. It had a smear of painted blood and a string coming out from the top. (You had to have been there, I suppose.) Rosenthal was charmed enough that he devoted half a column to the party and its hostess. "Bud was there, then Jap showed up," David recalled, "and they went into this routine that was hilarious and absolutely unscripted. We had a big Afro-style wig sitting around from some other costume event. Bud snatched it, put it on, and went into this act in which he was Dr. J."—the pro-basketball star Julius Erving. Rosenthal got into the spirit of the romp and started conducting a mock interview of the tall writer turned basketball star. "How can you achieve the kind of stardom that has come to you?"

"Learn to dribble, white boy," Bud replied.

Years later Rosenthal wrote again, "One of the best parties I ever went to was in Austin, Texas. . . . I realized later why I had such a good time. None of it was catered, a form of surrogacy that dominates evenings in most big cities. . . . The crayfish were cooked in Ann's kitchen and she spread them out on the table herself. There was music—not a hired pianist but some guest picking on a guitar. . . . There was a great stand-up comic—a novelist with a buzz on [Shrake]—right there in the living room, not on television. And the guests were not catered either—Ann invited them herself for her own party."

In his memoir David wrote about another night of festivity at the house in West Lake Hills. It was a fund-raiser for Vietnam Veterans against the War.

> The music was provided by a group that called themselves the Viet Gong or some such moniker. . . . At some point in the evening, the town marshal, who was our neighbor, arrived in response to a number of totally justified noise complaints. I remember thinking that I had placated him by toning the music down and promising to shortly end the band's efforts. The marshal's report to the town council was more alarming. He claimed he had been surrounded by a bunch of stoned hippies who kept screaming, "Off the pig." Who knows, it was a large yard, and I suppose something like that could have happened.

One afternoon in August 1973, Ann again displayed her gift of being in places where memorable events occurred—in this case, the daylong party following the recording of Jerry Jeff Walker's ¡Viva Terlingua! album in Luckenbach, Texas. A photograph of Ann appears in the album's liner notes. Thoroughly wasted, she looks primed to topple right off the picnic table. Eddie Wilson was fond of saying that life in Austin in those days was fueled by cold beer and cheap pot. Riding in a convertible one day with David and—who else?—Jap Cartwright, Ann had taken a few puffs off a joint and soon realized that she quite enjoyed marijuana. "But Ann was an alcoholic," insisted Jap Cartwright. "She had a vodka problem, she didn't have a drug problem."

More perilous to her health than the marijuana was her prescription medicine Dilantin. Since 1938, the Pfizer drug had been the standard preventive for epileptic seizures, but the National Center for Biotechnological Information eventually issued a stark warning: "Tell your doctor if you drink or have ever drunk large amounts of alcohol. . . . You, your family, or your care-giver should call your doctor right away if you experience any of the following symptoms: panic attacks; agitation or recklessness; new or worsening irritability, anxiety, or depression; acting on dangerous impulses; difficulty falling or staying asleep; aggressive, angry, or violent behavior; mania (frenzied, abnormally excited mood.)"

"When I was a kid," Clark Richards told me, "I remember Mom would be cooking dinner, and she would ask me to make her a martini. Mom's version of a martini filled up about the size of the glass you're holding there." He indicated a ten-ounce glass of water I had in my hand. "I filled it with ice," Clark went on, "and then to the brim with vodka, with a drop of vermouth and a twist of lemon. She would drink one without a problem, maybe a couple of them. I mean, I'm ten years old—what did I know about booze? That's just what Mom drank."

After the move from Dallas to Austin. From left, Ann, Clark,
Cecile, Ellen, Dan, and David Richards. Early 1970s.

CHAPTER 5

The Hanukkah Chicken

ANN AND DAVID ADDED another dimension to their lives by partnering with their carpenter friend John Huber in the purchase of a few hundred acres of wooded ranchland on the clear-running San Gabriel River, about an hour's drive northwest of Austin. The property contained a ramshackle house, which they gave up trying to make habitable, but the wooded banks of the shallow stream became their frequent weekend campsite. My wife, Dorothy Browne, told me of one campout: "The most impressive thing I ever saw Ann do was, after a full night of drinking, singing, and story-telling, she made pancakes over a campfire for the whole gang of us—without one hair out of place."

There were many outdoor adventures like the "Sam Rayburn Lake Caper," as Ann called it. Several families of friends had set out for a cabin reserved on the large lake along the Louisiana border. After many hours of driving, they almost never found the cabin, and then a tremendous thunderstorm blew up. It sent the barometric pressure plunging, and Ann could not get a large pot of water to boil for the night's pasta. Sue Sharlot thought the sparks blown out of the fireplace by gusts were going to burn the cabin down, and just as Ann's pasta water began to bubble, Sue dumped it all on the fireplace. Ann was furious. A while later, as they were trying to calm down and warm up, the door burst open with a bang. The adults gasped, children cried out. Standing large in the doorway was a frightful apparition: the tall *Texas Observer* writer Molly Ivins with a soaked sleeping bag over her head.

In 1974, Jo Cartwright walked downstairs in her and Jap's Austin apartment, dumped an armload of clothes, boots, and other possessions on the floor, and announced to her husband that their marriage was over. He looked down and wondered whether that could possibly be all in the world he owned. He moved to New York for several months, scaring up some freelance work, and then came back to Austin for a visit during the summer of 1976. He met a twice-divorced single mom named Phyllis McCallie who had grown up riding horses outside Wetumka, Oklahoma. In Dallas, she had been an animator and production co-ordinator for the Rocky and Bullwinkle cartoon series before going to work as an assistant and organizer for the photographer Shel Hershorn. They ran into each other again at one of Willie Nelson's Fourth of July Picnics, and afterward Jap canceled plans to go back to New York. Some months later, they got married on impulse in the back of a Capitol-area joint called the Texas Chili Parlor, their vows solemnly performed by Bud Shrake, who was an ordained minister of the Universal Life Church. The party moved on to another drinking establishment, where Jap jumped onstage with Willie Nelson and band and serenaded his bride with a spontaneous howler called "Main Squeeze Blues."

All this zaniness contributed to Austin's legend, but numerous marriages did not survive the strain. Doatsy Shrake would stay in Austin and remain Bud's devoted friend, and they shared great travels to Europe and other eye-opening places, but they were divorced by 1985. Despite running through booze and drugs like a man obsessed and becoming addicted to some of them, Bud was always a prolific writer. By his midforties, he had been married and divorced three times. Bud never suffered from a lack of women who desired his company.

In the meantime, accompanied by Jerry Jeff Walker as the team's catcher, Bud and Jap had once more taken to dressing up in the tights and capes of their acrobatic act the Flying Punzars. Ann and her Dallas friend Betty McKool were still producing their annual Christmas cards; the costuming for one of the card's photo shoots led Ann to sport a Santa Claus outfit to a party at the Cartwrights' house. Years later, Ann recalled what happened next. The sun was up, barely. "David and I had left and come home at a halfway decent hour, and when I woke up the next morning I could tell it was still very early. I was mixing in what I was hearing with whatever my dream had been, and somehow I thought my father was coming downstairs to my bedroom.

"My bedroom door burst open, and in came Jap and Bud, plus Jerry Jeff Walker, all dressed in what they insisted on calling their Flying Punzar outfits. They were attended by their wives, whom they were referring to as their groupies."

She said the Punzars wore long black tights, black T-shirts with lightning bolts splashed across their chests, and little capes that hung down as far as their waists. David reminisced, "In this instance, it developed that the Punzars had come to seek the assistance of Santa Claus. As best Ann and I could determine, the Punzars had reasoned that no pharmacy would turn down a request from Santa Claus." A doctor friend had written them a prescription for some amphetamines, and they were far enough gone to think that someone in a Santa outfit could walk in a twenty-four-hour drugstore, get that filled, and prolong the party for a few hours, perhaps days.

Ann and David talked them out of that idea, but the Punzars insisted on treating them to their new and improved act. The three of them flapped their winglike capes, Jap made another running leap at Bud, and as ever they crashed all over the deck outside the bedroom. No one was hurt, and the Punzars and their wives climbed in bed with Ann and David, with Jerry Jeff serenading them at one point and playing his guitar. I later asked David why he allowed this to happen. "Hell," he whooped, "I was the one who opened the door!"

The wildness of Austin in the seventies was one aspect of Ann's life. In another, she remained the diligent mom who was surprised and angered to find herself in an ongoing battle with the educators of her children. Cecile had always been the one who did everything right. Though shy, she studied hard and excelled at school. Their Dallas friend Mike McKool had won a seat in the legislature, and he made Cecile the state's first female senate page when she was in junior high. Cecile was such a model student and citizen, in her mother's view, that when the principal at Westlake High called and said her daughter had to leave school, Ann told him he must be making a mistake. "Indeed not," the principal replied, in her recollection of the heated conversation. "She will have to leave school immediately."

"What in the world has she done?"

"She wore a black arm band to school this morning."

Oh yes, the war. Cecile told me about that chain of events: "When I got to Westlake High, right away we were involved in the protests of the Vietnam War. And then if you wanted to be on the drill team, which was like the Rockettes or something, you had to be between five five and five eight in height." She brought home the paper announcing the rules and regulations of this elite group. Cecile was not eligible because she was five nine.

Ann was outraged, and she said that not long after that, "Dan came home really excited because his gym class had been given Gatorade as a reward for cleaning out the varsity football players' lockers. Dan was in junior high and, of course, thought it was a wonderful honor."

Ann asked Dan, "Son, why can't the football boys clean out their own lockers?" Dan replied that the football players were too busy, that they had to practice.

"That was it for her," Dan told me. "She gave up on public schools out there. She really pushed to get us into St. Stephen's." St. Stephen's Episcopal School was (and still is) a well-respected prep school on a campus tucked away in the hills above Austin. The faculty members had advanced degrees, and many of them lived on campus. Cecile and Dan were somewhat removed from their classmates who lived in the dormitories. But the new arrangement worked, especially for Cecile. "St. Stephen's was the progressive school, the alternative," she told me. "That was the first time I'd ever been in class with someone who was African American. Which was a real indictment of public school systems in Texas."

I asked, "Did you want to be on that drill team at Westlake High?"

"Oh no," she laughed. "I would never have done something that traditional and conformist. There were just a handful of kids like me. Just about everybody who taught at Westlake then was a coach. I had a coach for science, a coach for math—it was all about football, and we had to go to all these pep rallies. Two friends and I came up with the idea that we wanted to go to study hall instead of going to the pep rallies. That resulted in Mom getting in another big row with them. I wouldn't say we ever fit in at Westlake. Other people weren't having political fund-raisers on the weekends at their houses. But we were."

Dan recalled one party celebrating the release of the Watergate tapes and the downfall of Richard Nixon. "Mom and Molly Ivins were out there, and I think Maury Maverick, our friend from San Antonio. There were four or five of them. They each had parts they had chosen to read. They sat out by the pool, and they were wearing signs. One was [Bob] Haldeman, one was [John] Ehrlichman, and so on. And they'd picked portions of the transcripts to read and perform, while everybody sat around laughing and carrying on."

He recalled another gathering focused solely on the kids. "There was a Celebration of Life with us and the Whitten kids. It was almost like a teenager baptism ritual, but there were absolutely no religious overtones at all. We were all given a little silver sand dollar with our name on it. Mom and Dad and Sam and Virginia talked about how great it was just to be alive. I saw a keepsake from it recently. There was actually a printed invitation."

"A thing you have to remember about Ann," said her friend Sue Sharlot, "is that she was so pretty. And God, she was fun, including times when she was drinking. One time we went to New Orleans on a trip. Some guys wound up with our party but didn't really know us. Ann got us to doll up and come on to those guys like we were hookers. And when they found out we weren't the genuine articles, they got really pissed!

"She was like Marilyn Monroe. She got those lines in her face and throat pretty early in life—her mother had those, too—so some people who came to know her in politics never knew what a beauty she was. And she was incredibly generous to her friends. Sarah, our daughter, still talks about the Hanukkah Chicken. This was a character invented by Ann. The Richardses' home was Christmas in full bore, with a giant decorated tree and lots of beautifully wrapped presents. Ann felt sorry for our kids because we didn't celebrate Christmas, so she would dress up in a chicken costume and come to our door, announce that she was the Hanukkah Chicken, and give presents to Sarah and Matthew. She would show up in the chicken costume clucking and yelling: 'Braaaaaach! Braaaaaach! It's the Hanukkah Chicken!'

"When we had those parties at the Richardses' house, the kids would just be given free range—swimming and playing. There was a sign by the pool in Spanish that I think said something about a wet floor, *pisa*. The kids thought it meant 'Don't piss in the pool.' I remember spending lots of time around their big dining room table, stuffing envelopes for various candidates. There was always a lot of people and food and it was a very festive atmosphere. Like the Christmas gatherings but without Virginia Whitten's cheese grits and the venison."

In the summer of 1973, the Richardses embarked on the adventure of transporting the entire family to Europe. They had gotten the chance to trade houses with a couple living outside the quaint English village of Cookham. It was a large pastoral home with leaded windows and views of sheep and cattle grazing on a hillside, there was a garden of lettuces and green peas, and it looked out toward the verdant banks of the River Thames. They saw the Henley regatta, Stonehenge, and a play in London starring Alec Guinness. They had a pleasant lunch with a *London Observer* editor who had taken advantage of their hospitality in Dallas while covering the Kennedy assassination, and they tested the patience of Clark and Ellen by hauling them through countless museums. David fretted over the experience of driving cars that had steering wheels on the right, and he lost heart one day when he failed to properly set the brake of a neighbor's borrowed car, which rolled down a hill and bonked against an apple tree.

Ellen gave them a horrid fright by almost getting run over in traffic, snatched to safety at the last instant by her dad. David and Ann got drunk in a pub with a one-night gang of pals who were tossing down the house special—vodka and pineapple juice chased with beer. Unbelievable hangovers. Following a dash through Scotland, they flew over to Paris to meet their friends Betty and Mike McKool. Worried about the expense, Ann cooked meals whenever she could, instead of trying to feed her small horde in restaurants, but she sniped at David for being so cheap.

Ann was like any American dazzled and exhausted by a first exposure to Europe, but she had prepared to do one thing differently: she had alerted Eleanor Richards (her mother-in-law), Sue Sharlot, Virginia Whitten, and a few other friends to keep the letters that she and the rest of the family would write from Europe, and she would keep theirs. When they got back to Texas, she edited the travelogues and got them typed cleanly and bound. In one letter, she regaled the Sharlots with her critique of the Henley regatta and British people in general. The women wore "droopy, sweeping dresses and floppy hats with ruffled pink parasols. And the men! Migod! Sue, such peacocks! They're not a very handsome people anyway—ruddy—and they wore *ancient* (source of pride) moth-eaten blazers ('Bring down me blazer, dearie, it's Henley') with rowing club crests on the breast pocket and 'frosh' caps, crossed oars over the bill. Old school, m'dear, old school!"

Ann's only reason to assemble that journal, apart from the obvious pleasure she took in writing it, was to preserve some memories from that trip for her family. She had no ambition to publish any of it. From Edinburgh: "Clark can play 'Hail, Hail, the Gang's All Here' on the radiator! Gets lost *always*. Ellen wants to know what we're doing next. (Before we do what we're going to do first.)" Cecile was full of curiosity and an avid travel companion. Some nights she and Ann would take off together and leave David to entertain and feed the younger ones. "Paris is really beautiful, but the people look sneaky," Cecile wrote the Whittens. "We had our first (and probably last) experience with taxis. We were trying to catch one to go to Betty and Mike's hotel. After having about five empty ones very obviously passing us by, I suggested they were hesitant to pick up a family of six (the taxis are small). So we all stood behind a building while Daddy got one. The first one stopped and we all ran to it, only to have the driver floor the accelerator with us left behind. . . . The best thing I've seen since we've been in Paris was a pet store selling bats. They had a cage with these two bats hanging from the top, licking their teeth."

Toward the end, Ann wrote the Sharlots: "A boat trip down the Seine was a mistake. . . . The female narrator of the sights managed to speak French and English at the same time, which emerged as a hypnotizing double talk like playing an old 78 that's been in the attic and has mildewed. It would be wonderful to talk *with* or *at* some French people. We've encountered none of the hostility [toward Americans] of advance warnings. I respond to the scene more than England or Scotland, and I finally decided it was because of the multi-hued faces—England is terribly lily white but the skin hues of France run the gamut. If the damned people could talk! I don't think they understand each other either. The intensity of the listener is as great as the talker's. The women are beautiful. Men-dominated, I think."

Finally, they reached a chateau near Dijon where they could unwind and the kids could find friends and games that entertained them. One could tell by her writing that Ann was having what was then the time of her life. A world far beyond Texas had opened up to her, and she got on with it just fine, as people back home would say. But that may have been the last time those six people hung together as a family.

PART TWO

Superwoman's Chair

Ann addressing an audience of Democrats on behalf of her friend Mike McKool,
who won election to the Texas Senate. Dallas, late 1960s.

CHAPTER 6

Problem Lady

ANN SWORE WHEN THEY MADE the move to Austin that she was through with politics and campaigns, through with doing mundane office work for Democratic Party chieftains, and for almost two years she made good on her pledge.

Her first calling to employment in public life came from the Texas Legislature. The senators and representatives meet for 140 days every other year, though special sessions are often required. The governor, attorney general, other statewide officials, and some appointed agency directors drew reasonable salaries, but the lieutenant governor and all state senators and House members had a base income of just $4,800 a year (raised to $7,200 in 1975, where it still stands). The years when the legislature met, they could add a per diem of $12 for the six-month session, but even with that, their income barely exceeded $9,000. (The per diem is now around $170; to make up for their lowly base pay, legislators award themselves generous pensions.) How many people could afford to take leaves from their jobs, professions, or businesses for half a year, every other year, for that? The system guaranteed that rich white folks ran the legislature.

It was a slipshod way to govern such a large and complex state, but that was as much government as the writers of the Texas Constitution of 1876 had wanted. (Though amended 467 times, it still stands.) When sovereignty was regained by the southern states after Reconstruction, legislators wanted no more abusive governors like Edmund J. Davis. The Whig lawyer and judge turned Democrat had fled the state to avoid having to fight for the Confederacy, and Abraham Lincoln commissioned him a general and put him in charge of the Texas Unionists.

68   Elected governor in 1870 by the small number of carpetbaggers, scalawags, and freed slaves allowed to vote, Davis convinced the legislature to pass the Militia Bill, which enabled him to declare martial law in any county and suspend its laws, and it supplied him with a State Police force under his direct command. The Enabling Act allowed him to control patronage with the whim of a monarch. The Printing Bill established an official state journal and required privately owned newspapers to print all gubernatorial notices.

When sovereignty returned to Texas in 1874, a surge of voters awarded every congressional and legislative seat to a Reconstruction-hating Democrat. The Democrats' monopoly on power in Texas would last for the next century; almost all contests would be waged between factions of that party. President Ulysses Grant decided to let Governor Davis stew in his own broth. Davis quit the governor's office in 1874 but did not leave a key. His successor kicked the door in. Reconstruction in Texas had come to an end.

By design, the Texas Constitution left state government so limited that voters have had to approve amendments to allow cities to donate surplus firefighting equipment to rural volunteer fire departments, or to phase out the elected office of inspector of hides and animals. In the "plural executive" system, statewide elected officials direct agencies like the General Land Office, the Department of Agriculture, and the Railroad Commission. Those officials have their own ambitions and agendas and do not have to follow the orders of the governor. Those limitations have fueled a conventional wisdom that the most powerful official in Texas government is the lieutenant governor, who presides over the state Senate.

In Texas, it is against the law for corporations and labor unions to make political contributions in state campaigns, and all fund-raising must cease when the legislature is in session. But the state can hardly boast about the rigors of its limits on campaign finance. When the legislature is not in session, the sky is the limit for individual contributions as long as the gifts and favors are reported. When legislators retire, a large proportion of them never leave Austin. At once, they become lobbyists and take on as clients the same interests that in past years loaded them up with gifts and kept their political-officeholder accounts stuffed with money. On occasion, voters and legislators on the outskirts of power get disgusted and throw the rascals out. One such outbreak set Ann Richards on the course of becoming a politician.

During the 1971 legislative session, a House coalition of liberal Democrats and Republicans called the "Dirty Thirty" revolted against an autocratic Speaker named Gus Mutscher and his lieutenants over a stock-fraud scandal originating in the Houston suburb of Sharpstown. *The Handbook of Texas* describes the essence of the furor: "The scandal centered, initially, on charges that state officials had made profitable quick-turnover bank-financed stock purchases in return for the passage of legislation desired by the financier, Houston businessman Frank W. Sharp. By the time the stock fraud scandal died down, state officials also had been charged with numerous other offenses—including nepotism and use of state-owned stamps to buy a pickup truck."

Before it was over, the Democratic governor, Preston Smith, who had succeeded John Connally, ran a distant fourth in his bid for reelection; the attorney general, Crawford Martin, lost his bid for reelection to John Hill; Gus Mutscher and two of his business associates were convicted of felonies; and half the legislators were either voted out of office or shamed and bluffed into retirement. The Sharpstown scandal and the antics of the Dirty Thirty completely roiled the Democratic primary the following spring.

And simultaneously, something else happened that was pivotal. The U.S. Supreme Court ruled that two of the state's main urban counties—Dallas and Bexar—had to elect their state representatives from individual districts rather than allowing them to continue to run at-large. The lead attorney in that litigation was David Richards.

Politically, the biggest loser in the Sharpstown affair was innocent of most of the charges made against him. Red haired, personable, and slick, Ben Barnes was the overwhelming favorite to win the governor's race in 1972. From West Texas peanut-farming and ranching country, Barnes had been chosen by his colleagues as Speaker of the House when he was twenty-six, and then had risen to the post of lieutenant governor, presiding over the Senate. Barnes was on a fast track upward; Lyndon Johnson and John Connally both saw in him the next torchbearer in their line of succession. Mobilizing party functionaries and the LBJ machine's fund-raising behemoth in his behalf, they thought he would notch his belt by winning the governor's office, and from that base he might move quickly toward the White House—they envisioned him as a young, charismatic president, a cross between JFK and LBJ.

But a member of the Dirty Thirty used the onslaught of headlines and editorials to take Barnes down. Barnes's antagonist, state representative Frances "Sissy" Farenthold, came from a prominent family in Corpus Christi. Sissy was an attractive woman in her midforties, but her thick black hair was such a tangle that the look became a major part of her public persona. Barnes could only shake his head and smile as he watched her put an end to his career. He failed to make the

Once and future stars: Ann conversing with Ben Barnes, former speaker of the Texas House and lieutenant governor and a continuing behind-the-scenes power in Democratic politics despite his unexpected poor showing in a gubernatorial race in 1972. This was probably taken at a roast of Barnes, Austin, late 1970s or early 1980s.

runoff in the primary, finishing a battered and badly beaten third, running ahead of only Preston Smith. His downfall triggered the sudden and lasting collapse of LBJ's machine.

It was ironic that the Sharpstown scandal benefited Sissy Farenthold and other left-of-center Democrats, for the power manipulating the upheaval was the Nixon White House. The Republicans feared that Barnes, as governor, might challenge and defeat John Tower for his Senate seat in 1978. Also, Tower resented the influence that John Connally, still nominally a Democrat, had in Washington as Nixon's Treasury secretary. The timing of the investigations by the Securities and Exchange Commission and the Justice Department was designed to maximize the damage to Barnes and other Texas Democrats. When John Mitchell, Nixon's attorney general at the time of Sharpstown, got out of prison after the Watergate scandal, he apologized to Barnes for his role in targeting Barnes's political career. Tape recordings from the Nixon Oval Office substantiate the plotting to destroy Barnes.

Johnson had been a recluse since leaving the presidency amid the chaos of 1968; he seldom left his ranch, grew his hair long like the hippies who had so reviled him, and would die of chronic heart problems in 1973. Connally switched parties three months after the death of his mentor and benefactor, hitching his fortunes to Richard Nixon at the very worst time for choosing that man as his champion. When Connally finally ran for president in 1980, Ronald Reagan buried him—the Texan spent millions and wound up with one delegate vote. Unlike Connally, Barnes would remain a loyal Democrat; he became a major fund-raiser and power broker for both the state and national parties. He never ran for office again.

But Texas was still Texas. In the end, Farenthold's demolition of Barnes just made it easier for a rich rancher named Dolph Briscoe to dominate the runoff and once more carry the day for conservative Democrats.

In 1972, the whole country was awash in political scandal. The *Washington Post*, the *Los Angeles Times*, and other news organizations put forth a stream of stories about the Watergate break-in, but the Democrats' antiwar candidate, George McGovern, had no chance of making Nixon work hard or spend much to claim Texas's electoral votes in his quest for reelection. And yet woeful as it was, McGovern's race launched the careers of future leaders in the Democratic Party. His national campaign manager was Gary Hart, who would go on to win a Senate seat in Colorado and in 1988 would see his considerable presidential hopes implode in an adultery scandal. (He took a boat named, incredibly enough, *Monkey Business* to a private island in the Atlantic with a young woman who was not his wife and who was photographed sitting in his lap. That, plus his dare to news organizations to put a tail on him, spelled the end of a frontrunner's career.) For the McGovern campaign in Texas, Hart sent to Austin a young couple who had just graduated from Yale Law School and were living in Arkansas. Bill and Hillary Clinton didn't move the Nixon landslide in the state by one percentage point—Nixon battered McGovern in Texas by more than a million votes, a two-to-one margin—but during those months, they made friends of young peers who would be strong supporters decades later, when both of them got their chances to run for the presidency. The most visible ones were Garry Mauro, a future land commissioner and gubernatorial candidate, and Roy Spence, one of the partners of the fast-rising advertising agency GSD&M.

Ann crossed paths with the Clintons and their team during those months, and she educated a St. Stephen's history teacher named Don Roth on how to carry his precinct convention for McGovern over George Wallace, but she was not one who spoke of the good old days of the McGovern campaign in Texas. Her focused involvement in 1972 was in state campaigns. With the Sharpstown scandal growing ever larger on editorial and front pages, a woman named Caryl Yontz called Ann and asked her to talk to a young Austin lawyer who wanted to run for a seat in the state House of Representatives. Ann tried to convince Yontz that she wasn't interested, but she finally agreed to have lunch with Sarah Weddington. From the West Texas town of Abilene, the attorney had a round, pretty face—dimples when she smiled, and lots of blond curls. She was in her midtwenties but looked as if she might have been younger. Though she had a clear idea of what she wanted to accomplish, the only Democratic male politico who would give her the time of day was George Shipley, known in the trade as "Dr. Dirt." "She wanted legislation giving a woman the right to credit in her own name and not her husband's," Ann wrote in her book. "She wanted laws that would stop the practice of putting the woman rape victim on trial for her character rather than the assailant on trial for his assault. She wanted to make it illegal to fire a teacher because of pregnancy." Ann, who, at thirty-eight, was a dozen years older than Weddington, reflected, "I don't think I had been around any women who I would call out-and-out feminist activists until I met Sarah."

Ann signed on as Weddington's campaign manager, working with Yontz and Ron Weddington. Once the kids were off to school, she went to the candidate's law office, where they ran the campaign; she went home before sundown and resumed her life as a wife and mom. The Weddington campaign raised little money, and the candidate had no political experience. But she was running for an open seat, and she was a natural at thinking on her feet and framing short, quick answers to questions. Also, she looked good on television.

Within the Weddington campaign, Ann renewed her acquaintance with a volunteer who would become the most important strategist in her own political life. Mary Beth Rogers was the daughter of Anita Coniglio, one of Ann's friends from the Dallas years. A gifted writer, Mary Beth regarded people with a slanting, knowing smile and an exceptionally quick mind. Her husband, John, was one of the state's top labor organizers. For Ann and Mary Beth, it was easy enough to find out that the largest group of employees in Austin was the University of Texas's nonteaching staff. Mary Beth designed a striking purple postcard that reached all those employees they could find. "You have not been treated fairly," it read. "You haven't had a raise in years. Vote for Sarah Weddington." There was almost nothing Sarah Weddington, if elected, would be able to do to force the University of Texas to pay those workers higher wages. But Ann and her candidate knew that mobilizing constituencies ignored by everyone else was one of the ways underfunded long shots gained ground.

Weddington fired the imagination of Austin voters the same way that Sissy Farenthold did. The difference was that in the capital, a candidate like that could win. The Democrat who made the runoff against Weddington kept saying that one day she would wear her hair up, and one day she would wear it down. It was supposed to be a laugh line, but his stubborn theme was that no woman could serve effectively in the Texas Legislature. He played into the hands of Weddington and her campaign manager and team; she won her race handily. One of the great satisfactions of that race, Ann said, was that it was a campaign run by women. Always before, she had gotten behind a candidate because David spoke up for him first. This time, he followed her lead.

Ann's political instincts were not foolproof, and she often fired from the hip and from the lip. She took a position on one race in 1972 that she later didn't tell many people about. Bill Hobby was the scion of a family that was near royalty in Texas politics. Hobby's grandfather had served in the state Senate in the 1870s, and his father, the senior William P. Hobby, was a newspaper editor and publisher who acquired a controlling interest in the *Houston Post* in 1939 and brought the city its first radio station. Elected to terms as lieutenant governor in 1914 and 1916, the elder Hobby became the state's youngest governor, at thirty-nine, when James "Pa" Ferguson was impeached, and he governed impressively during World War I. His first wife died in 1929; President Eisenhower appointed his second wife, Oveta Culp Hobby, to his cabinet as the nation's first secretary of health, education, and welfare.

The younger Bill Hobby, whose mother was Oveta Culp Hobby, followed the same career track as his father, rising to edit the *Houston Post*, though a managing editor contended he was rarely seen in the newsroom. In Texas's fragmented environmental regulatory structure, he was an appointee on the Texas Air Control Board when, in 1971, he resigned to run for lieutenant governor, the office Ben Barnes gave up to run for governor. Rich and pedigreed, Bill Hobby wore bow ties, played polo, and fought all his life to overcome a stutter, which he covered when making speeches by continually clearing his throat. Though it took him a decade to assert his control over the state Senate, he eventually became the most powerful official in Texas government. In the coming years, he would do as much as any politician to tutor and help Ann. But at first she had a poor opinion of him. She supported Joe Christie, an El Paso senator whom she had admired since her first canoe trip on the Rio Grande.

In April 1972, she received a letter from their San Antonio friend Maury Maverick, Jr. Maury had his own pedigree. His family had arrived in Texas in the 1830s; the word "maverick" derives from the patriarch Samuel Maverick's aggressive roundups of unbranded cattle during the days of the unfenced free range. The elder Maury Maverick was one of Franklin Roosevelt's most loyal congressmen during passage of the New Deal legislation. Later, as San Antonio's mayor, he blocked developers' plans to demolish the city's colorful and historic old town and make its spring-fed river an underground sewer. Maury, Jr., was in turn a hero of Texas liberals; as a legislator in the fifties, he heaped scorn on the Red-baiting zealots who lionized Joseph McCarthy, and he energetically but unsuccessfully ran for the U.S. Senate seat that Lyndon Johnson gave up when he was elected vice president. Retiring from political life to his San Antonio law practice, Maury wrote tart and entertaining columns for the *San Antonio Express-News*— sometimes conversing with the ghost of his favorite dead bartender. Mention of an essay that Maury wrote for the *Texas Observer* had set off the blistering tirade that Johnson unloaded on David Richards at the birthday party in Washington ten years earlier. Maverick doted on the Richards children, sending them tree saplings to plant and signing his letters "Major Maury." But in 1972, Maury had a bone to pick with Ann, and as usual he spoke his mind.

> Dear Ann:
> I'm delighted you liked the wine. What follows is a reply to the rest of your card wherein you attacked me for being for Bill Hobby. You are a stunning, brilliant, and good-looking young woman, fine wife, and first-rate mother living on top of a modern Mount Olympus, [married to] a fairly wealthy man and one of the best men in Texas. It is too bad you are prone to flip remarks because it detracts from your otherwise many fine qualities.
> I never heard of your candidate in my life. I doubt if he is as good as you say he is or if Bill is as bad as you think he is. . . . Is there really a clear choice, is it really that important?
> Hobby is an old social friend—not close but we have close mutual friends. . . . Hobby gave me more space than any other newspaperman in Texas when I ran for the Senate 15 years ago, and at the time I said things like Red China ought to be in the U.N. He helped me more than you did.
> Suppose he does turn out bad? Have you ever known anything else in that job? Bill has a high sense of duty to country. He may not do any good with it, but I think on a comparative basis he will please you more than anyone

you have known in your life in the same job. He has a private hell of his own: Mother. That mother makes my mother, yours, and David's, rolled into one, look like a simpering worm. He desperately wants to escape.

No one knows I'm for Hobby except you and Bill. He is worried someone will find out about it. So what difference does it make? I hear in Austin circles that you're lukewarm for Sissy, and I haven't attacked you for that.

We both love David—so let us try to reason together.

Maury

The upheaval in Texas politics in 1972 and 1973 and the election of Sarah Weddington spun her life in a new direction. But events that had played out over decades on stages far from Austin instilled the philosophy of politics that drove and inspired her the rest of her life.

The American birth control movement essentially began with the suffragist Margaret Sanger. Sanger and her husband were members of the bohemian social community in Greenwich Village before World War I that included John Reed, Upton Sinclair, and Emma Goldman. Sanger wrote in her first pamphlet: "Stop bringing to birth those children whose inheritance cannot be one of health or intelligence. Stop bringing into the world children whose parents cannot provide for them. Herein lie the keys to civilization." Sanger coined the expression "birth control." She was the pioneer of an American women's movement that carried on for the next hundred years.

Haunted by the death from a second self-induced abortion of a woman she had encountered while doing volunteer social work in the slums of New York's Lower East Side, in 1914 Sanger started publishing a newsletter called *The Woman Rebel*, which advocated contraception under the slogan "No Gods and No Masters." Indicted for violating U.S. postal obscenity laws that year, she jumped bail and fled to Great Britain under an alias. Allowed to return to America the next year, she defiantly opened the country's first family planning and birth control clinic, in Brooklyn; for that, she served thirty days in jail.

Sanger was no advocate of abortion, but she called for the invention of an oral contraceptive, and in the 1920s her Clinical Research Bureau received generous anonymous grants from the foundation of John D. Rockefeller. Following a separation and divorce from her husband, she was reputed to have had affairs with the psychologist Havelock Ellis and the novelist H. G. Wells. If she was in the vanguard of free love, she had racially toxic views on who ought to be allowed to participate: "The lower down in the scale of human development we go, the less

76 sexual control we find," she wrote in 1920. "It is said that the aboriginal Australian, the lowest known species of the human family, just a step higher than the chimpanzee in brain development, has so little sexual control that police authority alone keeps him from obtaining sexual satisfaction in the streets."

In 1952, she and allies convinced a reproductive physiologist, Gregory Pincus, and a Harvard clinical gynecologist, John Rock, to increase research funding of birth control by as much as fifty times. Meanwhile, a Polish immigrant and research fellow for the Mayo Foundation named Frank Colton had discovered an improved way to synthesize cortisone, the first commercially available oral contraceptive. Sales of Enovid, first made available in 1960, netted G. D. Searle and Company profits of $24 million in the first five years. But the chemist credited for inventing "the Pill" was a Jewish man named Carl Djerassi, who was born in Vienna, Austria. His parents, both physicians, fled to Bulgaria to escape the Nazis. In 1939, he and his mother, though penniless, immigrated to the United States. Djerassi became an American citizen in 1945, and in 1950 he was an associate director of research at Syntex, a company in Mexico City.

Along with the Mexican researcher Luis Miramontes and the Hungarian George Rosenkranz, Djerassi first worked on a synthetic cortisone derived from a sweet potato that grows wild in Mexico. Later they synthesized a hormone called norethindrone, which could be taken as an oral contraceptive and proved to be more than 90 percent effective. It tricked a woman's body into believing she was already pregnant, so she released no new eggs for ovulation. About 100 million women worldwide came to rely on the pill. In the 1950s, American women had an average of four children. After the invention and legalization of the pill, the average steadily dropped to two. Produced and marketed under many brand names, the oral contraceptive pill was hailed by the philosopher Ashley Montagu: "In its effects I believe that the pill ranks in importance with the discovery of fire."

Still, the question remained whether all this fire would continue burning in American courts. Though Ann directed Sarah Weddington's campaign for the Texas House out of her law office, she was not directly involved in the historic lawsuit that consumed much of her candidate's time. But from that vantage point, she observed with fascination as the feminist attorney with the cherubic face took on the case of a lifetime.

In a landmark case in 1965, *Griswold v. Connecticut*, by a 7–2 vote the U.S. Supreme Court ruled that a state law that prohibited the use of contraceptives violated "a right to marital privacy." Then in the fall of 1969, Texas became the focal point of debate and litigation surrounding reproduction.

A young woman named Norma McCorvey had been working as an itinerant carnival barker when she learned she was pregnant. Friends in Dallas advised her to claim she had been raped: Texas law ruled that abortion was legal if the pregnancy was caused by rape or incest. McCorvey never filed charges on the bogus rape allegation, but she went to a Dallas clinic known to provide illegal abortions. She found that the police had shut the place down.

Referrals led her to a Dallas attorney, Linda Coffee, and Austin's Sarah Weddington. They filed a lawsuit in federal district court on behalf of McCorvey, hiding her identity behind the alias "Jane Roe," and named Dallas district attorney Henry Wade as the defendant. Seeking to allow McCorvey to obtain an abortion in the absence of rape or incest, they won in federal district court, whose judges cited the vagueness of the Texas law as well as guarantees of the Ninth Amendment, an article of the Bill of Rights that preserves, in James Madison's words, a "great residuum" of individual liberties that cannot be "thrown into the hands of the government." But the judges declined to grant an injunction that would enable McCorvey to have an abortion. She gave birth to the baby, gave it up for adoption, and years later completely changed her mind on the issue, becoming a pro-life activist who claims that she was a pawn duped by overly ambitious attorneys. But at the time, she told them to appeal the decision: "Let's do it for other women."

Ann was amazed by the way Weddington kept her poise and rolled with the punches. In a highly controversial ruling, Chief Justice Warren Burger declared in October 1972—right before the national and state elections—that *Roe v. Wade* had to be reargued for the benefit of the new Nixon appointees, William Rehnquist and Lewis F. Powell, Jr. Weddington flew back to Washington and calmly stated her case again. On January 22, 1973, the Court threw out the Texas law by a 7–2 vote. In his majority opinion, Justice Harry Blackmun did not emphasize the arguments of the lower court; he wrote instead that abortion in the first trimester of pregnancy was covered by an individual right of privacy guaranteed by the due process clause of the Fourteenth Amendment.

Two developments galvanized the sexual liberation of American women during the sixties and seventies—ready and safe access to birth control pills, and, thanks to the work of those two young attorneys from Texas, a law that prevented governments from criminalizing abortion.

AFTER SARAH WEDDINGTON'S successful campaign, Ann went back to her life of buying groceries, cooking supper, overseeing her children's educations, playing bridge with her friends, and hosting parties for Mad Dogs and Yellow Dog Democrats. But soon Charles Miles, a black friend who had worked on the

Weddington campaign, asked Ann to help Wilhelmina Delco in her 1974 race for the legislature. Delco, who had grown up in a Chicago housing project, was a member of the Austin school board and an experienced campaigner with a strong local organization. Ann said that Delco's campaign didn't need much of her help or time. But Delco recalled: "Ann Richards walked into my small office and said, 'Get your comfortable shoes on, we've got to raise some money,' and she did." It was a heady role for Ann to play in seeing the first African American, a woman, elected to the legislature from Travis County. Delco served with distinction for the next twenty years.

In that 1974 election, two Hispanic candidates were fighting for political footholds in Austin and Travis County. Gonzalo Barrientos had lost a previous race for the state legislature but was running again. Richard Moya had won a first term on the county commissioners court and was trying to defend it. "We rented a building over on the east side," Moya told me with a chuckle. "Gonzalo's sign marked the front door, and mine was above a side door. But inside, that operation was all mixed together. That was how I first got to know Ann. She and Claire Korioth and a couple of other women showed up to help, and they were good at it. They raised us some money." Both candidates won their elections, and Moya went on to become one of Ann's most important allies and followers.

Caryl Yontz, who had arranged Ann's introductory lunch with Weddington, took a job as the latter's chief of staff in the House of Representatives, but then got a job with the Carter administration in Washington. When Weddington asked Ann to take her place, she accepted. Offices in the House were very small; the representative and a chief of staff had a couple of assistants and perhaps a few student interns. During a legislative session, most staffers arrived early in the morning and continued long into the night. But Ann negotiated an agreement with Weddington that allowed her to go home early enough to cook supper for her family and to help, if needed, with her children's homework.

She loved the work of drafting bills, directing them to committees, and seeing them reach the House floor for a vote. There was plenty of social and working interaction among the members and staffs of the two chambers, so even though Bill Hobby presided over the Senate, Ann first came to know him during that session. And she changed her mind about the man she had blithely written off in the letter to Maury Maverick. Hobby became one of her mentors: "He was the first man outside my immediate circle of friends who ever talked to me as if we were on equal footing. . . . I was really taken with his easy manner and extraordinary kindness."

She was diligent about the work she did for Weddington during those months, and she was fully aware that they were part of a sea change in Texas politics. But she was still an irreverent and ribald character. This was before e-mail and the widespread use of fax machines; the legislative process in the Capitol lurched along with communications hand delivered by messengers. David and Ann had become friends of a young man from Iowa named Doug Zabel, who had come to Dallas and SMU in 1965. After graduation, he was about to accept a reporter's job with a newspaper in Karachi, Pakistan, when he received a tip that Ron Clower, a liberal state senator from the Dallas suburb of Garland, needed a press aide. Before long, Ann and Zabel had messengers galloping between Weddington's office in the House and Clower's in the Senate. Ann had some stationery printed up that read: "Memo from the desk of Ann Richards, Problem Lady."

She had a green rubber stamp that read "Bullshit." She used it often in her correspondence with Zabel. One day, she banged the stamp on a copy of a letter from a small-town district attorney who had written to a representative in support of a House bill that increased the fines in Texas for prostitution convictions: "The fine is still a maximum of two hundred dollars. It's a simple matter of arithmetic to see that a prostitute only has to have eight customers in order to pay a two hundred dollar fine. She can generally do this or more in one night." Beside her "Bullshit" stamp Ann wrote: "The insidious effects of inflation are felt in all segments of society. Eight tricks a night is damned hard work."

Another day, she read a copy of a profile of Marabel Morgan, the author of a best-selling book titled *The Total Woman* (1973). Ann underlined a passage in which Morgan announced, "God thought up sexual intercourse. In the marriage relationship, sex is as clean and pure as eating cottage cheese. Do it! Work at it! Your husband needs it every 48 hours!" Ann wrote in the margin, "Who needs an every other day kinda guy?"

Another time she wrote Doug a memo in response to a United Press International dispatch that Johnny Sartain, a city manager of the Dallas suburb of Lewisville, had been keeping a Thompson submachine gun in the city hall vault, sometimes under his desk, ever since dope-smoking hippies had danced naked and splashed in a crowd of 200,000 at an outdoor rock festival six years earlier, in 1969. Doug, one of the happy members of the throng at Lewisville, sent a courier to Ann with a copy of the machine-gun story. Sartain told the UPI he had several other Tommy guns in backup in case the hippies started a riot and stormed his office. In her memo to Zabel, Ann replied:

Dear Doctor,

My dedication to the council/manager form of government is renewed by the tenacity and good judgment of Johnny Sartain. "Preparedness" has always been my watchword and a riot without a machine gun would hardly make news much less put Lewisville on the map. . . . I once knew a fellow that carried a rubber in his billfold—hedging against emergencies and on the preparedness thesis, until one terribly hot summer day when the age and the heat of the appliance caused it to melt and adhere to his driver's license. He was much more law-abiding when driving as a consequence for fear of having to produce the bonded member. I would suggest that the moral is much the same in Mr. Sartain's case and that Lewisville is a morally tighter place, knowing that Sartain has his Tommy under his desk. All of this typing has exhausted me as [your] senator caused me to be over-served last evening. If I were not in such extremis, I would tell the story of the monkey and the chicken but that will have to wait until my next comment on the news of the day.

Oh yes. Please do not write suggestive things to me like "We do not have nuts like this in District 9." I am not interested in your nuts or the nuts of any of your constituents.

Mz Ann

CHAPTER 7

Landslides

ANN GAVE UP THE JOB on Weddington's staff after the 1975 legislative session, but the political pace only quickened in her life. In anticipation of the next year's local elections, a group of Austin activists approached David about challenging a veteran county commissioner who had started to rub some constituents the wrong way. The most persistent rap on Johnny Voudouris was that he no longer felt obliged to return constituents' telephone calls. Also, he just appeared vulnerable; the liberals thought they had a chance to insert another one of their own in Austin's power structure. David weighed the matter for a while and decided that he was not well suited to be a candidate for anything. It was a wise decision, Ann remarked afterward. David, she felt, would have made a stellar commissioner but a lousy candidate—he was not very good at suffering fools.

With David out of the picture, talk swung to Ann as a candidate. For several weeks the matter got a thorough airing at the customary watering holes. "I was the one who talked her into it," said Jap Cartwright. "We were at Scholz's one night and she was carrying on about how 'you guys' ought to get out there and do something besides just talk, and I said, 'Why don't you run, Ann?'" A politico named Carlton Carl contended that, in fact, he was the one who talked her into it. The two friends agreed, at least, that a conversation in the storied Scholz Garten launched her political career.

But the decision could only be Ann's, and she was inclined to turn down the opportunity—it frightened her, for deeply personal reasons. For someone who had taken up the intellectual cause of the burgeoning women's movement, she

To Miz Ann & David —
With love for the fine people you
are and with gratitude for your help, your advice,
your friendship and all the wonderful things you've
been in my life.
                                           Your devoted fan,
                                           Sarah
2-12-76

Sarah Weddington, former Texas state representative and one of the Texas attorneys who successfully argued Roe v. Wade, *presented this photograph with a note of congratulations to Ann, her former chief of staff, for her election as Travis County commissioner. From left are David Richards, University of Texas historian and friend Standish Meacham, Ann, and Weddington.*

clung to some rigid opinions about the adaptability of men. She wrote in her memoir: "In truth, I was afraid that if I ran for public office and was successful and served, it would be the end of my marriage.... I don't care how much things change, or how much men say 'I'm going to be a helpmate and I want somebody who is independent and responsible.' The truth of the matter is, men expect somebody to put food on the table for them, to provide for all of those little things that keep life together. That's all there is to it."

Their marriage had been adrift for some time. But David argued that it would be a mistake for her to pass up this chance. To her amazement, David wanted her to go for it. "He said, 'Don't do that. Don't tell them no. You will wonder all your life whether you could have done it or not. And in the end, you'll probably be good at it.'" Reassured, she was methodical and thorough in thinking the race through. She asked friends to help pull together totals of other races in which candidates had run against the Austin establishment. Then she and David and the kids drove to a condo on South Padre Island, where they often vacationed, and while the kids fished and beachcombed, Ann and David pored over the totals—not just races of comparable candidates, but also for elections involving low-turnout bond referendums and proposed amendments to the state constitution. They spent hours walking the long white beaches, comparing mental notes on the numbers they read. Ann came out of the exercise convinced she could win.

During the 1972 campaigns of Sarah Weddington and Sissy Farenthold, Ann had become the friend of Jane Hickie, a tall, abrupt, and intense young woman who would have a sterling career as a lawyer. She came from a Central Texas ranching family, but she was a graduate of Mount Holyoke and was the past president of the Texas Women's Political Caucus. "I thought at the time," Ann wrote in her memoir, "and I think today, that Jane was one of the brightest people I had ever met. She had tremendous organizational capabilities, unlimited energy, and real dedication. And she wanted to be a political player."

In strategizing Ann's county race, they bore down with yellow highlighters on a how-to campaign workbook published by the National Women's Education Fund in 1974. It posed a series of qualifying questions for potential candidates:

Home Life: What is the attitude of the candidate's family toward her candidacy? Are they willing to commit time to the campaign and sacrifice their time with her? Can they take criticism which is aimed at her? How can changes in lifestyle (housekeeping, cooking, driving the children) be accomplished most harmoniously to add campaigning to her schedule? Physical and Mental Endurance: Is her health good? Can she withstand a non-stop schedule day in and day out? What are her sleeping and eating requirements? If she smokes, can she abstain for long periods in "smoking prohibited" places? Can she withstand tension and frustration? Can she take public and/or personal criticism? Can she take defeat?

Ann and Hickie built their strategy on identifying three voting precincts that should be friendly, three where her prospects were probably so-so, and three

84   where she expected a hostile response. Ann's home turf in the county was not easy to figure. Many residents of West Lake Hills were affluent, had some connection to the university, and brought with them academics' customary aloofness regarding local politics. There was a varied assortment of hippies, musicians, recluses, oddballs, retirees, and drug dealers in the unincorporated developments strung along the shores of the Colorado River's connected reservoirs, Lake Travis and Lake Austin. And there were the cedar choppers—people who had hung on to fragments of families' failed ranches and farms and let old trucks and plows rust in the lower pastures and watched the water-sucking mountain cedars turn every acre of onetime prairie into impassable brakes and, during the frequent droughts, a terrible fire hazard. The only thing they could do with their land was to crank up chain saws and harvest some of the trees for sale as fence posts. Their hardscrabble way of life was threatened by the approach of Austin suburbs and a resulting spike in property taxes, and if they were even inclined to vote, they probably would not be thrilled to see a middle-class woman rolling up their unpaved roads at beer and suppertime.

Ann's strategy was to leave those people alone, allowing direct mail and radio and television ads to make the introductions and change a few minds. Of great importance, David Butts, Carlton Carl, and other emerging young politicos mobilized college students. Conservative legislators had for years fought to ensure that if university students registered and voted at all, they would have to go back to their hometowns to do it. In 1971, Congress and the states, with the support of President Nixon, put into law the Twenty-Sixth Amendment, which lowered the legal voting age from twenty-one to eighteen. The amendment was a concession to one of the bitter disputes over the Vietnam War, namely, that young adults could be drafted and put at risk of being maimed or killed, but in most states they were not able to vote for or against those who would send them into harm's way. Anticipating that the amendment would be ratified, conservative legislators in Texas passed a bill requiring collegians to register and vote in the counties where their parents lived. It was a brazen attempt to suppress turnout; the powers in control of Texas figured that not many students would do that, and it would negate their promise as a voting bloc.

Bob Bullock was the secretary of state appointed by then-governor Preston Smith. The ex-legislator from Hillsboro was regularly impugned in Austin as a drunk, a thug, a bully, and a bagman for Smith. One of Bullock's most fabled stunts came on the night he staggered from a house where he had been chased by a quarrel with his wife to a car that resembled one owned by Carlton Carl; he thought he had better snooze a little in the backseat before heading home. He sacked out in the wrong car, and when he woke up, a total stranger was speeding along. He sat up, thrust his hand over the man's shoulder, and in his deep growl of a voice scared the poor driver out of his wits: "Hello there, I'm Bob Bullock. I'm your secretary of state!"

Galveston's senator A. R. "Babe" Schwartz once said of Bullock, "He was the most atrocious human being who ever lived." When Smith was leaving the governor's office, senators rudely "busted" his nomination of Bullock as an insurance commissioner. Bullock said that rejection was one of the most painful things he ever endured, and for years he schemed ways to get even with those senators, who included Houston's Barbara Jordan. Even when she won a seat in Congress from Houston and became the voice of moral and constitutional authority in the televised Watergate hearings, he grumbled that she was a fraud and phony. Yet Bullock had many liberal friends and admirers, among them Molly Ivins, and despite his erratic moods and tantrums, people who worked for him tended to be extremely loyal.

As secretary of state, he was Texas's chief election officer. Around the same time, David Richards started expanding his practice to include cases involving voting rights and civil rights. In a case in behalf of students at Prairie View A&M, an all-black school in Waller County, he did not persuade a federal judge that their right to vote freely was being violated. Seeking a friendlier court, he got his friend John Duncan, the director of the Texas Civil Liberties Union, to round up some aggrieved students at North Texas State University in Denton. The case named Bullock as a defendant, along with the local tax assessor. David did not know Bullock enough to predict what he might say, but he was well acquainted with Bullock's staff expert on elections, Buck Wood, who signaled that despite being a defendant in the suit, the boss was sympathetic to the students' aims. The federal judge with jurisdiction over Denton County was William Wayne Justice, a hero to liberals and scourge of conservatives. Lyndon Johnson had appointed Justice to the federal bench, and he served notice of the power he would wield when he forced desegregation of the state's public schools in 1970. In this voting-rights case, he was quite pleased with Bullock's deposition. Bullock astonished lawyers from the attorney general's office, who were defending him, and infuriated the political old guard by his assessment of the election law: "I think it was placed there, to be very honest about it, to discourage students from voting."

Judge Justice thanked him for the input and declared the Texas law null and void. Justice's ruling transformed races in Austin and Travis County. And it is worth emphasizing: by freeing thousands of University of Texas students to vote, David Richards's courtroom activism and Bob Bullock's act of principle jump-started Ann's political career.

Ann had developed a strong belief that candidates who espoused the old saw of walking every block and shaking every hand were liars or losers or both. She relied on volunteers to roam through the city, putting up yard signs and handing out flyers. In neighborhoods that her numbers indicated should be friendly, she sent potential supporters two mailings of campaign postcards—ideally with some personalized handwritten note—and tried to visit every house once. When interrupting people's evenings, she knew to be friendly, brief, direct, and flexible. One time she came upon a house where a large flock of pigeons was cooing and rustling on the roof. She remarked to the woman who came to the door that she had some mighty fine pigeons. The woman snapped that she'd like to kill them all. Ann quickly changed her tune—oh, what a sorry mess they made! The woman went on that Austin's unpopular resident atheist, Madalyn Murray O'Hair, had lived a block away and put out food for the pigeons. Then she moved away, and the pigeons shifted en masse to the neighbor's roof, fouling the place and cooing their demands for birdseed.

Ann stated her positions and proposed solutions to pressing county issues to the editorial board of the *Austin American-Statesman* and won its endorsement; she believed that happened, in truth, because she charmed the editor, who had worked for a Waco paper in prior years and was fond of her Uncle Jimmie, the motorcycling photographer.

Ann had learned she had the gift for being a ham in the "Political Paranoia" skits in Dallas. In Austin, an all-male club of well-heeled professionals and business leaders called the Headliners Club entertained themselves once a year with a program of freewheeling humor. In 1976, the club invited Johnny Voudouris and Ann to the party. Voudouris ignored his invitation, but Ann conspired with a friend named Cactus Pryor, who had been LBJ's favorite comic, on an attention-getting stunt. In the county's parks, Voudouris had stenciled his name on all the heavy-duty trash cans. Pryor helped Ann get one of them onstage, and after he warmed up the crowd, she popped out of the barrel, swung her legs to the floor, whirled it around, and, with a grin, displayed one of her bumper stickers, which covered up the incumbent's name. Some of the most powerful men in the city guffawed in appreciation, and they later wrote checks to her campaign.

Ann also sought the advice and support of Commissioner Richard Moya. He shrugged and grinned in telling me how he played both sides of the fence. "I knew and liked Ann from the time she helped me in my second race. But I had my own seat to look out for, and the people who voted me in. Johnny Voudouris had been on that court a long time, and if he won again, I didn't need for him to be antagonized. Johnny thought the student vote wouldn't amount to anything, and he told me, 'A woman's never going to get elected county commissioner. People know that job's about roads and bridges.'"

Ann did not hesitate to call on her old friends for help. In October, on a fundraising letter thanking contributors, Ann added a handwritten postscript to Bud Shrake: "Since you have regularly financed my campaign, I want you to know that we can do some pretty progressive things at the courthouse. When you get a marriage license now, the woman is given a gift bag containing samples of (1) remover for neck rings on collar, (2) Rolaids, (3) Bufferin, (4) Massengill's douche powder. When I am elected, we are going to give the men something."

Years later, Clark Richards wound up living near Zilker Elementary School and served there as its precinct chair in elections. He told me that in that initial race, his mother and her team considered that precinct in the Barton Hills area the bellwether. Conrad Fath, whom Clark's father described as "one of the world's great fishermen, storytellers, and Democrats," was then the precinct chairman. As Clark tells the story: "She knew she was going to do well in the student areas, but she had to carry Barton Hills. That was the year punch-card ballots were being substituted for handwritten ballots. And the purpose of that was, the election judges had been able to unpack the boxes and look at the handwritten ballots and figure out who was ahead. And if a judge's candidate was behind, he could call up his crowd and say, 'Hey, we need to get some more voters over here.' The idea was that only computers could count the punch cards—so that until the final tally, nobody could tell who was ahead. That was supposed to take the election judge out of the picture.

"Well, Mom and her team were biting their nails about the race, and about two o'clock Conrad Fath called and said, 'You know, you can hold these cards up to the light, and they've got these holes in them, and you can tell how people voted.'"

Fath's discovery let her know there was no need to do anything more. She not only upset the incumbent, she trounced him, carrying 63 percent.

Eddie Wilson had left the Armadillo World Headquarters that year, exhausted by its success but exhilarated by the manic burst of creativity it help set off in his hometown. Always on the move and looking for something new, he found a

cramped little building on the east end of downtown, half a block from the police station, that he envisioned as a steak and beer joint where important and
entertaining people could just talk—there were by then plenty of places in Austin
where you could hear live music. Eddie was right about the Raw Deal's potential
as a hip salon, but the economic beating he had taken at the Armadillo told him
he had better have more going for his bank account than a downtown greasy
spoon. So he won a job as head of the local musicians' union. On January 1,
1977, a packed house of Austin liberals assembled for a party and swearing-in
of three officials: Eddie as the union leader; Frank Ivy, a lawyer friend of David
Richards, who had been elected a justice of the peace; and Ann Richards, the new
county commissioner. Virginia Whitten was a very witty matron of ceremonies.
A newspaper reporter asked Ann whether it was proper to get sworn into public
office in a bar. Ann shrugged and said that it was her chosen hangout, the people
crammed in the joint were her gang of friends, and people in Austin could probably live with that. She was right.

The race, victory, and the swearing-in had been rousing fun, but then Ann
and Jane Hickie, who became her administrative assistant, went to examine the
new digs in the courthouse. "We went in there the very first day," Hickie later said.
"We opened up the file drawers, and there wasn't anything in them. All the road
files were gone. Phones started ringing, and people would say, 'Why didn't I get
my asphalt this morning?' We'd say, 'Where are you?'" Hickie went on, "It doesn't
leave you with any information base to know what was done before—we literally
did not know where their road was."

In quick response, Ann asked the foreman of Voudouris's road crew whether
she could take him to lunch. A friend of the defeated commissioner, he did not
figure he would be staying on. But Ann coaxed him into seeing whether they
could work together. He took her out to meet the road crew, who parked their
trucks and heavy equipment at a precinct office and fenced yard in a part of the
county called Oak Hill. It was cold and rainy, and in going upstairs to the meeting
room, she encountered a soaking-wet coarse-haired dog lying in the doorway.
Trying to make conversation, she said, "My, isn't that the ugliest old dog you've
ever seen in your life?"

Inside, about thirty men sat stone-faced as she made her pitch to pull together
and work hard for the people who lived in Precinct 3. Finally, somewhat desperate, she asked them about their dog. "Texas men will always talk about their
dogs," she wrote, but no one said a word. Some shuffled their feet.

I thought, "There must be something unseemly about the dog's name, it's the only answer." I looked around and they were ducking my gaze. "Let me tell you," I said, "that I am the only child of a very rough-talking father. So don't be embarrassed about your language. I've either heard it or I can top it. So, what's the dog's name?"

An old hand in the back row with a big wide belt and a big wide belt buckle sat up and said in a gravel bass, "Well, you're gonna find out sooner or later." He looked right at me. "Her name is Ann Richards." I laughed. And when I laughed they roared. And a little guy on the front row who was a lot younger and a lot smarter than most, said in a wonderfully hopeful tenor, "But we call her Miss Ann!" From then on those guys and I were good friends.

Maybe she won over her road crew that easily. But the guys also found out things were going to be different when they invited her to the annual Christmas party. They paid for their beer and barbecue by cutting down enough trees in Pace Bend Park to sell a couple of cords of firewood. Located in the far west of the county, where the Pedernales River empties into Lake Travis, the park has a winding seven-mile road, nine miles of shoreline on the lake, many campsites, and, in its interior, a nature preserve accessible only by hiking and on horseback.

The men on the road crew were not thinning out the pestilent cedar. They were cutting down hardwood oaks and elms in the county's largest and most treasured park. Ann served curt notice that there wasn't going to be any more of that tree cutting in Pace Bend Park; and she canceled their Christmas party.

Reporters on the courthouse beat gravitated toward Ann, knowing she had a gift for colorful quotes, and she was usually glad to provide one. She was a heavy smoker in those days, and it made sense to her to use some leftover campaign money and have printed up a gross of books of matches with her smiling face on the cover. Jan Jarboe Russell later wrote about that stage of her political career in *Texas Monthly*:

Many of Ann's friends confess to being surprised when the former housewife and volunteer agreed to a full-time, high-pressure job. They must have been doubly surprised when she took to her new work so avidly—and not just by expanding the human services programs that came under the county's jurisdiction. Gone were the peasant blouses, blue jeans, and lectures on the rights of the oppressed; now Ann Richards could be found in a designer suit, out-bubba-ing the bubbas by picking her teeth with an ivory toothpick and cleaning her fingernails with a Swiss army knife during commissioners' meetings. (Read at least one story on the sports page a day, she'd advise her friends, so you'll have something to talk to men about.)

Ann's husband noted another big change—the hair. Gone was the look of the earth mother who had morphed into Mary Tyler Moore. The big hair of middle-aged Texas women would henceforth be part of her brand. "It was a straight-forward tactical decision," said David. "Now at night she wore all these curlers to bed."

For the most part Ann received high marks in Austin for running an office that few people in the city really understood. A politician with an urban base, she was catching a ride on a whirlwind of change—post-Vietnam, post-Watergate, post–*Roe v. Wade*. But she often remarked that the commissioners' courts are Texas's original form of local government. The courts are not courtrooms, and the elected leader, the county judge, is not a judicial official. The judge and commissioners administer the courthouse and county jail, appoint minor officials, offer public welfare services, set tax rates for the county, and issue bonds. Commissioners' courts maintain and build roads and bridges, yet they have no zoning authority over the hamlets and subdivisions that these roadways serve.

Jane Hickie had a grasp of large policy ideas, an occasionally abrasive man-ner, and the ability to drink most guys under the table—and she was proudly gay. Even in a city as bohemian and open-minded as Austin, out-of-the-closet lesbi-ans were not common in highly visible government positions. Ann's thirty-five-year friendship with Hickie was full of mutual respect, and it was complicated. In later years, allies and political enemies often claimed that the older woman kowtowed to the aggressive young lawyer.

Ann and Hickie found a crack appointments secretary in Nancy Cannon. Ef-ficient and funny, she resembled the actress Julie Christie, and, like Hickie, she shared a sense of mission with their boss. Following up on the themes that had gotten Ann elected, they made sure that constituents' letters were answered, that their telephone calls were returned. And along with that crew of guys with the ugly dog and equipment yard in Oak Hill, they tried to make sure that the narrow, twisting roads and bridges in her precinct were holding up to an ever-increasing load of traffic.

Ann didn't know how difficult that would be. She found out that she was re-sponsible for more than 500 miles of county roadways, while some of her fellow commissioners had less than 150 miles in their precincts, and budgets for maintenance were not divided up proportionally. She won the political support she needed to get her budget increased by $150,000. She said she would use it to hire more drivers and buy new dump trucks; the ones they had were spending too much time in the shop. Imagine that—Ann Richards, looking for the best buys in dump trucks.

Ann and her staff worked with the county judge, fellow commissioners, and their aides in budgeting expenditures for general sanitation inspections, food and milk inspections, vacant acreage cleared, air and water pollution samples collected, loose dogs picked up, dog-bite investigations, "loads of rodent harborage removed," and city and county acres sprayed for insects. They provided burials for paupers, appointed members to the Child Welfare Board and oversaw its meetings, and, enabled by the legislature and Governor Dolph Briscoe, founded an Austin–Travis County Mental Health and Mental Retardation Center. Ann

First-term Travis County Commissioner Ann Richards speaks to greater Austin's needs from a vantage point south of downtown and the Capitol, about 1977.

took great pride in helping develop Travis County Services for the Deaf, in fending off proposed budget cuts to Child Protective Services, and in improving the Infant-Parent Training Center, which provided particular help for children who were born with Down syndrome.

Lieutenant Governor Bill Hobby asked her to work with a committee—whose members included one of her drinking pals, the University of Texas regent Frank Erwin—set up to examine the state's delivery of human services. In the division of responsibilities, Ann wound up assessing the state's failure to steer juveniles in trouble with the law away from a future as inmates of state penitentiaries. At her direction, the committee devised legislation that would provide state money for a probation system dedicated to serving juveniles, but the money would be released only as matching funds to counties wishing to participate. "Seventy-two percent of the juveniles who are serving time in the state of Texas have abused alcohol or drugs," she concluded. "Many of them have reading or learning disabilities. The answer society has devised is, 'Let's lock them up and our problems will be solved.' But you can't build enough buildings to lock them all up, you just can't." That committee and its charge fueled her with a sense of mission she would bring to a much higher office than county commissioner.

The old Travis County Jail downtown was a constant headache for the commissioners. The roof was always leaking, and it was buckled enough that a pool of standing water became home to goldfish. In 1974, a federal district judge had ruled that the jail was detrimental to the health and safety of the inmates; he ordered the county to bring the lockup into compliance with requirements of the state Jail Standards Commission. "I would like to see it closed," Ann told reporters in 1978. "The number of violent deaths we've had indicates that rational behavior has no chance of survival in that type of situation." The incident that prompted her remark was the stabbing death of an inmate over a pair of shoes. The county judge and commissioners phased out the old jail and committed taxpayer revenues to construction of an expensive new one in the suburb of Del Valle, which later proved to have certain design problems of its own: with the foil of chewing-gum wrappers, the inmates found they could easily pick the locks. Design flaws delayed the opening of the new jail until 1986.

But all those issues paled in comparison to the fierce battle between environmentalists and developers. About half of Austin and its suburbs rest on thin topsoil and a substructure of limestone that is between three hundred and seven hundred feet thick; within that cavernous rock is a large circulating body of water called the Edwards Aquifer. Limestone is porous, full of holes big and small. Under the pressures of periodic drought, agricultural irrigation, and expanding residential development, artesian wells and springs often dried up. The holes and fissures in the limestone also let water trickle through a natural filtering system. Unlike San Antonio and several smaller towns and cities, Austin does not rely on the aquifer for drinking water; that comes from water rights to reservoirs on the Colorado River. But the aquifer lets out the clear-running Barton Creek and a jewel of a swimming hole called Barton Springs Pool. Shaded by a lush stand of oaks, pecans, and cottonwoods, the channel filled by the springs was treasured by Indian tribes centuries before any settlers of European heritage camped beside it. Barton Springs Pool and the swimmers who cherish its sixty-eight-degree water became the foremost symbols of Austin's uniqueness and self-possession.

By the time Ann was elected commissioner, the battle for the soul of the city was already joined. In 1974, John Connally and Ben Barnes had bought 2,200 acres on the aquifer's watershed and launched a lavish country-club development called the Estates of Barton Creek. That same year, the Texas Highway Department, later renamed the Texas Department of Transportation, built a bridge over Town Lake and extended past Barton Springs and over the aquifer's recharge zone a freeway called Mopac (because much of it ran beside a busy railroad track originally laid by the Missouri Pacific). In the 1920s, this road had been proposed as a short, nicely landscaped boulevard with a forty-five-mile-an-hour speed limit (some signs along the expressway still identify it as "Mopac Boulevard"). In opposition to the developers and the choked commuter artery that Mopac became, a nonprofit organization called SOS—Save Our Springs—grew into a major power in Austin and Travis County politics. Barnes and Connally went broke with their real estate development, but others took advantage of Mopac and other roadways, laying out grand schemes for subdivisions to be built over the aquifer's recharge zone and along Barton Creek. Two of those developers were Gary Bradley and John Wooley.

Bradley was smooth, handsome, and flamboyant, often a smart aleck. He said he grew up in hardscrabble rural Texas before he moved to Austin and began to chart his future, eyeing a 4,000-acre ranch south of town. Wooley was Bradley's opposite in many ways—soft-spoken, balding, and given to wearing glasses with translucent frames. Bradley eventually succeeded in turning that run-down ranch house and its pastures into a development of 3,700 homes called Circle C Ranch. Wooley was his main partner on the Rob Roy development.

Bradley and Wooley promised a development with first-rate schools, a paved course for bicyclists, and land set aside for what became the Lady Bird Johnson Wildflower Center. They later parted company in one of the most remarked-upon fistfights in Austin lore. But before that occurred, they had been friends of

94   Ann Richards and major contributors to her early campaigns. Ann was praised by many environmentalists in the community as a leader with a "neighborhood outlook," even as she demonstrated skill at knowing how to get state and federal funds channeled into road building. But like most politicians, Ann was loyal to old friends, even after Bradley went on to become an iconic villain in the view of environmentalists. One time, while being interviewed for *Texas Monthly* by Gary Cartwright, Bradley mocked and infuriated the SOS crowd: "Barton Springs? We'll fill it with Perrier!" Ann's friendship with Bradley would dog her the rest of her political career.

Ironically, given the distrust Ann aroused among some environmentalists, one of her greatest sources of pride as a county commissioner had everything to do with protecting water quality and the beauty of Austin and the Hill Country. A new multilane highway called Loop 360 was being built around the western edge of the city and through West Lake Hills, and it would cross a picturesque bend of Lake Austin, a winding reservoir on the Colorado River. Though the construction contracts were put out for bid, the real designers were engineers at the Texas Highway Department. They aimed to build the bridge the way they always had— straight ahead, lots of reinforced concrete, ample supports sunk in the lakebed. It didn't concern them that water skiers were in an uproar over landslides into the lake from the preparatory excavations, and they didn't appreciate being lectured by some pushy female county commissioner.

But in the end, Ann helped achieve what most people in Travis County would not have envisioned—a bridge that has the look of architecture and sculpture, a thing of beauty. It was a major part of Ann's legacy as a local official. Working with Evelyn Wanda Johnson, a local activist she had gotten to know while working on Ralph Yarborough's senatorial campaigns, Ann helped develop plans for a $10 million bridge, completed in 1982, that features a central arched span constructed from burnished, copper-colored steel imported in part from Japan and South Korea. Officially named for Percy Pennybacker, a longtime engineer for the highway department, the bridge has become one of the most stylish and frequently photographed landmarks of Austin. It reportedly cost less than the state design would have, and it is safer as well, since there are no piers for boaters to dodge. In 1984, after Ann had left county government, it won first place in the initial Excellence in Highway Design competition of the Federal Highway Administration.

CHAPTER 8

Raw Deals

BELLA ABZUG, THE OUTSPOKEN FEMINIST and Democratic member of Congress from New York, developed a particular affection for Ann, nicknaming her "Texas" and saying, "Texas, you've got spunk." Ann's emergence as a national figure in feminist politics began when she worked for Sarah Weddington. The United Nations declared 1975 International Women's Year, and Abzug introduced and steered to passage a bill that proposed a National Women's Conference as part of the nation's bicentennial celebration. Houston won the bid for the conference—which missed the bicentennial deadline and did not take place until 1977—and twenty thousand women attended. Moving through the crowd with retinues of photographers were Betty Ford, Rosalynn Carter, Coretta Scott King, Lady Bird Johnson, and her daughter Lynda Johnson Robb. "Total chaos," laughed Mary Beth Rogers, "the whole time."

Abzug chose Ann to make the initial speech at the conference and turn up the volume of organizational support for the pending Equal Rights Amendment. It was Ann's first major political address. She spoke, she said, for "those few of us who are fortunate enough to be in the positions we are in, but also for those who are voiceless, the divorced woman who may not get credit, the widows who are not capable of making a living, my own daughter who cannot find women in the elementary school history texts of this country, and the men who encourage us and support equal rights." She closed the speech: "Our problems are the problems of tomorrow. We don't just need to be right. We need to be in office."

The novelty of voting for herself: en route to an electoral triumph, Ann walks away
from Austin polls accompanied by her children Dan and Cecile, early 1980s.

Barbara Jordan, the Houston native and member of Congress, was the keynote speaker. Jordan brought the delegates roaring to their feet with her almost Shakespearean diction: "Human rights apply equally to Soviet dissidents, Chilean peasants, and American women! Women are human. We know our rights are limited. We know our rights are violated. We need a domestic human rights program. This conference should be the beginning of such an effort, an effort that would be enhanced if we would not allow ourselves to be brainwashed by people who predict chaos and failure for us.

"Tell them they lie—and move on."

AFTER THE HOUSTON CONFERENCE, Ann began to get requests to make appearances all around the country. At a three-day Campaign Techniques Institute conference in the Dallas suburb of Irving, she was photographed showing an

Oklahoma state legislator how to shake hands. "The secret," Ann was quoted in the caption, "is to be quick on the thrust, get the space between your thumb and forefinger to touch your constituent's thumb-forefinger first. Slow thrusters end up with crushed fingers."

On the home front, David and Ann and the family had gone down to San Antonio to tour the displays at the unveiling of the Institute of Texan Cultures. They saw a slide show that Ann thought was truly thrilling. But when it was over and they were lining up to walk through the exhibits, Ann's youngest child, Ellen, tugged at her mother's sleeve and asked, "Where were the women?"

Ellen Richards's question made Ann realize that the only women consistently mentioned in Texas history were Miriam "Ma" Ferguson, who served two terms as governor in the twenties and thirties; and Cynthia Ann Parker, the tragic nineteenth-century woman who was abducted as a child by Comanches and became one of them, only to be taken by force again and made to spend the rest of her life a captive of her Texan family. Ann served on the board of the Foundation for Women's Resources with Hickie, Sarah Weddington, Cathy Bonner, Judith Guthrie, and Martha Smiley. They engaged Mary Beth Rogers, a skillful writer, to take on what became a four-year, $400,000 project that profiled other influential and important Texas women: the pilot Katherine Stinson, who made her first solo flight in 1912; nineteen-year-old Emma Tenayuca, who led a bitter strike of San Antonio pecan shellers in 1938; Clara Driscoll, a young heiress who kept the Alamo from being demolished; Bette Graham, the inventor of the correction fluid Liquid Paper; and Katherine Anne Porter, the novelist and short story writer who boasted, "I was the first native of Texas in its whole history to be a professional writer."

At home, Ann and David clung to their evening routines, but now the telephone rang almost constantly. "David and I had a game we played," Ann reminisced. "The phone would ring and he would answer it, and if it was for me he would cup his hand over the receiver, point it toward me, and say, 'Ann, it's King Kong,' or 'Ann, it's the governor.'" It was a signal that the caller was probably someone Ann didn't want to talk to, at least not at martini hour. When the phone rang one night not long after a Democrat regained the presidency, David cupped his hand over the receiver and said "Ann, it's Midge Costanza."

Ann didn't believe it: Costanza was the highest-ranking woman in the Carter administration. As she later recalled, "I swept up the phone and said very cavalierly, 'Hi, Midge, what do you want? I'm cooking David's supper.'"

There was a stunned pause, then the caller said, "Ann, President Jimmy Carter has asked me to call you to see if you would be willing to serve on his Advisory Committee for Women."

Ann stammered and started apologizing as fast as she could. "My God, Midge. . . . I had no idea it was really you. . . . Of course I accept."

The invitation ushered Ann into friendships with the actress Anne Ramsey and the syndicated columnist Erma Bombeck, and it was a thrilling experience— at first. Funded by the Department of Labor, the committee met in Washington, focusing on the suddenly clouded prospects of the proposed Equal Rights Amendment. At the outset it had seemed that the amendment could not fail. By late 1972, the year that Congress approved the Equal Rights Amendment and submitted it to the states, legislatures in thirty of the required thirty-eight states, including Texas, had ratified it. Richard Nixon supported it. Then Phyllis Schlafly entered the picture.

Schlafly was a conservative attorney and activist from Missouri who had gained national footing with a self-published book called *A Choice, Not an Echo* (1964), which idealized Barry Goldwater's presidential campaign and offered dark intimations on why Lyndon Johnson won. Now she launched a grassroots campaign to stop the ERA, and her chiggers drew blood. She was pinning down state legislators with charges that the ERA would cause women to be drafted into the military, that they would have to use unisex bathrooms, that widows would lose their Social Security benefits as "dependent wives." And always between the lines of that rhetoric was fierce opposition to abortion and the Supreme Court's ruling in *Roe v. Wade*.

The committee was not able to debunk Schlafly's rhetoric or counter her organizing of conservative women. Ann was sick with the flu and unable to go to Washington when the committee imploded as a result. President Carter had grown suspicious that Abzug intended to embarrass him publicly, so his chief of staff, Hamilton Jordan, called Abzug aside and told her she was being relieved as the committee chair. More than half the women quit in protest. Members called Ann and urged her to resign as well. She listened to their complaints and reasoning, but she couldn't do that. The ERA's ox was in the ditch, as she often said in her speeches, and she felt obliged to try to help pull it out.

Months passed while the committee had no chair. Ann and other members decided that Lynda Johnson Robb would be an ideal replacement. She was the respected daughter of Lyndon and Lady Bird Johnson, and her husband, Chuck Robb, at that time a candidate for lieutenant governor of Virginia, was perceived as a rising star of the Democratic Party. Also, no one would ever say Lynda Robb was as abrasive as Bella Abzug. In a meeting the next day, LBJ's daughter began with a short statement, then turned to Ann. As Ann remembered it, she said, "Mr. President, it is our impression that you are willing to personally make some calls on behalf of our interests, and of central interest to us is the passage of the Equal Rights Amendment. We feel that there are areas and people that you might contact who would be helpful in the individual states."

Carter cut her off with the stern look and tone of a U.S. Naval Academy graduate and a rainless Georgia peanut farmer. The president scolded them: "Frankly, ladies, I am *very* disappointed." He said he thought they were going to tell him what *they* meant to do to get the amendment passed.

Lynda Robb was so thunderstruck by the rebuke that she told Ann that she had to talk to the White House press corps. Suddenly, Ann was trying to put words and thoughts together while Sam Donaldson, the walrus of the group, yawped, "Well, what's he gonna *do*?"

"Who knows?" was about all she could say. Ann was dumbfounded, too. She was proud of her performance with the White House press corps, but it was clear that Carter was not going to spend his dwindling political capital trying to rescue the Equal Rights Amendment. Congress had stipulated that the states had to ratify the amendment by 1982, and the growing resistance in several states set off an alarm verging on panic. This time Barbara Jordan had it wrong. The ERA was stymied, and Schlafly's forces were in a position to run out the clock. In its biggest test, the women's movement floundered in chaos and failure.

In the end, Ann's experience with the Carter administration, though fairly extensive, was hardly positive. In 1978, one of the president's aides, having heard of the Richardses' great love for canoeing expeditions, arranged for Ann and David to test their whitewater mettle on the Chattooga River in Georgia. Several scenes in the movie *Deliverance* had been shot on the Chattooga's fearsome rapids. David rented a Winnebago, and several Texas friends joined them in what was planned as a celebration of their twenty-fifth wedding anniversary. David and Ann had barely put their paddles in the water when someone photographed their vertical plunge over a churning six-to-eight-foot waterfall. Though they came out of that one grinning, the Chattooga's rapids far exceeded anything in their experience as well as their ability to navigate them. At one point, one of their most unflinching adventurer pals, the small-town lawyer and former legislator Bill Kugle, flopped on a rock and said he had had enough terror for one day.

But fear of drowning was just one of the dreads gnawing at David. On the way to the Chattooga, in some town in Tennessee, Ann—who was not the only elected official in that canoe caravan, nor the most prominent—and another member of the gang had run down a main street like a pair of chimpanzees gone bonkers, howling and whooping and jumping up and down on cars. It was a wonder they got out of that town without all of them going to jail.

David maintained his silence about the Chattooga River trip for more than twenty years, but he spoke up about it in his memoir:

> It struck me that Ann had fallen victim to the perennial risk of successful politicians—beginning to think they are bulletproof. The political life is full of hazards. The hours are long, the stress is high, and the temptations are great. Having a few drinks with colleagues becomes the norm, and before you know it, you're sloshed. But everyone covers for you, because they like you or because you have power or because it's our nature to look the other way. In any event, I did not step forward at the time and try to reverse the course, assuming I had the power to do so. I let the issue slide, and as a result, the gulf between us continued to widen as time passed.

David wrote that the next year he was "lured" into letting his name go forward as a possible nominee to fill a vacancy on the Fifth Circuit Court of Appeals. "I knew in my soul it was a mistake, but I wasn't thinking very clearly." He did note with gratitude that some friends brought a good deal more passion to the quest than he did. One of those friends was Jim Mattox.

Initially, David and Ann had not been close to Mattox during the Dallas years. At that time, Mattox was a young assistant DA on the staff of Dallas County district attorney Henry Wade. But in 1973, with some help from David on a redistricting case that, as a by-product, created a favorable map for Mattox, he won a seat in the legislature representing part of Dallas's blue-collar, multiethnic east side. He pushed an aggressive agenda of support for organized labor, ethics reform, open government, and consumer protection, and then, running in lockstep with the Jimmy Carter–Walter Mondale presidential campaign, he got elected to Congress in 1976. David was flattered and moved that Mattox kept up a continuing bombardment of the White House with calls and letters on his behalf. Also, Wilhelmina Delco told John White, the well-liked Democratic Party national chairman from Texas, that the civil rights movement wanted one thing from the Carter administration: David's appointment to the federal judiciary.

David Richards in a somber moment with Raw Deal co-owner Fletcher Boone (in glasses). Austin, 1980s.

Her invoking the entirety of the civil rights movement was hyperbole, but David couldn't complain.

By then Ann had developed an enthusiasm for smoking pot, especially when she was drunk, and she enjoyed being the bad girl—it did not really matter what company she was in. David told me about an incident when the judicial appointments were pending. There was no discernible regret in his account. "One time we were in Washington, riding in a car with Midge Costanza, when Ann fired up. I figured my goose was cooked, to the extent it wasn't cooked already."

But David conceded that one of the problems in their marriage was lack of communication. Ann believed she was doing all she could to *help* David get that appointment. She wrote Bud Shrake following an Austin fund-raiser that he had been unable to attend.

> Dear Bud,
> I got your check and I appreciate the help. The fund-raiser turned out to be one helluva party . . . and I paid off my debt to boot. It would have been more fun if you had been there. We started with chamber music, drink and food. Thinking that the older folks would enjoy themselves and leave before the disco show began. Ha! At one a.m. my mother was wildly waving her arms in the air with pulsating colored lights making her face a ghastly distortion. Gray heads outnumbered others . . .
> David has been interviewed by a citizen panel to elect nominees for the Fifth Circuit judgeship. He made the cut and is among fifteen nominees sent to the White House for consideration. There are five slots and it will be extremely difficult, but we have high hopes that he will make it. One slot will go to a Mexican, one a black, possibly one to a woman, which leaves only two for poor old white males. My work and association with Carter will not hurt a bit, and hopefully Sarah Weddington will do what she can.
> Jane Hickie and I had supper at the White House this week. An intimate little affair of the members of the President's Committee on Women who did not resign following Bella's firing. . . . Not much to drink though.
> We miss seeing you. Thanks again for being there with a check when your political hack friends need help.
> Love, Ann

Though David did not win the federal judicial appointment, it is unlikely that Ann's indiscreet tokes in that cab played any role in it. Midge Costanza had more pressing things to think about than marijuana smoked by the wife of a potential appellate judge appointee. She had been given a large office in the White House and the title assistant to the president for public liaison. But Carter had been in office only eight months when Costanza summoned thirty female presidential appointees to the White House for a show of protest against his opposition to federal financing of abortions for impoverished women. Months later, Costanza became the first member of the administration to call for the resignation of Bert Lance, the president's ethically challenged and embattled friend and director of the Office of Management and Budget. Costanza's goose was the one cooked. The Carter team stripped her of her staff and reassigned her to a basement office, where she quipped, "At least it's hard to commit suicide down here." She resigned from Carter's staff not long after that. Carter appointed Sarah Weddington as her replacement.

ANN AND DAVID WERE IN THE GRIP of a longtime marriage that was fast going wrong. Her qualms about what would happen if she went into politics had an element of self-fulfilling prophecy. In her book, she elaborates in a way that is both anguished and condescending.

> I had been so admiring of David because of how much he knew; the richness of his schooling and his background was far beyond anything that I would ever know. I could have started studying that day and I would have never caught up to him. David was so bright and quick. And here all of a sudden there were situations in which he was dead wrong. I was stunned.
>
> We had traveled along the same road for twenty-some-odd years and then suddenly my life just went straight up like a skyrocket. New experiences, new people, new ideas, new activities, and David was still doing the same thing he had always done. He was very good at it, but it was hard for him and a terror on me. I started thinking about it all the time, and what I saw happening was that my most valued relationship was beginning to spin out of my control. And the harder I reached for it, the more elusive it became.

David maintained that one side of his personality was dark and gloomy, but that wasn't how he was perceived as he walked about his office or the courtroom with his long stride, rubbing his hand over his bald scalp as if for luck. David and Sam Houston Clinton, who would soon be elected to the Texas Court of Criminal Appeals, had bought a large yellow-brick house on West Seventh Street and divided it into offices that housed the dominant forces in Texas liberal politics in the 1970s. One of the tenants in the building was the *Texas Observer*. For most of the seventies, that office was a place for the interviews, visitors, and contrasting styles of small, quiet Kaye Northcott and large, boisterous Molly Ivins, who was followed about by the devoted mongrel she named Shit. The other tenant in the building was the Texas chapter of the American Civil Liberties Union. The director, John Duncan, was a former academic economist who would lose his patience at a public forum in Amarillo in the early 1980s and delight reporters by erupting, "Ross Perot is a dumbshit." The staff lawyer was the California native Mary Keller, and the associate director was Dorothy Browne, who had watched her husband, Billy Lee Brammer, squander his writing talent and succumb to the drug culture—he died of an accidental amphetamine overdose when he was just forty-eight. David had not been close to Billy Lee, but he understood the lingering sadness of Dorothy and the writer's friends and admirers. *The Gay Place* captured the soul and style of Austin politics in the fifties and, better than any of the history and journalism at the time, the enigma of LBJ.

Some of David's most rewarding and important cases were undertaken pro bono for the Texas Civil Liberties Union, and whether they had an active case working or not, he liked to climb the stairs, lounge on the porch swings, and shoot the breeze with the drawling activist and two smart, pretty women. There were less inviting ways to spend the time. Such as going home.

In 1979, Eddie Wilson sold his little beer joint and greasy spoon, the Raw Deal, to two of Austin's great characters. Fletcher Boone and Jim "Lopez" Smitham had grown up together in Wichita Falls. Fletcher was a painter and sculptor whose boosters in New York included the influential writer George Plimpton, but Fletcher knew he would never be disciplined and productive enough to prosper as an artist. He ran an art gallery for a while in a rental property of Bud Shrake's. A street number on the door, 600, was hard to make out, and the place became known as Gallery Goo. Lopez, who had no Hispanic relatives, wore a hipster's goatee, dark glasses, and sometimes an ascot. He kept in his wallet a photograph of his profligate hero, Egypt's King Farouk.

Later they took on a third partner, Segal Fry, a banjo player of note, and they closed the original tiny place near the police station and opened two more Raw Deals. These joints had much more space, the owners had a liquor license, and the food was reasonably priced and more than passable; and if it wasn't, a sign above the bar read "It'll Be Better Next Time." For a decade, the Raw Deals were the salons that Eddie Wilson had envisioned: friendly places frequented by politicians,

lobbyists, real estate brokers, reporters, artists, professors, authors, and musicians—as long as that last bunch observed the house rule about guitars stated on
another sign: "Leave 'em in the car."

But for all the pleasure of that company, David admitted in his memoir that by
this time he was working up a keen distaste for Ann's political career, and what
its future might hold for him.

> Initially, being Ann's sidekick in the political mainstream was sort of fun.
> Shortly, though, I found myself uncomfortable. I don't think it was because I
> was taking a backseat to Ann; I had always done that in our social life, but that
> could well have been a source of discontent. I know I was not at ease in the re-
> spectable circles to which she was drawn. The anarchist side of me made me ill-
> suited for conventional behavior. For a while, I discharged my escort duties in
> reasonable fashion, but down deep this role did not square with my self-image.
> I thought of myself as a maverick, a dissenter, and a troublemaker. Much of this
> is now hindsight, but I am certain I was not destined to fit into polite society. . . .
> Somewhere inside me, I feared that my new role as consort was hurtling me
> toward the very life I had fled for so long.

Ann and David were among the regulars at the Raw Deal. The extravagance of
her drinking was becoming more and more apparent, and so was the conflict
between them. One time when she was really drunk at the Raw Deal, a friend
heard her attack David venomously, and the friend could only flinch and recoil.
"You are so perfect," Ann assailed him. "It must be hard to go through life being
so goddamned perfect."

Still, her offbeat sense of humor continued to attract people. Because of it,
she got a lot of constituent mail for a county commissioner, enough that she assembled one file titled "Weirdos." Most of its letters were harmless, to wit, one
that arrived in February 1979.

> Most Honorable Ann Richards
> Noble Person Dedicated to Human Interests
> Another dear soul told me maybe I should let you know what I'm up to. This
> "Bell of Human Being" is in the UN and the Kool-Meanie's Hands. The "spirit
> of humankind" has called me to defend my fellow human beings from a kind
> of mentality that seems running rampant world wide. . . . Feeling I am speaking
> for the people, I shot my "Mojo" to the world. This is the second edition. Please

"Grok" and if you understand that the higher spiritual powers are at work, my point is organic, not political; my values are human, not mechanical. My position is righteous indignation of my human dignity. I am merely exercising the right of free speech. Call the turkey hunters off if you can, please.

I give you my knowledge, I give my life. I am your servant.

The Hobo

Postscript: If you dig my rap please make copies for all humanistically concerned individuals in this area. I give the world a gift of an "early" Christmas. I want to give everyone in the whole earth a copy of this *free*.

Om Shanti,

Love peace

She was receiving invitations to participate in roasts of prominent individuals and to talk about politics with groups of progressive women. She didn't hesitate to make sport of powerful men. She introduced a comic act in which she pulled over her head an elastic band that was attached to a mask of a hog's snout. "Hi, I'm Harry Porco, president of Porco Electronics," she began one routine, as reported by the Austin-based magazine *Third Coast*. "I always say, when better women are made, Porco Electronics will make 'em. I'm good to my girls. We've had a number of firsts here. We were the first to put horoscopes on our bulletin boards. You know, for the girls. It's the little things that count. We were the first to give the girls on the assembly line hair nets made of real hair. We give them a plastic rose—we call it the "Yellow Rose" award—for five years' service. You just give your girls a hug and a pat on the fanny and they'll work like dogs."

When she wasn't off making speeches, she found bars to frequent after work that were more her place than David's Scholz Garten and the Raw Deal. One hangout near the Capitol, heavy in its politics, was the Quorum. The owner, Nick Kralj, was a former aide of Ben Barnes who now lobbied the legislature on measures that included legalizing pari-mutuel betting on horse and greyhound tracks. Kralj was as colorful and volatile as some of his customers. Molly Ivins passed on a tale that Kralj and Bob Bullock used to trade potshots at the building's large cockroaches. Kralj said that was preposterous; the bullets would have gone right through the hollow walls.

At the Quorum, Ann would laugh with the guys at some tale Bullock told about once doing legal work for small-time hoods who had monopolized the jukebox and cigarette-machine trade. Bullock had first been elected to the Texas House in 1955 from a district in the rolling farmland and small towns between

Waco and Dallas. In those days, he sided with the segregationists, but before long he changed his mind and proclaimed himself a liberal. He was elected state comptroller in 1974. "Bullock's Raiders" locked up businesses that ignored or fell far behind in paying their sales and franchise taxes—the Raw Deal was one such threatened enterprise, though it never happened—and he recruited a virtual think tank of professionals who became the state's de facto auditors and revenue estimators. Bullock was like the little guy in a leather sport coat who walks into some country beer joint, and for a few seconds the clatter of the pool balls stops and the place falls quiet, and then he laughs and becomes the life of the party.

Ann loved hearing Bullock's tales about his up-and-down road through Texas politics, and she welcomed him as one of her mentors. But she braced for the demons that could send him off in some direction that was just crazy. In the

Ann dons her costume as Harry Porco, sexist pig, in a photo shoot for the Austin-based magazine Third Coast *in February 1984. A few years later, when her profile was higher and her political calculus had changed,* Vanity Fair *requested use of this photo. To her relief the photographer declined.*

summer of 1980, she and Bullock traveled to New York City together for the Democratic National Convention. They were reportedly in the backseat of a cab racing through Manhattan when Bullock grew alarmed at the rate of speed and perceived nearness of car wrecks, and a couple of times he informed the driver of his wishes. His remarks went ignored. Bullock pulled out the pistol he carried in his boot, stuck it in the cabbie's ear, and snarled, "I said slow down, motherfucker!"

It was also widely reported that they boozed all over Manhattan but never got very close to Madison Square Garden, Jimmy Carter's renomination, or the high-profile speech he had to grant his defeated challenger, Ted Kennedy.

Back in Austin, she had some drinking pals who were surprising, given her self-description as a fuzzy-headed liberal. One was Frank Erwin. A jowly lawyer, he was the last of the old lions of the LBJ machine who still had political power. Erwin chaired the University of Texas Board of Regents with ferocity, especially when challenged by long-haired students and leftist professors. Erwin kept a large, detailed map of Vietnam at the Quorum, and periodically, as if he were an army general, he would deliver a briefing on the progress the troops were making over there. He personally ran off a group of brilliant academics that Chancellor Harry Ransom had recruited to the UT faculty in the sixties. His most flamboyant stunt came during the "Battle of Waller Creek" in 1969, when he ordered the chainsawing of some towering trees that campus rebels were desperate to save. (The trees were removed so that a street could be shifted and Memorial Stadium expanded.) A lonely widower, Erwin sometimes slept in a fraternity house where he was much admired. A mentor and friend of Barbara Jordan, he was a complex man. Ann wrote that one evening at the Quorum she turned to Erwin and said, "I've got to go home to be a wife and mother."

Erwin snorted. "You won't like it."

CHAPTER 9

Capsized

LIVING WITH MY DOG and cat in a cabin overlooking the valley that locals called Rogues Hollow, I was no stranger at Another Raw Deal, as the new one on West Sixth Street was called, but I also spent a fair amount of my leisure time in San Antonio. I had friends who lived in the King William district of restored and not-so-restored Victorian homes. Gerry Goldstein was a criminal defense lawyer of storied success and a protégé of the Richardses' old friend Maury Maverick, Jr. One day, I went to my mailbox and laughed upon pulling out an invitation to the thirtieth birthday party on September 27, 1980, of Gerry's tall, blonde, British-born wife, Chris, along with that of an Austin friend, Shelia Cheney. The graphic, done in the style of a 1920s *Vanity Fair*, featured the profile of a sleekly dressed woman with her index finger stuck down her throat. The caption read: "Boogie Till Ya Puke."

In San Antonio that night, I was at the foot of the Goldsteins' staircase, talk-ing to my friend Pete Gent, the former Dallas Cowboy receiver and author of *North Dallas Forty*, when Dorothy Browne walked over to us. She wore tan pants and a fitted top that complimented her short blonde hair and a lustrous pair of brown eyes. Pete introduced us, and she grinned and said she would rather talk to us than Fletcher Boone, the co-owner of the Raw Deal, who was carrying on at high volume. I knew who Dorothy was. Billy Lee Brammer, her first husband, had been one of my mentors, but I hadn't known them when they were married. Dorothy had ridden down from Austin for the birthday party with a group that included Fletcher and his partner, Lopez Smitham. Gerry Goldstein then owned

*The first Texas woman elected to statewide office in half a
century has a motherly moment with her son Clark.*

a part interest in a thriving little bar three or four blocks away called the Friendly
Spot. Chris shooed the party on to the bar, and I set out, intent on not losing
Dorothy in the crowd.

When we reached the bar, Fletcher became embroiled in some dispute with
his wife, Libby. He broadened the scope of their disagreement to women in general, whom he continually maligned by saying, *"You people."* After the first few of
these insults, Libby burst into sobs. I was happy where I was, but Dorothy told
me her friends clearly had to leave. We followed them at a distance on a street of
adobe houses. Libby would duck off toward a porch light or an alley and cry a
while. Dorothy and I were calling it the Trail of Tears.

I gathered up the Austin party in my car and drove them to their hotel. In the
large room the Boones had rented, Fletcher got in a raging argument with a cook
at the Raw Deal. Jaws and fists were clenched at one point. Libby sniffled and
wailed intermittently. As the evening tumbled on, I envisioned myself as riding a

quarter horse, trying to cut Dorothy out of that herd. I said at some point, "I really like you, Dorothy, but you've sure got some quarrelsome friends."

The next day I was back in my cabin on the hill, weathering a hangover and watching a football game, and they were on the interstate headed back to Austin. Whatever had bothered Libby so thoroughly the night before was forgiven, even if not forgotten, and she laughed merrily on hearing about my remark. I waited until Monday afternoon and then got the number from Austin information of the Texas Civil Liberties Union. Dorothy chuckled, "I didn't think I'd ever hear from you again."

"Yeah, you did."

I tell that story here because we were so smug in our self-assured hipness and hard-won hangovers; and because of the utter shock that awaited Dorothy, Fletcher, and Libby when they learned what that Sunday had been like for some of the people they loved and admired the most.

Dan Richards had gone to Texas A&M for a while and did not distinguish himself in his studies or the results. He came back to Austin and got a job on a construction crew, pouring concrete, but after several months he enrolled in the city's community college and won a part-time job in the warehouse of the comptroller's office. Bullock's Raiders had accumulated enough office furniture and the contents of enough liquor stores that the facility had to be managed like a true warehouse, with forklifts and such. Dan worked there happily for several months, and he dropped out of his community college classes so he could draw a full-time paycheck. He was twenty years old.

Cecile had meanwhile graduated with honors from Brown University and returned to Austin. The siblings shared an apartment, but she was gone most of the time, helping organize labor unions in El Paso. Clark and Ellen were away at school. Since he was the only Richards child living in Austin full-time, Dan got first notice of the pending upheaval of their lives. "Jane Hickie called me one night and said, 'Your mom's sick.' I jumped up like, where is she? I thought maybe she was in the hospital. Jane said, 'No, she's sick but doesn't know it. I've met these folks, and we need to do an intervention.'"

The intervention as outlined by the couple that directed it, John and Pat O'Neill, got mixed reviews. At first, David didn't want to have anything to do with it. Hickie asked Dan and their law professor friend Mike Sharlot whether they would come along and help convince David that this had to be done, and that he had to be a part of it. David at last relented.

"We got together and had kind of a pregame strategy session," Dan told me, "where we were going to figure out how we were going to convince Mom she had to quit drinking. There wasn't anybody in the room who was fired up about it at all." Hickie had painfully given up drinking herself; she knew what was going to be sprung on her boss and hero. Dan recalled the original plan: "The couple told us that we all had to write down something she'd done that was bad and hurtful to us and that we didn't think she would have done it if she hadn't been drunk. That was the plan, so we all did that. Then they said we needed to keep working on this for a week or so, and I remember everybody saying, 'No way! If we're going to do this we've got to get it over with.' They were thinking we were going to be able to tiptoe around this for a week or two? Then say in a chorus, 'The jig's up'? I think we rushed their schedule. I know we did."

"We had to do it!" Sue Sharlot told me. "Just the driving was insane, with Ann roaring around the narrow roads up in those hills. She was going to hurt or kill someone or herself." So that Sunday morning, Sue went over to Ann's house and told a lie about a health crisis of her father, and said she was terribly worried. Would Ann come over to Sue's house and stay with her?

Ann replied, "Of course," and rode the short distance to the house with Sue. When she walked in the door, she encountered David; her two oldest children, Cecile and Dan; and her best friends sitting in a circle. There were Tony and Claire Korioth, Jane Hickie, Sam and Virginia Whitten, Sue and Michael Sharlot, Sarah and Standish Meacham, and the two strangers—the O'Neills, the professionals.

In a mother's reflex, she asked about Clark and Ellen. She was assured they were all right, and the O'Neills took over. They offered a chair and said, "Won't you have a seat? Your friends want to tell you that they are concerned about you."

The chair was placed in a circle of other chairs, and each of those seated people had to read an essay they had prepared. These were articulate, well-educated adults, and they didn't let their stories wander or take on aspects of retribution. They couldn't have endured it themselves. They had all been coached to say at the end, "And I know you would not have done that if you had not been drinking."

The choreography was surreal. Ann was so furious at David she could barely look at him. The hypocrisy! She felt cheaply used by some of her friends too. She didn't lash out at them, though, which they appreciated, for they were well aware of her talent for sarcasm and ridicule. She did speak sharply to the O'Neills, questioning their authority, training, and qualifications. "She lit into those folks a couple of times," said Dan, "and I don't blame her."

Soon Ann was sobbing, and so were others in the room. "I was in such a state of shock," Ann wrote, "that I really don't remember much of what anyone said. Except for Tony Korioth. Tony said that one time I had been at a Fourth of July party at their house and Ann Korioth, who is my namesake and is their only daughter, had been sitting with me. I had held on to her hand and she had tried to get out of my lap, and I continued to hold on to her hand, and Tony thought that I had hurt her. I had certainly scared the little girl." Frightening and maybe inflicting pain on a child who had trusted you enough to crawl up in your lap—what a self-image to have to carry around!

"I had made a point of not knowing," Dan Richards said, "but I thought Mom and Dad were already breaking off at that point. So there was some talk about who would travel with her. And she was a county commissioner; that was another issue. But despite everybody's fears, at the end she said, 'I'll go. I'll do it.' I think usually it doesn't go like that. First they tell you to go to hell."

By three o'clock that afternoon, she had packed her bags and boarded a flight to the St. Mary's Chemical Dependency Services at Riverside Medical Center in Minneapolis. She had just turned forty-seven. In real ways, the life she had lived up to that point came to an end. David flew with her to Minneapolis, though they hardly said a word to each other. The place where they arrived was not one of those rehab centers set up like a spa. To Ann it looked more like an asylum than a hospital. Initially, she shared a room with a woman who was suicidal. Ann convinced the doctors and therapists that a private room was essential if she was going to make a recovery. She was lucky that she wasn't such a heavy drinker that she had to endure detoxification. One of the first things she surrendered in therapy was her anger at her friends and children who had taken part in the intervention. David, well, that was another matter.

At Ann's request, Richard Moya helped Jane Hickie cover for her abrupt and unexplained absence from the commissioners' court. David and her children came to Minneapolis toward the end for what the doctors and counselors called "Family Week." They were obliged to play a game called "sculpting," in which family members were told to mold Ann into a form that to them best represented her character and personality. She wound up seated in a chair with her arms upraised and her hands in fists. "In their eyes I had succeeded in what I had worked so hard to be, and that was Superwoman," she wrote. "But that was the last place in the world I wanted to be, and the last thing I wanted them to think of me. Even though my friends might doubt it, I have tried very hard to get out of that chair."

A few days before she came home, Ann wrote the Sharlots a letter that was hardly full of optimism.

> Dear Sue and Michael,
> How much fun to get letters from you. Everyone has been good to write but few have the flair for it. Your letters provoke a laugh and those occurrences are rare.
> I should write you an upbeat jolly jump-up letter but I need for you to know some serious things. I'm terribly fearful of coming home. As you say, Sue, our lives and activities are so centered around "using" (generic term for *take your choice*) that I do not know at this juncture how I can fit into the scene. We are told repeatedly what a threat we will be to our friends and family. We are taught techniques for dealing with situations but the bottom-line message is that when we feel we might succumb to *any* alcohol, dope, etc. we must "get the hell out of Dodge." An aftercare program is set up for each of us that includes at least two meetings of AA weekly. There is a lot of spirituality—"higher power," "god" concepts—linked to the program which is hard to deal with intellectually, but I accept it on the basis that if the program *works* I will learn to give up control and *let* it work. The total alteration of my lifestyle is overwhelming. I know that David and all of you will be as supportive as possible but the new me will wear off very quickly.
> The family week was torturous. It made the "interrogation" at your house seem like a picnic. I think it did the family a world of good, though, and we are doubtless the richer for it. I am now searching the deepest recesses of my guilt, anger, fears . . . which must be delivered orally next Monday. I seem to be getting a lot of intense attention because the counselor and staff are fearful that I cannot buck the ingrained drug usage in the political system and my lack of acquaintance with non-users.
> It takes a minimum of one year for the physical system to stabilize without chemical ingestion—particularly the blood—and a number of mood shifts occur as a direct result. We are told how to anticipate these situations but evidently they play havoc on everyone else.
> I feel better now that I've dumped all this stuff—I am so afraid that my homecoming will be a downer. Physically, I've never been better—EKG back to normal, no more heart pains, cholesterol stabilized. . . . I might add that my memory is also improving and it is great to be rid of hangovers.
> I love you both a great deal and for good or ill, will see you next week.
> Ann

When Ann returned to Red Bud Trail, she asked the people who had taken part in the intervention to come over to her house one evening.

> I wanted them to know that I didn't want them to feel uncomfortable around me, that their drinking was not going to affect me. My job was to take care of me, and their job was to take care of them. I was their first experience with Life After Alcohol. Most people don't know that you're still going to be you. . . . Things with David had not improved. They weren't worse, and I was better able to deal with them, but again our lives were drastically altered. I didn't want to leave work and go to the Raw Deal and sit and drink beer for several hours and listen to everyone get wise. So our whole pattern of living changed, and I think that was very hard on him.

Despite her bravado, she was not all that serene about what she had been through. She had lost quite a few pounds; people who were used to seeing her thought the strain was obvious. That fall, not long after she came back from Minnesota, she and David took part in another caravan down the lower canyons of the Rio Grande. The first four days were glorious—nothing but birdsong, canyon walls, blue sky. They came into a stretch of rapids that was difficult and dangerous. Some of the canoeists got out and ranged along the banks of the racing river in case anyone got in trouble. When David and Ann took their turn, they did not make of it an easy run. In the back of the canoe, he started yelling: "Turn right! Turn right! *Turn right!*" In exasperation and defiance, Ann pulled her paddle out of the water, gripped it with both hands, and held it high over her head. It was the same Superwoman pose she had been made to assume in the crowd of her family in Minneapolis. They crashed straight into a rock, though this time they did not turn over and lose everything.

Then the weather changed; a norther blew in. They had, by this time, made the pass around the river's dramatic bend, which meant they were now paddling back north, into the cold front's gale. "Ann literally turned blue," said their reporter friend Dave McNeely. "The clothes she brought were cotton, and she couldn't get warm. We finally found an overhang, a little cave, and we built a fire so she could recover."

Not long after the intervention, Ann was preparing to make a speech about her years as an alcoholic. The notes she jotted down, talking points for speaking off the cuff, were a fair measure of her self-esteem, and probably the voices in her mind at night.

Physical manifestations . . . shaking hands . . . coffee cup with two hands. Head-aches, hangovers, really needing a drink . . . because the only antidote to alcohol is more alcohol.

Accidents . . . prone to spatial distortion . . . driving home with one eye closed to focus on the yellow line . . . so there is only one.

Cut finger—broken leg—bruises.

Seizures. Combining diet pills and alcohol . . .

That time in the kitchen she had sliced herself so badly that Dan had to drive her to the emergency room for stitches; the other time she was unsteady on her feet and staggered on a doormat that shot out from under her, and there she sat on the porch of her home with a broken leg.

She had lied to herself about the seizures, holding at a long arm's length the epilepsy diagnosis in Dallas.

Personality manifestations . . . self-pity, fear, jealousy, feelings of isolation, rejec-tion . . . inability to accept affection . . .

How it is to want to tell someone . . . say how you love them but unable to do it unless you have enough alcohol to do it . . . and the horror of having your children listen to your maudlin talk.

Loss of memory and blackouts . . . vague notions that you were insulting or that you embarrassed yourself or someone in your family . . .

Carrying a drink in your purse and finding a soggy mess in your lap.

When people decide the loves of their lives no longer measure up, the outcome is seldom pretty for any member of the family involved. Ann and David hung on until the holidays of 1980, when the kids were coming home. Then something tipped the balance, and he moved out.

Roaring arguments seldom erupted in the house on Red Bud Trail, and the Richardses' kids were skilled at avoidance. Ellen, the youngest child, took the breakup of her parents hardest. "I had gone away to school for the first time that fall," she told me. "Mom didn't share a lot of things about herself with me. She kept them close to herself. It was a rough time for everybody in varied ways. I was aware there were issues between Mom and Dad, and her drinking was very difficult. It was something I didn't understand. I didn't have any perspective on alcoholism."

Some friends of the family have remarked that Clark was angry when he found out about his dad's relationship with Sandy Hauser, an attractive young woman who had been working at Scholz's and the Raw Deal while pursuing a degree as a nutritionist. Their romance began on a train trip to Laredo and rowdy, laugh-filled evenings beside a pleasant hotel pool and onward across the Rio Grande bridge. The Laredo jaunt was the first time I met David and several other close friends of Dorothy. Seeing my hesitation, David and Sandy, with great warmth, waved me into the gang. Fantasizing that the wild sixties and seventies were not yet over, two members of the party dropped acid and disappeared into Nuevo Laredo (which was a much safer place to be doing that in those days). The men missed the return train to Austin, and one of them was especially miserable on the slow bus ride north, knowing the reception that awaited him when he got back home.

Without question, that frolic, occurring just as Ann was adjusting to her new life of sobriety, accentuated a long marriage coming to its painful end, but just as truly, it did not cause that dissolution. Unaware of much in her parents' lives, Ellen Richards wrote in a letter to Ann that Clark might be happier if he stayed with David when he came home from school in Connecticut.

"I was an egghead kind of kid," Clark told me. "I was scrawny, couldn't play sports very well, so that put me sort of low in the Westlake pecking order. Of course, with Mom, anything that smacked of masculinity was not encouraged. School was a very different thing for me when I went to St. Stephen's, because out there I could be socially accepted. When I was a sophomore, I was an exchange student in Japan. I lived with a family in a suburb of Osaka. The school had some kind of Episcopal affiliation. There were two other American kids. I wrote a lot of letters back home that year, and got a lot of letters in return, but I don't know if we had more than one phone conversation. I was fifteen. I have children now, and I'm bewildered that it didn't seem odd to me then to be away from my family for a whole year."

Clark was a lawyer practicing with his brother and dad when he told me those stories. "Cecile and Dan had graduated by then," he said, "and when I came back to St. Stephen's, I felt myself invincible. I engaged in lots of things that were against the rules. I got kicked out between my junior and senior year. It was entirely my fault, and I owned up to it. Several of those teachers appreciated that. Right after that, I wrecked my dad's truck, totaled it, right down Red Bud Trail from where we lived—drunk as Cooter Brown, and I got a DWI as a juvenile.

"Mom, being a county commissioner, arranged for me to do some community service for a woman who ran the Travis County Alcohol Counseling Service. I went to a couple of AA meetings. Nobody said, 'You're drinking and smoking pot and it's a problem—we're mad at you.' There was none of that kind of discussion.

People in those meetings were in their forties and fifties. They looked like classic skid-row types. I couldn't relate to them.

"After that, Mom didn't really want me around Austin. They found a prep school for me in Connecticut. I made no lasting friends, and it was touch-and-go whether I'd get thrown out of there, too. But I did graduate. And then I started college at Northwestern in Chicago. My role in the family was being the kid who was off somewhere else."

When I asked him, "What did your mother do when she was drunk?" Clark was quiet for a moment. "Everybody drank a lot then. There was a lot of the pot calling the kettle black. I can see that being married to Mom would have been tough. Being married to Dad would have been tough. I can't say that either of them was wearing the black hat or the white hat. I can't judge them."

Clark worked his way around to answering my question: "In a lot of ways I'm a poor historian of family lore. I was gone so much. When Mom was in St. Mary's, at that Family Week we had no idea what to do or say. I couldn't stand those meetings, and I was just trying to get out of there. Mom had a real sarcastic wit, you know. It would seem like fun when she was tearing up George Bush, but for an eight-year-old it was a bit much. And then when I was in college, I'd be back in Austin for spring break or some other holiday, and I'd come home drunk at night. She'd be up, and she'd jack with me. 'Well, aren't you special?' I didn't really want to spend a lot of time around Mom. I tried to stay in Chicago."

He thought for a moment, and then said: "This is jumping ahead in the story a little. After I graduated from Northwestern I got in more trouble, and I had to go to drunk school, too. That was during the boom of Alcoholics Anonymous and 'Find Your Inner Child.' Everybody was on some kind of bandwagon about recovery paradigms.

"I spent several months backpacking around Asia by myself. I was coming to the end of my backpacking adventure and arrived in Tokyo. Somewhere along the way I'd picked up a copy of *Lonesome Dove*. I'd probably read a little bit of McMurtry, but I was so moved by that book, so full of nostalgia, and I wrote a long impassioned letter to Mom about how important she was to me, and how perhaps I hadn't communicated that. I remember getting a note back from her saying, 'Well, I guess I owe thanks to Larry, and I'll be sure and let him know the next time I see him.'

"In Tokyo, I found this guy who was a therapist. He knew about AA and all that, and I started seeing him. It was the first time I had been to a therapist who didn't already know who my mother was. And it dawned on me: one of my problems I had in Austin was that Mom had become sort of a demigod of the recovery community. She was a champion and everybody looked up to her. I saw her that way, too. But part of me wanted to say I was upset about the way things went when I was a kid. That part of me didn't have a chance to express itself. Any time I went to a group, I couldn't say, 'Godamighty, when I was young and Mom was drunk, she was *mean*.'

"Nobody wanted to hear that story. Part of me had a need to say to somebody, 'You know, that hurt.' So this guy provided me with an opportunity eight thousand miles away, and I could say when I was young, Mom would sometimes have these rage attacks, and boy, they scared the hell out of me."

In Austin in 1982, Ann and her daughter Cecile Richards enjoy a high point in the race for state treasurer. Cecile was a creative force in each of her mother's campaigns, especially on issues of organized labor. She later worked as deputy chief of staff for U.S. Speaker of the House Nancy Pelosi and since 2006 has been the national president of Planned Parenthood.

CHAPTER 10

The Class of '82

ANN AND DAVID TWICE attempted to reconcile, but it brought them no closer, and after a few months he left for good. "Why didn't you get divorced then?" I asked him once. He responded with an unknowing shrug, "She didn't want it." After all those years of marriage, they entered the purgatory of prolonged separation.

Ann's life narrowed almost entirely to her work as a county commissioner, the feminist friends she had made in politics and government, and sessions of Alcoholics Anonymous, which she sometimes attended several times a week. Cecile Richards was by then living in New Orleans and working as a union organizer for workers in service industries. In that pursuit, she met her future husband, Kirk Adams. Clark started college in Chicago, and Ellen was attending a school in Concord, Massachusetts. Dan was living alone in an Austin apartment and working in the furniture warehouse scavenged by Bullock's Raiders; at twenty-one, he was well out of the nest.

Ann cherished her sudden privacy and solitude—the increased time she had to curl up on the sofa with her feet under her and talk to friends like Virginia Whitten, Sue Sharlot, Claire Korioth, and Jane Hickie. But the sprawling place on Red Bud Trail would never again be the party house of Mad Dog, Inc. Many evenings, Ann put on some music, scarcely bothering with her own dinner, and with her dog and cat sat outside and watched the shadows of sundown move across the canyon they called Oracle Gorge. The message no longer held such promise.

A few weeks after the intervention, Ann won a second four-year term as county commissioner; the race was a formality—she was unopposed. But a succession of setbacks had left her in the political doldrums. Ronald Reagan was president, George H. W. Bush was vice president, John Tower was a senator with growing seniority, and Bill Clements was Texas governor, with little reason to think he might be denied another term. Clements had launched his first campaign by throwing a rubber chicken at John Hill, then the state's attorney general, at a joint appearance in Amarillo and declaring that he was going to hang Jimmy Carter around the Democrat's neck the way rural Texans punished a chicken-killing dog. And he lived up to his boast. The tough-talking driller wore loud plaid sport coats, walked with a limp, griped about the hitch in his get-along, and drove around in an old Mercury station wagon with fake wood panels. He had built his Dallas-based companies around a bunch of cronies with whom he had played high school football on a state championship team in Highland Park, back when helmets were made of leather.

Karl Rove was a face in the crowd back then. He had come of political age as a Goldwater Republican, but his real hero became Richard Nixon. When George Bush took on the thankless task of serving as national chairman of the post-Watergate Republican Party, he spotted Rove's talent and gave the young man a job with the party in Washington. Then he had to pull Rove back on learning that the FBI was asking questions about a tutorial on campaign dirty tricks that Rove had been conducting for the College Republicans. Rove bounced around the country for several months as the sidekick of another young GOP attack specialist, Lee Atwater. Rove arrived in Houston in a Ford Pinto, inspired to work on Bush's presidential race, which to his dismay would eat Ronald Reagan's dust. In the meantime, Rove offered brief political advice to George W. Bush, a congressional candidate who was then enjoying only spotty success in his attempt to match his dad's legendary success as a West Texas oilman. In 1978, the younger Bush impulsively plunged into the race against Kent Hance, a conservative Democrat from Lubbock. Bush later said he did it because Jimmy Carter was threatening to increase regulation of the natural gas industry. On an issue important to Panhandle farmers, Bush made a major mistake by supporting a grain embargo that blocked the sale of Texas wheat to the Soviet Union because of its invasion of Afghanistan. Bush had more than twice as much money in his campaign coffers as Hance, but the Democrat turned that against him—it was the money of "outsiders," code for "Yankees." Hance successfully cast him as an overage preppie who knew next to nothing about West Texas. His stump speech mocked his opponent with a joke that had Bush asking a fellow driver for some rural directions. The other driver told him to go down the road about a mile, turn left, and look for a cattle guard. To which Bush replied, "Now, what color uniform is this cattle guard wearing?"

Hance whooped with glee over an invitation to a "Bush Bash" at Texas Tech University that began "Dear Fellow Christians"—an ad for the same rally in the Tech newspaper promised free beer. Hance also scored with a letter castigating Bush for importing as campaign workers "Rockefeller-type Republicans like Karl Rove." It forced an exasperated Bush to protest to the *Midland Reporter-Telegram* that Rove was "a twenty-seven-year-old guy who works in my dad's office in Houston. He has nothing to do with my campaign. I doubt if he even supports Rockefeller." Hance defeated Bush with 53 percent of the vote, and the rout seemed worse than that. Bush's recent marriage to Laura Welch, a grade-school teacher and librarian from Midland, helped put the shambles of that race behind him. And Rove never forgot the first impression that Bush, who was then a graduate student at Harvard, had made upon him: "Huge amounts of charisma, swagger, cowboy boots, flight jacket, wonderful smile, just charisma—you know, wow."

The young politico's luck changed when he moved to Austin and caught on with Bill Clements. Rove, whose specialty was to raise money by writing direct-mail broadsides to fervent members of the GOP base, revered old-timers like Clements and another Dallas oilman, H. R. "Bum" Bright, who poured money into the Texas Aggie football program but was oddly indifferent to his acquisition of the Dallas Cowboys. Still, Rove thought they had no real sense of the opportunity for Republicans in Texas. They gave him a list of 5,000 donors from the 1978 campaign and said they wanted him to raise $200,000 in a couple of years. Rove expanded the list to 44,000 friendly names and raised $1 million for the Clements campaign during his first year on the job.

Despite the Republicans' hold on two of the top three political offices in Texas and confidence that the future belonged to the GOP, Democrats weren't acting as if 1982 was going to be a losing year. They were lucky to have Lloyd Bentsen running for reelection. Bentsen was hardly the liberal that Phil Gramm made him out to be in a failed race for the Senate as a Democrat. James Baker, who was Reagan's first chief of staff and George H. W. Bush's tennis partner in Houston, would have laughed at the notion. They knew Bentsen was of the same stripe. In 1970, Bentsen was the one, after all, who had retired Ralph Yarborough from the Senate with television ads that associated him with anti–Vietnam War protests and blazing chaos in American streets. That fall, Bentsen turned back George Bush, who was then a star GOP congressman from Houston; he had been licking his chops at the prospect of taking the Senate seat away from Yarborough. In 1976, the year Bentsen won his second Senate term, he felt he embarrassed himself with a feeble race for the Democratic presidential nomination. He never dreamed that Georgia governor Jimmy Carter could take him out so easily. As a politician, Bentsen was no LBJ, but he was smooth and urbane, and as he ran for his third term in 1982, his rough handling of Yarborough was forgiven, though not forgotten, by the liberals; he was the accepted leader of Texas Democrats.

In Austin, Jack Martin, a political consultant and public relations strategist, was closely aligned with Bentsen. Martin brought young computer wizards into the race on behalf of Bentsen and the rest of the ticket, and the Democrats campaigned with an uncommon air of discipline and a resolve not to repeat mistakes of the past.

And Bentsen drew a gift of an opponent in the ultraconservative Dallas congressman Jim Collins. After an irreverent and somewhat rocky ride with the *New York Times*, Molly Ivins had returned to Texas as a columnist for the *Dallas Times Herald*, and she lampooned Collins, no doubt to Bentsen's delight, with the line: "If his IQ slips any lower, we'll have to water him twice a day."

In the governor's race, the Texas attorney general, Mark White, from Houston, had risen through the organization of the conservative rancher and governor Dolph Briscoe. His political adversaries scoffed that he had been a lame Houston lawyer and an inert attorney general, but to win that office, White had defeated James Baker, one of the most skillful and prominent Republicans of his generation. To get the chance to challenge Clements, White had to get past both railroad commissioner Buddy Temple, the son of the East Texas timber baron Arthur Temple, and the liberals' favorite, Texas land commissioner Bob Armstrong.

Defeating Clements would be an uphill climb for any of them, but the governor had liabilities. Despite being a successful oilman, Clements got little credit for an economic boom in Texas that had been triggered by a sharp rise in oil prices in the seventies. And his popularity was not enhanced when his offshore drilling company Sedco, at one time the largest in the world, suffered a blowout in the Gulf of Mexico in 1979 in a partnership project with Mexico's oil monopoly, Pemex. It was at the time the worst oil spill the world had experienced. Clements's response was a shrug: "There's no use crying over spilled milk," the governor of Texas said. "Let's don't get excited about this thing."

In other top races in which Democrats were the incumbents, Bill Hobby and Bob Bullock had plenty of money and large, well-schooled organizations. Ann was closest personally to Hobby and Armstrong, but despite the occasional rancor between them, in that period of her life she really had the most in common with Bullock, who seemed to be on a tear of self-destruction. He had survived an early heart attack and the removal of a lung but went right on smoking. His love life was so tangled that he once tried to cook Thanksgiving dinners for his wife and an ex-wife on the sly. Since the summer of 1980, news reports in Austin had dwelled on FBI agents' seizures of typewriter ribbons from the office of an executive secretary who had worked for Bullock at the comptroller's office. He turned those stories into a public tirade over how long Travis County district attorney Ronnie Earle and his Public Integrity Unit had known about the FBI's activity. Bullock flung out a contemptuous press release that read: "Pretty boy Ronnie is caught with his pants down and his rear showing. It's long past time for little Ronnie to put up or shut up. His abuse of his law license is unforgivable."

A disenchanted aide had gone to the press with a description of booze-happy parties on state-owned airplanes. The comptroller all but dared the Travis County grand jury to indict him. "Yeah, I'm a crook," he blustered, "but I'm the best comptroller this state ever had." Later, after the statute of limitations had run, he admitted to Earle that he had been guilty as hell.

He was arrested for DWI one night, a marriage he cherished ended in divorce, and he talked about getting out of government and opening a car dealership. His reason: the people of Texas did not deserve him. Ann made some attempts to tease Bullock out of his funk, but he did not want her pity or help. He was holed up in a house out in the country, grieving over the loss of his wife, Amelia, when the climax came. It was alleged but not proved that he went off with a gun to rescue his son, whom he believed had run afoul of Austin's drug culture in the person, to make it worse, of a man who had gotten busted for dealing marijuana while employed as one of Bullock's Raiders. The Austin police officers who had been tipped off and subsequently intercepted Bullock said they found no guns in his car, and they discreetly gave him a ride back to his office.

The defense attorney Roy Minton was one of the friends who arranged for Bullock's admission to "drunk school." During the fall of 1981, Bullock appeared one night at the press's annual Boneheadliners show, in which he was given a Friendship Award. Mocking the reporters' assertion of his friendlessness, he said he could count many bartenders who were loyal friends, and he also had good friends named Remington, Colt, and Smith & Wesson.

Hours later, he got on a plane to Orange County, California, where he checked into the Care Manor Hospital, which was renowned for its treatment of Betty

Ford. "The last day I drank was when I went into that treatment center," he told Patrick Beach, an *Austin American-Statesman* reporter. "They told Minton, 'He can drink all he wants until he gets here.' Sure enough, I did just that. The first time I ever had the DTs was when I landed in Orange, California. I felt like I had snakes all over me."

That was the Austin milieu as Ann settled into her private life of solitude and sobriety. She recalled in her book that one Saturday morning in January 1982 when she was sleeping late, the telephone rang, she picked it up, and a completely unforeseen development gave a recharge to her political career. Her friend Bob Armstrong, the Democratic land commissioner, asked her whether she had seen the *American-Statesman*. She told him she was still in bed. Bob said, "Go get your morning paper and call me back."

She called him back a few minutes later and said, "Well, I have the newspaper but I don't know why you wanted me to get it."

"Do you see the front page?"

"Yes."

"Warren Harding is in trouble," Armstrong said.

Harding, who enjoyed the odd political advantage of having the same name as one of the country's worst and most corrupt presidents, was the state treasurer. He had been a veteran insider in Dallas politics and local government when Ann and David lived there. Ann read the story and agreed that Harding had a problem. Ronnie Earle's Public Integrity Unit had seized a large file of documents from the Treasury, and Harding and ten of his employees had been subpoenaed to testify before the Travis County grand jury.

"I see the story," Ann said. "So, what's up?"

"I want you to run for state treasurer."

She said, "Bob, you're crazy." For another thing, she told him, she had no idea what the treasurer did.

"Listen," he argued, "if Warren Harding has been treasurer, you can be treasurer. We're going to be in a fix if Warren Harding really is in serious trouble and is indicted; it will be an embarrassment to have him on the Democratic ticket." A corruption scandal involving a Democratic statewide officeholder would hardly boost his chances in the governor's race. "And," he went on cheerfully, "I think it's time for a woman to run statewide."

After the call, Ann spent a few moments thinking this was the dumbest thing she had ever heard of. But then the calls from old friends started coming.

Armstrong was a good politician, and he had been working the telephones hard. "You've just got to do this," cried Liz Carpenter, Lady Bird Johnson's former press secretary and LBJ's executive assistant. "What a great idea. What a great thing for women."

"Look, Liz, forget the great thing for women. Whatever I do, it has to be a job that I can do."

"Oh, Ann, you can do anything. Don't worry about that." That was easy for *her* to say.

There were two immediate and daunting obstacles. The deadline for filing for statewide offices was just two days away. And a Texas law held that an elected county official had to resign that position in order to run for a state office. Ann's separation from David hardly meant she was thriving on her own. Despite the large house in West Lake Hills, the acreage along the San Gabriel River, and her comfortable lifestyle, she relied on her paycheck from Travis County, which most months was $642.79. She didn't have a credit card in her own name. She was not wealthy.

But soon she was on the telephone conferring with Bob Bullock, Bill Hobby, Jane Hickie, Mary Beth Rogers, other feminist friends and tacticians, the Texas AFL-CIO chief, a prominent lobbyist for bankers, and David Richards: "If I made this race and had to resign as county commissioner, David would have to support me through nine months of campaigning, one whole pregnancy." She still framed time in the practiced rhythms of her life as a mother.

Clark Richards reflected on the upgrade of his mother's political career:

A large part of Mom's story is that she learned as a child that through force of will she could get to do what she wanted to do. She was encouraged to think that. But obviously some contextual opportunity had to be there. If she had married someone else in Waco, she might have had a completely different life. Dad's family was wealthy. Mom grew up poor—all those stories about her mother strangling and boiling chickens. And when Dad took her out the first time, she barely knew how to order off a menu.

In order for Mom to have that opportunity and access to politics, she had to have the financial platform Dad brought her. I always had the impression our lifestyle was enabled by Dad's family wealth. It wasn't like he was working at Vinson and Elkins and billing banks a hundred hours a week. He was representing the *Rag* [an anarchist student newspaper handed out on the University of Texas campus] before the U.S. Supreme Court, and his fee was a lifetime subscription to the *Rag*. Mom was a force of nature in her own right, and no doubt could have done amazing things in another context. But without Dad's financial security, it's very unlikely she would have had the chance to run for anything. She might have been chasing children around—and she did plenty of that. But we had a maid.

Mary Beth Rogers's husband, John, hatched the idea of calling all friendly hands and saying that if Ann could raise $200,000 in twenty-four hours, she would run. Liz Carpenter later tweaked the story, claiming that amount was raised entirely by women. But a subsequent memo from Jane Hickie, Ann's campaign manager, broke down the debt of $205,576.36 in this way: David Richards, $94,281.10; $6,250 from each of their four children; Hickie, $75,000; John Wooley, $70,710.83; and Gary Bradley, $23,570.28. Wooley and Bradley, recall, were partners in controversial Austin real estate speculations at the time. Wooley was Ann's campaign treasurer. And Bradley was the man that Austin environmentalists loved to hate.

Despite the contributions of David Richards, Dan Richards, Bob Armstrong, Bill Hobby, Bob Bullock, John Rogers, John Wooley, Gary Bradley, and many other men, Ann's campaign became a crusade for Texas feminists: it was their mission, their cause. Jane Hickie said that they were all "keenly aware of the importance of recording one's own history to find the . . ." She paused for a moment, searching for the right word. Then she said, "The *foremothers*."

In Ann's campaign office, no one knew then what a gifted speechwriter Suzanne Coleman would become—at that point, she was writing very detailed research memos, often with a polite request that Ann and others on the team take the time to read them. Pat Cole, who did fund-raising, had a doctorate in health and social-services policy and a rich, smoky, deep-voiced chuckle; she hoped they were looking down the road at prizes other than the treasurer's office. Lena Guerrero, a young House member from Austin on fire with her own political ambitions, recognized how important it was to make a strong impression as the Hispanic feminist protégée of Ann Richards.

Ann and Hickie got Suzanne to conduct some research on the Texas Treasury. She learned that the agency was small, never employing more than 300 people, but had a colorful history. In June 1865, as Texas Confederate officials fled to Mexico, Union troops arrived in Austin amid chaos and mob rule and found about fifty men sacking the Treasury. A few shots were exchanged, leaving one of the desperados dead, but the rest of them got away into the hills with more than half the gold and silver that belonged to the state, worth about $17,000. In the haste of making his escape, one of the robbers lost his hold on his valise, spilling across the floor coupons clipped from United States bonds that were worth $25,000.

After that, for more than a century the Treasury was run out of a tiny office in the Capitol that looked like a frontier bank lobby. From 1941 until 1977, the state treasurer was a man named Jesse James. With that name, he never had any trouble getting reelected. When the old man died, Governor Dolph Briscoe had appointed Warren G. Harding to fill out his term. On the odd strength of his name, the obscurity of the agency, and his connections in the conservative wing of the Democratic Party, Harding won reelection in his own right for one term. A hundred seventeen years after the shootout, everything at the Treasury seemed redolent of those origins. Clerks were still taking care of the state's banking business with hand-pull adding machines.

They discovered that Harding and his staff put a minimum of $5,000 in all the 1,400 approved depository banks in Texas. In most cases, those accounts drew no interest. Movers and shakers in the towns were supposed to raise money for Harding in direct proportion to the amount of state money deposited in the towns' banks. "This was on paper," Ann said. "Stupid. Really stupid. There may not have been anything illegal about it, but it was really dumb."

At the start of the race, Hickie sent around a memo on campaign letterhead with the shrill heading: "Important Facts About Contributions and Expenses: Read This Before You Do Anything!!!!!" The campaign finance law was tricky and full of nuance, though Hickie attempted to make it clear. But down the stretch, some worker sent in a note wondering whether Ann would have a problem accepting $500 from Rex Cauble, a horse rancher who had just been convicted of running a large drug-smuggling operation. The story would not be pretty if the press got wind of that. They sent the check back.

Questions arose of what exactly the reformer was trying to reform. "One of the challenges you have to realize," Hickie later said in an interview conducted by members of Ann's team, "is that if you're running for state treasurer, it's not what you'd call terribly exciting. I mean, if I talk to you about unclaimed property" —state-issued checks or other monetary credits that the recipients never came forward to accept—"your eyes are going to glaze over, and you just don't care. Only bankers and accountants and taxpayers who are really sophisticated love the hot issues associated with the Treasury."

For the ad campaign, they hired Roy Spence, a former Brownwood High School quarterback who was now the hottest creative advertising man in Texas. Hickie described their collaborations: "The jazziest thing that Roy and his company could think of to symbolize what Ann meant as an elected official was that she would bring a high standard of excellence and a new kind of management approach to the office—a new day, that Texas was really ready for a woman. . . . And the past practices of the offices in the state were antiquated, at the very best."

The campaign spots showed Ann walking beside purportedly state-of-the-art data-processing equipment that was really just word processors, computers. "Ann hammered away on that theme out on the road," Hickie said, "and we did it in the television spots and every other way we could think of. 'We've got to move that office out of the quill-pen, green-eyeshade era into what Texas is today.'"

Dan Richards had gotten a call from his mother during the two-day fire drill. She told him she wanted to come over to his apartment, and when she got there, she asked whether he was willing to give her the next nine months of his life. He agreed to it without hesitation, and the next day she filed her candidacy. "Mom and Dad had definitely split up by then," Dan said, "and they wanted somebody close"—a family member—"to travel with her. And I wasn't really doing anything."

Ann reminisced in her book about that time with her son: "He was very good at what he did. He was a very adept advance man; he kept up with the people that we went to see, he would stay right at my elbow in crowds; he would whisper in my ear, 'Miss Jones is coming up on your right,' and, 'Here's Mr. Smith, who we missed seeing last time,' and 'You remember that old drunk man that was here before, well, he's on his way over again.'"

"It was just you and your mother on those drives?" I asked Dan.

"Yeah, most of the time," he said. "Kaye Northcott, who had moved on from the *Texas Observer*, was handling press for Mom. I'd get my marching orders from Kaye, because basically that's what you're doing, trying to get somebody to write about the campaign. We traveled about six days a week. And that was a good deal for me. I was grown by then, although not in maturity. Usually by that time in your life you don't get to hang around much with your mom. That was nice, it really was. There would be four or five stops a day. And I understood what my job was—get her to the next place. It didn't matter if we'd had any sleep; she could get up and do her deal, make her speech. She'd go in there and make the same speech, time and again. And after watching a lot of other folks do the same thing, I started realizing, man, she is really good at this."

Despite the heavy-hitter candidates and the millions of dollars spent in the races 131
for the U.S. Senate seat and the governor's office, the campaigns that captured
the imaginations of Democrats and the press were further down the ballot. In
the race for attorney general, an East Texas U.S. attorney named John Hannah
had been one of the "Dirty Thirty" band in the legislature who turned Texas politics upside down over the Sharpstown scandal. A respected former state senator
from the Panhandle, Max Sherman, was also in the race. Ann would have liked
to see Hannah win, but after three terms in Congress, Jim Mattox had seen his
Dallas district's lines gerrymandered in a way that guaranteed he could not win
reelection. Mattox jumped in the race for attorney general, and he was a ferocious
campaigner.

In the General Land Office race, Garry Mauro was a curly-haired, former
Texas Aggie yell leader who had greatly dismayed his parents by postponing his
last year of law school to drive the car and carry the bags of Ralph Yarborough
in the liberal warhorse's last race in 1972. (After his defeat by Bentsen in 1970,
Yarborough attempted a comeback in the 1972 race against Tower, but he lost in
the primary to a freckle-faced Dallas judge and LBJ protégé with the wonderful
name Barefoot Sanders, who went on to lose to John Tower.) With time on his
hands, Mauro pitched in on the presidential campaign of George McGovern. Another member of that team was Roy Spence. Two years later, in 1974, Mauro and
Spence guided the Shakespeare scholar and New Braunfels native Bob Krueger
to a surprising win in a congressional district that stretched from northwest San
Antonio to Big Bend. It was the first of two years of backlash against Watergate.

Mauro later spent some years as Bob Bullock's protégé in the state comptroller's office. Along the way, Garry asked Bob Armstrong to let him know if he ever
decided to move on from the land office. Armstrong favored him with that call
when he decided to run for governor. Mauro was the underdog in his race against
Pete Snelson, a state senator from Midland, but he campaigned well by talking
about offshore oil leases and the state's public education endowment. Snelson
was no match for his ideas and energy, or his ambition.

Jim Hightower, from the Red River town of Denison, had worked for Yarborough as a legislative aide in the Senate. He cofounded the Agribusiness Account-
ability Project during his years in the Senate, and he was the national coordinator of the short-lived 1976 presidential campaign of former Oklahoma senator
Fred Harris. Wearing a cowboy hat and a closely trimmed mustache and driving
a sputtering white sports car, Hightower had arrived in Austin to succeed Molly
Ivins and Kaye Northcott as editor of the *Texas Observer*. Hightower's *Observer*

favored dry stories about agribusiness and bank holding companies and delivered almost none of the humor that Molly had brought to the muckraking journal, but the bone-thin populist was a laugh-a-minute demon with a microphone, becoming known for lines such as "There's nothing in the middle of the road but yellow stripes and dead armadillos." Hightower had run for a vacant Texas Railroad Commission seat in 1980 and lost, but he was back in the hunt against a Democratic agriculture commissioner named Reagan Brown.

Dolph Briscoe had appointed Brown, a real rancher, to the office Hightower sought. A conservative Democrat, Brown had made a name for himself with citrus farmers by requiring that all produce grown in California be fumigated before entering Texas in order to prevent an invasion of Mediterranean fruit flies. As the 1982 race warmed up, Brown emphasized the necessity of an all-out fight against fire ants, a species from South America that probably came into this country aboard banana boats docked at ports on the Gulf Coast. Anyone who had gotten stung by them or seen pastures overrun by their mounds knew they were a menace that could not just be doused out of existence with the poisons on the market. But Hightower got under Brown's skin by suggesting that he had invented a fire-ant crisis in order to get reelected. Out with a television crew one day, Brown took it on himself to demonstrate that the tiny insects were merely ants. He jammed his fist and forearm in one of their mounds, and was soon viewed grimacing and slapping, trying to put out the blaze of their stings. The Hightower and Richards road shows happened to wind up in the same town that night. They had a great time whooping and hollering over a race that Hightower had just won.

Ann stressed to her supporters that they were in this to win, not just to make symbolic gains for women, and they had to show they could play a game that could get rough. The campaign was barely a month old when it did. The incumbent, Warren Harding, was not Ann's only Democratic opponent. Also in the race was a state legislator, Lane Denton, whom Ann considered a friendly colleague, even if not a close friend. She certainly did not expect to get blindsided by him. She and Dan were in Tyler when a call came that Denton had just held a press conference at the Capitol. He told reporters that Ann was an alcoholic, that she had been treated for it, and that in the past she had sought counseling for mental problems. A former Travis County commissioner named David Samuelson stepped up and said that Ann was getting drunk during the workday, that her performance on the court had been erratic and poor, and that something appeared to be wrong with her. She was unstable—not someone to be trusted with taxpayers' money.

Also, Denton had obtained a copy of Ann's travel itinerary, and for the next week he would go into a town right before she did. When she arrived, what she heard about was not the Treasury but those stories about her alcoholism and psychological condition. Dan and Cecile, who took a leave from her job in New Orleans to help with the campaign, were outraged; they remembered Denton at friendly Austin political events. "Lane would go hit these places right in front of us," Dan said, "and he would cut and paste whatever he wanted under, say, the letterhead of the firefighters association. 'We support Lane Denton,' signed by somebody, and it was like this came from the entire organization."

Ann answered the questions about her character and mental health with nonchalant calm: yes, she was a recovering alcoholic, she had gone to Minnesota for a month of treatment, she was now a member of Alcoholics Anonymous, and as for the other allegations, she had no idea what those guys were talking about.

Denton's tactic backfired; the press jeered him as a cad. The *American-Statesman*'s cartoonist, Ben Sargent, caricatured him as a slug, leaving a trail of slime. The career that Denton sabotaged was his own.

The television ads and Ann's on-camera presence were effective, but they had not yet disposed of the incumbent with name recognition. "I think it is undeniably true," Hickie complained in a note to their Austin pollster, "that people in Texas do not know that Warren Harding has been indicted—just think what they will know by the time the Republicans get through with him by October of this year. What can we do to make the point?"

They didn't have to do anything different. A Travis County grand jury had indeed indicted Harding on two felony counts of official misconduct. The charges alleged that the treasurer had two employees working on political tasks while drawing a state salary. That is not a crime in many states—and certainly not in the White House—but the law is clearly written on the books in Texas. News of Harding's indictment broke at the end of March, just before the primary. Ann led him in the primary, and then, five weeks after his indictment, Ronnie Earle and his Public Integrity Unit offered a plea bargain that effectively handed the election to Ann. Harding pleaded no contest to a misdemeanor. "I remember being at the campaign office," said Dan, "and somebody called and said, 'He's getting out.' He's *what*? 'He's getting out!' We didn't have to raise money for the runoff."

Governor Clements reportedly persuaded the Republican who had won their primary that the GOP would be better served if he withdrew in favor of a candidate who had a better chance against Richards in the fall. The substitute candidate was Allen Clark. He had been a banker, and he had some definite ideas on how the treasurer's office ought to be run. But he was also a former Green Beret who had lost both his legs in combat in Vietnam. He laid a lot of wreaths on the graves of veterans that fall, and his wife followed him, carrying a tape recorder that blared "The Ballad of the Green Berets." Ann just worked harder. Her crowds were getting larger, and now she was being offered use of airplanes, which enabled her to cover more ground, to make personal contact with more people in more communities.

A major disappointment for Ann and other liberals in the primary was that Bob Armstrong ran a distant third in the Democratic primary for governor. Buddy Temple, the timber baron's son, made the runoff but looked at his totals and decided he was too far behind to catch Mark White, so he conceded and withdrew. Jim Mattox won his runoff and joined Ann, White, Bentsen, Hobby, Bullock, Mauro, and Hightower on the nonjudicial part of the ballot. Ann was one of the first friends who went to see Bullock after he returned from drunk school. But he directed little of his energy, organization, and money to the coordinated campaign. He had liked Bill Clements early in his term, but then had broken with him. On the other hand, he couldn't stand Mark White; he dispatched his press aide, Tony Proffitt, to help with Clements's campaign.

As Election Day neared, a Republican group prepared a print ad that showed Jim Mattox being handcuffed by Dallas police at a storied antiwar demonstration in Lee Park in 1969. The city's police chief had later apologized to Mattox for that detention. But the ad and the photo appeared in fifteen small-town newspapers and the *Dallas Morning News*. For Mattox, it was a point of pride and a show of his power that Republicans feared and disliked him enough to resort to that. It was also a hint that things were not going well in the GOP camps.

A former newspaper reporter named Bill Cryer worked for the Clements campaign the last three months of the race. It was an odd time in his life, because he would spend the next twelve years as Ann Richards's press secretary. In the campaign's swank Austin headquarters, he got to know Karl Rove fairly well. Cryer later told me about their experience the day of the election.

The exit polls started looking shaky, and it was raining hard over in East Texas. We got a call that blacks and refinery workers were standing in line outside the polls in a downpour. Something was happening out there, and it did not bode well for Governor Clements. Karl and the others were blindsided; they didn't see it coming. They felt terrible for the old man, wondered how they'd let him

down and all that, but they were pros. Karl had this gallows humor about it all.
. . . He could be a very charming fellow. What's the word for him in those days?
Puckish. He had a puckish sense of humor.

The most stunning thing about the 1982 election was the extent of the GOP disaster. Republicans thought they had the future of Texas politics firmly in hand; then they were routed from top to bottom. White ousted Clements 54 to 46 percent, and the down-ballot Democrats ran better—Hightower with 69.2 percent, Ann with 61.4 percent, Mauro with 60.9 percent. The established troika of Lloyd Bentsen, Bill Hobby, and Bob Bullock certainly helped the lesser-known

David Richards gives Ann a congratulatory kiss after her election as state treasurer in 1982. Though they were separated during that campaign, he provided generous financial support that enabled her to make the race. They divorced in 1983.

Identified in some accounts as "Yarborough Democrats," the down-ballot stars of the Democrats' class of 1982 take a celebratory stroll around the Capitol: from left, Ann, Jim Hightower, and Garry Mauro. Mauro and Hightower had worked for the populist liberal U.S. senator Ralph Yarborough, and Ann was close to him in her political career, despite an unpleasant experience when her then-husband David tried to go to work for him in Washington.

candidates, for their money and organization encouraged straight-party votes. And two popular congressmen, Mickey Leland and Henry B. González, boosted African American and Hispanic turnout in populous Houston and San Antonio. But Ronnie Dugger, the publisher of the *Texas Observer*, saw it as the triumph of a reborn liberal wing of the Democratic Party: "The claim of a Bentsen aide that Bentsen and Hobby practically picked White up and carried him across the finish line is less plausible than the likelihood that Richards and Hightower stimulated feminist and progressive voters to turn out, who then made the difference for White."

Taken during an impromptu nighttime stroll around the Capitol after the Democrats won, a widely distributed photograph ignored the populist Jim Mattox, but its "Gang of Three" captions and hype seemed to frame Texas Democrats' future: Mauro a shade too handsome, his hair a crown of long dark curls; Hightower ducking his head with a sly smile, wearing his mustache, cowboy boots, and a vested suit; and Ann with her hand flung high, grinning at someone she recognized in the crowd, just two years removed from the lowest point in her life, forty-nine years old and looking sleek and fine in a pair of high-heeled shoes.

Wearing a name tag for the benefit of her new employees, Treasurer Ann Richards conducts one of her first staff meetings at the small state agency.

CHAPTER 11

Raise Money and Wait

SOON AFTER ANN WON THE ELECTION, she received a letter from Nadine Eckhardt, who was living in Washington. Eckhardt proposed that she would get started at once organizing "the Austin-D.C. Axis" and Houston with an eye on grander campaigns to come.

Dear Ann,

Congratulations—again—on winning your race for treasurer. I'm writing you some thoughts before things get too hectic on the first of the year. First of all, the national press already loves you and I think you can be the first woman president (although you might have to be vp first) for the following reasons:

1. I haven't seen any other female politician in D.C. who has it together as well as you and you actually like it and have fun with it.

2. You're from Waco and went to Baylor and therefore can hang out with far-out folks and no one can criticize.

3. You're a "class" person and I perceive you as having the character it takes to make decisions which go against the party doctrine when it sucks. I can be an "Ann Richards" Democrat right now but I'm pissed at the national Dems and they'll have to woo me back somehow with new candidates and new ideas. You and Jim Hightower are the only ones who have turned me on and a lot of people who think with their heads instead of their gonads have told me they have the same position. You cut across party lines.

Nadine

Dear Nadine,

I've just completed the first agency department head meeting, addressed all employees in two separate meetings, and now I'm off to a luncheon with other elected officials. Oh! Glory! How much fun!

I loved your letter and appreciated the sentiment and the thoughtfulness in working out my ascendancy to the presidency.... Problem is, I'm not all that sure I want to be President or *anything* but treasurer. I suppose that I ought to be foresighted and plan all sorts of future activity but I've never been good at that ...

Ann

But she was still good at having a good time. That winter she went pheasant hunting in the Panhandle as a guest of Billy Clayton, a conservative Democrat and former Speaker of the Texas House who was now a lobbyist. She wrote him with the tone of an emerging good old girl. "Dear Billy Wayne, I cannot remember a hanging where I had more fun. You were a great sport. My office now proudly sports a stuffed pheasant. It is a beautiful reminder of one of the best times of my life. I cannot tell you how much it meant to me to be included in the hunt. Come see me!"

No doubt the lobbyist did just that. One night as Ann settled into the quiet time of her new routine, she read one of Jap Cartwright's hair-raising crime stories in *Texas Monthly*. She wrote him a fan letter at the magazine, addressing him carefully as "Gary." "Maybe age is upon us, but I think back on some truly insane adventures with real fondness. We may have slowed down a bit or redirected energies but you can't keep a mad dog down."

Almost immediately the happy family of the Democrats' class of '82 began to bicker. The previous land commissioner, Ann's friend Bob Armstrong, had won a multibillion-dollar settlement after suing the federal government over royalties from oil production in the Gulf of Mexico. (Texas's ownership of mineral rights extended miles farther offshore than that of other states because of its origin as an independent republic.) Armstrong and his successor Garry Mauro believed the windfall belonged to the Permanent School Fund, the endowment for public education. But Lieutenant Governor Bill Hobby directed Ann to put it in general revenue, which meant it could be spent on anything. Mauro consulted Bob Bullock and Jim Mattox, who said they agreed with him in principle, but wanted to stay out of his plan of action—which was to sue Hobby and Ann with a writ of mandamus. Both were livid and let Mauro know it. Ann particularly felt it was insulting and treacherous. She told Mauro that Hobby was going to crush him like an ant, or words to that effect. Mauro knew he might not be able to win the lawsuit, so he offered, and won, a settlement in which a third of the money went to general revenue and two thirds to the permanent school endowment and another fund reserved for public education. It would take a while for the hard feelings to heal.

Elsewhere in the Capitol complex, politics got off to an uncommonly fast start in 1983. As one would expect, the primary focus in the press was on Mark White's surprising ouster of Bill Clements. But White was not an exciting media figure, and before he could get his family settled in the Governor's Mansion and orient his staff, Bob Bullock announced that he would be running against White in 1986. Some of Bullock's aides said he declared his candidacy the day the winners in 1982 were inaugurated. Of White's performance as attorney general, Bullock asserted that some "dumb" legal opinions handed down by White made "about as much sense as a square bowling ball."

With the Texas economy tanking at the rate the price of West Texas crude plummeted, the comptroller battled White over revenue estimates and the governor's ideas of education reform and finance. But Bullock's marathon campaign lasted just a year and a half. By July 1984, his hope of wearing down and ousting White had dwindled to a brooding sigh. He acknowledged that his dream of being governor was over in an interview with Raul Reyes of the *Houston Chronicle*. "Here's a guy who's an alcoholic," Bullock said. "He's been a lobbyist. Divorced. The subject of a grand jury investigation that was crippling. . . . Would [Texans] want that type of individual in the governor's office?" In self-pity he said in quitting his race, "No one really gave a doggone whether I ran or not."

The comptroller's office shared a building on North Congress with the Treasury. Ann and Bullock parked their cars in the same lot. There were times when they cracked jokes like the buddies they once had been. But Bullock's ego was bruised, and he had begun to see her as a rival. He sniped at Ann as her positive press clippings grew, saying that he could do the job of the state treasurer with one telephone and two clerks. Remarks like that annoyed her, and she had ways of paying him back. Ann had the antiquated authority to commission and pin old-style badges on Treasury agents and declare them peace officers. Bullock knew this—he seemed to know all things about Texas government—and he decided he wanted such a badge. He pestered her for it, and he never took kindly to anyone turning him down. "I can't commission him as a peace officer and license him to carry a gun," she said with a laugh. "He'd be dangerous."

At that point in her political career, Ann had not given a great deal of thought to Jim Mattox. As attorney general, he issued opinions that affected Treasury operations, and for any kind of litigation, his office provided lawyers, but that was about it. She liked John Hannah and Max Sherman, but Mattox had beaten them; he seemed able, he was an unabashed liberal, and she had no reason to think he would ever be an enemy. In 1977, when he was in Congress, she had helped him out in a boisterous and well-attended fund-raiser in Dallas. Among the participants that day were Jim Wright, the congressman and future Speaker of the House from Fort Worth, and Hamilton Jordan, President Carter's chief of staff. Liz Carpenter kicked off the event in her usual drawling, uproarious manner. They had gathered, she declared, "not to praise Jim Mattox, but to bury him with greenbacks." Ann spoke next. "I didn't know there were this many Democrats in Dallas County," she bantered, "or this many reasonable facsimiles."

But then David accepted a job as executive assistant attorney general, the chief litigator on Mattox's staff. He had no more talent with a crystal ball than Ann did, and he foresaw no conflict of interest. The Democrats had rolled back Republican designs on state government, and a good number of the winners were liberals. In a way, Austin in 1983 resembled Washington in 1961. Jim Mattox was charting an urban populist agenda that David supported, and he thought it was time for him to get involved.

To the outrage of conservatives and the emerging Christian Right, Mattox and his legal team chose not to appeal a federal court ruling that voided a state law making sodomy a crime. And for the first time, an attorney general interpreted consumer rights as a responsibility of state government. He called himself the "People's Lawyer." During Mattox's terms as attorney general, his staff would handle and win judgments of more than $2.5 billion for the state. But he did have some unsettling personality quirks. After the Supreme Court lifted a de facto moratorium on capital punishment in 1976 (as a result of its ruling in *Gregg v. Georgia*), Texas became the country's busiest implementer of the death penalty, starting in 1982, and Mattox attended every execution. His presence in Huntsville seemed ghoulish: the attorney general had almost no authority in capital punishment cases, certainly not at the point when a convict was strapped to a gurney and someone was poking his arm with a needle and trying to find a vein and release the poisons.

Mattox looked like the comedian Buddy Hackett, but there was nothing lighthearted or funny about his approach to winning elections. His top political minions were notorious for shaking down people for contributions, and that promptly got him in a load of trouble. An investigation by Travis County district attorney Ronnie Earle and his Public Integrity Unit resulted in a 1983 grand-jury indictment of Mattox for commercial bribery.

The investigation came about because Mattox had jointly sued giant Mobil Oil with one of his major contributors, a South Texan named Clinton Manges. They were trying to void an oil and gas lease, an action that, if successful, would greatly benefit Manges and also earn the state some royalties. Mattox's brother and sister had given him $125,000 in campaign contributions, and a Seattle bank with links to Manges had lent them a large amount of money. Mobil's lawyers went after all those parties as well as the attorney general. Outraged by the attack on his siblings, Mattox threatened those lawyers, who belonged to the famous Houston firm Fulbright and Jaworski. Even though Leon Jaworski was the special prosecutor who helped bring down Richard Nixon, no Texas law firm was more aligned with the old moneyed establishment. In retaliation, Mattox threatened to take away the firm's tax-exempt status and its immensely profitable share of the state's bond business. It was open warfare. Ronnie Earle and his prosecutors did not bring the case to trial until 1985, and Mattox became a full-time defendant. David Richards functioned as Texas's de facto attorney general for nearly two years.

At the Austin trial, Mattox and his attorneys did not deny that he had threatened the Houston lawyers. But the prosecutors were never able to explain what commercial bribery was. The public and the press came to believe that Earle's crew had invented the crime in order to get the indictment. The jury walked Mattox, and when he strode out of the courthouse with that acquittal, he pulled a boxing glove on his left hand and in triumph thrust it high in the air. That was the man's style of political theater.

Ann had sworn on her first day in office that treasurer was the only job she wanted, period. But she was surveying the field of possible Democratic opportunities just a year and a half into her first term at the Treasury. Bill Cryer, the tall and wry former newspaper reporter who was her press aide, delivered in July 1984 a wide-ranging assessment of her prospects. The memo read in part:

> It seems to me that your choices for political office (other than state treasurer) are, in descending order:
> 1. Comptroller
> 2. Lieutenant Governor

3. U.S. Senator

4. Governor, if White does not run again for some reason, or in six years if he does.

5. U.S. Congress upon the retirement of Jake Pickle [a folksy, popular man who had represented Austin and been part of Lyndon Johnson's political team]

Politically, you are probably the strongest statewide office-holder at the present time, with the possible exception of Mark White and Bill Hobby. Mark White because of his strong showing in the special session is at a crest right now. . . . I think personally Hobby could be defeated in a tough primary [challenge for his seat] or for the governorship if his opponent were articulate and aggressive. I doubt, however, if anyone would be willing to take him on. He is one of those politicians whose name has a chilling effect on other people's political ambitions.

Jim Hightower is perceived to be strong, but his liberal image will be a big handicap in a high profile race at the top of the ballot . . .

Mattox is lucky to still be in office.

Mauro has an image of being thin-skinned, "spoiled," and tainted . . .

Bullock is tainted with his past beyond redemption. That, plus his early announcement for governor, has hurt him badly. He has never really had a hard-fought race and I think White would have rolled him over in any primary. . . . The betting right now is that Bob Bullock has made his last hurrah and is going to retire . . .

Ann Richards could probably win any race she ran for. She is seen as likeable, tough and honest. Her record at the Treasury is perceived as outstanding and her leadership in the national party [has] marked her as a winner and a Democratic darling. Furthermore, it is believed that it would be difficult for a male candidate to attack her.

Unfortunately, there doesn't seem to be an office open right now. She can keep the Treasury as long as she wants it. While comptroller is obviously a more powerful office, it is seen by most as a lateral transfer. She can bide her time until a senator retires. . . . The lieutenant governor's office is hers, if she wants it, and is willing to run against a rather large field, should Hobby retire.

Her option seems to be to hold on at Treasury, raise a bunch of money, and wait.

Almost nothing over the next several months played out the way Cryer predicted. For one thing, a major Democratic rival he neglected to mention was San
Antonio's handsome and charismatic mayor, Henry Cisneros. Not long after
Cryer wrote that memo, Cisneros was one of the politicians whom Walter Mondale seriously considered as a vice presidential running mate. In the end, Mondale
picked Geraldine Ferraro, making her the first woman on a major-party ticket,
but the episode emphasized that Cisneros was the elephant in the living room
of Texas Democrats—he commanded the Hispanic vote. In a crowded field of
Democrats who might run for governor, Capitol pundits, consultants, and poll-
sters generally ranked Ann no better than fourth.

For Ann and her team, the 1984 presidential election would have few high
points. Mary Beth Rogers laughed that, for her, it was when they got a close look
at the movie star Warren Beatty on the floor of the national convention in San
Francisco. Ann learned something valuable when she got to make one of the
speeches nominating Ferraro. Her performance caught the eyes of some party
insiders, but she was not enthralled by it, and she put down a marker in her store
of recollections: the lights of the Moscone Center were not turned down while
she was making her speech, and the crowd talked all the way through it.

*From right, Attorney General Jim Mattox and Treasurer Ann Richards stump in Texas for Geraldine
Ferraro and Walter Mondale, the Democratic nominees for vice president and president in the
1984 election. Ann made a speech seconding the nomination of Ferraro at the national convention,
exposure that contributed to her selection as keynote speaker four years later.*

In the election that November, Reagan and Bush carried Texas and forty-eight other states, with the Democrats winning only in Mondale's native Minnesota and the District of Columbia. The Mondale-Ferraro ticket suffered the second-worst blowout in a presidential election, gaining just 40.6 percent of the vote.

Whatever the future held in store for Ann, she and her team had a troubled and outmoded agency to run. During the 1982 campaign, Mary Beth Rogers had a full-time job working for the outgoing land commissioner, Bob Armstrong. When Ann won, Mary Beth talked to Armstrong about what she should expect. "He said, 'The legislature will be going into session, she'll have to compile a budget, and she'd better get an audit of the Treasury first.' So I relayed that to Ann," Mary Beth said with a laugh, "and she said, 'Well, then you have to come work for me, and do all that.'

"I didn't know anything about money, and she didn't either! I went to the university bookstore and bought a big old thick volume called *The Financial Handbook*. I took it home every night to learn those financial terms. We joked about how many terms we could throw around in meetings. God, it was interesting, and it was a lot of fun—and real hard. We worked our tails off."

Jane Hickie chaired the transition team. The state provided no budget for such a thing, and the changeover wasn't like the one that occurred at the land office across the street, where Bob Armstrong did all he could to make things easier for the newly elected Garry Mauro. Hickie described the surreal experience of their official first tour of the Treasury to Lynn Whitten, a student at the LBJ School of Public Affairs who was conducting in-house interviews at the Treasury.

> Warren G. Harding took us around to meet everybody and see all the departments, and as he introduced us in every department, he had our names written on a piece of paper—Ann Richards, Chula Reynolds, and Jane Hickie, and there were about seven departments, and as he introduced us in every department, he would read our names off the piece of paper, and not once in seven departments did he get our names right. The protocol in terms of dealing with Mr. Harding was pretty elaborate. We didn't want to upset anybody and inconvenience him, and we didn't want it to be awkward. But we found an atmosphere of real fear and distrust. . . . And the office was much more archaic than anything we had ever been led to believe. There was no mailroom, no mail processing system, and the data processing was like something out of an old movie. . . . And with people who had little to no experience with state bureaucracy, how

in the world do you get a handle on what was without a doubt the last little backwater of state government?

When we interviewed the department heads, we would be sitting there and the clock came to a quarter till five, and I swear if we had walked out of that door we'd have been stampeded by a hundred people rushing down the hallway. And we couldn't come during the lunch hour, because everybody got off from noon to one. It was the same stampede.

Mary Beth was organizing a fund-raiser to provide some operating cushion and reduce Ann's campaign debt. She also drafted a proposal that laid out the necessity of Ann taking command of the agency with a firm and confident show of control. "We thought that it really mattered that the first day we were here that this agency felt impact that we were in charge," Ann told Lynn Whitten, "and that it should not appear in the least to be business as it had been conducted in the past."

During recruitment interviews, they discovered Paul Williams, a twenty-seven-year-old prodigy on policy issues of banking and government finance. With Paul in charge, they could stop bluffing with big words out of an introductory college text. Now they had someone who really knew what he was doing. By the end of the month, Ann had made Williams deputy treasurer in charge of fiscal operations. She gave him no time to feel heady about his new position. She told him to talk to every department head and report back by the end of his first week on how they could install security measures in all those departments. The Treasury was handling a great deal of money, Ann told Whitten, but there had never been an internal audit system or a way to check off the procedures of one department against another's.

At the same time, they didn't want to heighten fear among Harding's employees. Department heads who wished to stay on were asked to fill out questionnaires that required writing short essays: "What were your responsibilities under Mr. Harding? Have they changed since Mrs. Richards took office? What were your first impressions of Mrs. Richards?" Note that the style used was "Mrs.," not "Ms." They took pains not to fuel rumors that the new treasurer and her executive staff were fanatical feminist ideologues. Ann and her team discovered some things that were just stunning. A man named Anthony Haynes had been the agency's chief accountant for ten years. Yet Haynes, an African American, had never been allowed to ride the elevator. Other discoveries left Ann just as speechless. A woman came in her office and asked, "Mrs. Richards, is it all right if we have doughnuts in our office tomorrow?"

"Of course it is," the new treasurer replied. "But why in the world would you ask me?"

The employee hesitated. "Well, Mr. Harding always thought it best to ask first." Every Thursday for years she had been coming in and asking the same question— could they please have their Friday-morning doughnuts?

The historian Ruthe Winegarten, another of Ann's friends from the Dallas days, arrived and took over the wide-ranging internal interviews. Ann told her about the quandaries her team had encountered at the start. "Day before yesterday, one of the employees came to tell me that we had $495,000 that had been willed to the State of Texas from a man in California in 1975, and the money had been in an escrow account since then, and my question was: Why hadn't any questions about it been resolved so that it had gone into the General Fund and the legislature could use and spend it? Okay? When we find out that we've got half a million dollars at rest somewhere and has not been acted on, previous experience tells us that there's a whole lot more we don't know about."

Ann elaborated on these discoveries when she wrote her memoir. "We knew how long it took us to get money into the bank, and so the next logical question was, How long does it take other agencies to get money to the treasury? How much time and money are we losing there? I called Garry Mauro, who had just been elected land commissioner, and asked, 'Garry, how long does it take to get checks from your office to mine?' He said he didn't know, he'd just gotten there too, but he would find out. He called down and found that [the General Land Office], which collected sizeable sums from leases on state-owned lands, delivered money to the Treasury *when the bag got full*. And we were literally across the street from each other."

Ann bragged on their installment of a new section called Rapid Deposit, which was derived, she said, from efficient cash-management programs. They rolled out a high-profile campaign with slick public-service television ads advising Texans on how to investigate the Unclaimed Property fund and find out whether there might be an unknown bonanza waiting for them. Harding and Jesse James before him had called this fund Escheat, an archaic and suspicious-sounding term that did not encourage inquiry. And the modernization of the office that Ann and her team achieved was genuine, not just a public relations campaign. At peak efficiency, Treasury employees processed 34,000 checks a day from other state agencies and earned the state $300 million in a fiscal year.

All that was the upside of the story. When Ann and her team took over the Treasury, state government was flush, operating with a large surplus. The OPEC oil cartel's boycott of Western nations had triggered a paradoxical boom in Texas. One saw bumper stickers that read: "Freeze a Yankee in the Dark." But the Texas boom went bust when the price of crude oil collapsed. Then a second economic blow battered the state. Texas senator Phil Gramm, who had been an academic economist, pushed through legislation to deregulate banking, and that contributed to the overleveraging of giant savings and loans. The savings-and-loan fiasco led to nearly 500 failed banks in Texas, and though some of these merged with banks that were on a sounder footing, the financial catastrophe caused a domino effect. The real estate market crashed, companies slashed discretionary expenditures on things such as advertising, another industry with a large payroll, and 300,000 Texans lost their jobs. Bankruptcies and foreclosures skyrocketed. In those first days after Ann took office, most letters she had received were giddy congratulations. Soon they came from people in search of employment.

Ann had corresponded with Bud Shrake for years, though she complained at times about the difficulty of cornering him. "I need the money and I'm grateful," she wrote at the end of one letter thanking him for a contribution. "I don't know how to get to see you. Is it best for me to call for an appointment? Do you ever eat out or should I cook something?" In another note, she fretted about the oil and gas wells that were not being drilled in Texas, and the banks and savings and loans that were failing. "It's more fun to be treasurer when there is a lot of money," she wrote. "This job is turning out to be work."

When Ann was running for treasurer, the headline for a *Third Coast* magazine interview read: "Ann Richards Goes Statewide." In an unsigned interview, the Austin-based magazine suggested that already a governor's race might be in her future. The interviewer asked her to respond to the "liberal" label that was being applied to her. "That's fine," Ann said. "It doesn't really matter to me."

The interviewer brought up the subject of her marriage. "You've been separated from your husband but coincidentally came to a reconciliation around the time you decided to run for statewide office."

Ann responded with her stock answer about not wanting to hang out at the Raw Deal anymore. "I wasn't happy. It didn't fit into my life. I no longer do things I don't enjoy. And part of that is I don't drink alcohol. I'd love to give up smoking." She laughed and looked at the cigarette in her hand. "That's my next goal."

The gist of the story came from this quote about her marriage and separation: "We didn't have to come to a reconciliation, really. We had been married forever, you know, and I was very busy—preoccupied, working hard. David was off working hard at his own thing. And both of us, after several years of a kind of evolutionary process, felt we ought to have a shot at being individuals. David and Ann Richards were an institution—you know what I mean? If I thought one thing, David was supposed to think that, too. It was as if we couldn't be ourselves—so we made the decision to live apart."

Texas Business ran a complimentary feature on the state treasurer, and then in February 1984 came a positively gushy story in *Third Coast*. Will van Overbeek shot the photograph of her grinning on the cover, the big-hair look evolving, though not yet into a helmet, with the caption "Ann Richards Laughing All the Way to the Bank." The loving set of photos of her by Overbeek and David Stark led off inside with Roberta Starr's text, and on another page was Stark's photo in which she donned a black turtleneck, black hat, and a mask composed of black glasses and the Harry Porco pig snout. Ann had volunteered a sample performance: "I put big lights up in the parking lot to cut back on rape, but I told my girls, 'Watch how you dress. Some women are just asking for it.' I just love women. Take my ball and chain, Gladys. Some woman came to me wanting me to support her for state treasurer. You know, she was just as cute as a bug. Anyway, I looked at her and asked her, 'Now, honey, why do you want to do something like this? Did you hate your daddy?'" (Years later, when Ann's profile and the stakes were much higher, *Vanity Fair* contacted Stark with a request to publish the Harry Porco photo. He thought about it and declined—and received a handwritten note from Ann, expressing her gratitude.)

And the parting with David was not as smooth as Ann implied in the *Third Coast* stories. "At the Treasury," Mary Beth Rogers told me, "Ann and I had a door between our offices. She insisted on it—had a door cut through there. I thought, 'Oh, god, I'll never have any peace.' But most of the time we left it open. That first year [after the election], David got a divorce lawyer and filed the papers. Somebody called Ann the day they were filed—she still had all those buddies down at the courthouse. And she called David and reamed him out. I got up at one point to close the door. She didn't care. She was crying, she was screaming. 'Who do you think I am, some *shop girl* at the dime store? You know, this'll be in the paper tomorrow. You get what's-his-name to go over there and pull those papers right now.' And he did. So it never made the newspapers. They still had stuff to work out. . . . I think she was concerned about how the children's trusts would be set up."

The end came when Ann's lawyer filed the petition in August 1983. Ann went into the office one weekend and wrote her lawyer a letter that contained some questions about the settlement. In the division of property, the house on Red Bud Trail would go on the market. Ann would get a half interest in the building on West Seventh and the acreage of the camping retreat on the San Gabriel. Counting the separation, thirty years and seven months of marriage came down to a division of wealth and real estate.

Ann wrote her lawyer: "This is being typed by my own poorly coordinated fingers on not-at-state-expense paper because I am a conscientious public servant. Please forgive." She ran down a list of four monetary concerns and then the sad fifth one. "When the divorce is granted, when do we close out, signing the papers?" She feared it would be like a real estate closing. "Do I have to be present with David at that time? I do not choose to do so."

In December 1984, Ann returned to Europe with her friends Jane Hickie, Chula Reynolds, and Claire Korioth. Once back in Austin, she wrote to people to apologize because she and Betty McKool had not gotten out their Christmas cards that year (they never revived the popular ritual). "The election did make me feel as though a truck had run us down," she wrote one friend, "and then backed over us for good measure, but I've bounced back. We have been beaten before and we will be again, but in the meantime we will have our share of victories.

"I just spent three weeks in Italy. It was a fantastic experience. The Rockefeller Foundation asked me to attend a conference of women from all over the world on population control. With my four kids, I'm hardly a good example, but I was pleased that I held my own with some pretty heavy duty folks."

On Treasury stationery, she wrote Bud Shrake after a silence between them of some months. He was off somewhere on a *Sports Illustrated* assignment or working on a book, as he always seemed to be.

Dear Bud,
If I had an address I would have written ages ago but I suppose it won't hurt if this sits in the mail basket until you come home.
I miss you.
Ann

Another day she spied a greeting card that seemed appropriate, and she sent it to him. The card's cover read "Don't Preach." Inside: "I'm Perfectly Capable of Screwing Up My Own Life." Under that she wrote: "And I've done a damned good job so far—but I must say that getting to spend time with you is a bonus I never counted on. For god's sake let's keep it up!"

The notes between them often traveled inside one of the *Far Side* greeting cards by Gary Larson. One of hers read:

> Dear Bud,
> I had been on the lookout for a good-natured, rich man who wanted to take care of me. Problem is, they don't come in that combination. There are a few who are borderline, but they want to talk and they want you to listen. This demand is a terminal liability since what they have to say is not worth listening to—even for a little bit. And since I am sober, I can't even build a fantasy about how it might improve. Maybe there are some of the female gender and I've missed them but my best guess is that they don't make them in either sex.
>
> Now—I have put the word out with the Texas Nurses Association that I am looking for one that will take minimal attention from me and for a short period of time, but who can still sign his name legibly. I can expand the call if you would like. I figure if they are rich enough, we can hire the "take care of" part.
>
> Jane Hickie has been working on a concept for years called "Curtains." The idea is to start buying good retirement sites now and getting the Filipino house-boys trained. Well, obviously it will take a lot of planning. . . . If I stay in politics, I've decided to take a graduate degree in zoology. This [legislative] session has reinforced the need.
>
> Ann

So there it was, she had said it—a joking suggestion that she might entertain no-tions of swinging both ways in her sexuality. More striking was her fear of being old and poor and not having anyone to "take care" of her. And the "if" in the last paragraph hinted that at least that day she was uncertain about her prospects, and that she might get out of politics should the right situation—and person—come along.

CHAPTER 12

Cheap Help

MY WIFE, DOROTHY, had left the Texas Civil Liberties Union, and in the spring of 1985 she was job hunting. She had known Ann a long time, and finally she wrote her a shy, tentative letter. A call came back at once. Ann had spent a good portion of her life answering to her first name, Dorothy, and she had a particular way of pronouncing it. "*Darthy!*" is the closest I can come to spelling it. "Come over here," she commanded.

Dorothy told her that the only thing she knew about the Treasury was that she, Ann, was the treasurer. "Oh, hush," Ann said. "You can do anything you set your mind to." She had Dorothy set up appointments to talk to Mary Beth Rogers and Suzanne Coleman; Dorothy was uncertain how well those meetings went. "Darthy," Ann told her in a follow-up, "I need somebody handling my correspondence that knows who Maury Maverick is." By that, she meant someone who had a sense of history, the state's and the country's and her own. She also wanted someone drafting letters who had a clue about what her voice sounded like. One youngster given the task had written a long letter expounding on the poetry of Rainer Maria Rilke, and somehow that went out above her signature.

"And I need someone rounding up people we have here doing research on various things that affect the Treasury," Ann said. "Can you do both of those things?"

Dorothy blinked and said she didn't know.

"Sure you can," Ann said, grinning. "You'll like it here, Darthy. We're gonna teach you all about *money*."

And so the bawdy woman who had commanded my attention at a bridge party in the house of Fletcher and Libby Boone entered my life in a continuing

Soul sisters: Ann as state treasurer greets county-western singing legend and new friend Dolly Parton in Austin, about 1983.

way. Dorothy downplayed her skill as a writer, keeping the letters short—seldom more than three or four sentences. But it was uncanny how much they sounded like her boss. Treasury employees worked hard, with Ann inspiring and driving them, many days well into the dark. When I was traveling for my work, Dorothy would pick up my stepdaughter Lila and take her back to the office with her homework. Ann liked to work in her stocking feet, and they got to where they could hear her padding down the hall, a letter in her hand. Dorothy came home one night marveling that Ann had been talking about some complex fiscal policy as she pulled out a needle and a spool of thread from a desk drawer and stitched up a runner in her panty hose.

Ann and David had sold the house on Red Bud Trail in the divorce settlement, and she bought a smaller one near the university, its porch and front windows looking out on some popular tennis courts and a handsome greenbelt along Lamar Boulevard and Shoal Creek. The first Christmas after Dorothy went to work at the Treasury, Ann had an after-work party at her house for members of her staff and their families. Everyone who came through the door was given a pair of white spongy reindeer antlers with a chin strap. Watching people like

Mary Beth Rogers, Suzanne Coleman, and Nancy Cannon, I put the thing on my   155
head because everyone else was wearing them, including the treasurer. It was odd
watching people converse and move through the house, their antlers bobbing and
weaving. Ann called us all into the living room, told us to take a seat if we could
find one, and with grand flourishes, like a teacher directing a grade-school class,
she led us singing, "On the first day of Christmas, my true love gave to me . . ."
What an entertainer! She didn't flub a line.

During that year, something terrible happened to two families and many sets
of friends, and it spelled the end of the Austin tradition called First Friday. Sam
Whitten had been diagnosed with lung cancer, the treatment punished him, and
in January 1986 he didn't survive a surgery. Virginia and her children asked David
to deliver one of the eulogies at the funeral in a Methodist church, and they asked
Ann to deliver another. That time Ann didn't ask for help from any of the gifted
writers on her staff. She composed the eulogy on a typewriter, making many mistakes, having never mastered those tricks with her fingers. Ann had made countless speeches by then, but both in words and delivery, this one was more heartfelt
than any of the ones she had made about government and politics or in humorous roasts of important people in her new milieu. It was her first masterpiece.

Well, Sam Whitten was a dancing fool. He would arch that skinny back, wing
out his arms, flash that smile, and his feet would step off into a life of their own.
No wonder Virginia was in love. Who could resist that sailor boy in his crisp
white bell-bottoms jitterbugging through "Tuxedo Junction." I can still see him
twirling Jill under his arm at Lynn's wedding.
  But Sam hated all forms of physical activity *except* dancing. David said, as a
friend, you knew Sam would do anything in the world for you, but he wasn't
worth a damn when you had a flat tire. . . .
  But he was a great listener. He loved conversation and he loved company. I
would come back from a long campaign trip and Sam would rush to the door
and as he saw me coming up the walk he would cry out, "Come in this house!"
as if I were *the* person he most wanted to see in the world. And he would listen
to my tale of woe or joy never really demanding more than I *just keep talking*.
  It was that insatiable love of good talk that made Sam tolerate camping—
and other forms of outdoor carryings on. . . . He froze in the winter. Bundled
and scrunched up into a fold on his camp chair by the fire, he would mutter,
"Why are we doing this?" But another song from Wayne Oakes or a jig from
Mary Holman would jolly him.

Always the last one to bed, he would crawl in the car, because he refused to sleep on the ground. Once, Virginia, who always did the driving, parked the station wagon on a slant. The next morning Sam complained bitterly that he'd been forced to sleep with his feet above his head and everything he'd drunk the night before ran to his brain. This condition was known as the Sam Whitten flu . . .

Sam is such a sudden and irreplaceable loss to so many of us. He and Virginia, through their First Fridays, helped us develop and preserve a circle of friends that spans generations. It was not unusual to find three generations of the same family at First Fridays, sometimes four. And he adored being at the center of all that. Because Sam loved each of us, too. We were all a part of Sam's family, after a time.

All politics is local, the old saw goes. Ann often made day trips around the state, and she was annoyed that when she passed the Treasury's offices on her way back home from the airport, all the lights were turned on. She complained of that one day to her developer friend Gary Bradley. The nemesis of Austin environmentalists told her that the wasteful lighting problem was easy to fix, and he could save the state some money. It was a motion-activated light switch that turned the lights off when, after a reasonable interval, no one moved. Bradley bought and sold Ann a batch of them, and the *American-Statesman* found out. The drift of the coverage was that Ann had done Bradley a covert financial favor when she should have put the job out for bids. Good grief, Ann reacted, but she had learned one more lesson about the press.

That fall, the *Houston Chronicle* sent a reporter named Barbara Karkabi to Austin to write about the new state treasurer. The angle of her story was not so much about how Ann got elected, or how she was transforming the Treasury, but why a prominent historian like Ruthe Winegarten was willing to immerse herself in recording Ann's first year in the new office. Karkabi asked Ann: "What do you think the general public will think about this? You know, this is a time of recession with all these cutbacks, but then there's a foundation giving a grant to do a study of the first year in office of the first woman elected in a long time in statewide office. Do you feel like there will be any negative feedback?"

"I have no idea," Ann said, but Karkabi pressed her. Ann replied evenly, "I don't answer what if, what if, what if because I don't know." Karkabi and Winegarten stepped out of Ann's office for a few moments, and when they returned, the interview ranged into Ann's perceptions of her new job as treasurer. She reeled off some pat answers about what a fantastic job the voters had given her. Then she blurted: "I grabbed a cigarette while you were gone."

Winegarten cried out in dismay. "What happened to your hypnotist and your stapling and your . . ." Ann had been trying everything, including the remedial fad of having her ear stapled. Karkabi said she had read about Ann's attempt to quit smoking.

Winegarten put in sympathetically, "I know, Ann."

"That's a miserable personal failure," Ann berated herself. "I was skunking again this week. . . . I hate it—it's obnoxious." As the women sympathized, Ann went on that she had been trying to quit in hopes of influencing her daughter to do the same. "Well, it was really funny. I was interested in myself. I took my youngest girl, Ellen, to school, then drove straight back from that college to the airport and bought a pack of cigarettes. Hadn't smoked in two or three days."

Interested in herself: she sure got that right. Ann was egocentric, principled, driven, caustic, and more than a bit cynical—qualities shared by many politicians. But she was a stickler about refusing to conduct politics on state time. Because they needed to talk about politics for the Treasury interviews, one weekend Winegarten came to her house in West Lake Hills. It was a poignant time for

Treasurer Ann Richards lights up as Karen Hughes observes, Austin, early 1980s. Hughes was then a television news reporter in Dallas. As executive director of the Texas Republican Party, she was a thorn in the side of Governor Richards and became a powerful figure in the gubernatorial administration and presidency of George W. Bush.

Ann—she was selling the house that contained so much of her personal imprint and history. Winegarten had been looking through boxes of mementos that an assistant had put in chronological order, for possible use in the documentary project. "Ann," the writer said, "I have a lot of original photographs that she found in there that I'm afraid I have to give back to you. You know, like pictures of you driving a bulldozer and taking a raft trip down [the] White River in Idaho, and—"

"Keep it, don't give it to me," Ann cut her off. "I don't want it."

"Do you have copies of all those things?"

"No, what would I do with them?"

"Well, I don't know," Winegarten said.

"No, I don't want any of that stuff," Ann said.

"But there's a picture of you with Cecile as a baby . . . and I guess your wedding picture with a candle, and . . ."

"Well," Ann hedged. "I can't imagine that anybody would be interested in that stuff. I am fixin' to move out of the house." But she relented and gave Winegarten permission to search through the bags and boxes that were about to be thrown out. "I had some things that it just seemed like I shouldn't throw away," Ann said. "Like I own all of the Dallas newspapers from the week Kennedy was assassinated, up to the time Oswald was shot. Scraps, God, there's a million scraps. All my old high school yearbooks still have these rotted corsages in them."

Ann had just come back from a San Antonio convention of the National Women's Political Caucus, where Bella Abzug had taken the lead in grilling potential Democratic candidates to oppose President Ronald Reagan the next year. Senators John Glenn, Gary Hart, Alan Cranston, and Ernest Hollings were there, along with Jimmy Carter's vice president and the eventual 1984 nominee, Walter Mondale. And as the race shaped up, *Time* had floated Ann as a possible vice presidential nominee for the Democrats.

"Well," Winegarten asked, "how did you feel about the discussion of yourself as a vice presidential nominee? I'm thinking about the fact that all the presidential candidates could really use a Southerner on the ticket—it appears that would make sense."

"It's ridiculous," Ann said. "It's ridiculous."

"For a Southerner to be on the ticket?"

"No, that I would be a vice presidential nominee or be suggested. It's hype; it's fodder for newspaper stories. That doesn't mean I don't think I'm capable. I think I'm perfectly capable of being vice president. But as a practical matter it's just not feasible. You don't begin with a base like I have and make a national base out of it."

As the conversation wore on, Ann talked about what neutral observers of that convention might infer about the ethnic makeup of the women's movement. "You know, you look around that hall, it is just a white bunch . . . We are slowly being able to get some Mexican-American women involved, but by and large, they are very angry. They are not only angry at men, they are angry about the Hispanic societal structure that's been more repressive toward them than what Anglo women have experienced. And the ones who aren't angry are, you know, still doing forty Hail Marys every morning and baking cookies for the church social in some little South Texas town." Ann was nothing if not blunt.

She elaborated on how dull, stiff, and inept the Democratic presidential candidates had been in trying to connect with women. "I went back around behind the stage, where there was a lady with a walkie-talkie. I said, 'Give me your walkie-talkie, and I want to talk to Fritz Mondale backstage,' because I knew he was the next one up. I called back there and I said, 'Fritz, I do not know what you're going to say, but you are going to have to personalize yourself to these people. Show some sense of humor. This is boring, what is taking place here.'"

After Ann's speech in San Antonio, a number of women had come up to her and invited her to address their state caucuses, and just to talk. Winegarten asked Ann what she told those women. "I encourage women in their workplace to talk with each other not only about their professional problems but their personal problems," she answered. "And I'll have women come up and say afterwards, 'You know, you're right, I was sort of locked into thinking that I had to compete with that other woman at the desk next to me.' They talk about problems with their kids, and they talk about feeling guilty, because they want to do something other than what they are doing, and they fear they'd be denying someone else if they did. And one of the ingredients I've been talking about for years is: Don't believe that stuff they tell you about the Superwoman. . . . You'll kill yourself trying to be the greatest professional combined with being a great nurse, lover, mother, and entertainer—whatever. I mean, all of that old garbage that we live by—or certainly I listened to and read in my generation. If we buy into that, we're just cheap help. Cheap help."

She went on: "The sustenance that comes with being needed is enormous. I'm the A Number One Worst. When my kids come home, I have to steel myself not to go in there and wash all those clothes. Last night my daughter who is just home for a little while came in the kitchen and said, 'Mama, I want you to relax while I'm here so that I can enjoy it.' And I was in there shucking corn and getting after those green beans."

Winegarten wanted to know what the most politically engaged women—potential candidates—said in San Antonio. "The same old questions," Ann replied, "about what role do you play in your family, or how can your relationship change when you are running for office. I said, 'Well, actually, when you are running for office everything is great. It's when you serve that's tough. . . . It becomes your life, and that's when things begin to fall apart. And no matter how enthusiastic your husband or your children might be about seeing you become an elected official, when it becomes a daily routine . . . you need to be prepared to give it all up and no longer have a family.'"

When Winegarten commented on how that must have shocked some of the audience, Ann stood her ground: "I say it all the time. . . . Some woman asked me, what did I mean? I told her, 'I mean exactly what I said. The back seat of my car is piled with clothes that I don't even have time to take to the cleaner.'"

She was amused by the way some Texans had begun to react to her: "Invariably I get compared to aging actresses like Doris Day—personally I think she's young—and Lana Turner, Joan Crawford, Barbara Stanwyck. About the only one I haven't hit is Bette Davis. The other day on a plane a stewardess kept staring at me, and she came over and said, 'How do you like your coffee?' I said, 'Oh, I like it fine, and I drink a lot of coffee.' And then she giggled and went to the back. I couldn't figure out what she was talking about. Later she came over and said something else, and it turned out she thought I was Lauren Bacall, who sells some kind of coffee on TV."

Winegarten asked Ann how she handled the press. "You just spend a lot of time on it."

"You don't refuse them?"

"Oh, goodness no," said Ann. "You don't dare refuse them. Lord, no. That spells disaster."

But she added that as the only female in statewide office in Texas, she received the kind of press coverage that other officeholders were constantly trying to generate. "Even when I was on the commissioners' court, I tried my best to get less press," she chuckled. "You stick out like a sore thumb anyway, for being the only woman there, and I think the public tires of you quickly."

Winegarten asked, "You think you can get too much press?"

"Oh, sure. You bet you can."

"What would the reaction of the public be? 'I don't want to read about her anymore. . . .'"

"Yeah. 'There she is again.'"

"Or they think you're out soliciting, trying to be a prima donna?"

"I don't know. I just know that I don't have to go get it. It comes anyway." She laughed again.

Ann's longtime appointments secretary, Nancy Cannon, was at Ann's house that day, and she walked in the room grimacing and trying to roll her head. "Nancy's having a 'neck thing,'" Winegarten explained.

"What's the matter with your neck?" said Ann.

"Beat around on me," Nancy jokingly invited.

"Is it stiff?" said Ann.

"Yes, it's like—"

"She can't move it," the writer interjected.

"—like I've been in a car wreck," Nancy said.

"Well," Ann said, "why don't you have something done about it? Is it more fun not to?"

"Well, no," the younger woman replied. "It just happened this morning. I guess I could put a sign on the walk for a masseuse, in-house."

"You probably slept wrong," Ann said, and then made an abrupt change of subject—as often happened, the more desirable topic of conversation was what *she* was thinking about and experiencing. "I had the weirdest dream this morning," she told them. "And it was so bizarre. A man banging on the door wanted to ask about mowing my lawn, since it hadn't been mowed in two months. And I said, 'I have to tell you this dream, I'm afraid I'll forget it.' He looked so startled."

"Inside the dream?" Winegarten asked.

"No! I went to the door with the man banging on it, in my nightgown and my bathrobe, and I said, 'Come on in, would you like to have some coffee? I have to tell you about my dream because I'm afraid I'll forget it if I don't tell you.'"

Winegarten asked, "Did he come in?"

"Yes. He was this kid, about nineteen or twenty years old. He looked so startled. In the dream I was at a funeral, and there was a young boy who was dead—I don't know who it was—in a coffin there, an open coffin. I don't know who all was there; maybe Ellen was with me. And the boy woke up and sat up in the coffin. And I said to this guy, the preacher or the funeral director or somebody, I said, 'This guy isn't dead, this kid is alive.' And he said to me, 'Oh, no—no, no, no—that's just the kind of dead he is. He's been getting up like that.' And I thought, 'Well, these fools are gonna bury this kid and he's obviously alive.' Oh, it was so bizarre."

Following the keynote speech at the Democratic National Convention that made Ann a national celebrity and gubernatorial contender, in August 1988 she accompanied Michael and Kitty Dukakis and Texas Democratic officeholders to a rally in Johnson City. She climbed on this longhorn as a lark, then laughed and yelled as the photographer came running, "Don't you dare take my picture, Scott; damn it, don't you dare!"

PART THREE

Only in Texas

Treasurer Ann Richards and Lieutenant Governor Bill Hobby don kitchen aprons and cut up with knives before a dinner party in Austin, mid-1980s. Hobby became Ann's mentor and close friend, though she did not support him when he first ran for his office in 1972.

CHAPTER 13

Poker Faces

IN THE 1986 ELECTION, almost all Texas news coverage focused on the rematch between Mark White and Bill Clements in the governor's race. Clements was not supposed to have been in the race. The former governor, who was sixty-eight and had sold his oil company for $1.2 billion, made the surprise announcement while standing in front of a urinal beside a *Dallas Morning News* Capitol beat reporter, Sam Attlesey. Lubbock's Kent Hance, who had become a political journeyman for both parties after handily beating George W. Bush in a 1978 West Texas congressional race, had hired Karl Rove and charted a GOP run for governor. Embarrassed and loyal to Clements, Rove recused himself from the Hance campaign and returned to help the former governor. With lavish money and a champion's standing with the party base, Clements brushed aside Hance without a runoff. He seemed motivated largely by desire to get even with Mark White.

White's term had been crippled by the oil boom gone bust, the banking and savings-and-loan fiascos, joblessness, tax increases, and the nature of the help he received from Ross Perot. White's abrupt, chatty education czar had authored a set of reforms that took dead aim on a hallowed Texas institution, high school football. The "no pass, no play" rule applied to all extracurricular activities in the schools, but if star tailbacks or quarterbacks didn't pass all their classes and thereby became ineligible for six weeks during a fall semester, that could sink whole seasons in win-hungry Texas towns. Bumper stickers appeared all over the state that read "Will Rogers Never Met Ross Perot."

Early in his term, White had been flattered by media chat that he would make an attractive vice presidential candidate in 1988. He may have found it hard to believe the early polls that had him thirty points down against Clements. But critics in the media were all over him. He later told Brian McCall, in an interview for his dissertation, published as *The Power of the Texas Governor*, "The *Fort Worth Star-Telegram* said there'll be no need for any new taxes in my term, but they didn't read my statement before that. I'd said that if everything stays as it is now, there will be no need for any new taxes. So they just cut out that phrase and said look at all the taxes I'd raised. Hell, I'd raised everything. I raised taxes on everything across the board!"

Clements spent $13 million—a million more than White—and reversed the score by 300,000 votes. But Clements had barely been sworn in to his new term when Texas football again raised its peculiar head. In the early to mid 1980s, with teams that featured the future NFL star runners Eric Dickerson and Craig James, Southern Methodist University had reclaimed the gridiron renown it had not known since the days of Doak Walker and Kyle Rote. Rich alumni had engineered this turn-around by paying top high school recruits and their families. It set off a covert bidding war and recruiting scandal that ensnared all the state's major college programs except the University of Texas's, and it led to the NCAA's imposition of the game's first "death penalty"—banishment of SMU football for an entire season. The shamed and scaled-down football program has never really recovered.

The scandal was germane to Texas politics because Clements also chaired the SMU Board of Governors. On discovering that twenty-six scholarship players were on the take, Clements ordered SMU subordinates to cover it up and turn off the spigot gradually, lest the athletes or their family members get upset and start talking loudly. When the *Austin American-Statesman*'s Dave McNeely asked Clements whether he had told "the whole truth and nothing but the truth" about the SMU payoffs, the old-timer replied, "Well, you know, we weren't operating like inaugural day, with a Bible, Dave, and there wasn't ever a Bible present."

At best, the champion of Texas Republicans came off as a liar and cheat. On top of that, the devastated economy and lost state revenues that had doomed Mark White in turn obliged Clements to sign a $5.7 billion tax bill, the largest in the state's history. Democratic heads swung quickly to the governor's race in 1990.

The Republicans made it easy for Ann to stay where she was in 1986, for they put up no credible opponents. A few days after her reelection, Ann, Mary Beth Rogers, Nancy Kohler, Sarah Meacham, and Mary Beth's son Billy Rogers, a young politico who had directed the campaigns of Garry Mauro, met after work in the office of the developer Gary Bradley. The purpose of the meeting was to organize for a race for an undesignated higher office and work out a plan to raise money. It was certainly not too early for that. In the meantime, Ann still had an agency to run.

That fall, Mary Beth Rogers had told my wife, Dorothy, that they wanted her to represent the Treasury's interests by guiding bills that benefited the agency through the 1987 legislative session. Dorothy pondered that and finally told Mary Beth that she just had no confidence she could do that effectively. Instead, they named her the Treasury's legislative director—the issues person—and hired Joy Anderson, a tall, confident preacher's daughter who had worked in advertising and public relations in New York, where her husband, Jim, was an advertising writer and art designer; she had also worked for a year in the office of Daniel Patrick Moynihan, New York's accomplished senator.

Joy came into the group by way of a friendship with Mary Beth's sister in Dallas. "We first talked about some kind of researcher's position," Joy told me, "but we agreed that what they had available then was not really a good fit for me. So I took a job working for Ben Barnes. When I called Ann to tell her, she said, 'Oh, that's great, you go ahead and see how the big boys do it, and then we'll talk when you get done with that.' Then I worked on a congressional campaign in Fort Worth. Our candidate lost, but I learned a lot about legislative districts and voter precincts. So Ann asked me to come work for them as the legislative liaison. I said, 'Ann, I have no idea how to do that.' She said, 'Oh, don't worry. We just want someone who's loyal and talented and that we know we can trust. We can teach you all you need to know about working with the legislature.'"

See how the big boys do it. That flip remark was such a revealing thing for Ann to say. Joy shared a handsome office with Dorothy—working knee to knee, as they put it. From that point on, Joy was a permanent part of Ann's team. She and Jim Anderson were our close friends before and after their divorce.

I had finished a couple of books and wanted a breather from the freelance scuffle, so I took a part-time job writing speeches for Garry Mauro. The General Land Office resembled the federal Department of the Interior, but with an elected director and almost no surface public land. (When Texas joined the United States in 1845, one of the conditions it negotiated was the retention of all public land by the state, but about 90 percent had been sold or given away to retire the republic's debts, pay veterans of its army, and attract settlers and railroad construction.) As land commissioner, Mauro framed his initiatives to maximize the state's oil and gas revenue—Texas wisely kept its mineral rights during the public-land fire sales—and its endowment of public education. He emphasized protection of the state's beaches, wetlands, and extraterritorial waters—his lobbying led the U.S. Senate to ratify a treaty that banned the dumping of plastic debris in the ocean, which had been normal procedure for the shipping industry and even the navy. And the office devised an innovative way to enforce the MARPOL treaty ("MAR-POL" is an acronym for "marine pollution"). Texas has huge reserves of natural gas, and he pushed plans to use the fuel in vehicles and industry as a way to bring cleaner air to its smog-afflicted cities. I enjoyed working there. Under the leadership of Mauro and his predecessor, Bob Armstrong, the land office was, in my view, the most progressive agency in state government for a quarter of a century. Ann liked Garry's ideas, but the time would come when her support of them cost her dearly.

Mauro was ambitious and made no bones about it. Reporters thought he was arrogant, that he cut too many ethical corners. Then one day late in his first term, as Mauro recounted it to me, he got a strange call from his mentor, Bob Bullock. They spoke by telephone almost daily, but the comptroller insisted that they go for a drive. "He told me, 'Garry, Karl Rove is in league with a guy in the U.S. attorney's office in San Antonio. He's an FBI agent named Greg Rampton. Their sole job right now, their mission in life, is to figure out a way to indict you, me, Jim Mattox, Jim Hightower, and Ann Richards. They're out to get us all.'"

Bullock had a paranoid side to his personality, but his political intelligence was renowned, and Garry had never seen the tough little guy so spooked. Mauro feared he was going to be the first one indicted when the FBI suddenly subpoenaed 70,000 pages of land office records. "There were fourteen of them," he said of the agents. "They showed up first thing in the morning, and we had rows and rows of boxes waiting. They'd demanded that we provide two computers, and they installed their software and started looking. They must not have found much, because by ten o'clock they were gone. Rampton's thesis was that any contribution from a veteran or a developer had to be quid pro quo."

Garry added: "I saw Rampton one time after that. I walked out in the hall, and he was just standing there. He handed me his card, and I asked him into my office, and we had a little chat. I never found out what he was doing there. I assume he was trying to intimidate me."

The investigation went away without any official notice that it was over or that Mauro's name had been cleared. Garry defeated an undistinguished GOP candidate in 1986, but gone was any perception of him as the Texas Democrats' Adonis.

Trashed as well were his fairly well-developed plans to run for attorney general, if and when Mattox left office in his quest to be governor. Garry had been keeping his options open for a dark-horse race for governor himself. He didn't share Ann's assessment of Bill Hobby as a candidate and campaigner. Garry got along well with Mattox, or at least thought he did. As Clements's second term fizzled, Garry asked me to write a speech in which he claimed that nothing good would come of an all-out three-year race for governor. At once Mattox snapped to the press, "I heard about that silly speech that Garry Mauro made." Later he came over and asked Garry whether he was going to run. Garry said he wasn't. Mattox then said he hoped to have Garry's endorsement. Garry replied that he couldn't promise that because he didn't know what Ann was going to do. In Garry's words: "Mattox said, 'I think I'd be a better governor than Ann.' I said, 'Hell, Jim, I think I'd be a better governor than either one of you. The question is, who can win?'" His chuckle in telling me that story was older and wiser. "I guess I was a little arrogant back then."

Such were some of the egos, fears, and jealousies at play among the Class of '82. And the enigmatic San Antonio mayor Henry Cisneros was in a position to step out and become the immediate front-runner—he had charisma, he had the looks, he was an exceptional orator, he had built a fairly distinguished record as mayor, he had been short-listed as a vice presidential candidate by Walter Mondale, and he commanded absolute loyalty from the huge but never quite awakened Hispanic vote. But nobody in Austin had a clue about what was on Henry's mind. Texas Democrats found themselves playing an endless game called "Waiting on Henry." It was a reference to Samuel Beckett's drama *Waiting for Godot*, in which characters hang about anticipating the arrival of someone who never shows up.

But Jim Mattox was not waiting on anybody. If Cisneros did not make the race, the conventional wisdom was that Bill Hobby would move up and run for governor and win the Democratic nomination. Ann and many others on her team believed that Hobby, the son of a legendary governor and former editor of one of Texas's major newspapers, was a powerhouse. But more than that, it was an emotional matter for Ann; she wasn't going to run against her friend and mentor.

Also, she loved the workings of the legislature. She liked the face-to-face negotiations, the swapping of yarns, and the horse-trading that got legislation passed. "I wasn't involved in the day-to-day stuff then, but I thought all the political focus was on the lieutenant governor's race," said Mary Beth Rogers, who was on leave writing a book about the Hispanic activist Ernesto Cortés. But Ann was forever attuned to the practical facts of making a living. Divorced and on her own, she had to wonder whether she was enough of a businessperson to maintain her ethical standards while making the side deals necessitated by the lieutenant governor's part-time salary. "I thought she was looking hard at the comptroller's office," said Bill Cryer. "The assumption was that Bullock would either retire or seek another office. Ann had learned so much about state finance in the Treasury, she'd done about all she could there, and the offices were so closely intertwined. Except the comptroller had much more power."

After fending off the indictment and trial for commercial bribery, Mattox crashed past his Republican opponent and won reelection as attorney general in 1986. He wasted no time in staking his claim to the governor's prize in 1990, and the only way he knew how to wage a campaign was to go after it like a tank battalion.

A political consultant named Kelly Fero was advising Mattox. They knew that Hobby kept a stable of fine horses in Houston, and every year he liked to vacation in England and ride in fox hunts. Unlike most Texans, Fero knew enough about the sport that he was aware the equestrian hunters referred to donning the traditional red outfits they wore on the chase as "putting on the pinks." Mattox got hold of that tidbit and raised an ongoing howl. "Do you know what putting on the pinks is?" he inquired in a speech to the League of United Latin American Citizens. "It's probably not part of your heritage, nor mine either. Putting on the pinks is when you go out there and put on your little red riding coat, and your little pants, your high-top shoes, and chase the foxes through the woods. Then you go back and eat your wine and cheese. . . . Some of these people have had the gold spoon in their mouth so long that they forget what it's like for the average person."

Just days after Mattox made that contemptuous speech, rumors started flying around the Capitol. As usual, Bob Bullock was the first to know: Hobby was about to announce that he would not be a candidate for governor—he was known to be weary of his battles with Clements and his staff, and he said the 1989 legislative session would be too critical for him to be a distracted and divisive figure.

Hobby had been a conscientious and distinguished leader of the Senate for fifteen years, and the prospect of a race against Mattox was unsavory. Hobby deserves the benefit of the doubt for his explanation of why he was getting out, but that summer morning got stranger as it went along. David Richards had not gone to work for the attorney general in the hope or expectation of becoming part of the political operation, but with Mattox those lines were always blurred. David, who had worked closely with Hobby and his staff on a case involving Houston's

Hermann Hospital Estate, got a call from the lieutenant governor. Hobby asked David to send a message to Mattox—that he was also not going to seek reelection as lieutenant governor—and he desired some sense of what Mattox would say. David passed on the message to Steve Hall, Mattox's good-natured and well-liked communications chief. Mattox sent word that, naturally, he would be gracious and complimentary. David called Hobby with Mattox's assurances, but the weirdness that morning just kept coming.

As recorded in Steve Hall's personal diary, which he shared with me, he was walking down a corridor and encountered two members of the attorney general's staff. One asked Hall whether he knew a man named Clyde. Hall answered that Clyde was a Houston private investigator who had worked with them on the suit involving the Hermann Hospital Estate. One of the men said that Clyde was in the building and was saying he had something important and urgent to tell Mattox directly. To Hall's surprise, Mattox chose to greet the investigator in his office instead of delegating the matter to him. The language of Texas government has a certain courtliness; the lieutenant governor is addressed as "Governor," the attorney general as "General." Hall wrote that the Houston private eye said, "General, I've got a favor to ask of you, and I've stuck my neck out a little bit in telling someone that I knew you well enough to be able to get in to see you and talk straight with you."

Clyde went on that he had been asked to come and talk on behalf of the lieutenant governor. "Hobby asked me if I had a file on him, and I told him, 'Well, Governor, you live in Houston, don't you?' He laughed, then he asked me if I'd done anything on him for you, and I said I hadn't. Then he asked me to come talk to you about destroying a file. I told him I couldn't do that. I didn't have anything to bargain with."

The investigator looked closely at Mattox and said, "You do have a file, don't you?"

The attorney general replied, "I do."

"Well, I know you play tough, I knew you would. The only thing that disappoints me is that you didn't call me to have me put it together for you."

"General," Clyde went on, "Bill Hobby is worried sick that file is going to follow him into private life. . . . I knew David Richards from the Hermann Hospital stuff, and I knew Hobby knew him. I said he ought to call Richards and have Richards talk to you. Now, General, I told him that after I did that, I'd be able to come talk to you, I'd have something to bargain with, and that I believed you were an honorable man.

"He did what I asked him to do. Now I'm asking you to tear up that file, and let me keep my word and go back to him and say: 'I told you Mattox was an honorable man. He tore it up in front of me and told me he would not use it against you.'"

The conversation veered off to other subjects but kept coming back to Mattox tearing up documents in front of the investigator. Mattox finally turned to Hall and said, "Bring the file."

There was no file on Bill Hobby. Hall went outside and scrambled, looking for anything, and finally he just started stuffing one full of old and useless memos. He carried the package back to Mattox, who tore the papers into little pieces as the investigator watched. He handed them to Hall, who walked into the private john that was afforded the office of the attorney general, dropped in the shreds and tatters, and officiously flushed the toilet.

Enormously pleased with his performance as a poker player and giant killer, Mattox didn't miss a beat. Signals went out to Cisneros that he would get the same rough treatment if he even thought about getting in the governor's race. Mattox knew that Cisneros was sitting on a personal time bomb. Cisneros had created a problem for himself that could be termed "Holier Than Thou." He and his wife had a little boy with serious health problems. He had consented to be photographed by *Texas Monthly* with his son in an angelic cuddle of white clothing and sheets. But he had also been involved in an affair, and after it ended, he had sent his former lover regular checks that could be construed as hush money.

Ann didn't want any noses poking around her bedroom. But she was trying to calculate what she could and should do next. Ann had the most curious and trying relationship with Bob Bullock, both before and after they quit drinking. It was a stew of friendship, condescension, rivalry, admiration, sexism, and envy. The jockeying in anticipation of the 1990 races found their relationship on one of its upbeat swings. One day he sent her a note with a single line of friendly advice: "Say nothing often."

CHAPTER 14

The Speech

ANN TURNED FIFTY-FIVE IN 1988. She had finally been able to quit smoking. She watched her diet more when an annual physical gave her an elevated reading of her cholesterol. She walked for exercise. She took a great deal of pleasure in being a new grandmother. But she had absorbed more personal blows as she pushed the Treasury agenda and spoke to Lions and Rotary clubs around the state. Her great friend Virginia Whitten had been diagnosed with breast cancer not long after Sam died, and though she lasted longer than he had, until 1997, the dread illness claimed her too.

Ann had periodontal problems that were getting worse by the month. She flew out to Seattle for difficult oral surgery that allowed her to avoid dentures by getting implants and bridges. She complained to her son Dan that the things made it difficult for her to carry on a normal conversation, much less deliver a rousing speech. "Dear Bud," she wrote. "Happy belated Valentine's Day. I went to Seattle and got a lot of teeth pulled and bought some new ones. They make me look like Mr. Ed"—television's talking horse.

She had recently taken part in a ceremony that honored Bud, Cartwright, Dan Jenkins, and Larry L. King with stars in a sidewalk in downtown Austin. A month after she sent him the Valentine, she got this letter from Bud.

You have been on my mind a lot lately, too, and not just because I saw you hugging and kissing a bloodhound in the newspaper. I got to thinking about all the nice things you said at the 6th Street ceremony, and how much I appreciated

"I don't believe it either, but I'm not going to turn them down," Texas state treasurer Ann Richards said to a press aide when informed she had been chosen to give a career-making keynote speech at the 1988 Democratic National Convention. Here she fields local questions at a press conference following the announcement.

what you did. Being kind to dogs and me is a sure way to get a front row seat in heaven, but let's don't go there until the last plane out. There are nights when I'd like to dress up like a dancing Tampax again and take you on a tour of Harlem. Can this be done sober? Yes, after you become president of the U.S. and make me culture exchange attaché. (Fletcher is too irritable for the job.) I miss seeing you.

"Speaking in public," Ann would reflect in her book, "is a very personal piece of business. Giving a good speech, especially one with some passion and emotion, you're revealing a lot about yourself. You're putting yourself in a very vulnerable position. It's sort of like Lady Godiva riding down Main Street without clothes on. Or stepping up on a scale and getting weighed. There's every possibility in the world that you'll be found wanting."

In the Democrats' 1988 presidential race, Delaware senator Joe Biden had barely gotten started when he was found terribly wanting because of one speech. In September 1987, he had made a self-aggrandizing reference to his blue-collar origins in language lifted almost verbatim from a speech by Neil Kinnock, the British Labour Party leader. The plagiarism may have been the sin of the speechwriter, not the orator, but in any case that blunder knocked Biden out of the race.

Another man hoping to challenge Vice President Bush was the former Colorado senator and initial frontrunner Gary Hart. He torpedoed himself when reporters annoyed him with questions about rumors of his possible adultery. "Follow me around," he dared them. "I don't care. I'm serious. If anybody wants to put a tail on me, go ahead. They'll be very bored." A pair of reporters from the *Miami Herald* took him up on it, and the evidence of his affair with Donna Rice spelled the end of his campaign and career.

Following the exits of Biden and Hart, Massachusetts governor Michael Dukakis emerged and won the nomination, fending off Missouri congressman Dick Gephardt, the Reverend Jesse Jackson, and Tennessee senator Al Gore. For a while during that summer of 1988, Dukakis's star shone brightly. He had an accomplished actress cousin, Olympia Dukakis, who that same year had won an Academy Award for her role in *Moonstruck*, the kind of credit that doesn't have anything to do with politics or government, but doesn't hurt. He spoke a great deal about presiding over a "Massachusetts Miracle" of economic policy and achievement. Ann was impressed when Dukakis chose for his running mate Lloyd Bentsen, whose credits included defeating George Bush in a race for the

U.S. Senate in 1970. She had urged Walter Mondale to put Bentsen on the ticket in 1984, even though Geraldine Ferraro got the nod.

Three weeks before the Democratic National Convention in Atlanta that summer, Ann was headed to make a speech about Treasury business in Houston when she called in from a pay phone at the Austin airport to get her messages. Her life would never be the same.

Bill Cryer was in Louisiana visiting his parents when the boss telephoned him. "She said, 'Bill, I'm going to tell you something you would never believe.' I said, 'What's that, Ann?' She said, 'I've been asked to deliver the keynote speech at the Democratic National Convention.' I laughed and said, 'Well, you're right. I never would have believed that.' She was laughing, too. 'I don't believe it either, but I'm not going to turn them down! I need you to get back over here.'"

A Massachusetts attorney named Paul Kirk chaired the Democratic National Committee. He had been impressed by Ann's delivery and style in a speech nominating Ferraro for the vice presidency four years earlier. Other fans of Ann were Dukakis's campaign manager, the feminist attorney Susan Estrich, and her then-husband Marty Kaplan, a movie and television producer who had been one of Mondale's speechwriters. Kaplan later reflected on the selection process: "We talked about what the themes should be. No one should try to out-ring the eloquent oratory of Mario Cuomo four years ago. This should be a speech for the working person. It should spell out the simple needs and hopes of someone like Ann. It should be funny. It should also be common sense. That's Ann."

Ann said that she was so naïve about politics at that level that she thought she could keep an appointment at a board meeting and field press inquiries by telephone. But by the end of the first day, the small press operation at the Treasury had been swamped with calls from reporters pressing for an interview with this minor official who was little known outside Texas and feminist circles. Jim Mattox tried to badger Kirk into withdrawing the invitation. Spokesmen for the national party responded that the 1990 governor's race in Texas was a long way off, that the party would stay out of that race, and that Ann's selection for the keynote was locked in.

The *Houston Post* interviewed Mattox's chief fund-raiser, Tom Green, who said, "I just don't think it'll have much impact on the Texas Democratic primary in 1990. . . . I couldn't tell you one thing Mario Cuomo said four years ago, and everyone thought that was the greatest speech since sliced bread." Mattox bristled: "It never ceases to amaze me that someone will get out there, get two or three blurbs on TV and in the papers, and all of a sudden they're considered great candidates." As Mattox's displeasure raced outward through his political network and staff at the attorney general's office, no one was more startled and uneasy than his chief of litigation, David Richards.

Mattox wasn't the only Texas Democrat jolted by the news. That afternoon, Dorothy and I were shopping for groceries when we ran into Jim Hightower and his longtime companion, Susan DeMarco. Dorothy asked them with a burst of excitement: "Did you hear about Ann?" Jim responded to the news with a quick, sharp frown and a glance at Susan that puzzled me. He was the former *Texas Observer* editor who had fought for liberal causes in David's office building, whose election as agriculture commissioner had been the entertaining highlight of the 1982 races. How could he begrudge this break going to Ann? It turned out that Michael Dukakis had been trying to ward off a rebellion at the convention by Jesse Jackson. The camps had been dickering back and forth, mostly about who would make what speech at what hour. In the trade-offs designed to make Jackson happy, Jim and some of his political allies hoped that *he* might get to deliver the convention keynote.

Ann's political office had just sent out 39,500 letters to supporters asking for donations to the Ann Richards Capital Council—a euphemism for her political operation. "Of course it was a coincidence," Jane Hickie said. "We'd been trying to get that out for months." A gushy profile rushed to print in the *Corpus Christi Caller-Times* noted that Ann kept a motto on her refrigerator door that read: "Women should be obscene and not heard." The writer told a story about how Ann had once startled a crowd of Wall Street bankers by pulling on her pig-snout mask and snorting her way through a Harry Porco routine; when the reporter asked whether she wanted to run for governor, she quipped, "It's about time we put somebody in the Governor's Mansion that knows how to clean it."

For a week after the keynote announcement, she had little time to do anything but respond to the press. By the end of that week, alarm had begun to overtake euphoria. Suzanne Coleman, Mary Beth Rogers, and Jane Hickie were all accomplished writers at her command in Austin, but at first she acted as though she had no faith in her team. Ann saw the looming date on the calendar and decided she had two good talking points and little more. "I think I know how to open and close it," she told Hickie, "which are the two tough parts. But we need a wordsmith."

Ann called Bob Strauss, a Texan who had been chairman of the national party, and he recommended John Sherman, a veteran Washington speechwriter. Sherman was already juggling several other speeches for the convention, but he flew down to Austin.

Suzanne Coleman was gay, wonderfully gifted, and dedicated to Ann, though the wear and tear brought on by that dedication was already considerable. She was also working full-time at the Treasury, and the boss was being very careful not to get dinged in the press over state employees working for her in national politics while they were on the state payroll. At the meeting with Sherman, Suzanne gave him some old speeches and a first draft for the keynote she had written. He gathered them into his briefcase, flew back to his home in the Virginia suburbs, and went to work. Ann was trying to keep up with Treasury business, all the while fretting about the speech. Of reading Sherman's draft, she said, "There were pieces in it I liked, pieces in it I didn't care for, so I did an edit on that and faxed it back to him. The political office fax machine never stopped."

The morning after Ann's selection was announced, New York's polished governor, Mario Cuomo, had called her with much encouragement but also told her, with a note of warning, that she had no idea how profound the change in her life was going to be. Her anxiety about the speech steadily mounted. She called former LBJ speechwriters George Christian and Harry McPherson—the latter had been a close friend of Ann and David during law school and their days in Washington—and she asked her pollster, Harrison Hickman, to draft a profile of a young middle-class family that was having a hard time making ends meet. That was the audience she hoped to connect with.

She called Ted Sorensen, JFK's speechwriter, whom she didn't know at all. She called Barbara Jordan, who sounded in her speeches as if she had invented the English language. Jane Hickie hired a former television newsman, Neal Spelce, whose mission was to teach Ann how to read and deliver text working off a teleprompter. She also hired an East Texas lawyer and convention veteran, Gordon Wynne, to manage the logistics of her entourage. An *entourage*! Ann now had a makeup artist from Washington. Women friends all over Texas were yanking fancy clothes off racks and sending them to her. She was a nervous wreck.

A new message from Bud came inside a card bearing a *Far Side* cartoon by Gary Larson.

Dear Ann: I just want you to know that if you get stuck for a big opening—or closing, for that matter—the Flying Punzars, feeble though we have become,

stand ready to rush from the wings and do our famous double-pyramid flip 179
that broke a table and three chairs at the University Club.

In case your early jokes about rabbis, nuns, Greeks, and watermelons don't go over, all you got to do is pucker up and whistle and the Punzars will be there. I am very proud of you.

Love, Bud

He was always good for a laugh and an encouraging word, but the lift was fleeting. Jane Hickie, Mary Beth Rogers, Suzanne Coleman, and Cathy Bonner were helping her edit Sherman's drafts. The political office didn't have enough room or furniture to accommodate them, so they moved to Bonner's office. They were cutting and pasting as Ann complained that it didn't have the flow she wanted, or the right tone. It was nice to know that Bullock had commented to a reporter, "There's fixing to be a real stem-winder. Mark it down." But Ann was aware that members of her team were starting to get pretty disgusted with her.

One of those days, she sent Bud a *Far Side* card and added a handwritten note.

Bud—
Book a flight for the Punzars. Crafting this speech is arduous and so far the only opening I like is "Here I am from deep in the heart of Texas whose history is principally the saga of what men do outdoors." The censors have doubts.

Any practice for the triple should be done on the capitol steps since the set in Atlanta looks like a Buzby Berkley [i.e., Busby Berkeley] extravaganza with a Mayan pyramid floor.

I'm pretty scared. The best thing in all this is getting two notes from you.
Ann

The line about the great Texas outdoors, on loan from the author Celia Morris, did not make it into many drafts of the speech, and Berkeley's name had faded from public awareness, except for moviegoers in the age group of Ann and Bud. Berkeley was a Depression-era choreographer of film and Broadway musicals, which included *42nd Street* and its classic "Lullaby of Broadway." He was also a rampaging martini drinker who disgraced himself by smashing into another car and killing two people. There but for the grace of God—as the saying goes.

"John Sherman was due to fax us more or less his final draft," Ann reminisced about the keynote writing, "when he called to say that his computer had eaten the speech. He couldn't get it out. The guy from the computer company was over there that moment and they were working on it, but he was afraid that the speech—and all of our work since the moment I had been chosen to deliver it—was gone forever. It was funny. I mean, I just thought, 'Whatever can happen will happen. And it's happening.'"

In the Atlanta airport, Ann was startled by all the shoving and the glaring lights of the media throng: "You feel like they've made a mistake. That they really don't understand that you're not that important. It was my first true moment in the eye of the media storm, and it took some getting used to. At first just the newness of it was a little distracting. But hour by hour, as it wasn't going away, I settled into it. I began to think of the attention as just part of my job: this is what I do and this crush is going to be part of it."

The Democrats had booked her party a number of rooms at the Omni Hotel—one suite became the keynote factory. "I was working the phones in the room adjoining," Bill Cryer told me. "I'd hear an ongoing chatter from all these women, then there'd be a whoop of laughter, and then more chatter. I wasn't on any terms at all with the Capitol press corps in Washington, and they were saying, 'Who is this woman? Why did she get to do this? What is she going to say?' The party people recognized the situation and sent me over some help."

From the outset, the speech had two constant components. In one, Ann would describe a scene in which she was pushing a ball back and forth across "a Baptist pallet" with her grandchild Lily. This would be her metaphor for how the good ideas, works, and vision of government were passed on from genera-tion to generation. The other key element was to be drawn from a letter Ann had received at the Treasury just days before her keynote selection was announced. Earlier in the summer, Donna Alexander had heard her speak to a professional trade group in the Dallas–Fort Worth suburb of Arlington. Alexander lived in Lorena, a town south of Waco that had 1,100 residents. She wrote that she and her husband had college degrees, she worked for a Medicaid-funded program, he worked for a public utilities company, and they had jobs with annual salaries that totaled about $50,000. She was the mother of three children, two of them teen-agers. Alexander wrote of her concerns: "I've written my representatives and have received polite letters back. We vote in hopes of electing people who understand and do something—and I'm not sure to do what. Listen maybe."

Ann had made a notation—"Needs a good response"—in the margin of the letter, and then passed it on to her Treasury staff. Then, suddenly, a thoughtful and moving letter from a constituent morphed into the linchpin of a prime-time television event. Cryer called Alexander to secure her permission for Ann to use portions of the letter in her speech. He assured the stunned and flattered woman that her identity would remain confidential.

Draft after draft appeared, in different typefaces from different computers and printers, with handwriting in the margins. One would begin with the woman's letter from Lorena, then that piece would slide downward in the next, and it would start with the ball patted back and forth between Lily and her grandmother. (Lily Adams, who was then sixteen months old, flew out from her home in Los Angeles with her parents, Cecile Richards and Kirk Adams.) Ann's large, forceful hand could be seen bearing down in the editing. With exasperation, she slashed the line "We've always believed what Ralph Waldo Emerson told us years ago, that this time, like all times, is a very good time if we but know what to do with it." Emerson wrote that? Who could even say that without getting tongue-tied?

Just in time, the team of Ann and Suzanne began to match eloquence with grit and imagery that distinctly came from their Texas roots. One line of attack on Reagan and Bush went: "Let's take the policy they're proudest of—their defense policy. We Democrats are committed to an America that is strong militarily. And quite frankly, when our leaders tell us we need a new weapons system, our inclination is to say, well, they must be right. But when we pay billions for planes that won't fly, billions for weapons that won't fire, and billions for systems that won't work, we have our doubts." Ann realized that last clause defused the ones preceding. She sharpened the paragraph into a rousing battle cry: "Billions for tanks that won't fire, and billions for systems that won't work—that old dog won't *hunt*."

They wound up using three paragraphs from Donna Alexander's letter. They debated back and forth about whether Ann should raise the pages as she read them.

Our worries go from payday to payday, just like millions of others. And we have two fairly decent incomes, but I worry how I'm going to pay for the rising car insurance and food.

I pray my kids don't have a growth spurt from August to December so I don't have to buy new jeans. We buy clothes at the budget stores and we have them fray and fade and stretch in the first wash. We ponder and try to figure out how we're going to pay for college, and braces, and tennis shoes. We don't take vacations and we don't go out to eat.

Please don't think me ungrateful. We have jobs, and a nice place to live, and we're healthy. We're people you see every day in our grocery stores. We obey the laws, we pay our taxes. We fly our flags on holidays. And we plod along trying to make it better for ourselves and our children and our parents. We aren't vocal anymore. I think maybe we're too tired. I believe that people like us are forgotten in America.

At which point Ann would bellow, "Well, of course you believe you're forgotten, *because you have been!*"

In addition to Dukakis and Bentsen, she had to work in praise of Jesse Jackson at some length. Following a three-hour summit between their teams of politicos, Jackson and Dukakis revealed at the last minute that they would henceforth be united—to the disappointment of pundits and commentators, who had been savoring a donnybrook.

No matter how late Ann and her team worked on the speech, during the day she had to bear up under public demands—a profile in the *Washington Post*'s "Style" section, a taped interview with Charlie Rose, a *Village Voice* profile, a stern command from *USA Today*: "Must report to boss—very urgent. Q: major themes she might stress."

She jockeyed for rehearsal and studio time with Ted Kennedy and the young Arkansas governor, Bill Clinton—enough bullshit gas in that studio to air a blimp. She saw the Texas-born columnist Linda Ellerbee at one rehearsal session and asked whether she wanted attribution for the line about Ginger Rogers matching Fred Astaire step for step in their movies while dancing backward in high heels. The writer told Ann it didn't originate with her, she may have overheard it on an airplane—she was welcome to it. (The line was eventually credited to Jill Ruckelshaus, who was prominent in Republican politics, but it likely originated in the Bob Thornton comic strip *Frank and Ernest*.)

Lily Tomlin's partner, Jane Wagner, weighed in with gusto. She offered the line that would make Ann Richards a household name. Ann's pollster, Harrison Hickman, argued that she ought to ditch that, it was an old gag—everyone already knew it. "Well, I don't know it," Ann replied. "And if I don't know it, Mama in Waco doesn't know it either." Ann's son-in-law, Kirk Adams, bolstered her trust in her instincts. "Don't let them talk you into taking that line out. It's too good."

A quiet, handsome man, the union organizer steadied his mother-in-law with a critique handwritten on pages of a yellow legal pad. He told her that the speech demanded three different styles and tones—wit, warmth, and charm. "I've never heard you put real anger in a speech but I think the feelings and issues of the woman from Lorena should be expressed that way; I think if you get that tone out right, it will really get the crowd going. But it is a very tricky tone to get across in the right way, especially on TV."

He offered one cautionary note involving his daughter. He urged Ann not to let her eyes tear up or her voice waver in expressing those sentiments about the little girl. And on the crucial ending: "Because you have no large established group in the crowd that will insure a standing ovation at the end, the windup must gradually build that final applause. The language is great; the trick is to have people already on their feet before the end of the speech, rather than forcing them to get up after the speech is over. It is an emotional ending. I even got misty!"

Recalling Ann's experience in San Francisco in 1984, when she made a speech seconding the vice presidential nomination of Geraldine Ferraro, she and her logistics manager, Gordon Wynne, got in a strenuous dispute with the convention manager. Ann insisted that she was not going to walk onstage until his crew dimmed the lights.

Ann was running for a second term as state treasurer when she met Lily Tomlin in 1986. The former star of Laugh-In, *who by then had a successful film career, became one of Ann's closest friends and a dedicated political supporter.*

"I want to tell you," he argued, "the networks are going to give us fits."

"I can't help it. It's going to be a worse fit for you if I stop talking."

Mario Cuomo came by that morning and gave her a beautiful sculpture of a good luck apple molded from Steuben glass. She made an appearance on *The Today Show*, then looked up Walter Cronkite in the convention hall and told him that she was going to be "talking Texan." She met at midday with Lloyd Bentsen and Fort Worth's Jim Wright, who had succeeded Tip O'Neill as Speaker of the House and was chair of the convention. She went back to the hotel at midafternoon and rested, listening to the soundtrack of *Chariots of Fire*. She dwelled on the Serenity Prayer of Alcoholics Anonymous: "God grant me the serenity to accept the things I cannot change, the courage to change the things I can, and the wisdom to know the difference." She saw Diane Sawyer in the rehearsal room and promised her that she would get to ask the first question after the speech.

Her hair was done up in a masterly silver pompadour, and she wore a simply cut, three-piece silk dress designed by the famous Adele Simpson; the remarkable thing was not the dress itself but the way its shade of blue exploded on a television screen. The climax of her performance came with three paragraphs that slammed the outgoing president, Ronald Reagan, and finished with comic ridicule of George Bush. She pulled off the last line with a slight tilt of her head, a gorgeous grin, all the right pauses, and an outward sweep of her arms.

> The greatest nation of the free world has had a leader for eight straight years that has pretended that he cannot hear our questions over the noise of the helicopters. And we know he doesn't want to answer. But we have a lot of questions. And when we get our questions asked, or there is a leak, or an investigation, the only answer we get is "I don't know" or "I forgot."
>
> But you wouldn't accept that answer from your children. I wouldn't.
>
> Don't tell me you "don't know" or you "forgot." We're not going to have the America that we want until we elect leaders who are going to tell the truth: not most days but every day—leaders who don't forget what they don't want to remember.
>
> And for eight years George Bush hasn't displayed the slightest interest in anything we care about. And now that he's after a job that he can't get appointed to, he's like Columbus discovering America. He's found child care. He's found education. Poor George. He can't help it. He was born with a silver *foot* in his mouth.

ANN BROKE HER PROMISE to Diane Sawyer and asked the first question herself. In the wings, she saw Wayne Slater, a *Dallas Morning News* reporter, and asked him, "How'd I do?" There were many reviews of just how well she had done, none gushier than the *New Yorker*'s imperiously phrased "Talk of the Town." A star is born.

> When Ms. Richards lit into George Bush in her flat Texas twang, we tore ourself loose from the screen and climbed the stairs to the curtain behind the podium, about twenty feet from her, and we could feel the heat. She was out there cooking. She had a hot crowd and a good piece of material, and she was playing it big and letting the crowd go wild. She got to the line "Poor George. He can't help it. He was born with a silver foot in his mouth"—and the roar of the crowd came in like breakers on the shore. You could hear the wave rise as she unreeled her line, and then it crashed on her and drenched her, and as it receded she paddled straight ahead . . .
>
> "I'm a grandmother now. I have one nearly perfect granddaughter named Lily," said Ms. Richards. "And when I hold that grandbaby I feel the continuity of life that unites us." We thought, What a great finish, and then felt a little dry heat in our eyes, then a tear in the corner. At the end, the crowd stood up and threw all the noise at her that it could make.

That night, Ann swept onward in an adrenaline rush to the *Nightline* booth of Ted Koppel, an experience that rattled her because in the earphones as she tried to keep up with what he was asking, unknown persons, editors, and directors of some kind were talking through every question and answer. She managed to say that she thought the audience needed to have a little fun with George Bush. Then it was on to all the night's parties. The next morning, she was besieged with requests for interviews and appearances: Reuters, *Business Week*, a newspaper called *India Abroad*, Larry King, Lesley Stahl, Diane Sawyer again, an invitation to sit between Michael Kinsley and Pat Buchanan on CNN's *Crossfire*. On the last one, Ann scrawled an emphatic "no."

Buoying her along the way was a wonderful fax of congratulations from Bud. Liz Carpenter barked directions from a seat in the second row at the press conference. Ann was holding her blond, ruddy-cheeked granddaughter, truly a beautiful child, who gazed about from that perch of love and safety with fascination. "Tell them how to spell her name," Carpenter hollered.

"Adams, as in Abigail. Lily, as in Tomlin," Ann replied. (Abigail Adams, the wife of President John Adams, was one of the earliest and strongest proponents of women's property rights in the newborn country and a fierce opponent of slavery.) In her newspaper column, Ann's friend Erma Bombeck related her quizzing of Carpenter on the exotic use of English in the speech.

> "What about 'He smells meat cookin' on the stove?'"
>
> "He's hungry for the job," Liz said. "Do I have to explain to you, 'You can't return 'em damp and hungry to the stable?'"
>
> "I think I figured that one out, but what's 'The cow ate the cabbage?'"
>
> "C'mon, you're kidding. It means those are real facts."
>
> "Oh. And 'I can still hear men laughin' about Mama puttin' Clorox in the well when the frog fell in.'"
>
> There was silence. "I haven't the foggiest idea what that means. But I do like 'putting down a Baptist pallet.'"
>
> "Spell it."
>
> "B-A-P-T—"
>
> "No, I mean pallet."
>
> "'P-A-L-L-E-T.' It's a bedroll. The one that's really meaningful was used by LBJ."

What? There was some lusty secret about Lyndon Johnson's sleeping bag? Everyone seemed to be having a blast except Jim Mattox and George Bush, his family, and his advisers. Ann's instant celebrity had repercussions in the nation's media capitals, New York and Washington. Bud's literary agent, Esther Newberg, caught up with him on a movie location. "Dear Bud, I forgot you were with Dennis Hopper. I've been trying to reach you because I think Ann Richards should do a book and I want you to call her for me. By the way, it might even be a book for you to write—*The Wit and Wisdom of a Down-Home Lady*—you know the kind of thing I mean. So call me when you return from the set."

Back home, *Texas Monthly*'s Patricia Kilday Hart visualized Ann in a race that had been a remote possibility one month earlier.

> As Richards enjoyed her big moment, her chief rival for governor, Attorney General Jim Mattox, was sulking in the thunderous ovation rocking the Omni Center. With no official reason to be at the Omni, he had nevertheless cajoled state party officials into giving him a floor pass. Then he sat petulantly in the front row, glaring at delegates waving "Ann Richards" signs, applauding weakly, and sitting glumly through her best lines. He spent the next day telling interviewers that the speech had been okay but no big deal . . .

Though it projected her personality brilliantly, the speech itself cannot answer the most intriguing question about Ann Richards: Can she broaden her appeal enough to become Texas' first woman governor in half a century?

She is certainly trying. Just as Michael Dukakis chose Lloyd Bentsen as his running mate, Ann Richards has embraced the Bentsen wing of the Texas Democratic party, even tapping Bentsen confidant Jack Martin as her campaign treasurer. Already some members of Richards' core constituency are uneasy. One Austin feminist even quibbled with her keynote speech, protesting that Richards had come off as a "clever grandmother," belittling her own importance. In coming months other ideologues will be watching Richards closely for signs of compromise and tarnished principles.

When Kilday Hart's story appeared, Ann was still uncertain what she was going to run for in 1990. Yes, she was a phenomenon. Esther Newberg was a force in both publishing and politics, and Simon and Schuster quickly offered a handsome contract and dispatched an as-told-to veteran, Peter Knobler, to help churn out her memoir *Straight from the Heart*. (Bud and Ann knew that his working on the book was not a good idea.) A Republican spokesman in Texas wondered just what the treasurer had accomplished to be worthy of writing a book for a big New York publisher. In the Democrats' camp, the jeering that Jim Mattox received over his appearance in Atlanta stoked the enmity of a man whose most abiding passion was fury.

And the uproar over Ann's speech produced an unintended victim. After the speech, Bill Cryer was besieged with press demands to know who this woman in Lorena, Texas, was. He doggedly replied that Ann had promised her anonymity. Okay, then—a horde of television trucks and block-walking reporters descended overnight on the little town of Lorena. Reporters and pundits accused Ann and her speechwriters of inventing the woman and her story—it must have been fiction. Ann, Bill, and the rest of the team realized they had no choice. Cryer had to call Alexander and tell her that the promise had to be broken; her identity and private life were about to be thrown into the hungry public maw. Adam Pertman of the *Boston Globe* wrote a profile under the headline "Thrust into the Limelight," which portrayed a naïve woman who had, at best, been used, and perhaps betrayed.

Waco, Texas—Donna Alexander is smiling, but the corners of her lips are quivering, just slightly. Behind the cheerful glint in her eyes is a hint of sadness. Last Monday night, words written by Alexander touched millions of Americans; she

188   knows she should feel flattered, probably even thrilled. Instead, she is overwhelmed, confused, worried.

Will the reporters' phone calls ever end? Will her neighbors resent her?
When will she and her husband resume the quiet lives they always cherished?
For a week now, her mind has been teeming with questions . . .

Alexander was wrapping up a Tupperware party in her home in nearby Lorena when she and a few friends heard their town (pop. 1,100) being mentioned.
Richards, at Alexander's request, did not reveal her name, but the impact was
still intense.

"Whooooooosh. It just came at me like a force through a wind tunnel," Alexander recalls, sweeping her hands toward her face. "Everything just stopped
and we all listened. When they asked me about using the letter, I expected her
to just use a sentence or two. It was a shock, let me tell you. It was so weird."

At first, Alexander was thrilled because Richards is "a personal hero" and
because she was allowed to remain anonymous. The next day, though, reporters swept through tiny Lorena, asking everyone in sight if they knew who the
author of the letter was. . . . So, last Wednesday, Alexander reluctantly agreed
to release her name, and the calls began to pour in, mainly from the local television, radio, and newspaper people. That night, about 10:30, she unplugged her
phone.

Alexander is recounting all this as she sips iced tea and lights an occasional,
anxious cigarette at a Waco restaurant. . . . She insists this will be her last
interview with a reporter, though she wonders aloud whether she is being too
dramatic, too sensitive about all the attention she and her family are receiving.
Her words are accented with a pleasant Texas twang, she uses her hands to
punctuate almost every sentence, and she is so ingenuous as to be disarming.

"I am not a political person, I'm really not," she says. . . . As she warms to the
conversation, Alexander slowly, hesitantly decides that she can talk about the
major cause of her discomfort since she became a minor phenomenon in her
community. The intrusion on her family's privacy is at the root, she says, but
there is a more specific reason.

On a local radio talk show the other day, people were calling in to criticize
her for complaining about making it on $50,000 a year. Alexander is afraid
such talk may be prevalent; she's apprehensive about picking up the newspaper
and seeing a letter to the editor ridiculing her, too.

"I know I'm lucky compared to a lot of people," she says. "The exact amount
of money wasn't the point at all. . . . I am so sorry, because I feel in a way that

I've alienated the people I was talking about. . . . All I want is to get back to what my grandmother used to call the rat's belly—you know, back to regular life."

Donna Alexander's marriage was shaken by the unwanted scrutiny. She was made to feel guilty for sharing something that had come, as Ann Richards put it in the title of her book, straight from her heart. But she didn't give up her admiration of the orator. In a photocopy of the story that found its way into Ann's archives, Alexander added in a handwritten note that Pertman had misquoted her in that last odd sentence. "Actually," Alexander wrote, "I said 'get back to rat killing.'"

For Ann, those were tremendous moments, days, and weeks. Her political career was like a NASA rocket given another boost into outer space. But the launch was supposed to fire up a winning presidential campaign. Dukakis enjoyed a fair bump in the polls after the convention highlighted by Ann's speech, but at the Republican convention weeks later, Peggy Noonan wrote Bush a polished and elegant speech—the speech of his life. Nobody knew exactly what Bush meant by "a thousand points of light," but it sounded good.

During the vice presidential debate, Democrats whooped with approval when Bush's running mate, Dan Quayle, flattered himself with a self-comparison to a president and set himself up for the devastating rejoinder of Senator Lloyd Bentsen of Texas: "Senator, I served with Jack Kennedy. I knew Jack Kennedy. Jack Kennedy was a friend of mine. Senator, you're no Jack Kennedy." By the end of the race, Democrats were wishing Bentsen had been the presidential nominee.

While Bush took pains to present himself as taking the high road, his young media and message adviser, Lee Atwater, destroyed Michael Dukakis. Atwater introduced the fearsome specter of the paroled murderer Willie Horton in television ads and captured a video that made Dukakis look like a fool. Riding a tank and wearing a combat helmet much too large for his head, the governor looked like a turtle with eyebrows. The governor spent the last part of the race looking dazed and numb. Perhaps he thought he was maintaining his dignity, that voters would respond to that.

After introducing Ann Richards at the national convention and then putting her on the road on the campaign's behalf, Dukakis had an occasion to join her on a short flight. In his reserved manner, he asked her how she thought the campaign was going. She leaned toward him and said, *What* campaign?" Then she tore into him over his listless performance until the wheels touched down. She spoke her mind, and she wasn't invited back.

But of course she campaigned onward—for Bentsen, for congressional and legislative candidates, for principles that Democrats believed in, and not least of all, for herself. In those days before e-mail, Bud and Ann had discovered that faxes enabled them to communicate in real time. She sent him this report from the road and the North Texas town of Bowie.

> Dear Bud,
> When we pulled into the parking lot of the Western Sizzler in Bowie, I was surprised to see so many law enforcement cars complete with officers. Sheriff, a deputy, Bowie police, a constable. Cy Young [not the ghost of the great pitcher] was really nervous but I attributed it to his advanced years—maybe his hearing aids were on the fritz. It turned out that we met at the Sizzler not because the event was to be held there but so we could be properly escorted into Bowie by all the aforementioned, whirling lights and all. Traffic is not all that heavy in Bowie at three o'clock in the afternoon, and the four cars and the pickup that we encountered got right out of the way.
> A big crowd—three hundred or so—was waiting outside Bowie Senior High *and* the junior high band (first time they had played together) playing a specially purchased rendition of "The Yellow Rose of Texas." A piece of red carpet was rolled across the sidewalk and a contestant in this year's Miss Texas pageant handed me the bouquet. Then I saw the source of Mr. Young's nervousness. Two kids were holding a six-by-eight-foot sign that read, "Ann Richards— These dogs will hunt."
> About eight or ten good old boys were lined up against a wall holding the chains and leashes on more than a dozen coon hounds. They had obviously been standing there in the hot sun a long time if the tongues hanging out of the dogs' mouths were any evidence. I made a commitment on the spot to come back and go coon hunting as soon as the campaign is over. After the mayor presented me with a Bowie knife mounted on a board, I made a stirring speech to the Montague County Retired Teachers Association. And you think I'm not having fun?
> I'd like to see you.
> Ann

CHAPTER 15

Dispatches

BUD AND ANN HAD BEEN INFATUATED with each other for more than twenty years, ever since the parties in Dallas on Lovers Lane. The mutual attraction was quite apparent when their lives intersected again in Austin during the madcap 1970s, but it is unlikely either one pressed to take things beyond the laughs and conversation into an affair. Their lives were too different, and they were friends with each other's spouses. The first part of Ann's adult life came crashing to a close at the end of 1980, with the intervention by family and friends for her alcoholism, followed by her separation and divorce from David in 1983. Bud's marriage to Doatsy ended in 1985. Doatsy stayed in Austin and became a prominent real estate broker, and she remained Bud's devoted friend, but she reflected on how naïve she had been when Bud plucked her off the Manhattan staff of *Sports Illustrated* and transported her to the mania in Texas.

Bud had written five novels and cowritten another with Dan Jenkins. When *Sports Illustrated* declined to publish his account of a jaunt with Doatsy into the rain-soaked, Deep South part of Texas called the Big Thicket, Willie Morris, the editor of *Harper's*, eagerly ran it and later said "Land of the Permanent Wave" was one of the two finest pieces he published in his fabled reign at that magazine. Bud's reputation as a novelist and journalistic stylist ushered him into the realm of writing screenplays. He worked on about thirty scripts for various studios and producers; most of those projects paid him well enough, though sometimes tardily, and several made it to the screen. The most memorable one, for which he shared credit with the famous novelist and Montana horseman Thomas

Following Ann's divorce from David Richards in 1983, the novelist, journalist, and dramatist Bud Shrake became the second great romance of her life; they are buried in adjoining plots in the Texas State Cemetery. This photograph was taken sometime in the 1980s or early 1990s.

McGuane, was the western *Tom Horn*, starring Steve McQueen in his next-to-last movie. Like all novelists entranced by the money and the mass audience of Hollywood pictures, Bud had his share of baffling and frustrating experiences. He told me that Eddie Murphy once berated Dan Jenkins and him over a cowritten script they mistakenly thought would get produced: "You don't write funny—*I'm* the one that's funny." Bud also wrote stage plays, the most successful of which were produced by an old friend in England. One of his dramas starred Mick Jagger's former wife, the Texas-born model Jerry Hall.

Bud was badly shaken when Joyce Rogers, an English professor who had twice been his wife and was the mother of his two sons, collapsed and died on a campus in New Mexico while in the throes of an asthma attack. Bud was not a recluse, but he was an expert at making himself hard to catch—a call to his house produced not the man himself or a recorded message, but the real voice of someone employed by an old-fashioned answering service. Yet he loved telephones; the conversations with Cartwright and other friends could go on for an hour or two.

Often the telephone marathons involved the numerous women who enjoyed and desired his company. After his friends Pete and Jody Gent divorced and Pete moved back to his native Michigan, Jody worked full-time for Bud, keeping the household running, any necessary repair crews called, and his manuscripts processed and proofed at efficient speed. On a secluded lane called Wildcat Hollow, Bud's house in West Lake Hills had a view of Austin as magnificent as the one Ann had enjoyed on Red Bud Trail. He doted on his dog and cat and decided that he was better off with only them as live-in companions. He had been married and divorced three times; marriage did not seem to be his calling.

When he was in town, he worked in the mornings and then played golf almost daily on Willie Nelson's golf course. Willie had bought a bankrupt country club on the westernmost fringe of Austin and refitted the clubhouse into a first-rate recording studio; until the IRS slapped him with an impossibly large tax bill, the nine-hole course was the plaything of cronies who included Willie, Bud, the western swing musician Ray Benson, the writer and moviemaker Turk Pipkin, and the former Texas Longhorns football coach Darrell Royal.

Bud had taken on as-told-to biographies of Willie and Barry Switzer, the former coach of the Oklahoma Sooners and, later, the Dallas Cowboys. Those were lively tales, but the projects signaled that Bud was in need of money. One day in 1985, he suffered what he called a "breakdown" on the golf course. Nick Kralj, the lobbyist and friend who owned the Quorum Club, took him to a doctor, who told him that he was diabetic and that if he didn't stop drinking and smoking and using hard drugs, he was going to be dead in six months. More than twenty years after this crisis, he told the interviewer Brant Bingamon, "I died in the hospital, but after I was with the spirits for a while, they brought me back to life. No kidding. Fantastic trip."

But he found that it was going to be very hard to just quit. Ann got him to try Alcoholics Anonymous. Though it must have helped, because he kept attending the meetings, he never talked about the twelve steps the way she did. He realized one day that fifteen years had sped past since he had written one line of a novel. He started a thriller in which he placed a foreign correspondent who resembled himself in a storm of 1950s history, the fall of the French Empire in Algiers and the Vietnam battle of Dien Bien Phu. That 1987 novel, *Night Never Falls*, became his favorite.

"The real reason this novel was so important to me," he told the author and archivist Steven L. Davis, "is it is the first long piece of prose I wrote after I had finally quit drinking booze and smoking cigarettes and snorting coke. I mean quit for good. Until this book I couldn't imagine writing fiction without the release of tension that you get from liquor and tobacco. I wondered if I could write at all without a cigarette smoldering in an ashtray near at hand and without knowing there was a cold bottle of vodka in the refrigerator."

And alcohol and tobacco were just parts of the difficulty. Bud had started taking speed when the NFL Cowboys and the AFL Dallas Texans set out bowls of Dexedrine and Dexamyl in the locker room like handfuls of chocolates—the players and reporters were welcome to them. After the wild shoot in Durango, Mexico, of *Kid Blue*, he had put amphetamines aside and become thoroughly addicted to the more expensive cocaine. Smoking marijuana and writing *Night Never Falls* enabled him to overcome the addictions that were killing him. "I had no DTs from quitting booze," he would tell the interviewer Brant Bingamon toward the end of his life, "which I had been drowning in for years, but quitting coke was a different and much more difficult matter. I haven't done coke in more than twenty-five years, but for a long time it was a struggle every day, and even now if I think about it and press my finger to a nostril and snort, I can feel the memory of the coke rush."

When Bud obtained the ministerial credentials that legally authorized him to read the marriage vows of Gary and Phyllis Cartwright, it was not the cynical prank that many acquaintances supposed. A belief in God and spiritual life was part of his complex makeup. That spiritual life would enable him to write the short novel *Billy Boy* (2001), which dwelled on games of golf in the presence of angels. Brant Bingamon asked him to elaborate on his experience of dying and coming back from it. Bud directed him to a passage in his 2007 novel *Custer's Brother's Horse*.

"I saw worlds and more worlds above them and below them, and there are a hundred thousand skies over them. I saw universe beyond universe. There are no boundaries or limits to God. I haven't been able to find words for what I saw. I am trying, but it's as if I am a worm under the crust of the earth trying to explain the stars to the other worms. That's what I heard in theological discussions—worms debating each other about the stars. What terms could I use to make you understand?" . . .

"You experienced this with your own soul?" asked the preacher.

"I did," Varney replied.

"You truly believe this happened to you?" asked the preacher.

"I used to wonder if I have a soul. Now I know for sure. This is not a matter of faith."

"You didn't see any people on the other side? You didn't see any friends or relatives?"

"The quiet people were with me. They didn't say anything. I understood. There was no need somehow. They were very well dressed."

"Were you in heaven, or in hell?" the preacher asked.

"The afterlife is far greater than either of those concepts. Hell or heaven don't exist in the afterlife."

Pastor Horry looked into Varney's eyes. "Were you afraid?"

"I felt excited but calm and curious," Varney said. "I was joyful. I wanted to stay. One of these days you'll see for yourself."

"Inevitably," said the preacher.

Bud and Ann sobered up at different times and under different conditions. After all those years of knowing each other, for the first time they shared the same footing, even if not the same world. Each was fascinated by the professional life of the other. And it didn't hurt that they had in common the intoxication of celebrity.

He was the most devoted, inexhaustible supporter she had—particularly now that both had discovered personal correspondence by fax. In addition to the bracing notes before her keynote and the rave following the speech, he fired off, via fax, a critique of the CBS News coverage of her role in the convention to Dan Rather at his home in New York. He was enough in the know to possess that number. Bud sent a copy to Ann.

Dan,
Please don't feel any need to answer this letter because basically it's just bitching and is not aimed at you personally, but CBS pissed me off so bad the first two nights of the Democratic convention that I had to get it off my chest.

Leaving aside all the ridiculous audio screw-ups, I was shocked Monday night to realize that while Ann Richards was being introduced and her great, touching story was being told on video (with Willie Nelson, yet) CBS was showing us a Texas delegate chewing gum and mouthing a bunch of garble that we couldn't hear.

Then, after the speech, you were trapped on camera with two characters out of *Limo* [the comic novel he had coauthored with Dan Jenkins]. "If you think this was a good speech, you should have heard the great stem-winder in 1948," they said, and such shit as that. I expected them to start any moment talking about the London blitz. "Rat-tat-tat-tat, kapow, boom! Take that, you Nazi swine! Yes, we had heroes in our day, not these country wenches from Waco speaking above their station."

The gum-chewing Texas delegate whom Bud saw on television was Bob Slagle, the chairman of the Texas Democratic Party—Dan Rather the newsman wasn't just grabbing the first yahoo on the way to the hot dog stand. Ann knew Slagle plenty well. Easing him out of his position of power happened to be high on her political agenda. In any case, on reading that fax, Rather could have been excused for being skeptical that Bud was clear of head and all chemical influences.

As the Dukakis-Bentsen campaign wobbled toward defeat, Bud wrote Ann a letter with a mock promotional campaign; he had picked up on Jane Hickie's idea of a retirement home for aged hell-raisers. Ann's reply contained a hint of how emotionally fragile she was.

> Dear Bud,
> The first two weeks after I received your promotional materials for the "Curtains" training school, I sort of moped around about how funny you are and how I could never compete with such wit . . .
> Then I hit the campaign trail through East Texas with Mark White, then South Texas with Oscar Mauzy, Jimmy Mattox, and Garry Mauro, and I thought, well, what the hell, of course I didn't have much sense of humor left and Bud wouldn't either if he did what I do for a living. The photograph of you and the trainees is filed in a fat folder called "Quality Stuff." It is the most interesting collection of things and contains everything but a love letter—since I have never received one of those of even passing interest, much less quality . . .
> Cecile and Kirk and Ellen and I are going to Italy on the 20th of this month and staying two weeks. When I come home, I have to get into the serious mode of deciding what to do about my future. Seems to me that you don't get much out of being governor except an old house with bad plumbing and velvet draperies. What do you think?
> Ann

In many ways, it was a sad letter. She wasn't sure she wanted to run for governor, and she verged on self-pity in the line about never having received a love letter. Bud wanted nothing to do with the clutter and stress of her political office—the Democrats' headquarters are always the grimiest things, while Republicans place a higher premium on order and cleanliness—but he kept up an unbroken stream of advice; many of the faxes were long and politically incorrect. But he was going his own way, and she understood that. Some of her assurances that she didn't want to intrude on time for his writing had the air of someone walking by his door on tiptoes. Few letters said more about their relationship than one concerning a New York fund-raiser and party hosted by Dan and June Jenkins and Liz Smith, the Texas-born gossip columnist of the *New York Daily News*. "Bud—Another day, another banquet in the glamorous life of a politician," she wrote. "Dan and June are hosting a cocktail party in New York. . . . Want to go?"

Bud replied:

Dear Ann:

I very much want to be at the grand party. . . . I will try my best to make it. But in case I don't, I want you to understand why.

For fifteen years Dennis Hopper and I have been trying to make a movie about Pancho Villa. . . . Years pass. Suddenly two months ago, Orion and Nelson Entertainment offer Dennis the job of directing a Pancho Villa movie based on a novel by Clifford Irving with a script by Oliver Stone and Alan Sharp.

Dennis told them no. He said he would direct the Pancho Villa movie only if I wrote it. They had already spent a million or more on the property. Naturally they wanted to know what Dennis and I had that was so good that they should abandon their original investment. I went to Los Angeles. Dennis and I met with the people at Nelson Entertainment, a British outfit. We met with the brass at Orion. We were great. They almost believed us. So they paid me to get with Dennis and provide them a scenario of our new script. . . . The date is important because (1) they want to start shooting *somebody's* Pancho Villa movie while they've got their financing together, and (2) Dennis is eager to go into pre-production, since a movie takes a year of a director's life and he is being inundated with offers after the success of *Colors* [the movie about Los Angeles gangs and cops that Hopper directed].

After we show the moguls our concept of the story, they can say: YES—and give us 35 million dollars to go make the movie our way. In which case, I write the script while Dennis does budgets and locations based on our plot outline. Then I go to Mexico for a crash course in Spanish. I have sworn to work with Dennis every day during the filming—a great adventure—probably in Argentina.

YES, BUT—they like our version but want to use pieces of the story they originally bought. In this case, it's up to Dennis. I go along with him either way.

NO—meaning I am out. Dennis quits the Pancho Villa movie and goes off to direct a different film . . .

The New York party is a wonderful event, and I want to be there with you, Ann.

But this is probably the last chance Dennis and I will ever have to make this movie we've wanted to do together for so long.

This being Hollywood, which is like a bubble floating on the water, everything could change in an instant and I might wind up flying to New York with the Austin delegation.

However, right now the dice have been thrown and we're supposed to play the game out. There is no way I would leave Dennis to play it by himself unless a sniper gets me.

My love and admiration will be with you . . . whether my body arrives there or not. But you knew that already.

Love, Bud

As it happened, neither of those scripts about the Mexican revolutionary found their way to the screen. Ann couldn't do anything to help as Hollywood whipsawed Bud from joy to gloom, but there could be little doubt all that came framed within a love letter, however inexplicit it was and others would remain. Bud's dispatches became a wellspring of support that helped Ann through the most exhilarating yet brutal months of her life.

Tense and pressured as her life became, Bud was her guarantee that she was not going to lose her sense of humor. In February 1989, she wrote him that she had received the first pages of her book from Peter Knobler, and she thought it was "pretty good, no literary epic, mind you." Her letter mentioned my wife, Dorothy Browne; our friend Fletcher Boone; and a story that suggested the spirit of Mad Dog, Inc., was not done for yet.

One afternoon in the Capitol-area joint called the Texas Chili Parlor, two women, longtime friends, were perched on barstools. Both were deep in their cups, and both had a gift for barbed remarks. Paula, having heard as much as she wanted from Cissi, whacked her hard with a longneck beer bottle. Both combatants were about fifty. Cissi, who already had lost one eye in a New York car wreck, went down howling and spitting, a furor erupted in the bar, the women were separated, no cops were called, but there was a fair amount of blood. Paula was consumed with guilt, Cissi tamped down her occasional rage for vengeance, and they became friends again, as close as ever. Cissi had been living with Paula's daughter, trying to help her through a siege of severe depression. Ann shared this choice gossip with Bud.

> Paula called Dorothy Browne and said Paula's dog ate Cissi's glass eye. Paula was looking for donations to replace it—$600 or so. Fletcher said he saw an advertisement in a magazine where you could get "lifelike" eyes for $39.50, so he wasn't going to pony up for much. The real question is how Cissi could help anyone with a depressive disorder . . .
>
> Tomorrow I leave for Laredo for George Washington's Birthday celebration where the goal is to wear as many sequins and rhinestones as your body weight. If I am lucky, I will dance with a drunken caballero and dine on potted meat sandwiches with the crusts cut off.
>
> Come home—then come to see me.
>
> Love, Ann

Ann waltzed through a continuing string of network-television appearances with an air of total aplomb. Texas, of course, was the real road test. In May 1989, word raced around the state about her cocky performance in Port Arthur at a roast for the football coach Bum Phillips, who had retired to breed horses at his ranch after his last coaching job, with the New Orleans Saints. Bum, who had established the Houston Oilers as one of the best teams in the NFL for a few years and ignited the "Luv Ya Blue" craze in the city, had worked his way up the hard way, starting as a high school coach in Port Arthur. Texans loved him for the boots, the cowboy hat, the old-school flattop haircut, and his sense of humor. The men who joined Bum at the long table that night were heavy hitters in that macho world—they included Earl Campbell, the Tyler kid who had trampled and outrun the best of the best for twenty years until his body just broke down, and Jimmy Johnson, a native of Port Arthur whom Jerry Jones had just lured away from the University of Miami to coach the Dallas Cowboys. The lineup included one other politician, Jack Rains, a Republican attorney who had been an insider, as secretary of state, on Bill Clements's team. Rains hoped to get elected governor in 1990. Ann brushed him off that night with a reference to his insistence on delivering the roast's final jokes and salvos. "I always like it when a Republican finishes last," she drawled with a smile.

Bud Shrake may or may not have helped her with the speech, but it contained inside-the-sport material not many women would have known.

"I love Earl Campbell," she teased the great runner. "He's been teaching me how to be a good old boy. We've had sessions where he's teaching me how to do

Skoal. What you do is put a pinch between your lip and gum." She pantomimed the ritual, poking her tongue through her cheek. "Isn't that right, Skoal Brother?"

Laughter erupted. She went on: "I love football. It's a great sport. Horse racing is the sport of kings, baseball is America's pastime, but football is the sport of good old boys—you know, weekends where they're bonding with their buddies, when they might be outdoors killing something, but watching football lets them live vicariously without all that sweat.

"You know, men and women react to football in completely different ways. Women react to a big play, but you watch a man, and you can see the drama— watch his eyes bulge and he licks his lips and leans forward in his La-Z-Boy recliner, and clamps his hands on his Miller Lite, and he tenses up like a cheetah ready to spring. . . . Now I have heard the complexity of football compared to chess, but you know, you don't see a lot of deep thinkers on the football field. Like Bum says, 'If he can count to four, he can play for me.'"

The whoops grew louder. "After long days and weeks of practice, running through all those used tires, they finally get to play somebody. They get to the stadium early, because it takes forever to get dressed. They shave their legs, and they wrap tape around them, and they put on these corsets—the kind of thing women wore when I grew up years ago—and they smear mascara *under* their eyes, and they put on the shoulder pads and helmets and color-coordinated arm bands, and they put on shoes that will keep them from slipping on the AstroTurf, and they wrap more tape over the shoes to make sure their ankles are protected.

"Well, they get all this rigging on, and they start making themselves into a state, and it's called psyching yourself, and it's all about convincing yourself that you're going to be involved with people who commit felonious assault for a living, and you *like* it. And when they're good and ready, they run out on the field, and the boys slap each other on the fanny two or three times, which produces an adrenaline rush. . . . To me, it seems kind of strange that they have a penalty called unsportsmanlike conduct. The uniform alone would make a normal person surly. What would you *expect*?

"Now, all I can say, Bum, is that it's a hell of a way to make a living. And I know you're glad to be out of it, and into something where you can deal with the front end of horses."

Instead of human horses' asses—she didn't have to spell it out. She was making fun of their manhood, nothing less. She had these men laughing too hard to take immediate offense, but she walked a fine line. Parody easily begets insult. She pivoted out of any trouble by borrowing a 1967 line from Senator Eugene McCarthy. "But I understand why you loved it," she told Bum. "Because you know what

they say, politics is a lot like football—you have to be smart enough to play the
game and dumb enough to think it's important."

Two years had raced past since Ann's friend and mentor Bill Hobby bowed out of
the governor's race and said he would not seek reelection as lieutenant governor.
The perception of Ann and her Treasury staff was that any function of state government financed by the taxpayers was fair game for them as a policy issue. That
led Ann and Dorothy one day to the women's death row in the prison at Gatesville.
Steel and concrete and a thick Plexiglas plate did not then separate condemned
prisoners from certain visitors. Dorothy was a nervous wreck in anticipation
of what awaited them. There were three women on death row at the time. One
was Karla Faye Tucker, a former teen groupie of the Allman Brothers who, in the
course of a boyfriend's amphetamine-fueled burglary, had murdered a woman, a
total stranger, with a pickaxe. What got her the death sentence was her statement,
admitted as evidence, that every time she struck with the heavy spiked tool, she
had an orgasm. The other women had been convicted of equally ghastly crimes.

But Ann and Dorothy were stunned to find that the women's surreal, lacy cells
were decorated with dolls they had sewn. They resembled Cabbage Patch dolls,
which were in vogue at the time, but these were Parole Pals—attached to every
one was an imitation sheaf of parole papers. The treasurer began, "My name's
Ann Richards, and I am an alcoholic." The ritual greeting of Alcoholics Anonymous dissolved the tension. The condemned women, who would all eventually
be executed, knew about AA, and they were able to chat with this politician as
if they were all just women grateful for the chance to talk about what had gone
wrong in their lives and what they were doing to try to make it right.

Ann's keynote speech had made her a national sensation, but she had to decide
what she would be running for next. She called her closest staffers together and
asked them what they thought, and then she talked it over with Austin feminists
who had been her core supporters since her time as a county commissioner. She
told them about her love of the legislative process, and that she was inclined to
run for lieutenant governor. But the women spoke up strongly.

No, Ann, *governor*. It is our time, and you are the one who can do it. You *have* to
run for governor.

Sheer luck and talent had put her on a trajectory that might be hell-bent. In
public, she could put on a completely self-assured performance like the one at the
Bum Phillips roast, but some people who saw her every day sensed a deep, brooding fear.

The speechwriting team: from left, Ann, Jane Hickie, Suzanne Coleman, and an unidentified fourth member (on the floor) craft a campaign address in a Fort Worth hotel during Ann's first race for governor, 1990.

"Goddamn Suzanne" had become an inner-office cliché that spoke to Ann's impatience and exasperation with Suzanne Coleman, the speechwriter on whom she relied so much. "I love Suzanne," Mary Beth Rogers told me. "At the Treasury, we'd have these meetings about all the things that Ann had lined up, and she'd say, 'Suzanne, where's my speech?' Suzanne would say, 'It's comin' along, I'm workin' on it.' And she would do some research, make some calls. But then Ann would just be reaming her out. 'God damn it, Suzanne, this is dull! It has to have a beginning, and it has to have a middle, and it has to have an ending! It has to tell a *story*.'"

Suzanne Coleman became one of the best speechwriters of her generation, and surely one of the most abused by her boss. But her tormentor was also her hero and friend. As Ann's anxiety increased about her prospects and options in 1990, Suzanne wrote her a deeply felt personal memo.

I may be out of line here but I am concerned about you. I pondered over our discussion about your political future last Friday . . . and, as is so frequently the case, it later occurred to me that I was not listening to you very well. On reflection, it dawned on me that what I was taking for road-weariness and understandable rebellion might be something more.

I have never known you to step back from a challenge or risk that you thought was do-able. I have never seen anyone else who comes as close to being a natural politician and who just honestly enjoys everything involved in the game. I cannot imagine anything to which you are better suited or at which you are more gifted than the holding of high public office. (God, that was a sentence. I think what I am trying to say here is that your career gives you more than pleasure and income—it almost seems to help you breathe.)

Given all of that, I was stunned to hear the deep equivocation you expressed. . . . So naturally, I have thought really hard—just about as hard as my meager mind will work. I asked if it was organization or money, but you said no. I mentioned that you did not have to drive yourself as hard as you have been; you agreed. I thought through the possibility that you might be getting bullshit from some of the players. But even if these things are screwed up, they are fixable—so that can't be it.

I thought, well, she figured out somehow that she has erred in her judgment of her chances—but I don't see anything on the horizon that would make me think that. If anything, the opposition is looking weaker all the time. . . . Then I thought . . . well, maybe she is truly sick of politics—always a possibility in a sane person. But, nooo—she gets too big a charge out of it. . . . At any rate, having reviewed all of these unlikely possibilities, I've got only one left . . . privacy over politics. I cannot figure anything else that would make you look as miserable as you do. Did I get it? Since I think I *did* get it, I'm going to stop being cute right here.

If I have hit on the right problem, I am a pretty sorry person to advise you. My concerns about how conventional society relates to me have limited me in so many ways. I try not to think about it much. I am a chicken at heart, but I am trying to outgrow it. . . . I have known you and Jane [Hickie] long enough to know that you could be worrying that 1982 could be small potatoes in comparison to what might come your way later. You told me once that I could not fuck up anything so bad, you could not fix it. . . . I honestly do not believe you could have done anything that cannot be mended politically. You have the best excuse in the world, you know: you took the cure and came out a better person . . .

All I know to say is this: after a certain age, your life is your own. You are always eager to tell me that you can only assume responsibility for your own existence, not everyone else's. (Don't you love having your own words thrown back at you?) You can take responsibility for others through love, but I do not think you can make yourself perfect for them or shield them from reality. . . . Is the burden of Texas women a fear of disappointing them? I doubt you can do that. They have known you long enough to know better—and forgive most things short of ax murder. And, they are a burden you have taken on pretty eagerly.

I trust your judgment—it is the main reason I asked to work for you. . . . I very much want my employer to run for higher office . . . because I think she would be good and that she would like it—a lot.

Even more, I want my friend to be happy—not just content (better than fine, as an old friend of mine used to say). And I am more than a little concerned that my friend will not be happy wondering if she could have pulled the big one off.

Before Ann could be certain about her plans, she had to be certain about Henry Cisneros. They didn't know each other well at that point. George Shipley, the Austin consultant called "Dr. Dirt," knew San Antonio's Hispanic politicians well, and he earned the task of arranging the meeting. "I drove her down there," George told me. "It was Henry's annual Christmas party, a big crowd. I managed to get them off together, and they had a good talk, really connected with each other. Henry told her that he wasn't going to run, and he was going to campaign for her. He actually made a couple of TV spots. We sent them up to Bob Squier, but they never ran." He stretched his mouth with some disdain. "That happened because of Lena Guerrero. She was going to make sure that if any Hispanic got to be on the same TV screen with Ann, it was going to be Lena."

Even if her campaign team was free of pettiness and backbiting, a governor's race in Texas was not going to resemble the Democratic outburst of hosannas that had greeted her speech that summer night in Atlanta in 1988. The first all-out attack against Ann was anonymous. Mailed in Fort Worth, one batch of letters went out to small-town newspaper editors and heads of select television and radio stations. Also bearing a Fort Worth postmark, a slightly revised version went out a few days later to Baptist preachers throughout the state. A minister in the town of South Plains forwarded his copy to Ann and her team.

Dear Pastor:

As a preacher of the Gospel and the leader of your congregation, you must be made aware of what I fear could be one of the greatest tragedies which could befall our state and nation lest you take action to prevent it.

Unless the truth comes forward, I fear that a person who has no business in a leadership role might have a chance of becoming governor of Texas.

The polls show Ann Richards leading her Democrat Party rivals. I never believed this could happen. But because she is clever and because secular humanists control the news media, she has fooled many people and could actually win her party's nomination and possibly even the election. This would be a tragedy for Texas because as an atheist, an admitted drug abuser and alcoholic, and as a homosexual, this woman has been an unfit wife and mother, and she is certainly unfit to hold the highest office in our state.

Dorothy Ann has a continuing history of drug and alcohol dependence and has been a practicing "bi-sexual" for many years. She masks herself as one who promotes strong family values, but her life and her beliefs are the opposite.

I must speak to you because I have known Dorothy Ann since she was a teenager in Waco. She and I attended old Waco High together. Ann now proudly talks about her debating in high school and how that taught her to be a public speaker. She learned a lot of other things in high school as well. Ann learned to drink, smoke, and curse in high school and hasn't broken those habits today. In fact she's refined them.

The Ann Richards of today is not the girl Cecil and Iona Willis tried to raise. But Dorothy Ann was always rebellious. She was always wanting to live out roles. At first it didn't seem odd that she should dress up in men's clothing. She was always hanging out with the guys and acting the Tom Boy. But after she got into her drinking state I understood what it could be leading to.

I don't know if it was the alcohol and drugs that led to the permissive lifestyle, but I do know that her contempt for the Lord did little to add to the quality of her life. I surely don't blame the Willises—they tried to raise her right, taking her to church and making sure she went to Sunday school. But Dorothy Ann was always running down the church and God himself. Using the Lord's name in vain was the mildest of her invective. She mocked God, His church and those who believe in eternal salvation. It was then I realized that Ann was an atheist who had nothing but contempt for God and God's people. I confess I ran with Dorothy Ann and her crowd when I was in high school. But I am now a born-again Christian and my sins are forgiven. I laughed at the filthy jokes that Ann told, but I never mocked the Lord the way she did.

I've kept up with Ann through the years. She's only changed for the worst. Over the years she's mocked Christianity. For a number of years she and her husband were members of the Unitarian church, if you want to call that a church. She recently became a member of a Methodist church in Austin, but only to hypocritically promote her political career. Her beliefs, I feel, should be well known and are known by many in Austin. One of her strongest supporters and friends is Madelyn Murray O'Hare. [i.e., Madalyn Murray O'Hair; the atheist was never close to Ann.]

I went to the Lord in prayer and was convinced to write this letter to you after reading in a newspaper what Ann said about her drug dependency. In the September 24, 1989 *Dallas Morning News* Ann said that "I have not had any form of mood-altering chemicals since I left treatment in 1980." First of all, that's a lie. I know from friends that she's a prisoner of the bottle to this day. She's even had to be sent out of the state to dry out at clinics because she's appeared in public drunk or high on drugs.

But even if her statement were true, should children have as an example as the state's highest leader a woman who abandoned her husband for the bed of another woman? A woman who abandoned her children for the pursuit of drug highs and deviant sexual gratification? Do we want a governor who would espouse radically liberal views and appoint fellow homosexuals and liberals to state boards and commissions as such? Should homosexuals set policy on the public education of our children?

The Lord says that none but the righteous should lead, yet we are risking the possibility of allowing a degenerate cocaine and marijuana addict to lead our state and our people. The governor's office is a public pulpit—shouldn't the person there be at least required to be of sound moral and spiritual character? Ann and her people (most of her key staff, both at the Treasury office and on her campaign, are radical feminists and homosexuals) would liberalize drug laws and laws regarding sexual conduct, as well as liberalize abortion laws and weaken the criminal justice system.

I've known this woman for many years. I can't understand how she is able to pull the wool over so many eyes. Most Bible-believing Christians in Austin, Texas are familiar with her behavior or the behavior of the people she associates with, yet no preacher has yet to speak out. Why?

A Concerned Texan

The attacks were vile and unbridled, and every accusation that would be made against her in the next several months was laid out in those letters. In the one to the small-town editors, the writer identified himself or herself as a Republican. The second one, to the Baptist preachers, sounded like it could have been written by a zealot in the Inquisition: "I pray daily she accepts Jesus as her Lord and Savior. But I also pray daily that her sin is exposed and that she is *defeated* spiritually. . . . I pray for your leadership in your congregation to fight the evil she stands for." It was as if Ann commanded a coven, and she was the bitch witch. The preacher in South Plains found his letter in the mail on January 1, 1990. Officially, the race had not yet begun.

Wearing a T-shirt blazoned "Another Man For Ann," Willie Nelson greets and encourages the candidate during her topsy-turvy first race for governor. Austin, 1990.

CHAPTER 16

Backyard Brawl

IN LATE 1987, GLENN SMITH was the Capitol bureau chief of the *Houston Post*. Caught in a continuing decline of circulation and revenue in its competition with the *Houston Chronicle*, the paper had been sold by Bill Hobby and his family to a group in Toronto, and now the paper had been sold again. Glenn had gone to the "Walk of the Stars" affair in Austin honoring Bud Shrake and his fellow writers. Glenn had not yet met the new editor, though they had spoken by telephone. "So we're all standing there, and this guy, the editor, is introduced to me, and he withdraws his hand, won't shake mine. Bud looked at me and said, 'What's up with that?'" Word of the insult got around Austin's political and media community in a hurry; one week later, Bill Hobby sent over his chief of staff, Saralee Tiede, to offer the furious reporter a job in the lieutenant governor's office.

A few months later, Michael Dukakis won the 1988 Democratic nomination and made Lloyd Bentsen his running mate. "Hobby was going to run for the Senate to fill the seat of Bentsen, if the Democrats won," Glenn told me. "So he jobbed me out to split time between Hobby's staff and Bentsen's vice presidential campaign. That's how I met Jack Martin. By Labor Day, it was obvious the Dukakis campaign was not going to have a happy ending. So I was going back to work the '89 session for Hobby, which was going to be his last one. A group of guys got together one weekend, and we went fishing down on the coast. On the way back, I was riding in the front seat with Jack. He said, 'How would you like to manage Ann Richards's campaign?' I said, 'Great,' because I didn't know what I was going to do after the session was over.

"Your ego tells you what your ego tells you," he went on. "I thought I must have really impressed Bentsen, that they wanted me to do this. At the time I was really flattered. But looking back I think they wanted her campaign manager to be a man, apart from whatever savvy I might bring to it. My role was to be the front man. Jack and Jane Hickie would be the ones really making the decisions."

Yet even that reading on his part proved murky. A few days passed, then Martin arranged a breakfast and formally offered him the job. According to Smith: "When Ann was treasurer and I was writing for the *Post*, I had gotten on very well with her. Her staff, especially Paul Williams, helped me break some difficult stories. She knew I'd worked for Hobby and Bentsen, and she thought I was funny and trustworthy, and the move made sense to her. But right after that breakfast she marched in Hobby's office and announced, 'I want Glenn Smith today.' Hobby said, 'Like hell. I've got to have him because he's filling a role for me in the session.' It was kind of a tip-off to a certain impetuousness on Ann's part that I should have been paying attention to."

A barrage of unsettling things continued to come the rookie politico's way. "Jack had told me to negotiate my salary with Ann directly. That just sounded like commonsense advice to me. But then someone brings all of Jane's files over, dumps them on my desk, and I'm told she won't be around anymore. I've never known what that was about. Ann never said a word about it. I didn't really know Jane then. Like I'd gone around her or something? I can't believe that was over my salary."

In a wide-ranging profile, "Ann Richards: How Perfection Led to Failure," in the October 1990 *Texas Monthly*, Mimi Swartz quoted the candidate: "Everybody wanted to let Ann be Ann. And they all had different Anns." Swartz wrote that the blowup with Hickie was not a minor tiff. Hiring Glenn at all had been the first problem; the second was that he demanded to deal directly with Ann on all matters. "When Smith took control," Swartz continued, "Hickie was clearly wounded. She and Richards stopped speaking for a time, and as the professionals gained more and more control, a schism formed between Richards's female loyalists and the male political consultants. . . . Like so many of the women there, Hickie could be rhapsodic on the subject of Richards, but she seemed barely aware of the male staffers. Perhaps the men were defensive, and perhaps Hickie was harried; either way, neither side worked well together, each claiming every small victory and laying blame for every small defeat. To the boys, the girls were amateurs obsessed with flow charts and schedules who wanted to manage the campaign like the treasury. To the girls, the boys were overzealous guerrilla fighters, dragging them into a needlessly dirty campaign."

But who was doing the dragging? "The thing between Ann and Mattox was extraordinarily pressurized," said Glenn, "even during those months in '89 while I was still working for Hobby. Mattox called me out at Scholz's one night. He said, 'I'm going to ruin you,' and was jabbing his finger at my chest. It was such a visible thing that a circle of people formed, like it was a fight. I did not antagonize him. But somebody took a photograph of that, and it wound up in the *Washington Post.* He accused me of setting him up. Later he did it again, right outside Hobby's office in the Capitol. 'I'm going to ruin you, you'll never work again in Texas.' We had some lapel pins made up: 'Mattox Threatened Me Too.' I was thinking, 'What the hell have I gotten into?'

"Another notable thing came in May of '89, when Ann took me out to lunch right before the end of the session. As intense as those months had been, I never took any of that drug stuff from Mattox seriously. I hadn't been in Austin during the party years. Just didn't know. She looked at me at this lunch and said, 'Okay, here's the deal. How are you going to get me around this?'

"I said, '*What?*' She was not explicit. She just said, 'There's some stuff out there, Mattox is going to know about it, and he's going to attack me for it. And I want to know how you're going to get me out of it.'

"I was noncommittal—said I'm sure we can get through it. But I was very surprised by how concerned she was. She was really, really worried, in a personal way. It's always been my impression that two things were going on with Ann about that. One, she was being told by Bob Squier [her famous media adviser from Washington] and Jack Martin that any contact with cocaine, however incidental, would beat her, period. But I've always thought she was more worried about her parents. She would talk to me more about that when I was alone with her than about any of the political ramifications. It really twisted her up—'I don't want my parents to be hearing about this.' She was quite emotional, and it affected her judgment. This was a problem I really didn't expect to have to deal with in my first time as a campaign manager. I was like, 'Holy shit.'

"But all that did lead to an event that still makes me smile. In December of '89, Anne Marie Kilday, a reporter for the *Dallas Morning News,* called me and said she was going to ask the drug question in an interview. We set up the call to come at three o'clock one afternoon when Ann was on a campaign stop in Lubbock. I flew out there from Austin, and Squier flew down from Washington."

At the time, the *Today* host and commentator Jane Pauley felt she was being squeezed out by NBC, and she was threatening to walk away from a multimillion-dollar contract. Squier, a friend of the network star, was incensed at how he believed NBC executives were treating her. "So I sat there for an hour and a half,"

Glenn said, "thinking we're going to construct the answer to the drug question. They talked about nothing but Jane Pauley. I'd interrupt them every fifteen minutes or so. 'Okay, we gotta deal with this. She's gonna call us at three.' And they'd start to deal with it, then they'd back up and it was poor Jane Pauley this, poor Jane Pauley that. We never did deal with it. Anne Marie called at the appointed time, and she never asked the question. She asked about drinking, but not the drugs. She backed off, for whatever reason, which was a damn good thing for us. But you know, Ann and Squier were part of that celebrity world, and that was what they wanted to talk about."

Since Glenn was committed to working for Hobby until the end of the legislative session, Ann hired Mark McKinnon, a young favorite of Jack Martin, as director of communications. Mark's resumé sparkled as much as his smile. After chucking college to go to Nashville, he had caught on, briefly, with Kris Kristofferson's songwriting team. After that, he returned to the University of Texas and won a student election to edit the *Daily Texan*. He dreamed of writing for a living, but in 1984 he volunteered for Lloyd Doggett, a state senator who was waging a doomed campaign against Phil Gramm for the U.S. Senate. Future campaign heavyweights Paul Begala and James Carville were working for the liberal Doggett. They mostly succeeded in taking out the favored Bob Krueger in his second run for the Senate, as well as the Democratic boll weevil Kent Hance, before serving Gramm with easy pickings in the general election. But in the process, Begala noticed McKinnon's talent and hired him for Doggett's press office. After that, Mark worked as a press aide for Governor Mark White when he was losing his rematch with Bill Clements. The next year, Mark caught on with Buddy Roemer, who was elected the "New Democrat" Louisiana governor. (That label was beginning to be tossed around, boosted by politicos like Begala and Carville.) After the Louisiana race, Mark went to New York to work in public relations for a while, but he had been looking around for a way to get back to Austin. He formed a partnership with Dean Rindy, a longtime liberal media consultant in Austin, and eagerly took on the task of managing Ann's media relations. Mark was charming, cool, and easy to like.

Particularly after the abrupt departure of Jane Hickie, another force on the campaign team was Lena Guerrero. She had grown up in the Rio Grande Valley town of Mission and emerged as an up-and-coming star in politics when she was in her early twenties. While attending the University of Texas, she was elected president of the Texas Young Democrats, and in 1984, at age twenty-six, she won an Austin seat in the Texas House of Representatives. Only the second Hispanic woman elected to the legislature, she distinguished herself with work in behalf of migrant farmworkers and the prevention of teen pregnancy. After the 1989 session, *Texas Monthly* put her on its prestigious list of the ten best legislators. She had unquestioned talent, and she was a favorite understudy of Ann, but I recoiled the first time I saw her in action. In the little office a few blocks from the Capitol, she was screaming at someone on the telephone. I wondered who in the world on the other end of that line would be putting up with that.

I happened to witness the outburst because I was one of the unpaid volunteers. Others who were still on the Treasury staff took pains to contribute only in their off-hours and on weekends. They included Suzanne Coleman, Bill Cryer, Paul Williams, Joy Anderson, and Dorothy Browne. Two of the essential players in the campaign were Cecile Richards and her husband, Kirk Adams, who lived in California but came over to try to help Ann blunt the attorney general's advantage with labor unions. At twenty-one, Ann's younger daughter, Ellen, was answering campaign correspondence, such as a letter that came from a gentleman in Beaumont. He wrote that Ann appeared to be only the women's candidate, and while he wished her well, he wanted to cancel his draft authorization of $22.03 a month as a contributor. Another campaign aide might have concluded that there was little to say in response, but after six impassioned paragraphs, Ellen concluded, "I am glad you shared your thoughts with me and I hope you will accept my response in the good spirit with which it was sent. I hope you will soon rejoin our efforts to elect Ann Richards the Governor of Texas."

Amazed at how this looming demolition derby had come about, David Richards told Jim Mattox he couldn't support him in a race against his former wife of twenty-nine years, and then beat a quiet retreat to his private practice and his new marriage to Sandy Hauser. David had managed the litigation that helped Mattox build his impressive record as attorney general, but Mattox never had much use for him after that.

The attorney general wasn't the only Democrat that Ann had to overcome. Just before the filing date in December 1989, Mark White muddied the water by jumping into the race. At the start of the campaign, Ann had only $30,000 in her political account, yet the first major poll showed her with 35 percent, White with 23 percent, and Mattox with a forlorn 8 percent. Mattox was outraged, furious.

Because she was so short on cash, Ann was the last of the seven major gubernatorial candidates to start airing television commercials. And when her ads appeared, their fuzzy, swinging-on-the-front-porch style made her look like a vacuous grandmother, not a governor. By the end of February, White had edged slightly ahead, with him and Ann each favored by about a third of respondents polled, and Mattox was rebounding with 17 percent. While the polls and the responses to the campaign ads pointed to a hard-fought and expensive primary race, in April Ann got a note from Bud that spoke to the improvement in their personal lives. "I have never received anything even close to a mash note from such a classy person before. . . . Thank you."

I had joined Ann's campaign team because I admired her, she liked me, and she knew I had been writing speeches on environmental issues for Garry Mauro, particularly those affecting the Texas coast and the Gulf of Mexico. And then was when she thought she had need of me. The die was cast, and on a sweltering day in June 1990, she officially kicked off her race for governor with a speech on the grounds of the Capitol. She had been weighing whether to go with Bud to watch Dennis Hopper shoot a movie that he was directing. "Bud," she wrote, "I spend next week on a coastal hegira—Corpus Christi to Port Arthur. After that I want to take you up on the offer to go see Dennis make his movie." Then she headed for the Rio Grande Valley and a controversial "boat trip" up the coast of Texas.

Glenn Smith later told me, "I think my contribution to Ann was basically that I was so damn naïve. I made judgments and did things that I wouldn't have done if I had been more seasoned in politics. But the fact that I did them helped her. Like the boat trip." McKinnon also deserved credit for the idea of the coastal cruise. The barnstorming would begin with a weeklong "fact-finding tour" of the state's 367-mile Gulf Coast. Ann reeled off the claims: it would take her past four million people, fifty million barrels of oil, and more than a hundred fifty school districts; and as some observers quickly noted, it would penetrate seven media markets. The premise wasn't entirely feasible. The coast between the Valley and Corpus Christi is a 165-mile stretch of sand dunes, long shallow lagoons, and flat, unhandsome, almost unpopulated chaparral. A boat journey up that part of the Intracoastal Waterway would have left her afloat far from any news cycle. So Ann spent a day touching base with the leaders of Brownsville and other Valley towns and the agricultural community. In a coincidental prescheduled event, she joined Mattox, Bill Hobby, and Jim Hightower in a show of support for a local bond referendum to bring safe drinking water and sewage disposal to some *colonias*— unincorporated subdivisions that had sprouted along the Rio Grande. Then she flew to Corpus Christi.

Dorothy had taken a week's vacation from the Treasury to be the candidate's chief aide on the trip. Also along for the duration was Monte Williams, a tall,

large, garrulous press aide. I signed on for the part of the float between Corpus
Christi and Galveston. Our task was to do all we could to ensure the candidate did
not get trapped in unpleasant corners in which her only means of escape would
be to jump overboard.

And what a boat we were on! A woman at the Treasury named Janet Allen-
Shapiro had, in an earlier period of her life, obtained a license to pilot an ocean-
going vessel, and she sure delivered in chartering this one. Dorothy and I were
amazed to find ourselves watching gulls, pelicans, and the sunset while sipping
drinks on a fifty-foot yacht. There was a great deal of jollity among the aides.
Most would be driving from port to port and making arrangements for her arrivals and schedules at night. Smith and McKinnon were close by their mobile
phones in Austin. But watching that splendid sunset, Monte, Dorothy, and I
had the rare luck to be making a private hotel of this yacht with decks made of
teak.

We pulled out of Corpus with the city's mayor, other officials, and a throng of
television reporters and camera crews on board. Ann wore jeans, sneakers, one
of her new campaign T-shirts, and a bandana knotted at her throat. For the benefit of the camera crews, she took the pilot's wheel for a few minutes. "Piece of
cake," she announced. As we crossed the bay toward the fishing town of Rock-
port, bright morning sunlight glistened off the water, and as if they had been
called up by central casting, several dolphins joined the show, cavorting in the
wake cut by the prow.

In the large air-conditioned cabin, Ann listened to briefings by an executive
at the Formosa Plastics plant and, as we passed the Aransas National Wildlife
Refuge, by a birder who told us the plumage of roseate spoonbills gets its pink
from a healthy diet of shrimp. That night in remote Port O'Connor, we wound
up in a fish and beer joint. It didn't bother Ann that the rest of us were drinking. She and Monte and the reporters, who included Wayne Slater, R. G. Ratcliffe,
Ken Herman, and Ross Ramsey, traded one joke after another, and they were hilarious. At one point Ann stuck out her tongue and, scratching it lightly with her
fingernail, informed us how salt affects the taste buds. The little darlings are trim
and erect, she claimed, but salt flattens out the tops like heads of mushrooms.
Dorothy squirmed, not too eager to see that in print, but we went to bed in our
comfortable berth, laughing at how well it was going.

The next day was a short one on the water. We put up in Port Lavaca, a small
town near the midpoint of an industrial complex that extends 400 miles along

the coast. After dinner that second night, a local host and campaign volunteer took us on a drive past plants that included Dow Chemical, Union Carbide, Du-Pont, Alcoa, BP Chemical, and Texas Liquid Fertilizer. This was country rich in organized labor votes for Democratic politicians, or at least it long had been. At night the plants put up a dazzling light show—I had never seen anything like it.

The third day was a long haul up the Intracoastal Waterway, which took on aspects of a large irrigation ditch. But then we came back into a lagoon, and a local official showed us how the erosion of one strip of dunes at a place called Sargent Beach was so severe that a direct hit by one storm could breach the waterway—which would be a commercial disaster, for the barges that used it could not navigate in heavy open seas. Fascinating as this exposure to a little-known side of Texas was to me, I had noticed something about the reporters onboard. Ann ran the briefings well, but as the talk about policy issues went on, the reporters' eyes glazed over. Their beat was politics for the state's major newspapers. Some of them had committed to accompany Ann all the way to Port Arthur, and the length of the voyage and relative pokiness of the yacht had begun to register. They had editors expecting them to file, and *there was no story*.

During one of the breaks midway through that afternoon, the reporters who had previously been such a close bunch of brethren started looking for places along the rails where they could speak with privacy. They had shoe telephones in those days, and they leaned far out with the clunky-looking things as if a few more inches would give them better reception and an edge over their competitors. Monte Williams walked the deck with a forced smile, trying to overhear snatches of what was going on. "There's something wrong with the boat," he came back muttering, no longer such a happy fellow.

The waterway ranged inland once more. In traffic, our captain would aim the yacht slightly right, and a barge bearing skull-and-crossbones signs would skate left, making just enough room for the two to pass. The skulls and crossbones indicated that the cargo had come from one of the many petrochemical plants along the way. A young lobbyist from the Chemical Council was onboard when we passed several of those barges. It was late in the day, everyone was loose, and the reporters merrily jumped all over him. It started with questions about how lethal those chemicals were, and in response to his claims that they were scientifically tested and perfectly safe, someone asked whether he would stir a couple of spoonfuls of them into a glass of water and gulp it down. "Yeah, I'd drink it!" he exclaimed. The ribbing got much worse after that.

Ann listens to coastal environmental activists on the controversial boat trip that launched her first campaign for governor. Galveston Bay, 1990.

The owner of the yacht, a burly man, was polite but kept his distance. He seemed to regard Ann with suspicion, but he had warmed to the task of manning the wheel and mugging for the television cameras. It turned out that the owner and his son, who piloted the yacht some of the time, did not have their licenses in order and could not legally operate the boat. That night in our cabin, as the boat rocked lightly in a slip near Freeport, Dorothy and I witnessed a campaign descend into jabbering panic. Total meltdown. Clad in his boxer shorts, Monte was jumping up and down on our mattress, yelling through his shoe telephone at Glenn Smith. The Mattox people were all over this! The Coast Guard was rumored to be searching for us! What if they boarded the yacht and arrested the captain?

Late that night, another young man with the campaign came around and announced that we were all jumping ship. The newborn Richards campaign was going to chug up the Houston Ship Channel the next day on a shrimp boat with no air-conditioning. While Dorothy and I slept on this alarming prospect, cooler heads prevailed. The owner and his son would leave the boat, and the tour would continue with the boat's properly licensed first mate at the helm. The sun was not up yet when Ann summoned me for my counsel. I said I thought the shrimp boat was a terrible idea, and then offered, "I just feel bad about the old man."

"What?" Ann said.

"Well, he's been enjoying this, and it is his boat."

The set of her mouth let me know that in politics I was a rank amateur. Here I was, sentimentalizing over a man who was being paid well for providing that charter, as if he were a child with hurt feelings. "Jan," she scolded me. "I didn't take him to *raise*."

The boat reached Galveston, and I caught a ride to the Hobby Airport in Houston. The driver was a young man named Chris Hughes. He had a sense of humor about it all, and wore a stylish, low-crowned western hat. His job, which he had lobbied hard to get, was to be with her wherever she went and never let go of her purse. On an impulse that was prescient at the time, he once shaved his head; she took one look at him and declared, "You're not going anywhere with *me*," and parked him at a desk until his hair grew out. Chris went on to have a fine career as a lawyer, but veterans of the '90 race forever typecast him as "the guy carrying Ann's purse."

I was on the last flight to Austin, as were the Democrats' comptroller candidate, John Sharp, and attorney general candidate, Dan Morales. The politicians and their entourages didn't mix with each other, it was a crowded flight, and I wound up seated right in front of Morales and a Hispanic aide. Morales was a small dapper man who wore glasses and kept his black hair very short. He and the aide chattered continually about their campaign. At one point, the aide chortled and said, "Now we'll see who's got the *cojones*," the Spanish word for balls, testicles. Somehow I knew Ann and these folks were not going to be one big happy family. I leaned my chair back, bumping someone's knees, and did my best to go to sleep.

The next day, the yacht made its way up the Houston Ship Channel without incident, except that it had to stop and refuel. Ann had some sharp words about that; it made her late to an appointment with some of Houston's most important leaders and contributors. But they arrived at the end of the week with Port Arthur television reporters hastening to wish her happy birthday, her fifty-sixth, at a campaign rally. She grinned and expounded on what a joy it was, just being alive and getting to know all these Texans. A television-news veteran in Houston editorialized one night that the boat tour was indeed a matter of little substance, but he ended by chiding Jim Mattox for his bluster. "The attorney general's problem is that he has a heck of a fight on his hands, one that he ought to be winning hands-down."

When Ann was back at the Treasury, she wrote Bud not about state business or politics, but about their time together on Dennis Hopper's movie set.

Dear Bud,

Okay, I'm a groupie. I had such a super time on Saturday. Everything that was supposed to happen in movies *did* happen. Someone out of sight shouted, "Rolling," and then Dennis would bark, "Action." If he wanted something different, he talked to the actors in a coaxing way. Seeing scenes shot in sequence gave me a real sense of the film itself. I ate lunch with a charming movie star and his winsome bride—and best of all, I got to listen to you tell me things that I don't know.

Love, Ann

Accompanied by her travel aide Chris Hughes, upper right, Ann observes a quiet moment at the announcement of her candidacy for governor. Austin, 1990.

CHAPTER 17

Answer the Question

A FEW WEEKS AFTER THE BOAT TRIP, Ann and her team had to go to a crucial AFL-CIO convention, where they found that the Mattox crew had people all over the crowded hall with walkie-talkies. "It was a disaster in the making," Glenn said. "We absolutely had to block a Mattox endorsement. We saw all those walkie-talkies, and his people were picking off delegate votes with them. I got Chris Hughes and Fred Ellis to go to a store and buy some models that covered all the bands. I put them up in a hotel room, and we monitored what the Mattox people were saying. They'd be saying, 'Go get Joe Blow, he's weak and we can sign him now.' And we'd get there before they did."

Some people thought Lena Guerrero had carried the day, though she was so aggressive that reporters wondered whether a Mattox staffer or the attorney general himself might punch her out. Irma Rangel, her House colleague, said emphatically, "Lena Guerrero won the primary for Ann Richards. *Pues, así es.*" Well, so it is, the phrase means. Maybe it was. But Glenn Smith said cryptically, "Lena kind of froze up," and maintained that Cecile Richards had been the heroic one working the floor. "I'd covered labor conventions before," said Glenn, "but these old pros were saying, 'At what point do we call for a vote?' It was pretty daunting. I finally said, 'What the hell, call it,' and we did, and we did block Mattox—labor chose not to endorse either candidate. Whatever momentum Mattox had then was gone."

Ann agreed with Glenn's assessment of her most important fighter on the convention floor. She wrote to Bud, sympathizing about an accident that had hobbled him, but it also allowed her to needle him a bit about the distance in their relationship.

Bud,

I suppose breaking a toe is better than breaking your nose. At least it is a *real* excuse for staying at home.

I just fought the battle of the state AFL-CIO convention where Mattox pressed hard, but we outdid him *and* the no-neck, gold-nugget-watch-wearing Teamsters. Cecile was the mainstay and did a fabulous job. What a job it is to fight a battle with one of your children. . . . I miss talking to you.

Ann

While that was an important triumph for Ann, it did not mean she was closer to winning the election. In June 1989, the U.S. Supreme Court had ruled in a trio of 5–4 decisions that states could carry out executions of murderers who were sixteen to seventeen years old when they committed their crimes, as well as of killers who were mentally retarded. McKinnon advised her on the politics of the rulings in a memo that was a model of bland caution. "The death penalty is, of course, an extremely emotional and volatile issue. I recommend that your response to any questions regarding this issue should be that as governor you would uphold the death of juveniles and mentally retarded killers. I believe you can safely, however, support . . . the Supreme Court in allowing consideration of a defendant's mental capacity by a jury." How did she really feel about the death penalty? She didn't like it, but if she wanted to be governor of Texas she *had* to be for it.

Ann's opponents perceived no nuance in the issue. White aired a startling ad in which he walked past a lineup of photographs of men who had been executed under his watch. "As governor," he promised sternly, "I made sure they got the ultimate penalty—death." Not to be outdone, Mattox came out saying, "I've carried out the death penalty thirty-two times." No, he had watched that many executions, rather creepily, was what he had done. But someone on death row published a newspaper for his fellow prisoners, and presented with the alternatives, the editorial of the condemned endorsed Ann.

Mattox seized on that with relish. He had been fuming about Ann's campaign ever since the keynote speech, and then the first major poll had him twenty-seven points behind her. Impossible! He had seen those anonymous letters to the small-town editors and Baptist preachers, and he thundered at one rally, "I just don't know if I can control my Baptist preacher friends any longer from attacking Ann about her drinking. I have many clients and many friends who have been on the wagon and then have fallen off. The statistics would show that a relapse occurs in a high percentage of cases." That torched any possibility of comity between the two camps—even though the candidates basically agreed on the major issues confronting Texas government. Mattox challenged reporters to confirm rumors that Ann had frolicked in a hot tub with Lily Tomlin.

Mattox could afford the help of heavy hitters. James Carville was advising him, and while the Louisiana native could get as down and dirty as anyone in American politics, he pressed Mattox to offer a panacea. He should promise that instituting a lottery would solve the ever-present problem of funding public education and other needs of state government, and people buying beer and Marlboros at the convenience store would gladly shell out a few dollars to try to beat the odds of a game that was all chance. Mattox was gaining ground with that.

"That early poll reflected the positive impression she made with the keynote and gave her a much bigger lead than she had," Glenn Smith told me. "What we saw from internal polling was that it was always tight, but when anybody got a lead it was usually Ann. A few times she got up to 35 or 36 percent, with everybody else in the high twenties. Mostly they were bunched up tight. I remember one poll that had Mattox ahead by a point or two. The press called us for a response, and Monte went out and photocopied a front page of a *National Enquirer* with a headline that read, 'Sixty Percent of Americans Believe Elvis Lives.' We faxed that to the press. None of us said anything else, so they had to go with that.

"But Mattox was a very savvy guy. I think he sensed Ann's fragility. I can't overstate the extent that Ann got into her own head. She had a lot of friends who were movers and shakers, big Democratic contributors. They had encouraged her. Celebrated her, almost. But they didn't think she was going to win, and now they weren't there. A lot of phone calls from her weren't returned, and these were to people she thought were going to help her. It hurt her feelings personally. 'These people told me they were going to be with me. What's going on?'

"Because she was in that frame of mind, she was full of self-doubt, and full of doubt about us. She was always bringing in new people to critique what we were doing. I had no idea how to navigate the ex-officio people she brought into the campaign. My reaction was to close the door and try to get stuff done. That campaign could have spun way out of control. We could have easily become a sort of giant therapy group.

"When I had known her as a reporter, she was a lot of fun to be around. During the primary, she wasn't that way anymore. She and I went round and round about her being so tough on the campaign staff. One day she came in and beat up on the people answering letters. They were working in just as intense a circumstance as she was. She was demoralizing people. So I talked to her in my office one day before a staff meeting, and I said, 'Look, Ann, you give them the pep talk, then I'll hammer them about the things that are falling through the cracks.' So we did that, she pumped them up and praised them, and I started in on the other, then Ann couldn't take it anymore. She jumped in and started calling people names.

"I always thought it was because Ann had the soul of a performer. She would project fears about herself onto people around her. I don't know how Suzanne Coleman took it. Ann could do some petty things, but she was never mean to me like she was to Suzanne. Ann knew what her race meant to Texas. She knew of its importance symbolically. She got it. It might have been easier if she hadn't got it so much. She was so afraid of failing, especially in the primary. All those young women around the state, she knew she was their hero. She saw it everywhere she went. She was terribly afraid of disappointing them; she didn't know how she was going to face them again if she did. It was very human of her. You have to wonder if someone with that much soul belongs in politics. Those are the people you want. But God, it's a soul-crushing machine."

Sometimes they all got caught up in the pressure, weariness, and conflict. Dan Richards told me, "I saw her light into plenty of people, but I was a protected class. Just once, during the governor's race, she did that to me. I'm not very combative—I think I got it from my father. I just went silent, and we didn't talk about it. But I knew what my plan was. 'When we get back to Austin, I'm done.' I think she must have known that, because before we got back to the airport she said, 'I'm sorry. I apologize. That was uncalled for. It'll never happen again.'"

It was ironic that Ann, the state champion debater who won a scholarship to Baylor for that feat, almost destroyed her campaign with her performances in debates. In the first one, she fielded a question about abortion—there was no issue she cared or knew more about. She said, "No legislator, no judge, and no bureaucrat has any business in determining whether a white woman has an abortion or not." After the audience gasps that night and her opponents' whoops over the gaffe, she remarked to Dan that she was having trouble talking with her new dental implants; her handlers tried to spin it that she didn't really say that—the imperfect audio made it sound that way. But she admitted that it happened, and apologized. It was a stock reply in which she said "whether or why a woman," not "whether a white woman." It was a slip of the tongue, but now she found herself fighting off charges that she was an elitist and a racist.

As Dan recalled: "It was almost a relief, dealing with the white woman remark, because of all the emphasis on drugs. Both the Mattox and White people
had been peppering her with that for a while. There were ten or fifteen people in
meetings we had with people about what to do. Someone would say, 'Here's what
she should say,' and someone else would make a different suggestion, then Mom
told them what she wanted to say, and everybody said, 'That's great, let's do it.'
I was thinking, 'Here are all these people who are supposed to know how to do
this, and the candidate is the one who's coming up with all the answers.' I think
that's why she was so nervous."

At the second debate, in the studio of a Dallas public-television station, she
may have been misguided by memory of her first race for treasurer, when an assault against her over her alcoholism and treatment had boomeranged against
her opponent. She couched her answer in language that a member of Alcoholics
Anonymous would recognize at once. But relatively few people belong to AA,

*Jim Mattox, holding pencil at left, challenges former governor Mark White and Ann Richards
during the first debate of the Democratic primary campaign for governor, 1990.*

and 1990 was not the same race as 1982, nor was it the same question. When a panelist asked the candidates whether they had ever used illegal drugs, Mattox and White said proudly that they had not.

Ann began her carefully rehearsed reply. "I want to address my answer to all of you out there who have had problems in your life." She said she wanted to assure them they could seek help for their problems without fearing the mistakes would be brought up to them again and again. Paul Burka, the panelist from *Texas Monthly*, later wrote, "I have never been in a place where silence was such a presence, except for her voice. A small audience was in the studio, and not even a cough broke the stillness. I thought we were watching Ann self-destruct on statewide television and that she had lost the race by dodging the question."

On the way out, she had to run a gantlet of screaming reporters. "Answer the question! Answer the question!" they yowled. Some of the most aggressive ones were the *Houston Chronicle* veteran Jane Ely, Robert Shogan of the *Los Angeles Times*, and Cinny Kennard, a reporter with WFAA-TV in Dallas who always seemed to show up wearing a bright red dress. (Kennard would become known in the Richards campaign as the "Red Dress"; Ely later apologized to Ann for her behavior.) "After that debate," said Glenn, "they got around her in an absolute lynch-mob mentality. 'You *can't* not answer the question!' It was just awful—emotionally wrenching. Ann thought the press was going to be her champion, that the reporters were going to lie down for her. She could not figure out why they were doing this to her. That was just a terrible night. We didn't know if Ann's race could survive it. We had no overnight polls or anything, but she hadn't done well in the debate, and that frenzy was just so bad."

On a hotel elevator with the young man carrying her purse, she said in a very shaken voice, "Chris, I am a good person," as if everything about her character had been cast in doubt. Meanwhile Glenn, Mark, Bob Squier, the pollster Harrison Hickman, and George Shipley were in a state of gloom. "It wasn't so much the way it was reported the next day," said Glenn, "it was that intense mean-spiritedness by the press. It seemed like just a total meltdown." Dan Richards told me, "Yes, yes, she had fears. One night we were in a hotel room, I'm not sure where it was. She said, 'This is over. I'm going to be out of this deal in a week.' It was a low, low point."

"There were a lot of people around Ann Richards who didn't like Bob Squier," Glenn said. "But he helped—it's a quality-of-mind thing. I don't know about catastrophes, you know what I mean? I was pretty sad after that deal with the press, but I didn't think the world was coming to an end. Ann later accused me of being too laid-back. But I also wasn't panicking, and Squier wasn't either. A lot of what he brought to Ann was a real fighting spirit. All he was going to do was throw the next punch. He wasn't going to stop a minute. It really helped her psychologically to have someone like that around her."

In the final debate, Mattox taunted her: "Ann, you look awfully sober tonight. If you're not off the wagon after what you've been through the last two weeks, then you're cured. But Ann, both Mark and I have known you too long, and we can understand why you don't want to answer the question. The Republicans won't be as gentle, regardless of how much you think it'll hurt you to answer the drug question."

Compounding the grim political outlook, an anonymous person called the Austin Police Department and Southwestern Bell and said Richards was going to be shot. Police traced the call to an Austin apartment complex but were not able to identify the person. The threat was judged serious enough that a Texas Ranger met Ann at the airport when she returned from the debate.

Ann's team knew that their hopes were fleeting and that they had better turn things around fast. One day when I was in the campaign office with Pat Cole, her close friend and adviser on health and human services, I said, "Pat, she's not going to make the runoff." She blew a stream of cigarette smoke and just shook her head.

The campaign had been stressing that Mattox had been indicted for a felony as attorney general, and that he had taken $200,000 from a man later convicted of racketeering. But the scoring punch targeted both Mattox and White. Ann had quipped that White's term as governor had been "like a B movie that you didn't want to walk out on, but you wouldn't want to see it again." But she hadn't really gone after him. Then they found out that when he had been governor, a large amount of the state's bond business had gone to a law firm in Houston, and after he lost to Bill Clements in 1986, he joined that firm with a high salary. Squier offered the stinger that White had "lined his pockets" as governor. The resulting ad had the condemning clause "White and Mattox, the best resumés money can buy." While Ann was reeling from the drug inquisition, her friend Jane Hickie reentered the fray. Hickie pushed hard for using the attack ad. "I said we ought to do it, and we did it," she told Brian McCall, the Republican chronicler. "And I do feel responsible for it. I don't regret it for a second. It caused us to win."

"That was a great weekend for the campaign," Glenn Smith agreed. "We managed to change the subject. Ann had used the line in a speech at an affair Willie Nelson put on for her, and we had all that research put together. We developed it to get to the press, we made the spot, the story ran, we put the headline on the spot, and got the ad on the air. We did it all really fast. Back then, you couldn't edit as quickly; it just took more time to do everything. We pulled it off, and it worked. Then she had a change of heart. I was in San Antonio when she called me and said, 'Look, I really don't want to attack Governor White like that.' But the ad had already shipped. I had to say, 'Ann, you already did.' That's the only time she ever yelled at me. She was really distraught. It was some time before Monte Williams could get her to leave the little holding room where she was and go out there and make her speech."

White called a press conference and exploded. "The true principle she's abiding by is to use anything to attack in order to save her failing campaign. That shocks me. I did not believe she had this in her. . . . I've never seen anyone dip to this low a level in making a scurrilous attack." One press account said he accused her of "tactics like those of the Gestapo chief Heinrich Himmler."

Ann responded mildly that she was surprised Governor White would call her a Nazi. But Jane Hickie said that Ann regretted running that ad for the rest of her life. For his part, White had the bitter rationalization for why he was going to lose. He later told Brian McCall, "That tape ran for about a week. I fell from thirty-three or thirty-four points in the polls to twenty in one week."

It is doubtful that White was ever in as strong a position as he claimed, and in the end it turned out that he had raised insufficient money to match the ad buys of his rivals. Ann led Mattox in the primary by 40,000 votes and a little more than two percentage points. White was embarrassed in his last campaign, getting just 19 percent of the vote.

To this day, Ross Ramsey, now an editor and analyst for the *Texas Tribune*, maintains with glee that the boat trip was exemplary of a foolish impulse that could have sunk Ann's campaign just as it was getting started. "Well," Glenn said, "we generated seventy-five free television stories of more than a minute"—claiming that they were worth $3 million in ad buys. "I would never do that today," he acknowledged. "It was too risky. But that really helped her. Those were beautiful pictures. And one thing I'm proud of—we earned our margins from those coastal counties where we'd done the boat trip. It surprised the heck out of Mattox, because he thought he had the southern coast sewn up. On election night when we saw the Nueces County numbers, that's when I was told to go tell Ann that she would finish first.

"There's another thing I never would have done if I had been a more sophisticated guy. We were pretty sure we were going to be in a runoff, and we'd be in a runoff with Mattox. So I took three hundred thousand dollars and hid it from everybody. Within a couple of days of the first race, we were back up on television. Mattox had spent his money. I got in a lot of trouble over that. The woman who wrote the checks got fired over it. Ann never said anything to me about it, but Jane Hickie thought the woman had a responsibility to tell her about it. Which I always thought was pretty weird, because that's how we won the runoff. They were saying, 'If we hadn't spent that money and come in third, what were you going to do then?' I don't know, I probably would have left Texas. But there was no way Mattox could outperform Ann in a Democratic Party runoff. She was going to have such an advantage with female and repeat voters. There were places where it was even, but there was no place where he had her outflanked."

James Carville kept trying to steer Mattox back to the lottery issue, which he thought was a winner. But Mattox's ads grew even more strident, stating flatly that Ann had used marijuana and cocaine. He claimed to know sources who had seen Ann use drugs when she was a forty-six-year-old county commissioner, but that he was not free to identify them. Ann called him "the garbage man of Texas politics."

Then it was his turn to be surrounded by a swarm of shouting reporters: the *Dallas Morning News* had published a sworn affidavit by a former Dallas vice officer and a Houston lawyer who claimed they had seen Mattox smoking pot on two occasions. In the four-week slugfest, Ann increased her lead over the attorney general to nearly 158,000 votes. In a headline about the outcome, the *Los Angeles Times* called the race and spectacle "lurid." The *Dallas Times Herald* ran its story under the headline "Richards Wins in Mudslide."

Mark White refused to take Ann's telephone calls in the aftermath of the lining-his-pockets television ad and the continuing election, but his temper cooled, and the time would come when he and his wife were Ann's guests at a reception in the Governor's Mansion. The bitterness and hurt of Jim Mattox did not heal so easily. He ran twice more as a candidate in Texas—once for the U.S. Senate in 1994, losing a Democratic primary to Richard Fisher, a wealthy and conservative Dallas businessman, and then in a 1998 bid to regain his office as attorney general. He lost that race to the Republican John Cornyn, who was later elected one of Texas's U.S. senators.

By all accounts, Mattox never quite got over losing that race to Ann in 1990. He was stung because he felt his long record as a progressive had been ignored, and the press was never his friend. After he died in his sleep in 2008, at sixty-five, he got what was probably the best press he ever received from the man caught in the middle of that furious strife eighteen years earlier—David Richards.

The *Texas Observer* titled his essay "Junkyard Jim," but David took pains to delineate what the man had accomplished in elective office. Their relationship began, he wrote, in 1972, when they successfully challenged the existing scheme to elect state representatives from at-large districts. Their lawsuit resulted in single-member districts that made it possible for black candidates to win; in addition, their "election guru," a man named Dan Weiser, drew up plans that were adopted by the federal court, and as a by-product they also created a district where Mattox could run in conservative Dallas and win. In two terms in the Texas House in the wake of the Sharpstown scandal, he battled for open-meetings legislation and more transparent campaign-finance rules, and when the aftermath of Watergate swept Jimmy Carter into the presidency in 1976, Mattox caught that wind in his sail and won a seat in Congress, defeating Tom Pauken, a Republican, in two extremely heated contests. "These races," David wrote, "became legendary for their vitriol and assured Jim's well-deserved reputation as a take-no-prisoners campaigner."

Bill Clements, he continued in the essay, was determined to get rid of the GOP's most loathed Democrat, and under the "utterly bogus cover of wanting to create a black congressional district in Dallas (the population wasn't sufficient at the time)," Clements proposed a district that would make Mattox's reelection impossible. "The battle continued through two special sessions of the Legislature, but the Clements plan was blocked in the Texas Senate. Then tragedy struck: Mickey Leland was killed in a plane crash, creating a vacancy in his Houston congressional seat. Craig Washington, the ablest member of the state Senate at the time, was elected to fill the vacancy. His election removed the blocking eleventh vote in the Texas Senate, and Clements's redistricting plan was shoved through in the closing days of 1981."

David wrote that Mattox persuaded him to file a suit challenging the Republican redistricting plan, but as the filing deadline for candidates approached, Mattox wanted a guarantee that the suit would be successful. David couldn't promise that, so Mattox quit his congressional seat and ran for and won the 1982 race for attorney general in another vicious battle, this time in the Democratic primary against John Hannah and Max Sherman.

So David once more answered the call of governmental service and became Mattox's chief of litigation, recruiting some of the brightest young lawyers in the state. At the end of Mark White's term as governor, a federal court in Dallas declared Texas's sodomy statute unconstitutional. Taking the side of gay-rights activists, Mattox filed a motion to dismiss the appeal that had been filed by Mark White when he was attorney general. That set off a furious legal fight in which Mattox's argument prevailed and the U.S. Supreme Court invalidated the Texas law.

"Perhaps even more controversial, though ludicrous," David wrote, "was the issue of women in the Texas A&M band." A federal court had ordered the university to accept women in the Aggie marching band, and in the ensuing uproar, Mattox said he agreed with the court's decision and was not going to appeal it. "A&M's regents went nuts, bombarding the office with threats and complaints. They even hired a lawyer to pursue an independent appeal. Mattox successfully scotched that effort, the court's order was implemented, and the band does not seem to have suffered."

On and on the wild eight-year run went, with the consumer protection cases, Mattox's feuds with Fulbright & Jaworski and Ronnie Earle, and his indictment and acquittal for commercial bribery. "Finally, in 1990," David wrote, cutting his personal feelings about that election to the quick, "Jim ran a deplorable campaign against my former wife, Ann Richards, for governor, which I am sad to say ultimately caused him, and many others, a world of grief."

David had certainly learned to be a master of understatement. He didn't have to elaborate on why so many of his colleagues and friends believed Mattox deserved to be the governor and thought the wrong person had won. David wrote that not long after the 1990 race, he and his new wife, Sandy, ran into Mattox, and the defeated candidate told her that he didn't know what to do with his life anymore. "She wisely suggested that the most rewarding thing he could do would be to get married and have children. As we know, he did, and family life seemed to soothe him, even as it gave him many opportunities, as Texas had in earlier years, to express his fierce loyalty and stubborn determination."

As the 1998 races approached, Attorney General Dan Morales, soon to be a guest of the Texas Department of Corrections, announced, just before the filing deadline, that he was not running for reelection, throwing Democratic plans up in the air. Mattox announced his candidacy at once, cutting off his '82 classmate Garry Mauro, who might have liked to try for attorney general, but not wanting to run against Mattox, instead soldiered on in a doomed race for governor against George W. Bush. Mattox lost his race to John Cornyn by more than 1.6 million votes. He practiced law in Austin for the rest of his life and remained a force behind the scenes of the Texas Democratic Party. Mauro put his occasionally bruising relationship with the man behind them and, on his passing, said Mattox was always "pounding on the table for the people. Anybody that thinks of Jim Mattox and doesn't think of the 'people's lawyer' really didn't know him. He never saw a fight he'd walk away from." To me, David Richards said the most about his perplexing friend and onetime boss at the beginning of his *Texas Observer* farewell.

> The least peaceful person I have ever known has died peacefully. May he rest in peace.
> Jim Mattox was restless, irrepressible, and combative on plenty of occasions. He was never one to let sleeping dogs lie. As a kid, I feel certain, he never passed a wasp nest without poking it with a stick just to watch the chaos. He was also, to my mind, the best Texas attorney general of my lifetime.

CHAPTER 18

Bustin' Rocks

CLAYTON WILLIAMS'S AURA of inevitability in the general election was partly a measure of how soiled in reputation the Democratic primary fight had left Ann Richards. It also stemmed from a television ad in which the Republican on horse-back chased some heifers out of a draw, vaulted off his horse, and swaggered up to the camera wearing a Stetson, long-sleeved plaid shirt, and chaps that flapped over his jeans and boots. It didn't much matter what he said—it just looked so good.

In the months leading up to the 1990 race, the Midland-based oilman and rancher had not been perceived as a politician at all. Two years older than Ann, Williams was the consummate West Texas rich guy. His Harvard-educated grand-father had come to Texas from Illinois in 1877 on the advice of doctors who told him he had tuberculosis and needed a more arid climate. Oscar Waldo Williams and his wife settled in Fort Stockton, where he worked as a surveyor of public land. He was twice elected county judge in Pecos County, once being voted out be-cause he favored Prohibition. That man's son, the elder Clayton Wheat Williams, was educated as an engineer and was an artillery officer in France in World War I. Though he had no formal schooling in geology, he discovered large oil and gas fields in the Permian Basin, in 1926 convincing the Texas Oil and Land Company to drill what was then the world's deepest oil well. He served as a Pecos County commissioner and as a trustee on the Fort Stockton school board. But for all his business, civic, and scholarly contributions—he was a regional historian—the elder Clayton Williams was not entirely popular out there.

The Republican gubernatorial candidate Clayton Williams displays his trademark grin and cowboy hat at a political rally in Floydada, May 1990.

The greater Big Bend area—everything west of the Pecos River—averages just eight to eighteen inches of rain a year. It is part of the Chihuahuan Desert with some handsome small mountain ranges and stretches of highland prairie. But it has groundwater, and ever since a Texas Supreme Court ruling in 1904, "the rule of capture" has, with few exceptions, granted landowners the legal right to use or sell all the water they can extract from their property. The elder Clayton Williams took brazen advantage of this descendant of English common law in order to irrigate his crops. Williams was blamed for extinguishing Fort Stockton's Comanche Springs, a fabled swimming hole and camping ground on one of the nomadic warriors' raiding trails to Mexico. In 1856, a traveler reported that cold clear water gushed from the earth and rock "like a sea monster." By 1961, the spring was bone dry.

Clayton Wheat Williams, Jr., knew all about the Comanche Springs controversy. It was one of many things he declined to apologize for. Born in Alpine in 1931, he grew up on the family's ranch outside Fort Stockton. As a rich and successful man, Williams reminisced that his dad gave him responsibility for running a cotton farm when he was fourteen years old. "The soil wasn't holding water, and boll weevils were attacking my cotton. The hail came and I couldn't collect crop insurance, then my hands quit and I was working around the clock. So when I went to college, I went to learn how to be a problem solver."

Williams was a proud Texas Aggie who graduated with a degree in animal husbandry and an army commission as a second lieutenant. He said that he invested his $2,000 in savings in an oil and gas company in 1957, following in the footsteps of his dad. He drilled his first successful well in 1959, and in 1961 he founded Clajon, which became the largest individually owned natural gas company in the state. Over the next twenty years, he established eight other energy companies and bought up more than 350,000 acres of oil and gas leases. In the mid-1980s, he branched out into long-distance telephone service with ClayDesta Communications. (His wife is named Modesta.) Unable to afford a professional actor, he starred in commercials that won trade advertising awards. He established the ClayDesta National Bank in Midland and backed a 186-acre commercial real estate development there. He bought large cattle ranches in Big Bend and started to farm alfalfa, a very thirsty crop, outside Fort Stockton.

The desert of West Texas and eastern New Mexico is given to sand, stunted mesquite, creosote bush, and tatters of trash impaled on the thorns by the ceaseless wind. Midland and Odessa began as railroad depots where cattle could be loaded and watered. Midland did not incorporate until 1906, and Odessa had only 750 residents in 1925. But a large sedimentary stratum called the Permian Basin had by the mid-1960s produced 11.3 billion barrels of oil. The twin cities of Odessa and Midland would scarcely have existed otherwise. Much of Odessa is a hodgepodge of pipe yards and wind-battered frame houses occupied by oil-field laborers. But Midland, the domain of landmen and wildcatters, has tall buildings and groomed neighborhoods with swimming pools and golf courses. In boom years following World War II, the iconic wildcatter of Midland was the heroic bomber pilot and transplanted Connecticut aristocrat, George Herbert Walker Bush. He later moved his business empire to Houston and launched his political career there. Clayton Williams, Jr., subsequently made a success of his exploration companies with innovative horizontal drilling and three-dimensional seismic technology. He founded the Chihuahuan Desert Research Institute for the work of biologists and botanists, and he put up half the money to build an alumni center at Texas A&M—the structure bears his name.

In 1973, OPEC embargoed oil sales to the United States and other Western nations that had supported Israel's rout of Egypt and Syria in the Yom Kippur, or

Ramadan, War. (The non-Muslim OPEC members at the time—Venezuela and Nigeria—went along with the embargo under pressure from the rest of the cartel.) The embargo lasted just a year, but America's attempt to lessen its reliance on foreign-supplied fossil fuels sparked a boom of production in the oil and gas fields of Texas, Louisiana, and New Mexico. Williams's corporate domain never flew higher than during that boom. But then the Saudis broke with OPEC and put the world awash in oil. Overproduction by American companies also contributed to the glut. The price of benchmark West Texas crude plummeted in a free fall that didn't stop until the price hit eight dollars a barrel. The oil bust plunged Texas into its very own depression. No longer did one see those bumper stickers urging the state to "Freeze a Yankee in the Dark."

Williams had to fight off creditors calling in loans that totaled $500 million. He was forced to sell Clajon, and during this time, he and Modesta realized that their fifteen-year-old son, Clayton Wade, was addicted to alcohol and drugs. They enrolled the youth in a Dallas rehab called Straight and flew out to visit and counsel him every other week.

The bright spot for Clayton Williams in those years was his success as a cattle rancher. In the lovely Davis Mountains and surrounding highland prairie, Williams bought the Henderson Flat Ranch and proceeded to alienate his neighbors. Long before Gary Cartwright had any inkling that Clayton Williams would get crosswise with his friend Ann Richards, he wrote about the ranching dispute in a 1985 *Texas Monthly* story, "The Last Roundup." Williams's horseshoe-shaped ranch enclosed the storied Kokernot o6 ranch on three sides. The Kokernot's young heir and his cowhands resented Williams's padlocking gates and denying them access to their own pastures. Traditionalists disliked him for plowing up native prairie and planting exotic hybrid strains from Texas A&M; they even bitched about his introducing Brangus cattle into a region long known for its Herefords (which were, after all, English exotics that had replaced the longhorns after barbed-wire fences closed the open range).

But the matter that caused Williams the most local grief was an outlook on water rights and use that he seemed to have inherited from his father. The Williamses and their landscapers kept a sprinkler system going continually around the big ranch house, keeping the grass as lush as the green on a country club golf course in Midland. When "Claytie," as friends called him, and Modesta planned one of their big cattle-sale parties, he sent trucks to spray water on his twelve miles of dirt roads and keep the dust tamped down, sparing the limos, pickups, and trailers hauling bulls and cows worth hundreds of thousands of dollars.

Williams was not a politician in 1985, and he spoke to Cartwright as if the possibility had never crossed his mind. At one point, he bragged about how a drought that ruined some of his neighbors was a blessing to him.

> Williams was an eternal optimist, but this was where his oil fortune came into play. While nature compelled the less fortunate to sell, it was inspiring him to buy. "A lot of ranchers around Austin and San Antonio were forced to quit or sell when the market was way down," he told me. "I bought a lot of heifers and some steers and sent them north, where a heavy snowfall made grass plentiful. I bought another fourteen thousand yearlings in South Texas and seven thousand in Mexico. I sent some to the Colorado cornfields and some to the Arizona desert and some more to Wyoming. Cattle cycles are supply and demand, pure and simple. When prices go up again, ranchers will be buying heifers to replenish their stock. I'll be selling heifers back to some of the same people that sold them to me. I usually make about seven dollars an acre here, triple what most cow-calf operations make. This year I estimate I'll make twenty dollars an acre. Next year, who knows? I might decide to let the grass grow."

In little cafés where old-school ranchers gathered to drink their morning coffee, Clayton Williams was the enemy—a man who made money off their failures and bad luck. But in politics far removed from the jealousies of a handful of ranchers in West Texas, he became an overnight sensation. Brushing aside the Republicans' longing for only high-profile conservatives to run—former Dallas Cowboy quarterback Roger Staubach and George W. Bush were among the names that came up—Williams jumped in the 1990 governor's race and spent $6 million introducing Texans to his big nose and even-toothed grin. He loved to ride his prancing horse in Main Street parades and wave his Stetson overhead like Gene Autry, using his fingertips to wobble the brim. That image was hard to beat on local television stations' six o'clock news.

He entered the Republican primary as a political novice facing a formidable lineup of opponents. Tom Luce was a handsome, intellectual Dallas attorney, the lawyer for Ross Perot and an expert on public education. Jack Rains had been Bill Clements's secretary of state. But the front-runner was Kent Hance. The former congressman and senatorial and gubernatorial contender now had an appointed seat on the Texas Railroad Commission, and against that strong field of Republican opponents, a poll in September 1989 showed him with an excellent 33 percent. Hance's impressive poll numbers were met by Williams's anemic 12 percent. But that same September, Williams launched his "Joys of Bustin' Rocks" anticrime ad campaign, whose buys soon reached $3 million. By February 1990, the polls were showing him with 33 percent and Hance, fading to a poor second, with 19 percent.

Then that same February, icing on one of his company plane's wings sent several of his employees and closest friends to their deaths in a crash near Abilene. Williams's show of grief for his friends during the suspended campaign made him an even more endearing figure to Texans. Friends said he came close to quitting the race. But when he decided to continue, he established himself as a character as much as a politician. He joked about himself in ways that resonated with some people: "Everybody always knows I'm an Aggie when they see my class ring while I'm picking my nose." He had millions of his own dollars he was willing to spend, and he hired a team of first-rate politicos. They provided the candidate with a twenty-five-point plan that included $1.6 billion for a war on drugs. Proposing budget cuts, privatization of many government programs, and a hiring freeze of state workers, he claimed he could balance the budget without raising taxes.

In the seventies, he had described himself as "an anti-environmentalist" to the *Midland Reporter-Telegram*, but in 1990 his eighteen-point plan for the environment was quite smooth. He was fond of the nostrum "We have to manage our state more efficiently, like the way we have been doing in the Texas oilfields."

But nothing caught on like his promise to double the capacity of the prisons, give drug dealers the death penalty, and introduce young first offenders to "the joys of bustin' rocks." Neither he nor the press remarked that his own son might have been one of the offenders slinging sledgehammers until they collapsed. He did catch flak, though, for proposing to put this hard-time boot camp for drug offenders in the state's largest nature preserve, Big Bend Ranch State Park. But Williams punched other favorite GOP buttons in offbeat ways. One day he spoke effusively of welfare reform: "One of the ladies on the Governor's Task Force—I probably shouldn't mention her name, but she's a very neat black lady—came up with this thought. It's not my idea, but I endorse it. A lot of the welfare parents are doing drugs. Her idea was that we should be sending anti-drug propaganda . . . anti-drug indoctrination, with the welfare. Second—now hold your hat on this— that we should have drug tests for welfare recipients, and if they test positive, no welfare check. *Pow! No welfare check.* If that's not a strong signal, I don't know what is."

Williams's accomplished opponents thought he would embarrass himself in debates, but he didn't. The younger George Bush was moderating one when someone brought up Williams's reputation for fistfights. "Dang right," he said quickly—he would fight for what was right. The audience guffawed. He elaborated another night when pressed on the number of his recent brawls. "Tell you about one," he volunteered. "It was this guy I'd fired from one of my companies. He kept coming around, harassing my employees, so I decked him. It was apparently an effective management technique, because he stopped coming around."

Williams said he would limit abortion in unspecified ways, protect Texans' right to bear arms, and support an amendment to the U.S. Constitution to ban flag burning. GOP operatives in rival camps passed on rumors that he held "honey hunts" at his big ranch—hookers made available to his high-rolling male guests. Nothing worked. Williams grinned, rode his horse in parades, and crushed his able opponents, carrying 60 percent and winning without a runoff. A Democrat who was friendly with Hance called on him after the rout. The Lubbock politician smiled and said, "He bought it fair and square."

Texas Monthly assigned Mimi Swartz and Jan Jarboe to write profiles of the candidates, planning to run them in tandem in October 1990. Jarboe's story was titled "Clayton Williams: Onward to the Past." It began: "Ten thousand feet above the state he wants to govern, Clayton Williams suddenly bursts into tears. A moment before, I had asked him if it was true, as I had heard, that he cries every time he hears 'The Aggie War Hymn.' The answer is swift and anatomical: The mere mention of the War Hymn triggers a fountain of tears. Here sits the Republican nominee for governor—the very man who is traveling around Texas representing himself as the last true cowboy—crouched on the edge of his cushy airplane seat, with his craggy face so wet with tears that it glistens in the bright August light.

"The 58-year-old oilman, rancher, and banker is a bundle of emotion. In the course of a 25-minute flight in his maroon-and-white King Air, Williams' vivid hazel eyes fill with tears three separate times—once over the War Hymn, again when he recalls his father's desk, and a third time when he talks about his grandfather. . . .

"Why does Clayton Williams cry so much? In every case what sets him off is a deep, personal sense of loss that carries over into politics—loss of his ancestors, of the Texas they knew that is no more, of the simpler, purer life he led at Texas A&M. It was while Williams was a student at A&M in the fifties that he learned the essential lessons of his life: Country folks are better than city folks. . . . Old values triumph over new ones. . . . Life is war. Most politicians can be heard to make glib references to the future, but Clayton Williams' heart is firmly fixed in the past."

Jarboe (now Jarboe Russell) asked whether "Williams' attitude about women raises the larger questions of whether he is too tied to the old codes and formulas to lead a modern state. Williams, of course, disagrees. 'Tom Luce got kind of stern with me during one of the debates,' says Williams. 'He questioned whether Texas can ride horseback into the twenty-first century. Well, my answer to that is you can if you have a good horse.'"

She finished her article with another telling quotation: "'I'm not going to force anybody to wear cowboy hats, jeans, and act like I do,' said Williams. 'But I've noticed that most people who hang around me long enough wind up owning a pair of boots.'"

Following his impressive primary victory, Williams made a triumphant swoop through Washington that brought him to the White House of the elder George Bush. The president was pleased to squire this new Republican star to church and introduce him to top congressmen. Williams declined to say that he hoped Jim Mattox would win the Democrats' runoff, but he did offer that he came from "the male world" and feared he really "wouldn't be comfortable battling with a woman." He elaborated for the *Dallas Morning News*: "I've never been in an adversarial position with a woman except once way back when I had a divorce, and I lost."

Ann replied, "I don't want to be his mother, I want to be governor of Texas."

A week later, Williams invited the press and his campaign aides to a genuine roundup on his ranch in the Davis Mountains. The late-March weather turned wet, foggy, and cold, just miserable, and beside a campfire he told a joke that likened their situation to a woman enduring a rape: "If it's inevitable, just relax and enjoy it." Then he didn't have the sense to let it go. Later in the day, at the urging of his aides, he offered an apology to anyone who might have been offended, but he continued, "That's not a Republican women's club that we had this morning. It's a working cow camp, a tough world where you can get kicked in the testicles if you're not careful." Oh, that helped. The reporters persisted, and he fired back, "I'm not going to give you a serious answer. It wasn't a serious deal. It wasn't a serious statement."

Women's groups jumped all over him, but Governor Clements quickly defended him, and Barbara Bush said the uproar wouldn't affect the president's support for Williams in any way. The polls still showed him handily beating either Richards or Mattox. Then, one month later, Williams was reminiscing about the tradition of Aggies "getting serviced" by prostitutes at the Chicken Ranch in La

Grange and the Boys Town brothels in Mexican border towns. A reporter asked whether he personally had taken part in that. "Why, of course," he said. It was just "part of growing up in West Texas."

That May, his campaign received a questionnaire about the pros and cons of six legislative proposals related to crimes of sexual assault. After four days, he and his team had not yet responded, and a *Dallas Morning News* reporter pestered him about it at a press conference. "I don't get my paycheck from you," he snapped, and stormed out of the room. A couple of months later, a reporter with *U.S. News & World Report* questioned him gently about his choice of verbs in describing young men's coming of age. "I was trying to find a nice, polite term for fucking," he said.

What the hell—that was Clayton.

As Glenn Smith predicted, with White out of the race, Ann drubbed the attorney general in the runoff. In the general-election campaign, Williams and his team left the drug-use issue alone, at least in public statements. Maybe they did that out of their candidate's courtly instincts, or maybe they figured Mattox had identified her that way and done all the mauling of her required. But in midsummer, they came out blasting with radio ads claiming that Ann sympathized with death row inmates, harbored desires to raise taxes and take away Texans' guns, and was allied with gay-rights activists and the traitor Jane Fonda.

The Republicans hoped to put the race away that summer, and it appeared they might. U.S. senator Phil Gramm was challenged at the top of the ballot only by an unexciting state senator who had no money. Running for the lieutenant governor post vacated by Bill Hobby, Bob Bullock had his hands full trying to fend off young Rob Mosbacher, Jr., whose dad was a Houston oilman, yacht-racing champion, past U.S. secretary of commerce, and close friend of President Bush. And Karl Rove was guiding two future GOP stars and combatants, Kay Bailey Hutchison and Rick Perry, in hot contention for state treasurer and agriculture commissioner. Of the Democrats' ballyhooed Class of '82, only land commissioner Garry Mauro seemed a reasonably safe bet to still be in elected office after 1990.

A native of Galveston, Kay Bailey had been a cheerleader at the University of Texas who went on to earn a law degree there. She claimed that because she was a woman, she had received no offers for employment as an attorney. She turned to journalism, working for four years as a political reporter for a Houston television station. That led her to a job as press secretary for Anne Armstrong, an heiress of a prominent ranching family and cochair of the Republican National Committee. From a district in Houston, Hutchison then won election to the Texas House, serving from 1972 to 1976. One liberal Democratic representative, Arthur Vance, told me that colleagues of all ideologies liked to see her in a bikini at Barton Springs. During her time in the legislature, she worked with Sarah Weddington and her chief of staff, Ann Richards, to pass legislation prohibiting publication of the names of rape victims. She witnessed Weddington's triumph in *Roe v. Wade* and at the time generally supported a woman's right to an abortion, though not if financed by federal funds.

Her second marriage was to Ray Hutchison, a wealthy Dallas Republican. She ran for a Dallas seat in Congress in 1982 and lost. When a Dallas newspaper ran a story that she had bought a candy manufacturer and was focusing on a new career as an entrepreneur and investor, Ann sent her a teasing letter about how much she loved the idea of Kay as a candy magnate. She changed her mind and set her sights on the office that had been a springboard for Ann.

Raised on a farm near the West Texas hamlet of Paint Creek, Perry, an Aggie and air force pilot, was elected to the Texas House in 1984. One of his best friends in the chamber was Lena Guerrero, and he supported Al Gore for president in 1988. But Karl Rove sensed he was primed to switch parties. He talked Perry into a race against the media star Jim Hightower and helped raise $3 million to make him a formidable GOP threat. For several months, Hightower had talked about challenging Senator Phil Gramm in his race for reelection, but Hightower was too skillful a politician to believe he could win that. He announced that he believed he could accomplish more working nationally at the grassroots level, and that he would seek a third term as agriculture commissioner. But the most entertaining candidate of 1982 was a listless campaigner this time.

Perry said he wouldn't be surprised if Hightower's emphasis on crop diversification had "encouraged the spread of marijuana in this state." The FBI agent Greg Rampton would succeed in putting two of Hightower's aides in federal prison for misuse of public funds; Hightower had to be nervous that the crosshairs were on him. Television ads highlighted the FBI investigation and forced Hightower to deny Karl Rove's remark to the press that he would soon be indicted. Perry aired an ad that showed Hightower shaking hands with Jesse Jackson, and another superimposed the incumbent's face over video of a man burning a flag. Another attack displayed a mean streak that would often be seen in Perry's races. When Hightower sliced off the tip of one finger with his lawn mower, Perry put out a gleeful press release that read: "It's probably a good thing Hightower is not a farmer, because there are machines much more dangerous than lawn mowers on the farm." Hightower had had a rare talent, but now he was putting up only radio ads in a feeble defense of his character and record. Perhaps he was overconfident. Perry painted him as a 1960s elitist who knew almost nothing about agriculture. Perry also demonstrated his gift for the biting, thoughtless turn of phrase. One night in Houston, he tossed out a story that could not have set well with a family named Bush.

Perry claimed he had made a speech about the state's vital stake in agriculture when George W. Bush tugged on his jacket sleeve and asked in all seriousness, "Rick, what's a mohair?" The *Houston Post* described Bush as "a worker on Perry's campaign." The candidate went off on how amazing it was that a son of a Texan president was not aware that mohair is the fleece of an Angora goat! A fleece harvest that Perry claimed was worth $11 billion a year to the Texas economy! There was never much love lost between those two.

George W. Bush quit drinking in the throes of a terrible hangover the morning after he turned forty. He attributed his becoming a devout Christian to a talk he had one day with the Reverend Billy Graham at the Bush family's compound in Kennebunkport, Maine, but he also credited Bible-study sessions that he had started attending during his time in Midland. The younger Bush was glad to be removed from the business setbacks that had hounded him in Midland. When he and his wife, Laura, and their twin daughters moved to Dallas, he borrowed $500,000 to purchase a small share of the Texas Rangers baseball team, and he emerged with the title of managing general partner. Bush knew his baseball, and he was proud of his active role in the Rangers' front office. He was in his element out there, spitting tobacco juice in a cup and calling the players by name.

He also played an active backstage role in the presidential politics of his father—he was the one who fired the elder Bush's first White House chief of staff, John Sununu. President Bush's father, Prescott Bush, had been a GOP senator from Connecticut and a staunch ally of the Eisenhower administration. With President Bush's approval ratings soaring toward 90 percent in response to America's triumph in the First Gulf War, thought naturally gravitated toward a dynasty in the persons of George W. in Texas and his younger brother Jeb in Florida. But for several reasons, it was deemed too soon for both of them. George W. moderated the Dallas debate in which the GOP candidates failed to yank Clayton Williams off his high horse over his record of fistfights. Then the Williams campaign released a direct-mail appeal from the oldest presidential son.

Dear Fellow Texan,

When Colonel Travis drew the line in the sand at the Alamo, he discovered immediately who had the courage to stand and fight for the Texas Republic. That line has been drawn again for the 1990 gubernatorial elections. On which side of the line do you stand? . . .

[Williams] wants to build more prisons and boot camps for first-time offenders. Bustin' rocks, as Claytie says, will set young offenders straight before setting out on a life of crime.

Ann Richards isn't sure about capital punishment, and just like Mike Dukakis she talks about "programs" for criminals rather than punishing them and protecting victims. . . . [Williams] shares the Main Street, mainstream views of the working men and women of Texas. . . .

Frankly, who could ever forget the outrageous attack she launched against my father, George Bush, at the 1988 Democratic National Convention?

Karl Rove, who handled direct-mail fund-raising for the Texas GOP at the time, may well have written the letter. But the presidential son signed it. Despite the silver-foot pendant, the notes of goodwill, and the peace offering, the last line in that letter left no doubt that the president and his family still had a serious bone to pick with Ann Richards.

CHAPTER 19

The Rodeo

FOR THE REST OF THEIR LIVES, Ann and Bud explained their relationship with the high school expression "going steady." In April 1990, when she was struggling to put away Mattox in the runoff, Bud wrote, "My prayers are with you (and also my cosmic powers which are better left undefined, sort of like Mad Dog). I can't even imagine how tired you must be, and how in need of . . . I started to say solace, but that's not the word. Maybe a good hug is all I mean."

"So far, so bueno" was Bud's droll, semioptimistic maxim of life. But even he acknowledged how bleak the situation appeared that summer. Amid reflections on the press's tepid response to her environmental policy plan—the one I wrote—and Saddam Hussein's provocative comparison of Britain's creation of Kuwait to a nipple carved from the breast of Mother Iraq, Bud offered an anecdotal detour and parable.

> Dear Ann,
> . . . I was kind of tired and my ankle hurt this morning, so I gave myself a day off. The dogs jumped in the car and I went to a long breakfast at Maudie's Cafe, where I read the *Dallas Morning News* and listened to Ab, Maudie's husband, the cook on Saturday mornings, as he would occasionally come out of the kitchen and make pronouncements. Once after he had been making a racket he came out and said, "No problem, folks. I'm just communicating with my ancestors."
> Later Ab sat down and said, "It's a beautiful day in Chicago."
> I looked up from the paper to listen.

"Back on the farm at four in the morning, doing the chores and freezing to death, milking the cows and slopping the hogs, I would be listening to this old radio in the barn, and every morning a man came on the air and said, 'It's a beautiful day in Chicago.' That's always stuck in my mind. No matter how bad it looks to me, it's always a beautiful day in Chicago."

Ann had been in the race for a year now, and like a long-distance runner, somehow she had to find the kick, the sprint to the finish. Bud's days of trying to overcome his crises had not all been beautiful, either, and she helped guide him toward AA. In those days, movies and AA meetings were how they often dated. In late June, she wrote him:

> I'd love to go AA-ing with you but I am off to Washington, New York, and Miami this week. Home on Friday. I had such a good time listening to the saga of your father at the nursing home that I can't wait to hear chapters 2-3-4.... I'll call when I can play. Hope you'll go to AA without me—great people.
> Love, Ann

Late that summer, Bud accompanied Ann to a benefit that Willie Nelson put on for her at the Austin Opry House. There was a good deal of laughter and much good music that night, but we had the air of people bunched up under siege. Glenn Smith told me that after the primary and runoff: "The first poll we got back showed her seventeen points down to Clayton. But that's a strange thing: Ann was way scared of losing the primary to Mattox—she just didn't know how she could face all of those people who believed in her—but she wasn't so afraid of losing to Williams. Those seventeen points didn't daunt her. She didn't think she had much of a chance of overcoming that, but she was much more relaxed. From the beginning, she just had a more happily aggressive attitude about it. That was a role Ann was very comfortable in—the liberal fighting an uphill fight against powerful good old boys. Her attitude was so much better in the general election. Even in those early days."

Glenn and the rest of the original team had reason to be proud. The primary had been a brutal contest in which they were backed to the edge of an abyss, yet they fought back and won. Still, Ann wanted Mary Beth Rogers to take over as campaign manager, with major help to come from Jane Hickie and Jack Martin. Mary Beth did not share Glenn's belief in the upbeat morale of the campaign team. And in her recollection, on the night of Willie's benefit at the Opry House, Ann was *twenty-seven* points down.

Several women who worked for Ann have said the campaign shake-up was necessitated by need to get rid of "the guys." But the dysfunction was not that simple, Mary Beth told me. "In the first part of the primary, the campaign was pretty much run by Glenn and Mark and Monte Williams and Lena Guerrero. And people wound up at each other's throats. Boy, that was a low point, even though Ann managed to squeak it out." Some of Ann's team thought that Bob Squier's ads had not measured up to his national reputation. Mark McKinnon was then in a short-lived partnership with the Austin politico Dean Rindy. The Richards team decided to give Rindy and McKinnon a chance to brainstorm and produce the ads for the general election. Before anything got on the air, half of that partnership departed when Rindy intimated to Ann that she dressed like hell; there were no more sightings of Rindy on the campaign team after that.

But Mark had been close to Ann for a few years; he had been one of the trusted readers of the manuscript of her book. "Harrison Hickman had conducted a poll about the general election," Mary Beth said. "It was about two weeks after Ann had won the primary. Mark in his innocent bouncy way just kind of blurted out how far behind she was in the polls, and how awful it was. Ann gave him this

Ann, conservationist and movie star Robert Redford, and Jim Hightower at a joint campaign event in 1990. Ann edged Clayton Williams in the race for governor, but Hightower's popularity with the media and figures in the entertainment industries was not enough to get him past State Representative Rick Perry in the race for agriculture commissioner.

look—I thought she was going to start crying, I think she held it back. She got so mad at Mark, after that meeting she didn't want to have anything more to do with him. That's when she got Jane and Jack and me to come in and take over."

George Shipley recalled a campaign ad that Cathy Bonner produced during that period of flux. "It had rodeo footage, and the theme of it was that Ann was going to put Texas back on top. They ran it for two or three days. But the sexual innuendo that Ann was going to be 'on top' was offensive to a large number of white men." Squier came back aboard to do the advertising, while Glenn and Monte started a consulting team and continued to play a role in the campaign. "I was a lot happier," Glenn said. "I was exhausted, and there was nothing I could do to recast the way Ann thought of me. She didn't really think badly of me, to my knowledge. It was more like, 'Where are all the people who said they were going to be with us? I thought this guy was going to be a figurehead, and here he's been making real decisions.' I didn't feel any resentment when Mary Beth came in. She took a lot of pressure off me. Also, I wanted Ann to win."

Glenn smiled, remembering a debate prep that turned out to be one of his favorite moments in the campaign: "Somebody had given us use of one of the big houses above Town Lake. I was sitting on a sofa with Ann, and she said, 'You know, Glenn, I don't know how to deal with you because you're not obsessive-compulsive enough.' I had a pen in my hand, and I leaped up and threw it against the wall and said, 'Fuck you, bitch!' Then I sat back down and said, 'How was that?' She doubled over laughing, but nobody else knew what was going on."

Mary Beth recalled that evening quite another way. "The situation was real delicate," Mary Beth said of handoff from the primary team. "To his credit, Glenn made it easy, and we've been friends to this day. But we also had to get Lena out of there. There was going to be a coordinated campaign for all the candidates under the direction of the party. I was being given the role of having to do all the dirty work for Ann, and I had to convince Lena she would be more effective, and play a greater leadership role, if she headed up the coordinated campaign. And then we had to convince everybody else on the coordinated campaign that Lena could do it, and that took a month. During the primary there had been a debate preparation in which a developer had loaned us his big house. I'd never seen anything like it—such out-and-out animosity on Lena's part. It was one of those things where you're thinking, 'I don't want to be in this room.'"

My wife, Dorothy, had vivid memories of that evening as well. Bob Squier had flown down from Washington for the debate prep. Perched on a steep hillside, the borrowed mansion had a deck where people could enjoy the view—also a sturdy railing to keep them from toppling off if they had had too many. Dorothy looked up at one point and saw Squier out there in his solitude, walking the railing like a gymnast on a high wire. The Richards campaign had been a circus up to that point, and the big-name pro from Washington was an oddly perfect fit.

———

"CLAYTON HAD BEATEN a big field of opponents," Mary Beth said. "He was just so arrogant, so contemptuous of Ann. He was on track, and he would have beaten her. The demographics in the state, the number of self-identified Republicans, were changing fast. And Clayton was doing very well until we began to pressure him." One of those times, they believed, came in July. The press had carried stories of Williams saying that Ann was sympathetic to traitors, followed by a former prisoner of war questioning her patriotism on Williams's behalf. Then came a barrage of attack ads in that vein on radio. At a joint appearance in Plainview, Ann walked up to him and said, "You've got to get this stuff off the air." His adversaries in the primary had not confronted him that way, and it seemed to rattle him.

Two events in the Gulf of Mexico worked to Ann's advantage that summer. First the *Mega Borg* tanker exploded, releasing around 4.6 million gallons of oil, then a tanker-barge collision sent 500,000 more gallons into the wetlands of Galveston's Seawolf Park. The state had no workable plan in place to deal with calamities of that scale. Ann raced down to Galveston to view the muck and said, "I am horrified that Bill Clements has failed to act to protect our fragile environment. Clayton Williams brags that he is cut from the same cloth as Bill Clements. Right now that cloth is soaked in oil and is wearing mighty thin."

Mary Beth said, "We came up with this seven-point strategy for the campaign. We had to tell Clayton's story. We had to tell Ann's story. We had to galvanize women voters. Especially suburban women. We had to raise six million dollars. We had to turn out our Democratic base in East Texas, the inner cities, and along the border. And we had to have some good luck.

"We started doing crash research about Clayton Williams's businesses. Paul Williams was discovering things that had never been out in the open before. And people couldn't believe it. At the start of our focus groups, voters would start out being for Clayton Williams. But when we laid out facts about his career, they'd switch. So we knew that if we could get the money to put that on television, we'd have a shot. We started targeting big donors. Fred Ellis and I went down to see Walter Umphrey [a personal injury lawyer in Beaumont]. I told him, 'Look, we have poll results and we have focus group results. If we can put this argument on television, we can knock this guy down. But we've got to get on TV.'"

There were about six Democrats with that kind of wealth that they called on. A pariah to Republicans, who loathed all "trial lawyers," unless of course they gave money to Republicans, Beaumont's Walter Umphrey contributed a little more than $100,000 and lent her campaign $200,000.

The first draft of "Meet the Real Clayton Williams" read: "Over the next several weeks, the Ann Richards campaign will begin a series of public service press releases to introduce the public to Clayton Williams.

"These releases will introduce the real Clayton Williams, the man behind the $6 million television campaign, the junk bond wheeler-dealer whose big grin shows that he thinks he can do what has never been done before: the leveraged buyout of the State of Texas."

It was a joke that the attacks were "public service announcements," and many of the accusations were too wonky to catch on with voters. But some of them stuck. Private property rights are sacrosanct in rural Texas; the Richards campaign found a 1981 *Houston Chronicle* article in which Williams spoke in heavy-handed fashion about using eminent domain—or condemnation law—to force his oil and gas pipelines across anyone's land: "They can protest as to what we pay them, but we have a right to lay our pipelines across anybody's property at any time."

Paul Williams found that in 1984, the Texas Railroad Commission reported that one of Clayton Williams's oil companies and a contractor called Bulldog Construction Company had been cited for intentionally dumping 25,000 barrels of waste mud and oil into a tributary creek of a lake that provided drinking water for the small town of Brenham. Partners and competitors in the oil and gas industry had sued his companies more than 300 times. Two large federal suits, which alleged fraud, deception, restraint of trade, and illegal fixing of natural gas prices in order to cheat royalty owners, had been settled by Williams's lawyers. The most recent lawsuit involved his long-distance telephone company, ClayDesta. One of his first employees claimed Williams lifted his business plan, promised him 30 percent equity in the company, and then fired him two years later. Williams bristled in the deposition, "I fired him and gave him fifty thousand dollars because he wasn't doing his job. That's more than the man deserved."

Ann released all her income tax returns and challenged Williams to do the same. He bragged that it would take an eighteen-wheeler to haul all his personal and business tax returns. A young member of Richards's campaign team, John Hatch, had friends in the trucking business, and they arranged to haul an eighteen-wheeler to Williams's campaign headquarters. A Williams spokesman responded haughtily, "Ann Richards is a liberal elitist who is comfortable hobnobbing in the boutiques of San Francisco and Greenwich Village with the likes of Jane Fonda and Michael Dukakis." But the counter did not line up with the gibe—boutique liberals were not often acquainted with people who knew how to park an eighteen-wheeler.

None of the charges could have overcome Williams's lead in the polls and huge advantage in funding. But the accusations about his business practices angered him. In September, he bragged that he was going to "head and hoof her and drag her through the dirt." That is a reference to roping cattle, which did not play well among women who were already put off by his roundup rape joke.

Inexperienced aides in the campaign office responded with a colorful non sequitur. Mark Strama, whom Ann would later help win a seat in the legislature, was then a twenty-two-year-old, fresh out of college in Rhode Island; his job at the campaign was to run errands. Strama and some pals came up with a top ten list of silly characterizations of the Republican and posted it around the office. Chuck McDonald had joined the team as a press aide; he later became a sought-after public relations consultant, but he got the campaign job in part because his mother was a prominent Democratic legislator from El Paso. When Williams made the crack about Ann falling off the wagon, reporters started calling for a response. McDonald was caught off guard, and both Bill Cryer and Margaret Justus, the seasoned campaign press aides, were out of the office. His gaze fell on the top ten insults the young staffers had compiled. Reading the first one, he told a reporter from Amarillo, "Clayton Williams is a fraudulent honking goose." The odd rejoinder sped around newsrooms all over the state. "Ann and Bill Cryer were driving in Nacogdoches and heard this on the radio," recalled Mark Strama. "Bill said he literally had to pull the car over so she could stomp around. Oh, she was pissed!"

Williams had declined to participate in any debates with Ann. He didn't need to. But they scheduled a joint appearance before the Dallas Crime Commission in early October. Williams's handlers had publicly distanced themselves from their candidate's blunders a number of times, but according to the *Dallas Times Herald*'s Ross Ramsey, while the rape joke and other sexist cracks were totally consistent with who he was, the handlers put him up to a stunt that was out of character. Although Williams bragged about his fistfights with men, his code of honor demanded chivalry in encounters with women. But with cameras all around them, he punched a friend's shoulder and said, "Watch this." He walked up to her and declared, "Ann, I'm here to call you a liar today. That's what you are. You lied about me. You lied about Mark White. You lied about Jim Mattox. I'm going to finish this deal, and you can count on it."

"Well," she drawled. "I'm sorry you feel that way about it, Clayton." She had extended her arm for the ritual handshake and was so surprised that she just left her hand out there. He turned away and snapped, "I don't want to shake your hand."

Chris Hughes, the young travel aide and carrier of Ann's purse, had seen her in emotional and psychological despair following the screaming press gantlet she had to run at the Dallas primary debate. Now he and McDonald were in the van riding away from this episode. Chris was shocked when she looked back over the seat and said, "Boys, this sucker is over. He must have lost his mind."

To Ann, the turning point wasn't the joke about the rape, or the story about getting serviced in whorehouses, or the boast about roping her and dragging her in the dirt. It was that image that could never be erased of a grown man aggressively refusing to shake a woman's hand.

Bill Kenyon, a Williams spokesman, had told the *New York Times* the candidate was aware of the damage he was doing to himself, well before the handshake incident—an indication that he was getting conflicting advice. "He's going through this inward-looking process of saying to himself for the first time that politicking is a ton of grief. . . . Instead of sliding around in the muck the way we have been lately, we decided to take a break, start over, and try to come out like in the good old days."

But that was a hard pivot to make. Ann had claimed that she was closing in the polls, and on camera Williams was shown giggling, "I hope she hasn't started drinking again." Then Richards put up a negative campaign ad that showed him saying that over and over. Molly Ivins provided her completely biased view of the race in a *Dallas Times Herald* column that later appeared in her book *Molly Ivins Can't Say That, Can She?* (1991).

But the polls still showed Williams ten points ahead, then seven points ahead. The Richards campaign was praying for Williams to screw up again, and he cheerfully obliged. Williams's people had to sagely dodge all requests for a debate, since Williams knew almost zip about state government, but two Dallas television stations, KERA and WFAA, managed to rope him in to "in-depth" interviews. He gave a shaky performance, his ignorance more visible than usual. Then one interviewer asked, almost as a throwaway, "What's your stand on Proposition One?"

"Which one is that?" Williams inquired.

"The only one on the ballot."

He was still lost, so the interviewer told him what the proposition was about—concerning the governor's power to make late-term "midnight" appointments. Williams still didn't know if he was for it or against it.

"But haven't you already voted?" inquired the interviewer. "You told us you voted absentee. Don't you remember how you voted?"

"I just voted on that the way my wife told me to; she knew what it was," Williams explained.

He was so clearly a candidate in a world of trouble, the clip made the national news. The polls showed her within three points.

Ann's crowds were enormous now, and the rallies had taken on the air and tone that this was a cause, not just another race. Almost too late, Ann had become the campaigner that people had envisioned when she made that speech in Atlanta. In her speeches, she kept going back to an image that had inspired her since 1982, in her first race for treasurer. She had gone to the Rio Grande hamlet of La Joya and a gathering for old folks called Amigos del Valle. Put on by her friend Billy Leo, who owned the general store, the occasions resembled Meals on Wheels, except

Holding a cup of coffee and an issue of the local newspaper, Ann is greeted by Democratic supporters in the Big Thicket town of Kountze, 1990.

the old friends and kinfolks gathered for fellowship as well as food. They played dominos and did needlework. Ann had made the scene the endnote of *Straight from the Heart*. She compressed it in her speeches, but it always came out more or less the same.

> It was late afternoon by the time we were going to leave, kind of dusky on the highway. And as we were pulling away I saw a little woman, she couldn't have been over four and a half feet tall, probably in her early eighties, standing by the highway waiting for her ride. She was a frail woman, in a cotton print dress that hung straight to her ankles.
>
> I really thought, looking out that window, that that little woman is what our business of public service is all about. She has faith in us to do right by her and by the place where she lives. She will never know the intricacies, the machinations, the pull and tug and hardness of politics, and it doesn't matter. What she does need to know is that there are people serving in public office who care about her and her community. That's all she needs to know. And it's important that we be true to her . . .
>
> She had a mask. She was standing in front of Billy Leo's store wearing my face. I waved at her. She waved back.

Bud Shrake's coauthored book with Barry Switzer, *Bootlegger's Boy*, had spent nine weeks on the *New York Times* best-seller list. But a sportswriter who covered Switzer's career for the *Dallas Times Herald* and Oklahoma City's *Daily Oklahoman* took sharp exception to a chapter alleging that the reporter had participated in an attempt to entrap an Oklahoma Sooner in a cocaine sting. Calling the chapter "vindictive fiction," he sued Switzer, Bud, and their publisher for libel, slander, invasion of privacy, emotional stress, and loss of consortium. Bud was irked at having to sit for depositions in the suit, which was eventually settled, as they waited for the election.

> My dear Bud,
> I hate the answering service and don't leave messages because I'm not here enough to get a return call.
> Polls are even. I'm in a snit. I can handle real crisis but good news threatens me.
> The only thing I have worth reporting was a press conference in the metropolis of Fannett.

It took place in a feed store and they built a podium out of eight sacks of mule feed.

I'll miss Jap and Phyllis's party. I'm in South Texas with Henry Cisneros.

Light candles. Say mantras.

Love, Ann

On the last weekend of the race, a bombshell burst. The Williams team had arranged an old-style whistle-stop train tour, and in his beloved Aggie town of College Station, Williams was pestered by reporters with questions about his tax returns. "I'll tell you when I didn't pay any income taxes was in 1986," he volunteered. "When the whole economy collapsed." He was being honest, as he often was in making big mistakes. He went on about how the oil bust cratered the entire Texas economy that year, forcing him to sell off companies and fight to stay out of bankruptcy. It was true that his losses far exceeded his income, so he owed no income taxes when his accountants got through with that year's return. But that was not how the story was bound to play in the press.

Reggie Bashur, a publicist for the campaign, said that one of their efforts at damage control was to open the bar early for the reporters on the train, which was racing toward the Mexican border. They wanted to get those folks good and drunk and out of the reach of their editors. According to Molly Ivins, they even went so far as to cancel the reporters' Laredo hotel reservations and put them up in Nuevo Laredo, where they would have no telephone service to the United States. "Oh, my God," Mary Beth Rogers giggled to Dorothy and me the night the story broke. Cathy Bonner put together a campaign spot, Monte Williams provided the voice-over, and aides all over the state were racing to hand deliver the tapes to station managers and get them on the air.

Bud knew that now was the time he needed to come out of hiding and join her. In a fax, he proposed that he accompany her to another event hosted by Willie Nelson. She replied:

Bud m'dear. Don't know if we will connect by phone. I would love to have you take me to the Willie event tomorrow night. . . . Clayton Williams lost his cool today—big time. You're still #1. Ann

Then almost in the next breath, it seemed, she sent him a fax full of weariness, hesitation, and uncertainty. She was laying herself wide open.

Nose to nose: Ann Richards and Clayton Williams did not have a formal debate in their race for governor in 1990, but in Plainview that May Ann challenged the rancher and oilman and told him to pull down radio ads that questioned her patriotism.

Dear Bud,

It is almost midnight. Long day. Texarkana, Longview, Nacogdoches, Richmond, Angleton and Houston. Pay dirt today—Williams says he didn't pay income tax in '86. We'll see if it plays big . . .

It would be a treat for me to have you in the mayhem of election night. I'll be home in the afternoon on election day. Call and we'll plan.

Some of the kids and I are going to Padre Island after the election. Depending on the outcome I've been thinking about asking you to come for some part of the time and have feared that we might not like each other with constant exposure. Does that make sense?

I know that the root of it lies in the lingering anxiety I have about rejection. . . . The fatigue is invading my brain and this probably makes little sense but there won't be time to write from here on. I'll be home again Sunday night late.

It's great to come home to your fax notes.

Fondly, Ann

Bud later told her that he would be glad to join them at the beach, and would bring his sleeping bag, but for now, with a metaphor that mixed Texas hooey with a line from the Beatles, he emphasized that she had really scored this time.

Dear Guv:

Great going! I'm proud of you!

Keep pounding the little cowboy with that big Silver Hammer.

Don't let him get away with confusing his business losses with his personal income.

I was surprised to see you paid such a high percentage of income tax in '86.

I wonder how many billionaires paid 30 percent taxes?

None, I'm sure.

I could have fixed you up with my CPA and he would have saved you from paying the IRS anything in '86. Of course, you would now be a fugitive.

I'm praying harder than ever . . .

I'll see you Tuesday. Get someone to tell me when to show up and where.

Love, Bud

On election night, the Democrats' coordinated campaign made the Hyatt Hotel in Austin its headquarters. In one large ballroom, anxious faces and gulps of booze prevailed as the returns came in. Handsome Rick Perry, who proved to be no upstart, was edging ahead in the race for agriculture commissioner. With 99 percent of the precincts reported, Perry had 49.1 percent to 47.9 for Jim Hightower, ending the colorful populist's career in electoral politics. The office they sought had little relevance in the lives of most Texans. It was a historic race because one liberal Democrat's downfall was matched by the ascent of a conservative, new-born Republican who would never lose an election in Texas, and with much initial fanfare and subsequent flameout he would one day seek the presidency. Karl Rove had schooled Perry in his breakout campaign. He also guided Kay Bailey Hutchison to a win in the treasurer's race. The time would come when his two protégés couldn't stand each other.

In the lieutenant governor's race, Bob Bullock had bluffed, bullied, and out-hustled two attractive, younger opponents. McNeely and Henderson wrote that for almost three years he had run like a man possessed. The first credible challenger was a Democratic state senator, Chet Edwards. Mark McKinnon had worked for Edwards before signing on with Ann Richards. Bullock raised nearly twice as much money as Edwards did, and lined up an intimidating list of endorsements of elected officials. At the last moment, Edwards decided to run for a vacant seat in the U.S. House, which he won. "Thank God," McKinnon joked to McNeely. "It saved us from having Bullock tear off our heads."

George Christian, the veteran consultant who had been Lyndon Johnson's press secretary, was close to Bullock, and he feared the comptroller might underestimate the GOP's Rob Mosbacher, Jr., who grew up close to the Bush family; to burnish his governmental credentials, Bill Clements had appointed him chair of the Texas Department of Human Services. Christian urged Bullock to hire Jack Martin to run his campaign. He argued that bringing in Martin, who had run Lloyd Bentsen's campaigns, would signal Bullock's alignment with the party establishment. Bullock consented to a meeting, and then, to Christian's astonishment, he tore into Martin. Christian said Bullock "chewed Martin out worse than I ever heard a man chew out another man." Consider for a moment: that came from a man who had witnessed LBJ's tantrums.

But that was often Bullock's perverse way of measuring a new acquaintance. He hired Martin to run the campaign. Geared up for a vicious fight, Mosbacher ran an ad with a photo of "old Bob Bullock," who wore a hearing aid, with his hand cupped behind his ear. Bullock countered with taunts of "Little Lord Fauntleroy" and an ad with a soft-looking child moving to knock down a sand castle as a voice-over blamed Mosbacher for a $340 million budget shortfall at the agency he chaired. Bullock's ads blamed Mosbacher for oil spills in the Gulf; the only basis for that was a barge company owned by the Republican's father. In the end, Bullock won the heated duel by 260,000 votes, a majority of 51.7 percent—and 75,000 more votes than Ann Richards received. Everyone said the lieutenant governor in Texas had more power than the governor. And Bullock had the votes to start proving it.

The morning of Election Day, a former county judge from West Texas named Bill Young was holding down his job in the veterans programs division of the General Land Office. The judge and others liked to hang out in the speechwriters' office, because we closed the door when we wanted and we didn't mind them smoking in there. Dorothy was pretty confident that she would be on the governor's staff if Ann won, but she would be jobless if her boss lost. Young told us he always consulted a favorite barber on the morning of important elections, and in the course of our jitters during those hours when nothing about an election is known for sure, he walked in, took off his cowboy hat, and told us the unscientific polling result was in. Jim Hightower and the Democrats' treasurer candidate were in trouble, the barber figured, but he said that when he got in the voting booth and started to vote in the governor's race: "I looked at that ballot, and the face of that ignorant son of a bitch just *swum* up at me."

Clayton Williams's election-night affair was by invitation only, and when he came down to concede, a torrent of catcalls and slurs erupted when he spoke Ann's name. It angered him, and he snapped, "Now . . . now . . . you owe me that courtesy!" The rich old-boy establishment in Texas was coming apart on live television; the candidate was having to shout down his own supporters.

A short time later, Ann climbed on a stage and in exultation jammed her fist high in the air. She grinned and held up a T-shirt with an illustration of the Texas Capitol with the caption "A Woman's Place Is In the Dome." The explosion of noise was deafening. On the floor beneath the new governor, I saw Cinny Kennard, who had been one of the leaders at the mauling of Ann after the Dallas debate—the reporter we called the Red Dress. For the occasion, she again wore red. She looked forlorn and lost.

From left, Richards aide Don Temples, Bud Shrake, Ann Richards, and her son Clark Richards watch the returns in the race against Clayton Williams. Austin, 1990.

*The newly elected governor of Texas holds up for her joyous supporters a
T-shirt that became ubiquitous in the final days of her 1990 campaign.*

The next morning, the *Dallas Times Herald* headline declared, "Ann Whups Him!"
True enough, but it was no landslide. A Libertarian candidate denied her a majority; she finished with 49.6 percent of the vote. But 99,239 more Texans believed
the liberal grandmother from Austin made a lot more sense than the conservative Midland oilman and cowboy. Many of her voters were middle-class women
who couldn't wait to get to the polls and send that perceived yahoo back out to
his pipelines, whirlwinds of dust, and creosote bushes. Ann had come from a
long way back and run a stellar finish, but she also benefited from one of the
most spectacular self-destructions in Texas political history. Williams had spent
approximately $22 million, including $8 million of his own money. He was no ignorant fool—he was just out of his element. "I'd shoot myself in the foot," he later
reflected, still with that infectious grin. "Then I'd load 'er up and blast away again."

Jim Hightower's concession in the Capitol the morning after the election was
short and sad but good-natured. He described his feelings sagely: "One day you're
a peacock, and the next you're a feather duster."

When Bob Bullock made his appearance in the Senate chamber, John Sharp,
the new comptroller, and Dan Morales, the new attorney general, were eager to

stand close to his side. Sharp presumed to give the smaller man a friendly hug. Bullock's expression went ice cold.

Ann also held her press conference in the Senate chamber. The room was packed as she slowly made her way through the applauding crowd. It was a cold day, and most of the people were bundled up in coats. The crowd of reporters around the microphone tried to back up and give her room, as if in recognition of her revised status. In the front of the pack was the *Houston Chronicle*'s dark-haired, mustachioed R. G. Ratcliffe. He had been laughing with us as hard as Ann and Monte Williams and everyone else that first night at the beer and fish joint on the boat trip, but he had gone after Ann and other elected officials with skill and doggedness that was unmatched by his colleagues in the Capitol press corps. Ann threw her head back on seeing him, they traded smiles, and she said, "O ye of little faith, R. G."

That week, Bud Shrake had promised to attend a Fort Worth reunion at his alma mater, TCU. Once more at an important time he was away from her. Ann's fax read:

Dear Bud,

The crown got heavy today. No list of things that *must* be done. No hourly frenzy. I tried some Christmas and inaugural shopping for the family but I could not get much done for shaking hands. I feel trapped in the house and outside too. All of this will take some getting used to—and I am a little frightened.

Just got back from the Claus and Sunny von Bülow movie and it was surprisingly good. I went with my friend Pat Cole—another manifestation of my weird state of mind is that I don't feel like I have anything to say—even to old friends. I'm tired of talking about the race. Transition talk spurs gossip or breaks confidences and I think I am tired of being entertaining.

I'd *love* to go to the movie Sunday. What time shall I expect you? I only wish it was not such a long time until then.

Maybe I'll clean out some closets.

Love, Ann

PART FOUR

The Parabola

Accompanied by her children, Governor Ann Richards exchanges grins of delight with Texas Supreme Court Chief Justice Thomas Phillips immediately after voicing the oath of office.

CHAPTER 20

The New Texas

SPIRITS RAN EXCEPTIONALLY HIGH in the days after the election. Unfortunately, for those of us who still drank, the last of Austin's Raw Deal saloons and chophouses had run its course during Texas's economic bust of the 1980s. It would have been so fitting if Ann's electoral career had come full circle in the joint where she was sworn in as county commissioner. One of the Raw Deal partners, the ribald sometime artist Fletcher Boone, had found needed work in the treasurer's mailroom. Bud suggested that as governor, perhaps Ann could offer him other options. "Dear Gov," he wrote. "Good morning to the Renaissance! Now that we've got one, I'm going to learn how to spell it. . . . How about Fletcher for Wrestling Commission?"

Ann faxed him back: "Fletcher would be dynamite on the Board of Barber Examiners. No work, some pay. Wrestling Commission, [he] might become embroiled in the dwarf tossing controversy."

A week after the election, Ann sent Bud a note remarking that her longtime hairdresser Gail Hewitt had been besieged by requests for interviews and by the scramble for access to the new governor. Asked how she made Ann's big hair stand up so well, Gail had told Ave Bonar, a photographer, "I rat the tar out of it. Then spray the hell out of it. We defy gravity." Other calls to the beauty parlor required evasive activity.

Bud initially accepted the invitation to join Ann and her family at the beach retreat, but then didn't make it, and she made him pay for it in small ways: "Hi

Bud—I found someone to go to the movies. I'll be home tonight about 8 p.m. or in the morning. The gulls missed you. A."

Bud was getting enough intrusions on his routine to make him testy. He was asked to line up Willie Nelson, Kris Kristofferson, Johnny Cash, Asleep at the Wheel, and many more musicians for the big blast of an inaugural party; the political folks who passed on these requests obviously knew very little about the minds and habits of musicians. Back in Austin after traveling, he was delivered another order, this one from the comely wife of Jerry Jeff Walker, or Jackie Jack, as Bud nicknamed him. He complained about it amiably to Ann:

Dear Gov:
When I returned home I found another assignment from Susan Walker. You know how I love assignments.

This one is to get you to a boot shop to have your feet measured for some fancy custom-made cowboy boots that are a gift to you from Susan and JJ, Jap and Phyllis, Sally and Bill Wittliff, and Jody [Gent] and me.

I said, "The one in the boots lost."

Susan said, "Don't be so stupid, the Governor of Texas must have cowboy boots ready by inaugural time." I said I had never seen you wear cowboy boots and doubted if you would want them, though you would no doubt gracefully accept them.

She said, "Well, these are great boots," and that I had better ask you, or else. . . . JJ is going to design the boots himself.

Maybe they're protection during our dancing things—in case I nail you with a spiked heel.

On the other hand, what do I know? Except I'm accepting no more assignments, regardless.

Love, Bud

Bud was correct; the polite reply went back that Ann would not wear the boots if she had them. (Then again, when she practiced firing a handgun under FBI tutelage, she wore a tight pair of blue jeans and bright red cowboy boots.)

Days later she got a reasonable request from Bud, and a present, and she began to let go of small squabbles and her insecurity. She addressed her letter to him as if to George Bernard Shaw and signed it "Mrs. Patrick Campbell," referring to the actress with whom Shaw conducted a forty-year correspondence.

Dear Mr. G. B. Shaw—

Who felt safer in print than in person. Of course I'll call your aged friend—he will go into the teetering stack, and I am wise enough to know that he won't be the last to get to me through you.

The mailbox got so full during my absence that they took my mail back to the post office and now delivered it in a *huge* box. Your silver chain was amongst. I like it better and will give the other back.

If you will call me, we will discuss Thanksgiving, [going to the play] *Greater Tuna*, AA, etc. I don't have time to keep writing.

Mrs. Patrick Campbell

During the holidays Gary and Phyllis Cartwright invited Dorothy and me over one evening. As demonstrated by his performance with Willie Nelson on their wedding night, Jap was given to spontaneous bursts of song. On a balcony overlooking the Zócalo, the great square in Mexico City, we once watched him stand like a king or dictator and sing "The Internationale" as a band was playing. This night as Ann and Bud came through the door, Jap waved his arms and sang, "It's the governor! It's the governor! It's the governor!" Dressed to the nines, Ann laughed so hard she nearly tottered into the Christmas tree.

On Christmas night, Ann and Bud celebrated together; he had received another fax from her that day:

Bud—A couple of years ago there was a ceremony at the little church on the square in Laredo. It was in honor of an icon that travels to Texas once a year from Mexico. I had a long talk with the Virgen do los Lagos about the governor's race. Since she made a miracle for me, perhaps she will do the same for you or at least keep you safe from tigers and recovering women.

Love, Ann

Mary Beth Rogers whooped with laughter when I asked her how the Richards team had made the transition from politics to governing: "We were so far behind that we hadn't given much thought to what we'd do if she won."

But for nearly two years their minds, memos, and speeches had been drummed full of policy needs and initiatives—they just had realistic doubts that they would ever be in a position to implement those ideas. After the card games and reading and walks on the beach with her family, Ann and her inner circle had gathered in condominiums on South Padre Island. Ann often said, "Sometimes you'd rather set your hair on fire than go to another meeting." But she was disciplined. The sessions on South Padre were in dead earnest. After all the effort and stunning success, Ann's team had to deliver.

Most of the participants in the South Padre sessions were women who had played leading roles in getting her elected, including Jane Hickie, Suzanne Coleman, Pat Cole, Cathy Bonner, and Claire Korioth. Mary Beth led them through flip charts on goal after goal, and when they came back to Austin, she wrote a thirty-day plan. They continued with a series of meetings with state auditors at the office of Jack Martin, whose power, gravitas, and fund-raising mastery had flowed from his close relationship with Lloyd Bentsen. According to *Texas Monthly*'s Paul Burka, on just the third day on South Padre, the subject swung to politics in 1994.

Jack Martin . . . posed the initial question: Do you plan to run again in four years?

The implications were clear to everyone in the room. Richards was the first person from the liberal wing of the Democratic party to be elected governor since the early days of the New Deal. . . . Did Richards want to stock the government with her buddies, declare war on business, come out swinging for an income tax, and retire, voluntarily or involuntarily, after four years? Or did she want to govern in a more pragmatic way?

Her answer was immediate: Yes, she wanted to run for reelection.

In the last stretch of the campaign against Williams, Ann had started wrapping up her speeches with the promise: "Come January, you and I will meet on the Congress Avenue Bridge. Together, we will march up the avenue arm in arm—and we will take back the Capitol for the people of Texas."

From all over the state, thirty thousand people assembled to be a part of that march on the cold, blustery morning of January 15, 1991. The crowd assembled at the south end of a Congress Avenue bridge that would one day be named for her, and then she strode out among them and led a multiethnic throng on a twelve-block hike to the grounds of the Capitol. She walked with her mother; her children; her son-in-law, Kirk; her grandchild, Lily. Back in March, someone had called the Austin Police Department and Southwestern Bell with a threat that Ann was going to be shot. Under the new governor's white wool coat, state troopers had fitted her with a bulletproof vest. It was a sensible precaution, but it was hard to imagine anyone harboring such dark thoughts that morning.

The marchers were singing, yelling, and skipping arm in arm. As we passed through downtown, I glanced above the sidewalk at the windows of one of the office towers. White guys in suits and shirtsleeves were looking down and smiling, charmed by the spectacle, willing to give her a chance.

Hardly anyone who witnessed Ann's inauguration has any idea of what she said in her speech on the steps of the Capitol. "Welcome to the first day of the New Texas," she began, "and welcome to the official representatives of thirty-five countries and the governors of the four Mexican border states who have joined us. ¡Bienvenidos, amigos!"

Her New Texas had begun as an ad man's lame creation, and on first hearing of the idea, she asked, "What the hell does that mean?" But now she promised that barriers of race, color, gender, and sexual preference would fall away, and that the doors of state government would swing open with opportunity for all. It was going to be a state with clean air and water, good jobs aplenty, help for those in need, and a public education system that enabled all children to attain the full promise of their lives. She wound it up in cadences she employed when she spoke to the congregations of black churches: "And I hope that as we invoke the blessing of God in the questions we must ask, in the words of the old gospel song, may the Lord lift us to higher ground, and that we can be wise enough and strong enough to do what we have set out to do."

The speech contained just one concrete proposal—the creation in her office of an ombudsman who would respond to people's complaints about state government. But Ann's first speech as governor has not been forgotten because of the vagueness or clichés. No one could *hear* it. A smart-mouthed woman had come out on top of what was then the most expensive gubernatorial race in the nation's history, and she was a national figure now, the politician as celebrity. Intent on scooping the image of her ascent to power, one television-news crew ignored its competitors' restraint and continually hovered in a helicopter over the Capitol's pink granite dome. The roar and echoed whacking of the rotors was like the opening credits of the sitcom M*A*S*H*, without the bittersweet score.

Still, anyone who doubted that Texas government had changed would have been convinced by following a group of Ann's aides into the Sam Houston State Office Building after the speech. Those aides included my wife, Dorothy; I jogged along with them. Their attire ran to jeans, sneakers, and the campaign's satiny blue and white windbreakers, modeled on those of the Los Angeles Dodgers. The jabbering crew ran along a corridor to a set of elevators; they were eager to claim their new desks and offices and *get started*. As the elevator doors opened, they lurched one step forward and then braked. The newly hired Richards staff stood face-to-face with aides of the outgoing governor, Bill Clements. Riding

Bud Shrake and newly elected governor Ann Richards proceed in formal dress between the ranks of an honor guard of National Guardsmen at an inaugural ball, January 1991.

the elevator for the last time as the governor's staff, Clements's aides were well-groomed men in suits, all of them white, all carrying briefcases. They took one look at the new crowd in power and blanched. They slipped past without a word, awaiting another election, a new day.

Ann was not the only Texas politician who made a speech on the Capitol steps that day. The marked distance that Bullock had kept from Ann's campaign had drawn considerable notice and comment. But when Bullock had come back from his necessary enrollment in drunk school, Ann was the first one to welcome him and counsel him about the new world of sobriety. And that night at the inaugural balls, the new governor and lieutenant governor put on a show that was almost mushy. Ann said of Bullock, "He knows more about government than I could learn in a lifetime," and he introduced her as "her excellency, Ann Richards, my love."

Austin's downtown hotels had long hosted balls following gubernatorial inaugurations, but the city was not accustomed to seeing the festivities extended into presidential-style galas. People outside the University of Texas's basketball and concert arena, the Erwin Center, were hawking cotton candy shaped to resemble Ann's hair. (One could wonder what its namesake Frank Erwin, the late LBJ confidant and onetime drinking pal of Ann, would have thought of all that.) Dolly Parton flew in for the festivities and quipped to a *Houston Post* reporter, "Ann and I have a lot in common. We both have a heavy load on our shoulders." Ann looked out at one of the crowds and drawled, "This proves what Mae West said. And that is, too much of a good thing can be *wonderful.*"

That night, Ann wore a floor-length rose-colored gown designed by the Texan Michael Casey. Bud Shrake was comfortable in a tux, but ever since she had won the election, he had feared he couldn't do a passable waltz. They took to the dance floor at the first ball, flanked by squads of young soldiers in dress whites who were holding sabers pointed upward at their jaws in a stance of utmost attention. Bud said that when she looked up and moved in his arms, it was like they had been waltzing together all their lives.

Ann declared that the former Flying Punzar, Jerry Jeff Walker, performed her favorite act of the night. He and the Lost Gonzo Band brought down the house by singing and playing Ray Wylie Hubbard's anthem of the cosmic cowboy seventies, "Up Against the Wall, Redneck Mother."

The rebels and Mad Dogs were winners at last.

Proud parents: Cecil and Iona Willis at the time of their daughter's election as governor of Texas.

CHAPTER 21

Fast Start

"THE AMAZING THING ABOUT ANN'S ELECTION," mused her former husband, David Richards, "is that it could have happened at all. It wasn't like she had been patiently working her way up through the Yarborough liberal wing or any other faction of the party." Politically, the word "liberal" was now almost a curse word in Texas; electoral power was swinging fast toward the conservative wing of the Republican Party, which had been a boutique gathering thirty-five years earlier. President Lyndon Johnson is often quoted for his belief that by signing the Civil Rights Act and the Voting Rights Act, he had delivered the South to the Republican Party for a generation. But in his home state of Texas, perhaps, the election of Ann Richards as governor had called that into question. The pragmatist governor that Paul Burka and other centrist pundits raised as a standard was always LBJ's understudy, John Connally. Ann was not going to go down the path of that snob and strikebreaker, but Connally epitomized another truth about the governor's office: those who delivered on their promises were ones who used personal charisma to its best advantage. Though it had been bludgeoned almost out of sight by the brawls on the campaign trail, Ann did have that going for her.

And she had plans to turn Texas government on its head. Ann and her team wanted to do it with the staff they were recruiting, and they also knew that the governor's power to make appointments belied the conventional wisdom that it was mostly a ceremonial office. They wanted to consolidate the byzantine boards and commissions, and they wanted to enforce the changes they desired by eliminating the staggered terms of those officials. This part of the agenda was nothing new; the system stymied all governors in their first terms by making them play tug-of-war with agency heads who owed their appointments and loyalties to a predecessor.

As her team was being put together, areas of responsibility and top management were assigned to women who had driven her campaign. Mary Beth would again be her chief of staff, and Suzanne Coleman continued to be the indispensable lead speechwriter. Jane Hickie took initial charge of appointments, and Claire Korioth managed the transition. Susan Rieff was a skillful environmental specialist who had backed out of a job she had accepted on the staff of Bob Bullock so she could work for Ann. It was no coincidence that he gave her almost continual grief. Pat Cole oversaw social services, Sonia Hernandez took the lead on education, and Cathy Bonner was assigned to find ways to clean up a junket-crazed Department of Commerce that had spun out of control under Clements.

Annette LoVoi and Rebecca Lightsey had worked for a nonprofit consumer protection organization during the campaign (and their embrace of Ann's candidacy infuriated Jim Mattox, who had made consumer rights a hallmark of his time as attorney general). Annette's job was to analyze and respond to citizen complaints, launch investigations when necessary, and focus particular attention on problems that had arisen concerning the Texas Alcoholic Beverage Commission and the regulation of nursing homes. She was soon fielding two hundred gripes about state government a week. Rebecca came aboard as assistant general counsel charged with helping reform the state's insurance industry. She had testified several times before the insurance commission and offered some sharp remarks about its operation, so the hiring of a consumer advocate sent a jolt of alarm through the board and an agency that for decades had agreed to whatever the insurance companies wanted. She found herself immersed in disagreements related to car insurance rates and policy cancellations, the safety of railroad crossings, and allegations of child abuse and unpaid child support.

Joy Anderson was deputy chief of staff, again employing her legislative skills and also working with Nancy Kohler to keep the governor's scheduling manageable and efficient. Mary Beth told Dorothy they wanted her to serve as deputy director of the Criminal Justice Division of the governor's office. Former cops prominently staffed that clannish outfit. Millions of dollars flowed through it in the form of federal grants for law enforcement and the war on drugs. Narcotics task forces that crossed county lines and local jurisdictions were funded by such grants, and were always skirting some kind of trouble. Ann and Mary Beth told Dorothy they wanted someone who would keep close tabs on all that money.

And they took pleasure in the prospect of those hard-bitten ex-cops reading the resumé of this new superior and discovering that for several years she had been employed by a branch of the American Civil Liberties Union.

The coterie of impassioned women was no welcome sight to the old-boy types who had long ruled the legislature and the lobby. But there were plenty of able men on Ann's team. Her press secretary, Bill Cryer, and the financial whiz Paul Williams came over from the Treasury and assumed important roles in Ann's inner circle. Williams would later serve as one of Ann's chiefs of staff. The governor's legislative director was traditionally a former legislator; that job first went to Jim Parker, a genial fellow from West Texas. Dave Talbot, the general counsel, was a droll black man who had practiced law for the state his whole career. Bill Ramsey was a gay-rights activist who had performed yeoman's service in lining up political support for Ann in metropolitan Houston, and he became one of her favorites—she trusted him to make sure her office attended to the needs of legislators whom they wanted to keep happy.

Ann's style of matching individual talents with staff needs was intuitive and unconventional. One political insider complained to me that no one in her administration was really vetted. Richard Moya, Austin's pioneering Hispanic politician and her friend and ally on the Travis County Commissioners' Court, had left government for a while and helped start a housing development company. The economic crash of the eighties drove him out of that business, and he took a job on the staff of Jim Hightower. He later recalled the circumstances of his hiring by Ann: "She called me one day when she was treasurer and asked me why I was over there working for Jim. She sounded kind of irritated. I said, 'Well, Ann, I needed a job.' She said, 'Okay, if something like that ever comes up again, I wish you'd call me.'

"Election night in '90 I was in the wrong ballroom at the Hyatt. Jim was losing to Rick Perry, and it was real gloomy in there. I was wondering what the hell I was going to do after the first of the year. Then after a few days Bill Cryer got in touch with me and said she was going to be calling. She said, 'What are your plans?' I told her I was just looking for a job. She said, 'Well, stop looking. I'll hire you.' That was about as formal as it got."

Moya was one of the deputy chiefs of staff working within the policy council headed by Susan Rieff. In the early days, Mary Beth issued orders about firings that were deemed necessary; later, Moya gained a reputation as Ann's hatchet man. He was also her guide concerning the politics of regions stamped by their proximity to, and shared ethnicity with, Mexico. "Whenever she was going to San

Antonio, El Paso, anything along the border, I'd go with her," he told me. "She liked to go to the dog tracks, and we attended some great *pachangas*"—Hispanic barbecues that mixed politics with music and booze, the latter of which they had to decline. "I'd quit drinking by then, like her. But it was a lot of fun traveling with her. One time we were in the Valley, and she had a meeting with some officials on the other side. She always had a couple of state troopers with her. They were still packing heat. I told 'em, 'Guys, you can't be coming over here with guns.'" That prohibition against American guns, which is hugely ignored by smugglers, is in the nation's constitution and is posted at every border crossing. He lectured the troopers, "This is *Mexico!*"

Ann knew she had to move fast in order to succeed. Her hires and appointments and policy initiatives were full of political dimensions, calculations, hunches, wagers—they had to be. Two days after the inauguration, she spoke at the swearing-in of John Hannah, her secretary of state, who was a former U.S. Attorney, three-term member of the legislature, and loser of the fierce 1982 attorney general race against Jim Mattox. Ann said that his principal task would be to help craft her ethics legislation.

A week later, she appeared at the Capitol swearing-in of Lena Guerrero, whom she had appointed to a vacant seat on the Railroad Commission. Guerrero had been a first-rate legislator, and no one could fault her quick study and her incisive votes regarding regulation of the oil and gas industry, pipeline safety, and the like.

The day after Guerrero's swearing-in, Ann was back at the Capitol in support of her nominees to the Texas Board of Criminal Justice. The one who caused the most stir was Ellen Halbert. In 1986, a man had broken into her Austin home, concealed himself in her attic all night, and then attacked her when her family was gone the next morning. In riveting testimony to the legislature, she had described the horror of her experience: "I remember the thoughts that went through my mind: 'Oh, God, please let this be a nightmare. Well, it wasn't a nightmare. It was real life. Through the next hour and a half I was raped, stabbed four times, beaten in the head with a hammer so many times [the doctors] were unable to tell how many, but they think probably eight to ten times." Ann couldn't have stressed more strongly her approach to violent crime than by making this well-spoken advocate of victims' rights the face and voice of her penal authority.

Ann also introduced at that press conference Halbert's fellow appointees: Josh Allen, a black contractor from Beaumont, and Selden Hale, an Amarillo defense lawyer and her new chairman of the prison board. Selden was a good friend of mine. The press release identified him as a former chairman of the Potter County Republican Party and a member of the National Rifle Association. That was true. But it was also a feint to the press, the legislature, and the public. Selden was reviled in some Amarillo quarters for defending in court a vicious and nutty criminal known in that locale as "the Nun Killer." When I met Selden, he was a cooperating pro bono attorney for the ACLU and a member of the NAACP. His wife, Claudia Stravato, was a senior aide to Bob Bullock. Selden enjoyed his maverick reputation in Amarillo; he often jogged his saddle mule down their street, past the houses of neighbors who included T. Boone Pickens.

Ann chose Selden in part because she trusted him to be her advocate in an attempt to settle a federal lawsuit that for years had resulted in the prison system being under the control of the federal judiciary. In 1972, a thief and self-proclaimed writ writer named David Ruiz had alleged that by measures of violence, overcrowding, and indifferent medical care, his incarceration in Texas amounted to cruel and unusual punishment. (The term "writ writer" refers to lawsuits written

Ann Richards and the Amarillo defense attorney Selden Hale, whom she will appoint to chair the Texas Board of Criminal Justice, strike a hunting pose in the Panhandle during the 1990 race for governor.

278   by hand.) Other inmates and President Carter's Justice Department joined a class action suit, *Ruiz v. Estelle*, and in 1980 the plaintiffs won. While appeals dragged on without resolution, the East Texas federal judge William Wayne Justice effectively ran the Texas prison system. Bill Clements's officials had spoken about giving criminals long hard sentences, but in order to comply with the overcrowding formulas set up under Justice's watch, many of those criminals were being quietly released through early "backdoor" paroles. The state also allowed felons to sit for months in county jails instead of bringing them promptly into the prison system after their convictions. County commissioners and sheriffs were in an uproar over the cost of feeding and doctoring them and protecting them from one another. Harris County took the lead in suing the state over the logjam of prisoners. No issue was more important to Ann than resolving those suits and correcting the situations that had caused them.

Selden giggled in telling me the story about his escorting the new governor on a tour of Amarillo's maximum-security prison: "There was a big sign over the main gate that said: 'No Hostages Will Be Allowed Beyond This Point.' What it meant was that convicts trying to escape should not bother attempting to force their way out behind a shield of hostages. They would get the hell shot out of them if they tried it, hostages or no hostages.

"Ann took great exception to that sign. She told the warden, 'I want that taken down. *Now*.' After she left, phones in wardens' offices were ringing and teletypes were clacking all over the state. 'She said that? She really did?'"

Another early hire arrived because of Hightower's defeat. Joe Holley was a journalist who had grown friendly with Ann when he was editor of the *Texas Observer*. Ann liked him because of complimentary things he wrote about her during her initial term as treasurer, and because he hailed from the same Lakeview outskirts of Waco where she had spent her first years. They spoke the same dialect, knew many of the same hometown stories. During the eighties, Joe had gone to California as an editorial-page director for a newspaper in San Diego. He managed a move back to Austin by landing a job with Jim Hightower, expecting that he would be writing press releases and research papers for the agriculture commissioner. But then Hightower lost his race to Rick Perry. Joe was wondering what lay in store for him when Bill Cryer and Dale Craymer, an ace budget analyst and another one of Ann's senior aides, asked whether he would be willing to digest her varied position papers and work them into a single document. He went off with a thick bundle of papers and delivered a tome that thrilled Ann and Mary

Beth. They titled it *Blueprint for the New Texas*. The document contained sections on eighty-two priorities.

Weeks later, the governor had Joe Holley working on the most important speech she had made since the keynote two years earlier. And this one was not show business. Texas was a mess, just as measured by the daunting lawsuits it faced. In addition to the prison court cases, Texas faced an uphill fight in another suit filed over reductions of payments to hospitals through its $2 billion Medicaid program. And just a week after Ann's inauguration, the state's supreme court held that the method of funding the public schools was unconstitutional.

"Ann liked the *Blueprint for the New Texas*," Joe said, "and she asked me, 'Can you make this into a State of the State speech?' So I took it home and made it into a speech. I'd never written a speech for anyone before. But as I typed, I heard that voice. It was the voice I'd heard all my life—not just the Ann Richards voice, the Waco voice. It's something different from the East or West Texas manner of speaking. Central Texas, I guess. I swear I could hear it through my fingers as I wrote it. I gave it to her and her staff. There was a lot of stuff to add, and I was concerned that it was getting unwieldy. Suzanne Coleman and I were working on it right up to the last ten or fifteen minutes before Ann went out to make the speech. And then I was mesmerized by how this woman could take those words and make them connect."

The new governor delivered a stinging, ambitious, bravura performance in her first State of the State address to the legislature. She began with an assertion that she would take her progressive cues from the revered Father of Texas.

> In 1841, when Sam Houston took the oath of office for his second term as President of the Republic, the frontier was still a dangerous place, only three or four towns had a population of more than a thousand—and Texans were in the midst of a gnawing recession. In his inaugural address, Houston faced the unhappy duty of informing Congress that the cupboard was bare; there was not one dollar in the treasury. Listen to what he told them: "Patriotism, industry, and enterprise," he said, "are now our only resources." . . .
>
> We will not sit back and let crisis overwhelm us. We will not wait until prodded by court order.
>
> We will be active, alert—as even the most conservative businessperson is alert, on the lookout for opportunities to make the business of government work better.

Texans will know that the reins of government are in the hands of officials ready to make the difficult decisions they were sent to Austin to make. They will see us making changes that should have been made a long time ago.

Those lines brought the first burst of applause. Then she bluntly shared her opinion of what Texans thought of their government and its officials.

They are suspicious about our motives, yours and mine. They are distressed about the seductive smell of money in the political process and the influence of narrow special interests. Sit in a barbershop some afternoon or on the stool of a small-town drugstore counter and listen to what the people say.

They hate the bureaucracy. They come to Austin looking for answers, for help, and what they get is the runaround. They get bounced from one office to another until their eyes blur and their feet give out. That is going to stop.

The chamber resounded with more applause and a few hurrahs. She said that the boards and commissions would no longer be allowed to go their independent ways. Chairs of boards and commissions would meet regularly with her as an Executive Council. By audacious fiat, she was pledging to transform the wide-ranging authorities into a real cabinet system of government. In this New Texas, she said, her appointees and staff would be guided by principles of public service and ethics, not personal gain, and would be sworn to eliminate inefficiency and waste.

She turned to the Texas Supreme Court's ruling that the system of public school finance was unconstitutional.

After all the years you have struggled with the beast of school finance, you know better than I do that it is a devil of a task. But the payoff makes all the effort worth it. We are working for that little guy who was carrying a Ninja Turtle backpack as he walked to school with his buddies this morning, past the ice houses and modest homes of San Antonio's West Side, and for that little girl in the saddle oxfords who rode with her friends in a car pool Suburban past the manicured lawns of Highland Park. For both of them. They both deserve a chance.

She was saying that the court's unanimous decision was going to force the legislators and her administration to confront the fact that the funding disparity was nothing less than a clash between those school districts that were privileged and those that were not.

You know, we have perpetrated a hoax about local control. The hoax has been
that school districts had control because they could assess and collect taxes. In
fact, state government usurped their power years ago with mandates that require local tax increases and regulations that turn local educators into Austin-
controlled robots.

She left a pause after throwing down those challenges to the legislators, and then
turned to the environment. Every major city in the state was dealing with critical levels of air pollution. In addition to threatening the health of its residents,
the pollution put the cities in danger of noncompliance with the Clean Air Act,
which could lead to a cutoff of federal highway funds. Texas was the worst state
in the in the country in the Environmental Protection Agency's inventory of toxic
polluters. She voiced support for land commissioner Garry Mauro's alternative-
fuels programs, especially the use of compressed natural gas as a motor fuel,
which could help urban areas curb the air pollution caused by vehicle traffic. She further praised Mauro's legislation regarding coastal protection and oil
spills. And she said her administration was going to close the "revolving door"
that shuttled former officials into cushy jobs with the industries they had been
charged with regulating.

In one of the thunderbolts that drew loud applause but also set some of the
legislators and lobbyists buzzing with concern, she promised:

> We are getting serious about hazardous waste. No more will hazardous waste
> facilities be rammed through the permit process, over the objections of local
> communities. No more will they be located near schools or residential areas or
> water supplies. We are calling on the Water Commission and the Air Control
> Board today to institute a two-year moratorium on permits for new commercial
> hazardous waste incinerators, cement kilns, or injection wells involving salt
> domes.

Turning to crime and punishment, she promised that the construction of prisons
with enough space for 27,000 new beds would be finished within the next two
years. (Twelve thousand had been built during the Clements administration.)

> But we will go further. We will ask the hard questions about the roots of
> crime—in social discontent and despair, in poverty, in racial oppression and
> ignorance, in suffering and deprivation. We won't excuse criminal behavior; we
> cannot wait until we understand crime before we protect our citizens from its

dire consequences. But we would be foolish if we did not try to dig up the fetid soil where criminal behavior takes root.

The day after Ann's inauguration, she and a small group of her policy advisers had decided that the first fight they were going to pick was with the insurance industry and the state board appointed by Bill Clements.

> Just last week, after I pressed the board to hold off on a 30 percent auto rate increase, they announced a delay so they could audit the data the industry had given them. Isn't that what they are supposed to be *doing all along*?

That line got the whoops of laughter Ann wanted. In a big chair behind her, Bob Bullock was watching with apparent admiration how the legislators watched her. She went on:

> The board's rubber-stamp increases have cost Texans millions of dollars. The board has also refused to protect consumers from failing and disreputable insurance companies. Its foot-dragging response to insolvencies has earned the ire of a grand jury as well as of independent management and financial experts. The State Auditor has warned that more than $3 billion in premiums are at risk today because of the state board's mismanagement. This gross neglect of duty must stop now.

Then came her boldest power play. She demanded that Clements's holdover appointees to the State Board of Insurance resign one week after her speech, and warned that if they did not, she would move to put the regulatory body under the direction of a conservator.

> I am determined that the State Board of Insurance will protect the public interest of Texans. Older Texans on fixed incomes, young families, small business owners—they all must be assured that the State Board of Insurance is working for them.

Many senators and representatives were on their feet, applauding. She challenged them to approve bills that scrapped the overlapping terms of boards and commissions and would allow future governors to appoint a majority of board members during their first year in office. She closed with an anecdote about her first days in office.

When I moved in the Governor's Mansion the other day I found a gallon of honey waiting for me. Attached to it was a hand-written note on a scrap of paper. The hand that wrote that note was old and shaky. It was written by a man who had worked hard all his life but didn't mind sharing some of the fruits of his hard labor. The note said, "We believe we finally have a governor who cares about ordinary people and the poor."

As we begin the task of building a New Texas, I promise myself one thing: I will always try to remember that beekeeper's hope. . . . I intend to remember that man and his hope that we will make a difference in his life.

In that speech, Ann reached for a great deal more than she could achieve, and she rubbed some powerful men the wrong way. Lieutenant Governor Bullock and a prominent senator, Lubbock's John Montford, were offended that she hadn't consulted them in advance about her threat to place the insurance board into conservatorship if two members did not resign. Bullock found out about it from a staffer the night before the speech. But the veteran reporter and Capitol observer Sam Kinch wrote that it was the most dramatic speech in Texas government since John Connally launched his administration in 1963. It was not the mark of a governor wounded by a brutal campaign and intimidated by poor opinions of her character in the polls.

The insurance fight proved ugly. Before it was over, dozens of employees of the insurance commission would be ordered to turn in their keys and pagers and be out of the building by the end of the day. Ann appointed her friend Claire Korioth to chair the commission and applied hardball pressure to get the resignation of holdover appointees of Clements. One of them was not just any Austin banker with a receding hairline. He was James Saxton, a former All-American running back for the University of Texas. He had been an undersized and electrifying jitterbug runner on the first national-championship-contending team of Darrell Royal, who contributed to his lore with a tale that when Saxton was a teenager working on a farm during the summers, he would jump off a tractor and run down jackrabbits for fun.

Symbolically, Ann couldn't have picked a more dangerous fight with the Texas establishment—with white males—than by singling out James Saxton. So this was what her New Texas was about, the old guard steamed.

Saxton stood his ground for a couple of weeks and then resigned, saying he wanted to spend more time with his family and wasn't cut out for politics. Ann wrote to a House committee with oversight of the commission and agency:

My interest is in having an Insurance Board that will be responsive to business and individual taxpayers in this state. During recent months, I have expressed concern about the direction of the agency and structural constraints that make it difficult for an incoming governor to change the direction of the agency without having a majority of appointees on the Board. Mr. Saxton's resignation will provide that opportunity and I am grateful to him for this decision. I have known Mr. Saxton for many years and consider him an honorable man of high integrity. My disagreement with the State Board of Insurance does not involve Mr. Saxton personally. I wish him nothing but good will in his future endeavors.

Her State of the State speech was a rousing success, but the insurance companies and the Chemical Council were gathering forces and lobbying money in preparation for a long-term battle. But Ann had done something extraordinary in just one month: she had completely reversed the public perception of a bloodied candidate who had things in her past she wanted to hide. Her public approval ratings soared higher than those that Bill Clements and Mark White had enjoyed at any time during their terms. She received more than 3,600 letters during her first month in office; they were flooding in at five times the rate Clements's administration had seen in the last year of his term.

Nine days after her speech, the *Houston Chronicle* ran a telling photograph about the permit request of a company called HIFI (Hunter Industrial Facilities, Inc.), which wanted to open and operate the state's largest hazardous-waste disposal site in an underground salt cavern between the small East Texas towns of Dayton and Huffman. The applicant maintained that the toxic waste could not possibly leak out of the cavern into the region's groundwater. But the Texas Water Commission agreed to the governor's moratorium on such permits for at least eight months, even if not the two years she wanted. This was not the kind of public-relations fight that a company like HIFI could win. The *Chronicle* photo showed two smiling children, a boy and a girl, running through a pasture with a large billboard in the background. It said: "Thank You! Governor Ann, for Protecting Our Children from Poisonous-Toxic Waste. Families Against Contaminated Environment."

CHAPTER 22

Ethicists

PAUL BURKA, THE *TEXAS MONTHLY* political writer, thought he was watching Ann destroy her political career the night of the debate when she refused to say whether she had ever used illegal drugs. What a difference a year could make: the magazine's headline over his story about her first months as governor sang of her as "Ann of a Hundred Days." Burka gushed that she was the first governor in "goodness knows when" to have a true vision for the state: "She has turned an office from one that's supposed to be weak—the Texas governor has no direct control over state agencies and doesn't even get to appoint a majority to their boards for at least two years—into one with muscle. . . . Ann Richards *is* a politician, in the true sense of the word—someone skilled in using the political process. She is the first governor since the fifties to push her agenda by testifying at legislative hearings."

Burka relayed some concerns, though: "The biggest threat in this regard [if voters ever get the idea that her values exclude traditional Texas notions] is not Richards herself but ideologues and advocates around her. Some are members of her policy council, a group of around ten staffers with individual control over areas like budget, crime, education, energy, environment, insurance, economic development, and human services. Any outsider with a problem in one of those areas has to go through the appropriate policy-council member. No one else on the staff is supposed to intervene; everyone has been admonished to 'stay in your lane.' This doesn't sit well with business lobbyists, who are used to dealing with fixers but—to hear them tell, at least—now find themselves forced to deal with purists."

Passing the torch of opportunity for women in politics and public service are, from left, Hillary Rodham Clinton, Ann Richards, and Lady Bird Johnson in 1993. Governor Richards introduced the speech of Clinton, who was then First Lady and later a U.S. senator from New York, presidential candidate, and secretary of state.

Nonetheless, Burka ended his piece with a scene in which Ann saw a group of friends at the Capitol, threw her arms wide, and hollered, "Isn't it great I'm here?"

She made speeches or took questions in press conferences thirty times in the first thirty-one days of her term. When she testified at legislative hearings, her aides made sure she was seated front and center. In addition to wrestling with issues as complex as prison crises, the financing of public education, and budgetary short-falls, she roamed the state addressing the Texas Chamber of Commerce, the Texas Abortion Rights Action League, the Texas Association of Rural Schools, the Communications Workers of America, a Boy Scout convention, the Commission for the Blind, the South by Southwest Music Festival, and the Texas Bluebonnet Queen pageant.

She stressed again and again that the top priorities of her administration were to open doors that had been closed, to bring new people with fresh ideas into leadership roles, and to serve as a model of ethics in government. She knew that her appointments were the source of her real power, and she put people with high profiles in important places. Frank Erwin had personified the old-school University of Texas Board of Regents. Erwin thought he alone ran the state's flagship university, and in chasing off a slew of gifted left-leaning academics who had been recruited by president and chancellor Harry Ransom, he pretty well proved that he did. Ann appointed as regents the Reverend Zan Holmes, a highly respected black Methodist pastor in Dallas, and Bernard Rapoport, who used the fortune he had made from a Waco-based insurance company to agitate for countless liberal causes, such as bankrolling the muckraking *Texas Observer*. Those appointments sent a message to the university's scholars that under her watch, the regents were not going to impose conservative political dogma and dictate the range of their teaching and research.

Ann was in a much stronger position than her narrow victory over Williams suggested, for Democrats held strong majorities in both the Senate and the House, and committee chairmen were willing to follow her lead. Ann blasted the Commerce Department's board and administrators for spending $16.5 million on European and other travel junkets between 1988 and 1991. Bill Clements had nominated his secretary of state (and gubernatorial also-ran) Jack Rains to be director of the department, and Rains had been one of the high rollers on those junkets. The Senate heeded the governor's wishes and "busted" his nomination. She said the treatment of Rains, like that of the insurance commissioner James Saxton, had not been of a political nature.

The loudest partisan exchange erupted over Clements's proposed appointment of Karl Rove as a regent of East Texas State University, which later became Texas A&M–Commerce. One might wonder why Rove would want such a backwater appointment, but he did. He considered himself an intellectual, and he was sensitive about failing to get a college degree while scrabbling his way upward in GOP politics. Senator Bob Glasgow, a Democratic former district attorney, took the lead in quizzing him. Without much success, Glasgow tried to get Rove to talk about the widely reported story that he had planted a listening device in his own office while working for the 1986 Clements campaign, intending to blame it on Mark White. But the politico grew flustered when Glasgow asked, "How long have you known an FBI agent named Greg Rampton?"

"Ah, Senator, it depends. Would you define 'know' for me?"

Glasgow said Rove knew what the word meant and pressed him to answer the question. "Ah," Rove said, "I know I would not recognize Greg if he walked in the door. We have talked on the phone . . . a number of times. Ah, and he has visited me in my office once or twice. But we do not have a social or personal relationship whatsoever."

Glasgow persisted. "Do you know why Agent Rampton conducted a criminal investigation of Garry Mauro at a time you were involved in [opposition to] that campaign? Why he pulled the financial records of Bob Bullock at the time you were involved in that campaign? Why he pulled the campaign records of Jim Hightower at the time you were involved in that campaign?" The committee chairman banged his gavel as the men tried to shout each other down.

Glasgow turned to higher education funding and the state budget. "Senator," Rove cried, "I'm a nominee for the board of East Texas State University, not the comptroller or Legislative Budget Board."

Laredo's Judith Zaffirini took her turn: "I was told that you made a statement that you do not expect to be confirmed by the Texas Senate but that you welcome the opportunity to 'confront' this Democratic body." Rove denied it: "I did say that I did not think I've got a particularly good chance of getting confirmed in the Senate, [considering] all your declarations that you've got twenty votes in your back pocket to bust me."

"I don't even have a back pocket, sir. My pocket's up front."

Rove's nomination received some Democratic support on the Senate floor, but was rejected by a vote of 16–13. "He's simply not qualified," Zaffirini stated as a parting shot. "It's not a question of vengeance or vendetta."

Opening up state government was the promise on which Ann best delivered. In the first 100 days of her term, she made 384 appointments: 192 men and 192 women. Fifty-four percent were white, 25 percent were Hispanic, and 21 percent were black. Those percentages roughly matched the state's demographics without resorting to quotas, she proudly said, and most were highly qualified for the jobs. (She had to hedge on that claim over a few who did not work out. Ann appointed a man to the Pest Control Board who was subsequently arrested for murdering his wife and burying her in an oil barrel in their backyard. An emissary from the governor's office hustled to the jail to see him and ask him to resign. At first the man resisted; he may have thought it would help to have his seat on the board as an inferred character reference.)

Despite the long friendship between Molly Ivins and Ann, Molly blasted Ann in one of her *Dallas Times Herald* columns for accepting $300,000 in campaign cash and loans from a controversial plaintiffs' lawyer and then appointing him to one of the most sought-after boards in state government. "Lest anyone assume that Governor Richards walks on water," Molly wrote, "I point out that among her many fine appointments is one big fat awful one, made for the tawdriest of reasons. P. U. This lawyer, Walter Umphrey from Beaumont, whom Richards appointed to the Parks and Wildlife Commission, has a grim environmental record. Talk about a fox guarding the hen coop." The man was notorious, Molly wrote, for destroying wetlands, which in his neck of the woods were customarily called swamps.

Ann had been fascinated by the workings of the Parks and Wildlife Department ever since she was the legislative chief of staff for Sarah Weddington, but for a while, that agency was a pain in the neck for her as governor. Ann was impressed and intrigued by the record of Andy Sansom, who had been director of the Texas Nature Conservancy and then had worked in purchasing parkland for

Unlike most Texas governors, Ann Richards often pressed her legislative agenda in person at hearings of the Senate and House. Here she discusses public education with Mount Pleasant senator Bill Ratliff, at left with glasses. Austin, 1991. Ratliff stunned and disappointed her in her 1994 race for reelection by calling a press conference and denouncing her for allegedly filling her staff with gay activists.

the state agency before becoming its executive director. Andy's office walls featured photos taken of him with the likes of President Bush; he was a conservationist Republican in the tradition of Theodore Roosevelt. "I had never met Governor Richards," he told me. "I had made some remarks about her appointees that got back to her. She called me in and said, 'Andy, I like what I hear about the way you're doing your job. But see, I have this philosophy—you do your job, and I'll do mine. Your job is to manage that agency to benefit the people, the wildlife, and the parks. My job is to appoint people to boards and commissions. Now if you can live with that arrangement, I think you and I can get along just fine.'"

Andy has a ruddy-cheeked, joyous grin. "I had a solid relationship with Ann Richards."

That spring, Ann appointed to the commission Terry Hershey, a well-heeled conservationist in Houston. In one public hearing, after listening to a staffer rhapsodize about the promoting of trophy hunting in Texas, Hershey said she wished the agency would "cope with hunters rather than encourage them." All hell broke loose among the legions of Texas hunters; Ann felt she had to go to a meeting of the commission to calm them down. The governor could go overboard in her mastery of old-boy horseshit: "I remember my father taking me down to the Bosque River to set trotlines—blood bait was the bait of choice in those days. And when my father had the opportunity to get on a deer lease, he'd always take me with him, and I remember those times fondly, with the smell of kerosene oil and wet wool jackets and gun oil mixed with tall tales and men's laughter. Of course, much of my courtship was spent cleaning birds that were taken during outdoor adventures with my future husband. And I might add that I hope to be able to take my limit this year."

That might have been true, but in David's many tales about outdoor adventures that I heard, he never mentioned firing a gun at anything. Still, she was an avid bird hunter, especially in dove season, which marked the end of summer. And she occasionally braved cold weather to hunt geese on the coastal plains and pheasant in the Panhandle. Those were great photo ops, with her out there in her camouflage shirt and cap, shouldering a gleaming shotgun.

Prominent friendships came Ann's way because she had been a leading public figure in Austin for fifteen years before she was governor, and people of national prominence were drawn to the city. The former CIA deputy director Bobby Ray Inman, for example, was one of her supporters. Barbara Jordan became a good friend of Ann's. She suffered from multiple sclerosis, which shortened her time in

Congress, so in 1978 she joined the faculty of the University of Texas's LBJ School of Public Affairs, where she taught courses in ethics and political values. (This was fitting, since Johnson had been one of her early supporters.) Ann appointed Jordan as her ethics adviser as soon as she was elected, and they became close. They were a whooping and commanding courtside presence during years when the University of Texas's Lady Longhorn basketball team was a national power. Ann told a story about going out to the house that Jordan and her partner, Nancy Earl, had bought on Onion Creek. The property was a beautiful hideaway on the southern outskirts of Austin. They walked and talked, getting away from it all. Jordan walked with difficulty, and one day on encountering an obstruction that a neighbor had put on her path through the woods, she fumed that it was nothing but racism and meanness. Another time, Ann said, they walked past the same spot, and she asked Jordan what happened in her trouble with that neighbor. "Well," she said in her magisterial voice, "that old man got sick, and he was old and weak. And so he died." She left a pause, then added, "And went to hell."

Ann's second major priority was ethics reform. But on this, she found that she could not just hold forth and expect the world to applaud. Ann and Bob Bullock wanted to create an ethics commission that would be independent of the legislature, that would advise lawmakers on proper behavior, and that would have investigative power. Ann presented a thirteen-point plan, but she wound up supporting a bill and proposed constitutional amendment authored by the Stephenville senator Bob Glasgow, who had taken the lead in busting Karl Rove. House conferees balked at several of the ethics bill's provisions, and the wrangling dragged on throughout the session. One major sticking point was House members' rejection of any cap on lobbyists' expenditures. Ann said she would veto any bill that did not have teeth, and tempers flared as no agreement was reached.

Ann's warning that she would immediately call them back in session if they did not send her a bill that she could sign heightened the pressure. At one point, Glasgow erupted at the governor, accusing her of hanging him "out to dry" by retreating on critical language defining bribery. The negotiators finally agreed that to make a bribery case, prosecutors had to present direct evidence—eyewitnesses, videotape, or voice recordings.

Bullock had reservations about the ethics bill, which came in just under the wire. Several of Ann's demands, such as requiring lawmakers to disclose their sources of income, were lost in the bargaining. But she said, "I take a lot of heart in having passed what is really progressive ethics legislation." Then she was blindsided by another member of her own party.

Though Ronnie Earle's wife, Twila Hugley, had drafted correspondence for Ann at the Treasury, and his daughter Elizabeth Earle was my wife's assistant in the governor's office for several months, Ann's testy relationship with the Travis County district attorney went back to her days as a county commissioner. Ronnie had grown up on a cattle ranch near Birdville (present-day Haltom City), outside Fort Worth. He played high school football with some distinction and was an Eagle Scout. After graduating from the University of Texas Law School, Earle was elected a municipal judge, and then served two terms in the Texas House in the seventies. He got along well with the conservative Democratic governor Dolph Briscoe, who supported his drive to free convicts who were serving insanely long sentences over minor marijuana convictions. That played well with Austin voters in the heyday of Mad Dog, Inc., and the Armadillo World Headquarters, and in an upset Ronnie was elected Travis County's district attorney in 1976, the same year that Ann was elected to the commissioners' court.

In the wake of the Sharpstown scandal, Briscoe supported Earle's founding of the Public Integrity Unit, which expanded his office's jurisdiction over offenses by state officials that might or might not have transpired wholly in Travis County. The legislature began funding it in 1982. Ronnie was a quirky Democrat and policy wonk who once prosecuted himself for missing a finance reporting deadline by one day; he pleaded guilty and paid a $212 fine. In large part, Ann owed her election as state treasurer in 1982 to the Public Integrity Unit's takedown of Warren Harding. Ronnie and Ann had plenty of things in common, but he once told me: "I don't think she liked me much until she quit drinking."

But that had been ten years before, and their most heated crossing of swords came at the end of the first legislative session when she was governor. In the first week of June 1991, after the ethics bill's passage, Ronnie wrote the governor and the members of the House and Senate a letter that bluntly challenged her and was at once made public.

> Dear Gov. Richards:
>
> The purpose of this letter is to provide you with an analysis of the ethics bill from the perspective of those whose job it is to enforce the ethics law.
>
> The most volatile issue concerning the subject of ethics is the gap between public expectations and reality. The result of that gap is a media bonanza, because conduct taken for granted in the capital community frequently is shocking to the public and is therefore news.
>
> That is the primary reason for an ethics commission: to provide a fresh

perspective from outside the capital community on the behavior of public officials.

Not only does the ethics commission created both by this bill and by the constitutional amendment not provide for a public perspective, it aggressively keeps outsiders' comments out by giving the legislature a way to silence complaints.

The legislature gets to hand-pick who will be considered for appointment to the commission, which then gets to punish those who file what the commission decides are "frivolous" complaints. Who would be willing to raise an issue in the face of a $10,000 fine? It is a standing threat to anyone who dares question the ethics of a member of the legislature.

. . . I strongly advocated creation of an ethics commission for years, but this is not an ethics commission. It is a new rug to sweep things under.

. . . Offering this analysis to you and to the public is not a pleasant duty, for I know how much you believe in effective ethics legislation and how hard you worked for passage of this bill. But after close and careful reading it is my opinion that this legislation is not in the best interest of the public.

It has been suggested that its problems can be fixed (if those who wrote it are given another chance in a special session). Maybe so, but that is a gamble with the public trust. It will require all of our best efforts to keep ethics legislation from becoming a cynical hoax.

Sincerely,

Ronald Earle

His most serious complaint was that the bill would make it practically impossible to prosecute lawmakers who took bribes or those who offered them as long as the money was reported as a campaign contribution.

The governor was furious, and with characteristic sarcasm she fired back the same day.

Dear Mr. District Attorney:

Your letter concerning the ethics bill is interesting in several respects, but after reading it carefully, I am left with the feeling that there is no ethics legislation known to government that would satisfy your requirements. In examining your letter, it seems to me that the only ethics commission that would pass muster is one that descended from the heavens, with the angels singing. In response to your concern about how members of the ethics commission are to be selected, let me pose a question: How can they be chosen without politics being involved?

If the commission members were picked by the governor and subject to Senate confirmation, would you also consider them "hand-picked"? Shall we elect them? If so, then elected politicians are the commissioners . . .

I was fascinated by your suggestion that there is something wrong with doing the initial stages of an investigation in secrecy—particularly from such a strong advocate of the secret grand jury process. An ethics commission needs secrecy at the initial stage of an investigation for the same reasons a grand jury does—to ensure protection of the innocent, due process, and to allow a full examination to determine if serious charges are warranted.

Frankly, the critique of the bill is much like the woodsman standing with his nose pressed against the tree bark, unable to see the forest . . .

I am sure that your letter was meant to be constructive and I appreciate that. We all acknowledge that there are matters in the bill that should be addressed in a special session, once the questions about the budget and government consolidation have been completed.

Like any other complex legislation there will continue to be future activity on this bill in the legislature, and by the ethics commission itself as it begins initiating policy.

We both know that neither this legislation nor any action by the ethics commission will supplant the activities of the District Attorney of Travis County.

Sincerely, Ann

For all her indignation at having her legislative integrity questioned by a local prosecutor, this was a problem for Ann. She regained some footing and leverage by calling on the moral authority of her friend Barbara Jordan, but Jordan's statement of support was quite measured: "On a continuum of ethics reform, the bill is a good place to start. It is not what I would have written, but I believe that, on the balance, it is a worthy effort."

As it happened, on that day of dueling letters with Ronnie Earle, she was scheduled to go to her hometown of Waco and address the annual reunion of the Texas Rangers, whose museum is located there. The Rangers had evolved from being paramilitary fighters of Comanches and borderland *bandidos* to ranking as the state's elite force of uniformed criminal investigators, a branch within the Department of Public Safety. In districts that covered multiple counties, they were called in to help investigate crimes that local authorities found too hot to handle. They were prized in many quarters as Texas's Stetson-wearing equivalents of the FBI. Ann was fully aware, too, of the Rangers' history of lynching and other acts of brutality during the Rio Grande border scrapes around 1900, and as intimidators when John Connally tried to halt the peaceful march on Austin of farmworkers from the Valley.

Her speech didn't dwell on those things, of course. She began by reminding them of questions Rangers had to answer in the old days: "'Can you shoot? Can you ride? Can you cook?' Those were the criteria of Texas Rangers a hundred and fifty years ago." She chuckled with the men and their wives and went on with self-assurance: "I'm pleased that retired senior Ranger Captain Clint Peoples, now in Waco after a long and distinguished career, is with us. I heard a rumor that this is the very same Clint Peoples who said during the governor's race last year that he would never support a 'petticoat governor.' It's good to see you, Clint."

Governor Ann Richards and Lieutenant Governor Bob Bullock strike a telling pose that signals the deterioration of their relationship during the second half of her term.

CHAPTER 23

Odd Couples

ANN SAID SHE HAD NO social life after she took office as governor. An Associated Press story on her first hundred days reported that she carried two hours' worth of paperwork to the Mansion every night, and according to her staff, she worked forty days straight between February and March 1991. "I try hard once a week to do something I think is fun," she told the reporter, "like go to the horse races, or go to a basketball game, or go to a movie, or something that's just what normal people do."

But she exaggerated that claim of her life being all work. At a movie matinee one Sunday, Dorothy and I saw Bud and the governor looking very much like normal people in the lobby. They were chomping handfuls of popcorn amid folks whose expressions ranged from startled to dazzled.

"How are *you?*" Ann greeted the ones who overcame their shyness and came up to have a word with her. She said it in a way that seemed to make them think she was raptly interested in their answers. Perhaps she was.

Yet in real ways, she had surrendered much of her freedom and privacy. She said that, at first, on Sunday mornings she would put on her bathrobe and slip outside through the Mansion grounds to get the newspapers, as she always had in her private houses. But one time when she did that, this man just appeared, looking like a derelict and talking nonstop, apparently with a gear loose. "All right, I'm going to have to have some security," she conceded.

The Governor's Mansion (which would be almost destroyed by an arsonist's fire in 2008) was ornate and gleaming—a tribute to nineteenth-century and early-twentieth-century southern style. The bed she slept in had been passed down from Sam Houston, the George Washington of Texas. But Ann was not a captive of the place. She brought to the showpiece residence her own wry touches. While interviewing Ann there, *Texas Monthly*'s Paul Burka encountered a green parrot first on top of its open cage, then hanging upside down, pecking at the bars. Ann told him, "That's Gracie. It's short for Amazing Grace." The rear stairs passed under a large print of an alleged quotation from Richard King, the frontier patriarch of the King Ranch: "People who come to Texas these days are preachers, or fugitives from justice, or sons of bitches. Which one fits you?"

In their communiqués by fax, Bud often added updates or gossip about Austin friends she didn't see much anymore. One concerned Jim "Lopez" Smitham, one of the partners of the late and lamented Raw Deals. "Lopez has a beautiful beard and Kerouac scowl—lost in the 50s, his favorite era. Maybe we should open a coffee house for poets and angry novelists. I could get angry myself, if I don't watch it."

He may have been referring to his roller-coaster ride as a screenwriter. As Ann was launching her gubernatorial campaign, he wrote her one day:

> I think I've taken about all the bites out of Hollywood I can swallow. And prob-
> ably vice versa. If you have a nice bank you'd like to have me run, please call. I
> wouldn't make foolish energy and construction loans. I'd give the money to Jap,
> so it stays in circulation.
>
> Sorry I missed seeing you. Know any rich good-natured women* who'd like
> to take care of me?
> *Or guy. This is the '90s already, isn't it?

But then the movie business served up a break. In the early seventies, Bud and Jap Cartwright had written a screenplay they called *RIP*. The central character was a Texas Ranger; the script drew on material they had observed or heard about during their crime-beat days in Fort Worth. It was often optioned, but they were turned down by one production company because the script contained a scene in which the Ranger got a confession out of a prisoner by "taking him for a ride." A studio executive said, "Nobody would believe that, not even in Texas." Was he being ironic? They shrugged and went their way, having learned not to brood too much over Movieland after the experience with Cliff Robertson as their convict bull rider.

Two decades later, the red lights suddenly turned green; the producer Stan Brooks started a company that would deal exclusively in television movies, and Bud and Jap found themselves positioned to deliver bankable stars, Kris Kristofferson and Willie Nelson. Kristofferson played the Ranger, Rip Metcalf, and Willie played a safecracker named Billy Roy Barker, who swore he was innocent of his alleged crimes and teamed up to help the Ranger protect his daughters from a serial killer who preyed on high school cheerleaders. It was not the best movie ever made. But *A Pair of Aces* (1990) scored well in the ratings.

In April 1991, Dorothy and I were invited to the home of Jap and Phyllis one afternoon to watch the sequel, *Another Pair of Aces*. Bud and Jap had graduated to the title of executive producers. A pair of state troopers accompanied Ann when she ventured out now. The ones we saw most often were tall, rangy Billy Rhea and his handsome black partner, Sam Maxey. In the new movie, Kristofferson got to play the love scenes, but Willie, whose character was now named Billy Roy Rodriguez, was on such a tear with his music that now he was billed as the higher draw in the film's promotion. I sneaked glances at Billy Rhea, who stretched out amiably in his chair and watched Texas's most flamboyant and unapologetic dope smoker enjoying his time as a movie star. I also watched Ann as she watched the movie. A couple of times, as the snappy comic dialogue sped on, her features seemed to restrain a wince. Billy Rhea later remarked that the governor liked a lot of movies that frightened him.

That year, Ann sold her house on Shoal Creek, and Bud gave one of her prized possessions a new home. Ann had bought a large abstract sculpture from their friend Fletcher Boone. Bud, along with Ann's sons, Clark and Dan, took on the task of moving the weather-fast sculpture to its new place as sentinel of Bud's home on Wildcat Hollow.

Dear Guv:

Muy implantes buenos!

This is an idiomatic way of saying the Boone stands handsomely in the flowerbed beside my front door, looking as if it has grown there.

Soon as Dan and Clark drove off in the red pickup, I let my dogs out the front door for what we call a "Runaround."

The dogs raced up the driveway, did a screeching U-turn, raced back, and started barking at the Boone!

But they like it now.

I like it, too.

Come visit it sometime.

I love you, Bud

Christmas 1991 found Bud off on some travel. He sent her a card that was captioned "Mad Dog Enjoying a Smoke."

A few laughs . . . a little music. . . . Thank you for the great stuff you have let me share with you. It has been an extraordinary experience for me—even more fun than running around with pro athletes or movie stars. Or musicians, I hasten to add. Feliz Navidad y prospero Año Nuevo.

Love as always, Bud

One of his roles was to shelter her from too many social demands by her old friends, and he admitted he valued the perks that came with the assignment. A few weeks into the new year, he wrote her about their joint invitation to a birthday party for Jerry Jeff Walker.

Dear Guv:

You are off any kind of hook tomorrow night. Susan [Walker] called this morning with another assignment (for me to get Dennis Hopper to come to JJ's birthday), and I told her I wasn't going with her group tomorrow night, no matter what. I said I no longer go out with anyone who can't park where they please.

Love, El Punzar

Friends of the pair wondered what went on between them when the lights were turned down low. Even Jap seemed to have no clue. Was it platonic? Did Sam Houston's famous bed creak when its occupants got rowdy? I figured then, and still do, that what happened in the governor's bedroom was none of my business. Their correspondence was voluminous but never explicit, yet there was no question their romance was profound. An undated card from him supplied a hint. Bud could have been a professional cartoonist or graphic artist, and in a hand-drawn mock-up he composed a pitch for a daring new magazine, the kind one might see in a publisher's office. If Ann still believed she had never gotten a love letter, she was one demanding soul.

In this issue
Endless backrubs
Constant cuddling
Willingness to talk about the relationship
Endless foreplay
Plus
More backrubs
Flowers for no reason at all
Romantic nuzzling
The sexual prowess of a jungle ape

Bud was sure enough of his place on earth that he was not ill at ease or too surprised to find himself seated beside Ann in the presidential library of Lyndon Johnson at a formal dinner honoring the queen of England in May 1991. Others at Table 1 were Lady Bird Johnson; Bill and Diane Hobby; the library's director, Harry Middleton; and Ann's old friend, the distinguished historian Standish Meacham. At Table 2 were the Duke of Edinburgh; Lieutenant Governor Bob Bullock and his wife, Jan; the Speaker of the Texas House, Gib Lewis, and his wife Sandra Majors; the *RoboCop* actor Peter Weller; and Nancy Lee Bass, the wife of Perry Bass, the Fort Worth oil and gas tycoon and philanthropist. Thirty more tables were populated by the likes of LBJ's daughter Lynda Robb and her husband, Virginia senator Charles Robb; Texas treasurer Kay Bailey Hutchison; former governor John Connally; the veteran CBS commentator Harry Reasoner; Ross Perot, growing more political by the day; and Ann Richards's first and only boss in politics, Sarah Weddington. President Bush and his family were not invited. That was explained as just protocol, a belief that those greetings should be arranged in the nation's capital.

At the welcome ceremony at the Governor's Mansion, the queen's visit was choreographed down to bobs and bows every five seconds. The matter of who sat where at the LBJ Library affair became an issue because a snub was perceived by the lieutenant governor's office. No offense to the Duke of Edinburgh, but the *number two table*? Drafted by a member of Bullock's staff, a bristly letter went out over his name to the governor's aide LaVada Jackson:

Regarding your call from Houston this morning and your and Cathy Bonner's confusion, please know that we clearly realize the Governor's lead role. It was not our intent to signify otherwise. It had been our understanding this visit was a mutual leadership function—a joint effort that involved the Governor, Lt. Governor, and Speaker. Since you indicated that that was not the case, we regret any confusion that was caused. We do hope, however, you will consider our request for some additional seating.

This was just what Mary Beth Rogers and Paul Hobby, the past lieutenant governor's son and the new lieutenant governor's chief of staff, needed—another spat between Ann and Bullock. But as the royal visit unfolded, the principal hosts brushed that conflict aside.

Ann was in a near panic because her voice was a croak; Bullock prepared to fill in for her. But she got over the laryngitis in time to carry on. The queen arrived with her husband in a carriage with a team of richly groomed black horses they evidently transported all over the world. Ann said she and the queen had a nice chat about horses. The outdoor reception for the royal couple took place on an uncommonly windy day. It was reported that the only thing that didn't flap or flutter was the governor's hair.

Bob Bullock had more things to be annoyed about than his secondary role in welcoming the First Brits to Texas. Suddenly, he spoiled for fights with Ann. In a story told by his biographers Dave McNeely and Jim Henderson, Ann asked Bullock and the House Speaker to come to the Mansion for Monday breakfasts so they could address pressing issues in the legislature: "After one breakfast, according to the House Speaker Gib Lewis, Bullock had about $100 worth of groceries delivered to the Governor's Mansion, along with a note: 'Next time, I'd like to be fed.'"

Bullock had nothing against the governor rubbing shoulders with movie stars and foreign royalty, if that was what turned her on. But he felt that when it came to actual governance, he was doing all the heavy lifting. Early in the 1991 legislative session, Ann had proposed a school-finance plan that would essentially be based on a statewide property tax. She dropped that like a hot rock when school boards, superintendents, and Republicans raised a howl and legislators showed no interest. And on schools and their performance, she relied on a New York educator, Lionel "Skip" Meno, to trim and reform the beast of the Texas Education Agency, which he was not able to do. Bullock scorned Ann for, in his view, hightailing it to the sidelines on public education. (And that view was increasingly shared by a parent and private citizen in Dallas named George W. Bush.)

As long as property taxes were the primary source of revenue for schools, students in the Edgewood school district in San Antonio (the lead plaintiff in the lawsuit against the state) were never going to have the equivalent opportunity of rich Dallas kids in Highland Park. Property taxes were determined by property values—it didn't take the best tax collector the state had ever been blessed with, as Bullock perceived himself, to divine the inequity in that.

Early in the legislative session, Bullock had gone over to the Governor's Mansion to meet with her and major newspaper editors and editorial writers. He climbed a few steps up the flight of the grand staircase and told them in his resonant growl, "Texas needs an income tax."

It was definitely not what the public wanted to hear. Paul Hobby told Bullock's biographers, "We literally had two fax machines melt into the corner over the weekend." Under fierce attack, Bullock declined to back off. He sent the newspapers an op-ed explaining the logic of his position: "Full implementation of a state income tax would let us completely eliminate the school property tax on all residential property. A Texas income tax would apply to people and corporations from out of state who do business and make profits in Texas. For the first time, out-of-staters would be paying a Texas tax on the money they make here."

Bullock embarrassed Ann in her own damn house, and she let him hang out on that limb and get blistered. She said she didn't believe an income tax was necessary, commenting accurately that the chances of it getting through the legislature were "slim to none." For Texas politicians, calling for an income tax was tantamount to throwing open the doors to vampires and werewolves. The only thing as bad was to oppose the death penalty.

From the outset, Ann had stressed that one of her most important priorities was to reorganize and streamline Texas's outmoded bureaucratic and regulatory structure. But only one major consolidation of agencies occurred, and Bullock quickly claimed that as his turf. Both the governor and the lieutenant governor backed a bill carried by Carl Parker, the voluble senator from Port Arthur, to create a new, overarching environmental department. Bullock wanted nothing less than a rigorous state equivalent of the federal Environmental Protection Agency.

Ann had started out with a bang on the environment—demanding a moratorium on hazardous-waste permits and the passage of a statutory no-hire policy to help slow the "revolving door" of regulators who made good contacts on the state's payroll and then became highly paid lobbyists as soon as they quit. I wrote the swearing-in speech of John Hall, her choice to chair the Texas Water Commission and manage its consolidation with the Texas Air Control Board, the Texas Water Development Board, and the Water Well Drillers Board, along with other areas of regulatory oversight, into a new Department of the Environment. One of her most praised appointees, John was a tall, deep-voiced black man who had grown up on a cotton and hay farm near the hamlet of Washington-on-the-Brazos—the birthplace of Texas government—and had worked in the Carter White House and for Senator Lloyd Bentsen; he had become my friend while he was the chief deputy of Garry Mauro at the General Land Office. My gaze happened to fall on a veteran lobbyist when John raised his voice and said, "The revolving door *will be* closed." The lobbyist shook his head on hearing that, and with a disgusted grimace walked away.

John's fellow commissioner Peggy Garner was an engaging woman with a dry sense of humor whom Ann had befriended when Peggy was a county judge in small-town West Texas. Ann also appointed Pam Reed, a smooth, attractive woman who had won the Travis County commissioners' court seat she once held. Peggy remarked to one reporter, "There have been nothing but all-Anglo male boards here in the past, and now here we are without an Anglo male. It's been quite a culture shock around here."

Though groups like the Sierra Club were cool and suspicious during Ann's campaign, she had won considerable credit for her record on environmental issues by the end of that first legislative session. Her efforts helped bring safe drinking water and sewage facilities to *colonias*. She championed landmark legislation that empowered the land office to respond to oil spills in the Gulf of Mexico and its estuaries in hours instead of days; the bill also established a fund to help cover cleanup costs, compensate Texans for damages incurred, and advance scientific research into the long-term effects, prevention, and remediation of spills. She signed a bill aimed at reducing municipal solid waste through novel programs to recycle or safely dispose of used tires, newsprint, motor oil, and car batteries. The moratorium she announced on the Water Commission's granting of new hazardous-waste permits drew raves from environmentalists. "This is sending shock waves through the environmental community because it's so sweeping and it happened so quickly," said Brigid Shea, a leading Austin activist.

But the EPA's Toxic Release Inventory announced once more that Texas had the worst record of all the states. A number of serious problems contributed to this unenviable status. An alarming legislative standoff arose over the Comanche Peak Nuclear Power Plant's inability to properly dispose of its nuclear waste. Similarly, the governor overruled a plan to put the low-level nuclear waste of other states in desert caverns along the Rio Grande, claiming it would endanger groundwater. And even though the quite conservative Texas Medical Association backed the Democrats' contention that children with asthma were placed at greatest risk by the state's urban air quality, the plan offered by Garry Mauro, the governor, and other key Democrats to utilize the state's wealth in cleaner-burning natural gas to essentially burn up the pollutants of coal fell by the wayside when consumer advocates and lobbyists for electric companies raised a howl that it would increase utility rates.

A second part of Texas's plan to reduce noxious emissions was to mandate the use of compressed natural gas as an engine fuel in state fleets of trucks and vans and public school buses, and to encourage the conversion of private-sector fleets that covered about the same route each day and could be accommodated by strategically placed refueling stations. The plan won the praise of the U.S. Senate majority leader, George Mitchell, of Maine, and then from President George Bush when he unveiled the 1990 renewal of the Clean Air Act, which he considered one of the highlights of his administration. Bush caused a stir in Texas when he targeted Houston, New York, and Los Angeles as the metropolitan areas with the most polluted and harmful air in the country.

Mauro's ideas and programs were twenty to thirty years ahead of their time, and though gasoline refiners and school-board transportation chiefs hated them, they were no pipe dream. The dominant motor fuel in Pakistan, for example, became compressed natural gas, not gasoline or diesel. In this country, the energy tycoon and corporate raider T. Boone Pickens promoted natural gas as a panacea and proclaimed himself the man with the answer to America's dependence on foreign oil. And in 2012, as this book was going to press, the GOP presidential candidate Mitt Romney made natural gas the linchpin of his energy and clean air policy. But in the end, Ann's dogged support of Mauro's ideas cost her plenty.

Adding to the mess, Bullock's style alienated House Speaker Gib Lewis and ignited talk of a feud between the two chambers of the legislature. As reported in the *Austin American-Statesman*: "Lately, in addition to irking some staff members of Governor Ann Richards, Bullock has gone to chewing the behinds of several powerful House members, and they don't like it one bit." He steered Senator Carl Parker's bill creating a new Department of the Environment to unanimous Senate approval, but the House offered a quite different bill. House members heeded lobbyists' pressure to strip a provision that would keep landfills at least 500 feet from residences and 1,500 feet from schools, and the new agriculture commissioner, Rick Perry, balked at losing control over the regulation of pesticides. The Democratic House sponsor of the bill, Bruce Gibson, claimed that Bullock finally said, "Just send me something." In joking contempt for his own bill, which he did not believe would pass, Gibson branded the new agency the Texas Natural Resource Conservation Commission—soon called, just to make sentences possible, the TNRCC. And that soon spawned the mocking nickname "Train Wreck."

John Hall got high marks on his performance from Ann, the business community, and the press, but he told me about being summoned to Bullock's office and tongue-lashed. His veteran staffers called the experiences "drive-by asschewings." The rebukes occurred often enough that John sought advice from Mauro, who was once known by comptroller employees as Little Bullock. Garry told him, "You've got to hire a Bullock-ite." John found one of these mediators, and his trips to Bullock's woodshed stopped.

Bullock's mistreatment of another head of an important agency would become the stuff of legend. Andy Sansom, the director of Parks and Wildlife, went to the lieutenant governor's office one day to discuss his agency's budget. Two cents of each dollar collected from the cigarette tax had been going to Parks and Wildlife; Andy had hopes of doubling that to four cents. But the Senate under Bullock's leadership had eliminated the funding arrangement altogether; the agency would now get zero pennies out of that tax dollar. John Montford, chair of the Senate Finance Committee, told Andy he had to talk to Bullock if he wanted to complain. He made the appointment and presented his case for how that revenue would finance the improvement of state parks, how they needed the resources to do a better job of managing the state's wildlife, and how it would fulfill the state's obligation to its many hunters and anglers.

Bullock chain-smoked cigarettes as he listened. He blew a stream in the general direction of Andy and said, "The cigarette tax should be earmarked for cancer research and treatment." Andy asked unhappily if any options were open for him. Bullock leaned toward him and suggested, "Suicide."

In the next session of the legislature, Andy had to go back to Bullock, braced for more punishment. After much jovial chat with the lieutenant governor about hunting and fishing, Andy feared they were running out of their scheduled time, and he reminded Bullock that the subject of their discussion was the Parks and Wildlife budget. Bullock shot up from his chair and said, "You're the most disloyal son of a bitch I've ever known. Get out of my office, and don't ever come back to this side of the Capitol again."

I asked Andy whether he ever found out what he had done to get thrown out of Bullock's office. He shook his head: "I think I was just in the wrong place at the wrong time."

Bullock wanted to create a budget policy committee composed of the governor, the House Speaker, and himself. When the legislature was in session, the committee would recommend funding priorities. But when the legislators were out of town—the majority of the time—then this powerhouse trio would have budgetary authority to do anything. House members declined to pass legislation that would put them aboard that. Bullock did not get laws passed that would have greatly increased his power, but neither did Ann. Mary Beth Rogers told me that except for the environmental agency nicknamed the Train Wreck, all their talk in *Blueprint* and the State of the State speech about streamlining and reorganization just went away. "Foosh," she said. "Never heard from again."

Jim Mattox had tried to rescue his gubernatorial campaign by advocating a lottery that would help finance the public schools. During her campaign, Ann regarded the lottery idea with distaste, but she spoke up for a lottery at a press conference fourteen days after she was inaugurated. She swore then that the proceeds would be channeled directly into public education. Yet when a lottery bill finally won passage and received her signature, it turned out most of the proceeds would be diverted into the general revenue fund. That was the state of affairs until 1997, when the legislature established the Foundation School Fund.

With the Texas Supreme Court's ruling on school finance hanging over their heads, legislators eventually arrived at a solution in which school districts with an abundance of property-tax revenue would share some of it, under a complex formula, with districts that had an abundance of broken-down old buildings, portable classrooms, and trash-filled lots. Residents of the wealthy school districts branded the compromise "Robin Hood," and the notion of robbing the rich to give to the poor was not as lofty sounding to conservative voters and parents of school children as it had been to young David Richards.

During her first year in office, the governor had to call four special sessions before she could wind up the state's business and send the legislators home. In April 1991, Comptroller Sharp's revenue estimators had claimed that the state was $4.6 billion in debt—and the Texas constitution required a balanced budget. Ann said she would not call a special session on the budget until July, when

308 a comprehensive audit of all agency spending was in hand. Tempers frayed. At a conference committee on the budget, according to Dave McNeely, Bullock dressed down Representative Bruce Gibson in front of legislators and lobbyists in language that was described as verbal abuse. Gibson told Speaker Gib Lewis, "I'm taking this personal. I've had it. You just don't treat people this way. I'm going to bust him." (One year later, Gibson accepted a job as Bullock's chief of staff.)

In the special session, Ann, Bullock, Lewis, and key staffers holed up in the Wynne Lodge on Matagorda Island to write a budget. There are no bridges or ferries to the preserve. Reporters and editors yelped about violation of the state's open-meetings law. Some of the journalists rented boats and tried to force their way through security. The state's leaders cobbled together a budget that featured sales and cigarette taxes, projections of escalating property taxes, and a lottery.

When they got back to Austin, according to Paul Hobby, Bullock called in lobbyists who had killed all tax proposals during the regular session, predicting that he was a sure dead-duck one-term lieutenant governor over his proposal for an income tax. He said, "The state of Texas has gone as far as it can go without additional revenue, and I am going to take a little chunk out of each of your asses and put a tax bill together. If you whine, I'm going to take a big chunk out of your asses. So you just decide what you want."

Whatever motivated Bullock, it was hard to lay it off on some secret compact with the Republicans. In the infighting over redistricting that year, he excluded and bullied GOP senators so rigorously and tried to protect Democratic incumbents with such a heavy hand that lawyers with the Mexican American Legal Defense and Educational Fund persuaded state judges that the plan undercounted minorities in violation of the Voting Rights Act. Because of a past history of discrimination, Texas was one of the southern states that had to win approval for its redistricting maps and plans from the U.S. Justice Department. Ann had issued a statement about how pleased she was that the Justice Department had preapproved the Senate plan, but now she had to call yet another special session, this time for redistricting. She didn't lay any public blame on overreach by Bullock in a January 2, 1992, letter to the *Dallas Morning News*: "Frankly, I do not see the issue as one of partisan disagreement: Rather, the issue is whether the State of Texas will surrender another area of local jurisdiction to the federal courts. The people of Texas are tired of court intervention and so am I." On a civil rights matter that grew out of racial prejudice and exclusion, the doctrinaire liberal was now taking up the banner of states' rights.

But before that special session could convene, a federal court imposed its own redistricting plan on the state. In the account that Paul Hobby related to McNeely and Henderson, the pressure and disagreement over redistricting brought his boss into heated conflict with Dan Morales, the Democratic attorney general. To protect Democratic interests and abide by federal law, Bullock had hired the best voting rights attorney and expert on redistricting that he knew—David Richards.

Hobby said that Morales first complained to him: "Paul, how do you think it feels? I'm supposed to be the lawyer for the state. These guys don't have the authority to hire separate counsel. We've got lawyers to do that. How do you think it feels to be the first statewide elected Mexican American and have this sort of slap in the face?"

Morales got the meeting with Bullock that he wanted. The lieutenant governor listened for a while, then got to his feet, bumped Morales in the chest (in the kind of antagonism I used to know as a rooster fight), and gave him a real slap in the face, though it was a light backhand. "You skinny-assed son of a bitch," he snarled, "you're squealing like a pig stuck under a gate."

Hobby jumped between them, wondering how in the world his life had come to this. Once, after getting home from work at one o'clock in the morning, he said this about his boss to his wife: "I might kill him. I might literally use my bare hands and kill him."

Not quite a year earlier, Paul Burka had lavished praise on the governor for her political skill, and so had his colleague Patricia Kilday Hart. But in October 1991, they sang a quite different tune in *Texas Monthly*'s critique of the Democrats' leadership.

> The best that can be said about the long struggle of the Seventy-second Legislature is that it is over. This was a year when the Legislature was as bad as the public has always suspected. . . . Eight months of work produced only patches on leaky tires: a school-finance law that hurts as many schoolchildren as it helps; new prisons but no change in the practice of crowding them with non-violent felons; and new taxes on the same old taxpayers.
>
> The Legislature . . . must be judged on the gut-check issues—and on these, it failed. The main reason why is that none of the legislative leaders was willing to demand that it succeed—not Governor Ann Richards, not Lieutenant Governor Bob Bullock, not Speaker Gib Lewis.

On a host of issues Ann Richards and Bob Bullock fundamentally agreed, and for years they had periodically carried on like good friends. I asked Mary Beth Rogers how things got so haywire between them. "I don't know," she replied. "I really don't. I know bits and pieces of it. Ann learned a lot from Bullock, and in the early days he was willing to teach her. I think it started when we were in the Treasury. It wasn't constant. They might have a tiff about something, but then it was over, and they'd be big buddies again. But I can't see into the mind of Bob Bullock. He was unpredictable. Bullock was the smartest man in state government. He knew everything, and he had all that power in the lieutenant governor's office. Yet Ann was out in the spotlight all the time—she was the star. And it came to a point of him thinking and saying, 'She doesn't know as much as I know.' Which was true.

"That first session, if Ann wanted something to happen in the Senate, she'd pick up the phone and call Carl Parker or whoever the lead senator was on a particular issue, and it just pissed Bullock off. He thought it was *his* Senate, and he felt that somehow she was violating the protocol. She was supposed to call him first. Bullock was learning during that first session, too. As smart as he was, presiding over the Senate with thirty-one prima donnas was difficult. He had to get all of them in line, which he did. He enforced his will; they used to come in and complain about it.

"Pretty soon, they didn't try to cut a deal with Ann without Bullock's knowledge and permission. I remember one time, we were trying to finalize something—I think on insurance. Some senators came over, and Ann said, 'Did Bullock give you the authority to make a deal?' They hemmed and hawed and wouldn't give her a clear answer. She just got up and left. Paul Hobby and I got along great. But it reached a point where there was just no communication between Ann and Bullock."

In the privacy of his chambers, the lieutenant governor referred to the governor and her staff as "a bunch of hairy-legged lesbians." Chuck Bailey was legal counsel for the lieutenant governor and later his chief of staff. "Back when they were still speaking," he told me, "sometimes I could sit there and hear them saying words, but I had no idea what they were talking about. I finally realized it was AA stuff, like they had some secret code. And there was something chemical going on with him. You could see it happen. He'd be all animated about something, and then his face would turn gray, and he would lose all expression."

He used to erupt and fire people without warning—tell them to turn in their keys and pagers and empty their desks, get out of his sight. In a morning or two, he would call them at home and ask them why the hell they weren't at work.

On one occasion, the governor came to his office alone to talk to him. He started in on some differences in policy, but soon made it personal. He commented on her appearance. Why, look at her legs, he remarked with disdain—she had a *runner in her hose*. "He knew what buttons to punch," Bailey said. "By the time he finished, she was in tears, she was so angry." Aides of Bullock didn't want the governor going out like that into a crowd of legislators, aides, lobbyists, and tourists. One of the state troopers made a call to her office and then ushered her to a private way out.

Governor Richards and her escort for the evening, Congressman Charlie Wilson, are greeted by First Lady Barbara Bush and President George H. W. Bush at a formal White House dinner.

CHAPTER 24

Favorables

IN LATE OCTOBER 1991, Morley Safer chortled, just beside himself, through a
60 *Minutes* profile of this new sensation, the governor of Texas. The liveliest exchange came when the veteran newscaster had Molly Ivins hooting and reminiscing about Ann with the Governor's Mansion in the background. The governor
burst out the front door waving her arms and laughing as she approached, but
there was a hint in her words of the tension between the two women. "Don't talk
to *her*," Ann yelled. "She makes it up! I'll tell you, Molly Ivins and I've been through
a lot together. When she tells a story I know she was there, but it doesn't bear any
relation to what *happened*."

Safer cracked up. "Ann, just a minute here, I'm trying to get a little bit of the
truth—"

The governor looked about in mock wonder, as if to the people who voted her
into office. "Well, y'all—he wants the truth and he's asking Molly!"

Paul Burka started his critique of the program with a jeer. "What a puff piece!"
It sure was that. But give Ann credit for knowing how to score some payback on
prime-time national television, and it didn't cost her a dime. The creeping frosti-
ness between Ann and Molly may have been simple jealousy over turf—which
one was the grande dame of Texas liberals?

That same year, in addition to the three or four newspaper columns a week
that Molly continued to churn out, she became a national figure in her own right
with her surprise bestseller *Molly Ivins Can't Say That, Can She?* (In a breakthrough
contract, Random House agreed to publish the collection of columns—a genre
famous for selling poorly—as a favor in anticipation of a long book on Texas

politics that she proposed but, in the end, never wrote, because her collections and collaborations with Lou Dubose sold so well.) There was plenty of ego and sarcasm at play in the relationship of Ann and Molly. Also, after the divorce, David Richards was a much closer friend of Molly than Ann was. In 1993, she devoted one of her columns to her admiration of him.

> One of my favorite David Richards cases was the tuba player who taught at the community college in Dallas. He had one tuba student for one hour a week and was paid all of $3.50. In those days, we had a lot of wiggy, leftover laws from the McCarthy era—in order to teach, or even attend, a Texas college you had to sign a pledge saying you were not now and never had been a member of the Communist Party, despite the fact that the Communist Party was perfectly legal. Now Richards' tuba player was not a communist (I think he was a Methodist), but he felt strongly that he shouldn't have to make any kind of political commitment to teach tuba. (Given our Lege in those days, we're lucky they didn't outlaw being a Republican: Come to think of it, not a bad idea.) The college wouldn't give the tuba teacher his $3.50, so David took the case (I assume for a handsome contingency fee, like half of the $3.50.) And lo, at long last, at the end of the legal process, Richards triumphed and got this silly little menace to freedom of thought removed.

On the greater arc of his legal career, Molly wound up that column:

> Richards has not only fought for freedom himself; he has inspired a generation or more of young lawyers to go and do likewise. During Jim Mattox's first term as attorney general, Richards was his top hand, and that office almost crackled with energy and idealism. Everyone who was there seems to remember the speech Richards made at a farewell party they gave for him. He closed with a favorite line from one of the Mexican revolutionary leaders, who had been offered a share of the spoils, a big hacienda, when it was over: "I did not join your revolution to become a hacendado."

Anyone reading Molly's columns on Ann's performance as governor would not sense the rift between them. Molly was generous in her praise, sparing in her criticism, and she made no bones about their being on the same side in the partisan trenches. But in private, they were no longer the soul sisters of popular perception, if they ever had been.

About the same time the *60 Minutes* profile aired, Mary Beth Rogers received a memo from a young pollster at Jack Martin's firm, Public Strategies, Inc., named Matthew Dowd. Martin had assigned Dowd the task of analyzing a poll of 1,000 likely general-election voters in 1994, which had been conducted by Harrison Hickman. Dowd wrote:

> Overall the numbers look very good for Governor Richards. Her favorability rating is 63 percent positive to 22 percent negative which is nearly 3 to 1. (One week before election day 1990 Richards' favorability rating was 39 percent positive and 51 percent negative.) Richards' job performance and favorability are strong among Democrats and Independents. Moreover, she has a net positive of 11 percent among Republicans.
>
> Concerning expectations, 39 percent said Richards has done much or somewhat better than expected, 48 per cent about as well as expected, and 12 percent somewhat or much worse than expected. Thus more than 3 to 1 say she has exceeded expectations. Also in rating past governors, 11 percent say Richards is one of the best, 25 percent say Richards is above average, and 4 percent one of the worst. Again, these are very strong figures.
>
> These numbers contrast somewhat with the "re-elect" question where 45 percent of the electorate said they would either definitely or probably vote to reelect Richards as Governor; 40 percent said they would definitely or probably vote for someone else. The 40 percent basically consists of Republican men and women who, even though they have a favorable image of Richards, say they will vote for someone else. There is no gender gap among Republican men and women—Richards does not garner a significant portion of either vote.

But she still polled eight to ten points higher with Democratic and independent women than with men of the same persuasion, and that margin had been a crucial part of her victory over Clayton Williams. In not quite a year, Ann's performance as governor had raised her favorable rating by *twenty-four* points and decreased her unfavorable rating by *twenty-nine* points. This despite the haggles in the legislature over school finance, the lottery, and the budget; the appearance of ineptness caused by being forced to call multiple special sessions; and the overriding specter of President Bush, who was at the height of his popularity after leading a rout of Saddam Hussein's Iraq in the First Gulf War. Bush's expected blowout of whoever surfaced as the Democratic presidential nominee would spell trouble for Democrats everywhere, especially in Texas.

The Hickman poll, wrote Dowd, indicated that likely voters believed the governor had done well in providing strong leadership, passing her programs through the legislature, appointing competent people, dealing with the lottery question, and fighting for average people: "Voters see Richards as a strong and decisive leader who has ideas to improve government. They believe she stands out in front on important issues, presents a good image of Texas to the rest of the country, and is active and aggressive. The areas of concern are: a slight majority believe Richards is 'just another politician' and no more honest than other politicians."

On the issue she believed in most of all, a whopping 59 percent of the sampled voters supported a woman's right to choose, while 30 percent opposed it. But there was an element of distrust, or perhaps just of misreading her, as well. Forty-three percent of the sampled voters believed she supported a state income tax, while 39 percent said she opposed it.

In the preceding twelve years, neither Bill Clements nor Mark White had come close to matching her popularity. "Basically you are in great shape," Mary Beth Rogers started a cover letter with Dowd's report, "held in affection and respect by a majority of Texas voters." The reversal of her positive-negative poll numbers, she exclaimed, was a "remarkable achievement! . . . But the poll also shows that voters are waiting for you to produce results. To date, they have not seen their insurance rates go down, or new jobs come to Texas, or the early release of criminals stopped, or the cutting of waste in government. While we know that it is too early to produce these results, the voters do not yet measure you as effective in these areas. And in truth, although we have set in motion efforts to solve some of these problems, we don't know if we will actually be able to succeed."

Rogers continued:

January, 1992 to January, 1993 is a critical time for your administration. It is the true "governing" period, where results have to be the goal. But the year is also the time for some essential base building for the 1994 election. This includes raising $8 million (to reach our goal of $10 million in the bank) by the fundraising cut-off in December 1992 . . .

You are experiencing extraordinary demands from important people for your time and energy. Legislators, lobbyists, business leaders, friends and staff—all want you to operate on an agenda that is important to *them*. You could spend all of your time responding to these requests (as we are doing in October, November, and December), and make some key people happy, perhaps even

achieve a few good things. Following this path, however, will drain your energy
and leave an unclear and uncertain legacy for your administration . . .

Instead of having 14 or 15 goals (insurance, education, crime, jobs, energy
policy, higher education, expanding the power of the governor, reorganization,
environment, etc.), we should have two or three, with a major emphasis on
only one. The most important question is: *What do you want to be remembered for?*
[Rogers's emphasis]

. . . This background leads us to a checkpoint for you to reaffirm or recon-
sider the most important decision you made last January: do you want to run
for reelection?

If you do, we must follow a course in 1992 that focuses on producing some
very specific results and we must carefully "market" the results to the target
audiences you need to win reelection.

A reelection decision will involve staying closer to home, with a significant
amount of in-state travel and carefully orchestrated events, such as town meetings, built around the issues identified in our poll and the limited goals you
want to achieve. It will also involve paying very close attention to the budget
and tax situation, including developing a revenue strategy that will head off a
major tax bill in the 1993 session . . .

The reelection campaign begins immediately after the 1993 legislative
session. As you look at the attached calendar for 1992, you can see that the
available time for base-building and fundraising activities is limited. . . . I would
suggest only one major foreign trip in 1992. Also, a high-profile national Democratic presidential campaign role—both at the convention and during the general election—could be risky for you in Texas, particularly if George Bush wins
decisively in November. That, plus a difficult legislative session in 1993, could
create a hard reelection campaign.

If you decide you don't want to run for reelection (a decision only Jack, Jane,
Kirk [Adams, her son-in-law and trusted adviser] and I need to know about),
you have a wider range of options for both politics and pleasure next year.

You could concentrate on becoming a national political player, including
taking a shot at the 1992 vice-presidential nomination—which quite possibly
could be yours if you want it.

Or, you could choose to simply enjoy the remainder of your term, doing
what you consider to be important, without undue concern about the political
consequences. Unfortunately, this is the only option that allows much time for
a personal life.

318   There the choices lay for Ann, her options outlined with great frankness. She
could win the reelection her polls seemed to indicate or strike out for national office—the vice presidency or even, in time and with great luck, the presidency—or
have a personal life. (One of her show business fans, Bill Cosby, inscribed a photo
of them together with the line that Ann was going to be president whenever "she's
damn well ready.") On the March 1992 calendar, she had trade meetings lined up
in Japan, South Korea, Taiwan, Hong Kong, and Singapore. In September, there
were trade talks in Spain, Germany, France, and Britain, and then in November,
talks in Canada. To run and win, said her most trusted adviser on both politics
and policy, Ann needed to give up all or most of that, and by that time in her life
she was a dedicated world traveler.

Mary Beth urged her to keep a low profile at the Democratic National Convention, this one scheduled in glorious New York City. But Ann's answer was like the
one she gave to the question of what had prompted her to run for the office in the
first place: too many people were counting on her—she felt she *had* to be there.
Plus, the spotlight she first discovered in Atlanta in 1988 was terribly hard to give
up. As her political advisers in the 1990 campaign found, she was quite taken with
being a celebrity. In the end, she tried to be a successful regional politician *and* a
superstar in the national Democratic Party and the celebrity mills of New York,
Washington, and Los Angeles. And also nourish a midlife (which really means
later-in-life) love affair.

———

ONE OF THE MOST URGENT policy issues she had to address was near chaos in the
prison system. She had not been ignoring it. Since 1972, the Texas prison system
had been embroiled in litigation brought by an inmate named David Ruiz. The
outcome of the federal lawsuit *Ruiz v. Estelle* determined that Texas had violated
the Eighth and Fourteenth Amendment rights of inmates—namely, the right not
to be subjected to cruel and unusual punishment and the rights to both due process and equal protection under the law—through overcrowding, poor medical
care, and institutionalized savagery by prison guards and the trusties called building tenders. The Carter Justice Department intervened on behalf of the plaintiffs,
and since 1980, a particularly demanding federal judge, William Wayne Justice,
had held a tight rein on the Texas prison system through a court-appointed
master, Steve Martin, a Pampa native who had gone from being a collegiate
prison guard to an assistant attorney general and an international authority on
penal policy. But state district courts did not have to heed the demands of Justice
and Martin; the sentences imposed by juries and reelection-minded judges grew

ever longer. The prisons were so packed that in order to comply with *Ruiz* standards, Bill Clements, certainly no friend of criminals, had been forced to quietly order the Board of Pardons and Paroles to release about 750 inmates a week, and many of the convicts sprung early were vile people. The state contributed to the crisis, too, by leaving convicted criminals in county jails instead of transferring them immediately to state prisons. Harris County was leading a multicounty suit against the state over its costly failure to assume its legal responsibility for convicts and move them to penitentiaries.

At the very start of Ann's term, when members of the transition team were formulating prison policy, Jane Hickie had interrupted my wife in a meeting and said, "Dorothy, all we're going to talk about is treatment." That declaration on her part was vastly oversimplified. Goaded by the lawsuits, Ann and the legislature launched the largest correctional construction project in the country. By 1996, more than 70,000 additional correctional beds had been added to the system. The state's capacity for inmates that year, about 128,000, more than doubled the prison capacity, 55,000, at the start of Ann's governorship. Parole policy was toughened so that the most violent offenders had to serve at least 50 percent of their sentences, and capital murderers sentenced to life had to serve forty years before they could come up for parole. In 2000, Texas was projected to have the largest prison population of any Western democracy—one out of every twenty-one adults, compared to one out of fifty-eight in 1982.

Ann Richards's election and term happened to coincide with a horrific rampage and manhunt that sent shock waves through the state. After growing up a dropout and thug and serving time for fourteen counts of burglary, a man named Kenneth McDuff and a friend decided one night they would torture and kill two Fort Worth boys and a girlfriend in the Fort Worth–area town of Everman in 1966. They raped the girl with a broken broomstick, and then McDuff slowly strangled her with it. Though sentenced to the electric chair, McDuff twice received last-minute stays from the courts. The U.S. Supreme Court's 1972 moratorium on capital punishment resulted in his death sentence being commuted to life imprisonment. He offered a member of the parole board $10,000 to arrange his early release. Then in 1989, when Bill Clements was governor, McDuff somehow qualified as one of the 750 "low risk" convicts paroled each week.

He was out three days before he murdered a prostitute. He was once more free to be a drunk, and he added an addiction to crack cocaine. Another prostitute died at his hands in 1991. Later that year, he and a low-life friend abducted a young accountant named Colleen Reed from an Austin car wash. They tortured and raped

320 her as she begged for mercy, and when McDuff parted company with his friend, he said he was going to "do her." And he did. The killing of Reed, a pretty and popular woman from Louisiana, raced through the state's news media. McDuff's accomplice was arrested, and he talked. But the brutal psychopath killed another prostitute and a Waco convenience store clerk before an *America's Most Wanted* item on television led to his arrest in Kansas City in 1992. Gary Cartwright wrote a *Texas Monthly* cover story with a mug shot of McDuff and the caption "monster." McDuff sneered through the Reed murder trial; he was finally executed by lethal injection in 1998.

No one on earth was going to reform or find mercy in the soul of Kenneth McDuff. He was the poster boy for Texas serial killers and the symbol of all that was wrong with a prison system that the public expected to impose punishment on violent criminals. When Ann was treasurer and running for governor, she remarked to my wife, "Dorothy, I just told the board of the *Texas Observer* that I support capital punishment. And you know what? I'm all right with that."

On the other hand, she was a recovering alcoholic, and she was aware of credible evidence that 80 percent to 85 percent of Texas prison inmates had convictions that were drug or alcohol related. And they managed to get high and drunk while locked up by the state. If they were addicts going into prison and addicts coming out, what were the odds of their going straight while seeking the sort of jobs that they could obtain with criminal records?

Ann's senior aide Pat Cole and others on her staff worked closely with Senator Ted Lyon, a former Dallas-area policeman, and Mount Pleasant's Sam Russell, the House sponsor, in crafting Senate Bill 828 and guiding it to Ann's signature in June 1991. Lyon chaired the Criminal Justice Committee until his defeat in the 1992 elections. His successor as chairman, John Whitmire, of Houston, and Lieutenant Governor Bullock played important roles in putting the legislation on a fast track to passage and implementation. The bill created two series of initiatives, including those that developed into the In-Prison Therapeutic Communities and the Substance Abuse Felony Punishment (SAFP) program. The first program set up prison units segregated from the general population. After being screened by professionals at the Texas Commission on Alcohol and Drug Abuse, the convicts entered prison units removed from the general population as a condition for their parole, and for up to nine months underwent highly structured work, education, and treatment schedules supervised by licensed chemical-dependency counselors, physicians, or psychologists. Many of these convicts had already spent years in lockup. Most were volunteers; some were ordered into the program. If they

completed the program, they would remain apart from the general population   321
until they were discharged or released on parole, and then they had to participate in mandated aftercare. The second program provided six or nine months of
intensive substance-abuse treatment in specially designed SAFP facilities to individuals on probation or parole.

Ann promised, "We will have created a model for other states . . . and generated proof that we can use this kind of program to reduce addiction and crime . . .
that we can break the cycle . . . that we can take back the night and awake from a
long nightmare of violence and fear."

The legislation for the in-prison therapeutic communities required the Department of Corrections to provide at the outset at least 800 beds for the new
program. The hope in the governor's office was that the capacity would increase
to 2,000 by the end of Ann's term, in 1994. Private organizations bid for the contracts to work inside the prisons. No legislative accomplishment was a source
of more pride to Ann than this one. And in a breathtaking development in our
household, the governor charged my wife with the task of getting the program up
and running. It would be the most challenging and rewarding period of her career
in government.

All this created a scramble among small towns that wanted the prisons for the
jobs—advocates of Beeville showed up at a hearing in bee costumes—and among
companies that wanted to see the prisons privatized. Also in the 1991 session,
Ann signed legislation designed by Senator Whitmire to address overcrowding in
county jails by creating "state jails" for nonviolent offenders. But a condition for
passage of the bill was acceptance of a settlement in the lawsuit by the counties,
and Ann almost had to beg Harris County to go along with it: "I am hoping the
commissioners' court of Harris County will not single-handedly act to defeat this
legislation. It is important to remember that taxpayers served by the state and its
counties are the same Texas citizens."

In March 1992, Selden Hale, my Amarillo friend whom Ann had appointed
chair of the Texas Department of Criminal Justice, sent her a letter full of news
that might be a blessing and might be a curse. Selden wrote that negotiations with
the plaintiffs' lawyers in Ruiz had produced a compromise and a settlement offer.
If the state would immediately raise the system's inmate capacity by 2,300–3,000
new beds, the convicts' lawyers and the Justice Department would terminate the
lawsuit. Among the reasons Selden cited for accepting the offer was a staff esti-
mate that it would save the state $100 million over the next eighteen months.

He warned, though, that two dramatic turns of events could torpedo the proposed settlement: "First, Jail Commission figures indicate that the overcrowding in the Harris County jail is reaching crisis proportions." Also, one ranking assistant attorney general, Bob Ozer, raised the possibility of returning to federal court, reopening the *Ruiz* case, and attempting to remove the prison system from the jurisdiction of the federal court. After noting that the case had already been in the courts about fifteen years, and that the state was already involved in a vast prison-building program, Selden posed some tough questions to counter this proposal: "In a return to federal court, after expensive legal discovery, when would the case actually be tried? How long would the trial last? How expensive would it be for the litigation costs, not only for the State, but also on behalf of the inmates?" He wondered also on whose side the U.S. attorney general and Justice Department would intervene this time. And he closed with his strongest reason for not reopening the case: "If we spend anticipated months in a court battle and anticipated millions of dollars in staff time and legal fees, can Mr. Ozer give us any assurance as to a final victory?"

Ann supported the *Ruiz* settlement, and in time so did Dan Morales, but estimates from the Texas Criminal Justice Policy Council projected that 24,000 more prison beds would be needed to accommodate all the inmate growth projections—on top of those already budgeted and under construction. Dorothy recalled, "Ann said, 'All right, if they're going to do that, twelve thousand of them have to be treatment beds." At a cost of $1.6 billion, the governor's demand sailed through the legislature. Texas had gone from last or nearly last in the country to first—at least on paper—in providing drug- and alcohol-treatment programs in its prisons. Dorothy and a few devoted colleagues had to find a way to pull it off. "What would these prisons look like?" Dorothy said. "How would they train guards to administer them and counselors to run these programs? We visited treatment prisons in Chicago, Staten Island, and Tucson. The joke around the country was 'Have the Texans been to see you yet?' We didn't know how to do this on such a grand scale."

Ann had been tacking fast toward the center since before she took office. Despite the fiscal restraint and skill she had shown as treasurer, the business community had wanted little to do with her as a gubernatorial candidate. They didn't trust anyone who came billed as an Austin liberal. Yet despite the continuing animus of the insurance, petrochemical, and oil-refining industries, she turned out to be a pleasant surprise to many business leaders. In late 1991, General Motors announced plans to close its assembly plant in Arlington. Working with local governmental and union leaders, Ann took the lead in offering GM $30 million in tax incentives if the plant stayed open. In addition, to advance the clean-air initiatives she and Garry Mauro had promoted, she promised that if GM would manufacture vehicles that could be fueled by compressed natural gas, the state would buy 1,000 of them. The plant stayed open, and although GM never started production of these clean-air vehicles, executives said they were impressed by the state's offer.

A month later, in a drive called "Texas Commitment," the governor, Mauro, and Cathy Bonner, Ann's director of the Department of Commerce, invited chief executive officers to hear how both the people's health and their companies' prosperity could be strengthened by the plan to exploit the state's proven natural gas reserves. The invited business leaders represented Southwest Airlines,

Ann strikes a characteristic pose while answering questions at
a fund-raiser in Dallas. The man at right is unidentified.

324   Frito-Lay, Chevron, Sea World, the *Houston Chronicle*, Lone Star Steel, and Dow
Chemical among other large corporations. She was trying to sell them on the
entrepreneurial and innovative spirit of Texans. She was also trying to sell herself.

She flew the next night to New York, where she explained the reason for her
visit on *Good Morning America* and then met with executives of Chemical Bank.
The next day she sat for interviews with *Newsweek*, *Financial World*, and *Fortune*.
Then it was back to Dallas–Fort Worth and a day with business leaders, chamber of commerce officials, and reporters, where she emphasized the merits and
profound importance of the Superconducting Super Collider, which if finished
would be the most powerful particle accelerator in the world. The quest to find the
so-called secret of the universe had begun with research physicists courting the
administrations of Ronald Reagan and George Bush. When the site, in the area of
Waxahachie, was completed in 1999, the governor reported, it was going to trig-
ger a surge in housing construction and other economic activity. Ann was making a hard pitch that the Super Collider's promise was not a grandiose pipe dream.

Two days later, she was off to San Francisco, where she had lunch with executives and staffers of Chevron, trying to dissuade them from downsizing its Port
Arthur refinery. That day she also met with the group president of Lockheed's
Missiles and Space Systems. She told the executive, who was a former deputy
director of the CIA, that aerospace research and technology had product applications as varied as thermal insulation for the Alaska pipeline, solar energy collec-
tors for drying grain, polarized sunglasses, graphite golf clubs, digital television,
coatings to preserve works of art, fracture tests for steel in bridges, electronic de-
icing of aircraft wings, and weather satellites, among other things.

That night she had dinner with the president of Apple Computers, which had
chosen the Austin suburb of Round Rock as the location for a customer service
center. Ann's briefing paper said, "Ask if we can do anything to make their move
into Texas easier or more pleasant."

Ann roamed the country armed with "Texas Facts," which had been compiled
by Bonner and the Commerce Department. The governor stressed that Texas
had the fourteenth-largest economy in the world, comparable to that of Spain
or Brazil. It employed more than 8.5 million workers. Texas was the third-largest
producer of electronic components in the United States, the fourth-largest developer of software, and first in production of computer clones (200 million units
a year). It was the largest producer of plastic materials and resins. It led the nation in the production of natural gas and possessed 30 percent of proven U.S.
reserves. Its ranchers grazed 90 percent of the country's Angora goats, and the

seasonal shearing of their mohair fleece brought millions of dollars into Texas 325
agriculture. (The ranchers also enjoyed an outlandish federal subsidy; when Congress took that away, most of the longhair goats vanished as well.) Texas farms,
she went on, harvested a fourth of the nation's bales of hay. Texas had no income
tax, and it was a right-to-work state—workers could not be compelled to join
labor unions. Her liberal supporters, including her former husband, could not
have been thrilled by that gubernatorial endorsement; "right to work" also meant
anyone could be fired or laid off at an employer's whim. She was singing a very
different song about labor unions since that contest to block the AFL-CIO's endorsement of Jim Mattox in 1990.

Politically, all this seemed to be paying off for her. Ken Lay, the CEO and chairman of Enron, told the *Wall Street Journal*, "Overall, she has tried to do the things
that would be helpful for business and the economic climate of the state. I have
been somewhat surprised. I didn't expect her to be quite as pro-business or as active in supporting business as she has been."

Ken Lay. Enron. Neither of those were household names yet. Lay was one of
the executives who agreed to join her advisory council of business leaders.

Ann supported the emerging North American Free Trade Agreement (NAFTA), a
pact with Mexico and Canada. At the time, I happened to be working on a magazine assignment that took me one evening to a popular bar in Nuevo Laredo. She
was making a speech on television to Mexican leaders and citizens about NAFTA's
promise to both countries, with a Spanish translator; the men standing around
me at the bar seemed to hang on every word.

She explained her belief to American audiences that opposition to the trade
agreement was built on a number of myths—that Mexicans could not afford to
buy U.S. goods, that Mexico would export its horrendous environmental problems, and that NAFTA would cost the U.S. jobs and destroy its manufacturing base.

This is a lot like trying to put the blame for rain on the people who make
umbrellas.

There is no question that during the eighties some American companies
took manufacturing business overseas.

But when you buy clothes and VCRs and cars you see more "Made in Taiwan
or Korea" than "*Hecho en Mexico.*"

The fact is that companies that want to go to Mexico because of wages—or
for any other reason—will do so without NAFTA.

As many have pointed out, if low wages were the key to profitability, Bangladesh would rule the business world . . .

This is not an easy vote for many members of Congress.

They are scared. They face the loss of longtime friends and allies. . . . They face the loss of crucial financial and political support.

I honestly believe the well-intentioned people who oppose NAFTA have dumped their concerns about larger issues of the new international economy on this agreement.

The bottom line is this. We have been begging, badgering, and bashing Japan to give us a level playing field, open markets, and an opportunity of friendly competition and cooperation.

Now the Canadians and the Mexicans are freely offering us the same thing.

Now our friends are willing. And we ought to take them up on the offer.

Back in her Austin office, after remarking to Nancy Kohler how short the man was, she admonished the president of Mexico, Carlos Salinas de Gortari, who was soon to enter voluntary exile in Ireland because of corruption allegations, that his country had to respect and adapt to the very different environmental standards in the United States. He agreed enough, and they got along well enough, that he urged her to take a vacation at his retreat on a bay along the Pacific Ocean.

She took him up on the offer, inviting an entourage that included Jane Hickie, Suzanne Coleman, and her old friends Mike and Sue Sharlot. "Jane told us *after* we were there that we had to pay for it," Mike told me. He smiled and said he understood it was good for Ann to maintain her positions on ethics and junkets. "You can tell from the pictures that it was a very swell place. There were mountains to the rear of it, and one day we made our way over them so we could see the ocean. We were surrounded by all these warships of the Mexican navy."

CHAPTER 25

White Hot

IN 1986, WHEN ANN HAD JUST WON her second term as treasurer and had little idea about her future in politics, she became acquainted with a young Californian named Marlene Saritzky, who was then working for an organization called the Hollywood Women's Political Committee. She had grown up in the San Fernando Valley. She was in the business of knowing about women in politics, especially Democrats, and she was aware of the regional success and talent of Ann Richards. Through that organization Lily Tomlin had gotten in touch with Chula Reynolds and Jane Hickie. Later Reynolds contacted Marlene and said Ann wanted to come to California. Could Marlene set up some meetings with helpful people—and pick her up at the airport?

"You can imagine how easy that was," Marlene told me. "Many people I called in L.A. said, 'A woman govenor in Texas? Sounds like a long shot.'" A number of people replied politely that their schedules would not allow them to make any time available for Richards, but Marlene was good at that kind of work, and she managed to schedule some meetings with well-heeled people in the movie business who made no bones about being leftish in their politics. According to Marlene: "When Ann walked in and started talking, it was like another set of lights came on."

When Marlene was driving her around Los Angeles, they talked constantly about movies. And Ann had gotten her foot in the door with the liberal celebrities. The third time Ann went out there, a small crowd of movers and shakers

Governor Ann Richards receives a Harley-Davidson motorcycle from Texas dealers. Austin, 1992.

invited her over for dinner. At the table that night, a woman wrote a check, handed it to Marlene, and whispered, "Do you think this is all right?" She had written the check for $10,000. Marlene whispered, "I think that will be fine." Ann flew back to Austin with about $100,000 in contributions.

When asked by *Savvy* about her ethnic background, Ann had replied, "I am about three-quarters WASP—That's Waco and Sure Poor—and twenty-five percent Brazos River Rural." She was not poor by the time her parents moved to Waco. But how could she not be dazzled by being introduced to the stars of show business? For several months while Ann was treasurer and then through the '90 campaign, Marlene Saritzky found herself being interviewed in a laid-back and curious fashion by Bud Shrake and Gary Cartwright. Ann had asked them to check her out. Ann wasn't sure how she could manage to help build a Texas movie industry, but she had a hunch this young woman could help. During the governor's race, when producer Stan Brooks brought out Bud and Jap's Kris Kristofferson–Willie Nelson television movie *A Pair of Aces*, Bud went with Ann to Los Angeles for another dinner with the players. As the conversation ranged from Ann's campaign to why more movies weren't produced in Texas, Brooks remarked to Bud, "Marlene should be the film commissioner."

After the election, in one brief conversation Ann told her, "I'm trying to get the Film Commission away from the Department of Commerce and in the Governor's office. If that happens, I'll call you." When they spoke again, Ann offered her the job with the condition "I'll give you a week to decide." One week! That was how Ann operated. And when Marlene looked at the reasons why she should stay in California and pass up the opportunity, they didn't add up to as much as her desire to work for and be around this woman. Marlene was chary about Texas, but she wound up living there for the next six years.

"I was young and made a lot of mistakes," she later told me. "I knew nothing about Texas. I didn't really speak the language. For a long time, nuances and rhythms that everybody else understood were mysteries to me. But a lot of that job consists of just calling up a mayor and the Department of Public Safety and asking them to reroute traffic for a few hours in some town." And it wasn't as if Ann had no case to make for films to be shot, and crews hired, in Texas. Texas productions had given the world classic movies like *Giant*, *The Last Picture Show*, and *Tender Mercies*. Bill Wittliff's adaptation of Larry McMurtry's novel *Lonesome Dove* as a miniseries had been a big hit; Terrence Malick, the artful director of *Badlands* and *Days of Heaven*, had long made his home base in Austin; and the year Ann took office as governor, the young director Richard Linklater launched his career with *Slacker*, followed months later by Robert Rodriguez's *El Mariachi*.

These things were cyclical, Marlene said. The incentive dealing could be won by Canada or Louisiana—and often did—but Ann was determined that Texas was not going to lose out on getting a bite of the apple. And it was not a passing fancy. Southwest, American, and other airlines were soon providing nonstop flights between Austin and Los Angeles. Under her "Film Texas" initiative, she hosted receptions for Gary Goldberg, Cybill Shepherd, Lily Tomlin, Norman Lear, Richard Zanuck, and Jack Valenti. She sent letters of congratulations for their pictures and awards to Oliver Stone and Tommy Lee Jones, went on *The Jay Leno Show* and steered the chat around to the Texas film industry; at the end of her letter of gratitude to Leno was a handwritten "Get out of the hut and see the real world, we want you here." She did, however, pass on Paramount's invitation to cast her in *Clear and Present Danger*.

Despite the long hours and frenzied activity, she did what she could to ensure that Bud did not disappear from her life. She invited him to move his regular poker games with pals to the Governor's Mansion. They had dates as often as their schedules permitted, even if it was just to a session of Alcoholics Anonymous. In their unremitting correspondence, they shared their impressions of movies they hadn't viewed together. Ann had pronounced herself a movie-world groupie the first week of her campaign, when Bud took her to watch Dennis Hopper directing a movie on a Texas location, but she turned on the director with a vengeance after seeing the finished product. She had gotten Claire Korioth to go with her to see *The Hot Spot*, which starred the dimpled *Miami Vice* hunk Don Johnson and a young actress with a bright future, Jennifer Connelly. Johnson played a drifter turned used-car salesman who hatched a scheme to rob a small-town bank. Hopper indulged himself with a scene in which Connelly and a female friend went skinny-dipping and on the creek bank slid into a steamy nude sex entanglement.

> Dear Mr. Shrake,
> We regret that you have failed the Richards/Korioth movie review test. *Hot Spot* is not only a bad movie, it has space and time dimensions that make two hours seem like twelve and causes the theater walls to press inward. . . . Much like what real life must be like when you make the center of your life a used car lot office.
> Ann

After she became governor, she had less time to enjoy Bud's company, but their time together had never been constant. While she was speeding around being the governor, he embarked on a project that his agent had warned him would be a waste of time. A small, frail Austin Country Club golf pro named Harvey Penick had been the tutor of the University of Texas and pro tour stars Ben Crenshaw and Tom Kite, among others. Penick was in his mideighties when Bud got to read the red notebook that the old pro was always scribbling in. Bud thought it was magic—secrets of golf, philosophy, life. He asked Penick for permission to help turn it into a book, and was disappointed when the old man frowned and declined, as if a friend had violated his privacy.

Then Penick explained that he and his wife couldn't possibly dig deep enough in their savings to pay Bud to do such a thing. No, no, Bud clarified: "The idea is that I'll write it and someone will pay *us*." An editor and golf fanatic in New York snatched up the manuscript, and *Harvey Penick's Little Red Book: Lessons and Teachings from a Lifetime in Golf* (1992) went on to become the best-selling sports book of all time.

Good deeds can be rewarded. Bud's gesture on behalf of an old man he revered set him up for the rest of his life. He could write his novels and plays at his leisure. He didn't need Hollywood anymore. But Ann did.

One thing Ann couldn't abide in Mary Beth Rogers's memo about running for reelection, quoted in the last chapter, was the suggestion to keep a low profile in national politics. Ann couldn't do that; if she were going to work that hard being governor, she was also going to have some fun. In the midst of her 1991 coast-to-coast blitzkrieg in search of more jobs for Texans, Ann flew back to Austin to rehearse her appearance at the annual Washington Gridiron Show. The young Arkansas governor, Bill Clinton, wondered whether sparks would fly between Ann and President Bush.

"So this is what you all do up here on Saturday nights," she said to the celebrities of government and media. "I don't know why anyone would think you're out of touch. But Mr. President, distinguished guests, and stuffed shirts, I'm having a great time tonight. And what a good-looking audience you are. As my mama would say, 'You look as good as a new-scraped carrot.'

"In any event, I'm proud to be out with such a high-class crowd. But I've been wondering, Mr. President—to overcome the image of attending a white-tie dinner like this, how many pork rinds do you have to eat?

"And Mr. President, putting aside partisanship, I can say that in all honesty that it will be hard to beat the kind of strength, energy, and grace under pressure that we have in the White House today. You are really one of a kind, Barbara."

One more shot across the Bush family's bow.

Democrats in their twenties were thrilled to have a chance to work for Ann Richards. Shawn Morris, who was my wife's administrative assistant, said that almost all of them spoke of "her constant ability to scare the daylights out of people." The travel aide Chris Hughes recalled the angst of trying to frame the context of some mistake he had made. *"Don't get started,"* Ann cut him off. "Just tell me what happened."

And she didn't unload only on the youngsters. One evening Bill Cryer, the communications chief, and David Talbot, the lead general counsel, were having dinner in a Washington restaurant, where they were relieved that no one in the classy place would know about some mistake they had made and the vocal and psychological pounding they had been taking from the boss all day. And then her voice boomed out, in reference to the popular animated series, "Well, if it's not Beavis and Butthead!"

But she inspired her staff as much as she drove and, at times, belittled them. "Ann showed me how to focus on issues, on what I was trying to say," said Joy Anderson. "She wanted you to have thought through the issue, to bring in all the pros and cons. She really taught me how to have more self-confidence. Nothing focused you like knowing you had to go in and talk to Ann. She would push back and question you. Every time she would come up with something you hadn't thought of. And you'd do a better job the next time you had to go in. She was just as hard on herself. Wanting to be perfect, while knowing she couldn't be."

A young man who worked on the communications team—and for professional reasons preferred to remain unnamed here—winced at the memory of a day when he was supposed to fax three sets of briefing papers to Ann regarding an engagement in San Angelo. To his horror and the joy of the people who received the fax, he had punched in the number of the *Houston Chronicle*; the next morning, the paper ran the story with much humor. The aide was scheduled to travel with her, and she didn't have to say anything, just give him the *look*. Bill Cryer and Chuck McDonald put their hands on his shoulders and welcomed him to the club.

He marveled at the teamwork of Ann and Suzanne Coleman. "Suzanne was so close to Ann," he told Shawn. "She really was the quiet partner. She was well educated, and was a voracious reader with huge intellect. Ann also had the intellect, and she was a great storyteller, a precise political thinker, and a pragmatic political thinker. Their combo was incredible. But there weren't too many times when Suzanne would get good feedback."

He noted that for all her faults: "Only Ann could do what she did with such authentic Texas experience. Going hunting, canning food—only she could have created this kind of change, combining her Texas experience with her progressive core values. That wouldn't have had a chance of working if she weren't as true to Texas as she was. She could disarm people."

But there were currents of staff dissent. "During one of the more publicized death penalty cases," Shawn Morris said, "everyone was writing to the governor.

David Talbot's office was inundated with mail." But the execution went forward. "That was one of the things that seemed to be counterintuitive to her progressive status. I would be out protesting on the Capitol steps, and the next day I'd come to work in the office. It seemed like it was expected that we *all* would feel like protesting the death penalty. No one felt too strongly in favor of it, I'm sure of that."

Still, Shawn and others were caught up in the sheer exhilaration. One day, all the talk at the Capitol was about politics. President George Bush's seemingly overwhelming popularity after the First Gulf War was vanishing with the sucking sound that the Texas billionaire Ross Perot ascribed to the loss of American jobs overseas. The little Texan with the gleaming crew cut, bent nose, and whinnying voice and laugh was offering himself as an independent candidate for president. Perot intrigued the public; he was climbing fast in the polls and getting a largely free ride in the press. And a strong showing in the New Hampshire primary by a nativist opponent in Bush's own party, Pat Buchanan, added to the president's difficulties. On the grounds of who was more conservative and alarmed by deteriorating American culture, the former Nixon speechwriter got 38 percent to Bush's anemic 53 percent.

One day in early 1992, Garry Mauro urged me to come over to his political office and meet his friend of twenty years, Hillary Clinton. I told him that I was then leaning to support Nebraska's senator Bob Kerrey. "Oh, that's all right," Garry said. "Come on over anyway." At the small reception, he embarrassed me thoroughly in our introduction by telling her what I had told him—I was interested in Bill Clinton's candidacy, but at the moment I was supporting Kerrey. "Well," she said, "we'll have to take care of that." And they did. In a very few weeks, Kerrey had been bulldozed out of the race.

A short time after Hillary's pass through Austin, tall Bill Clinton strolled into the Capitol. "We were talking about him," Shawn Morris recalled. "He seemed to come out of nowhere because everyone was so focused on Perot and Bush. Clinton gave an incredible speech to the Texas Senate about the out-of-work guy. We were all floored. Jesse Jackson was also running and was here at the same time. Some of us on the governor's staff were giving him a tour, and under the Capitol dome he was signing autographs when Bill Clinton tapped me on the shoulder and said, 'Can I say hi to the Reverend?' Suddenly the photographers came running, and Hillary and I were shoved together so hard our heads bumped. She was no passive wallflower. She snapped, '*Excuse* me!' to one of them. It was one of the most profound moments of my time working for Ann."

Arkansas governor and Democratic presidential candidate Bill Clinton greets Ann and her daughter Ellen on his campaign jet. Hillary Rodham Clinton is likely the woman in the foreground. Note the sticker on the luggage compartment stating that President "Bush Couldn't Run a Laundromat."

On May 1, 1992, the nation was transfixed and horrified by three days of rioting and violence that erupted in Southern California after the acquittal of four white Los Angeles police officers who had been videotaped beating and kicking a black man named Rodney King with the apparent intention of killing him, or at best leaving him in intensive care. The verdict had been rendered in Simi Valley, a Ventura County town whose residents were so white, conservative, and prosperous that it had been chosen as the site of Ronald Reagan's presidential library. The three days of rioting, looting, and arson in Los Angeles resulted in more than 50 deaths, some 2,000 injuries, anywhere from 7,000 to 18,000 arrests (accounts vary wildly), and $1 billion in property damage.

But it was not just that these horrid events occurred. In seventeen incredible and electrifying months in 1990 and 1991, the United States and the world had lurched into a new age of constant, real-time television with CNN's coverage of the air assault on Baghdad in the First Gulf War and the collapse of the Soviet empire. The savage violence and burning buildings in LA held America in thrall even more than the King videotape had. The image that dominated the news and stirred the conscience and anger of America captured an attack on a white truck driver named Reginald Denny, who drove his eighteen-wheeler into Inglewood, southwest of downtown LA, unaware of the riots there. As television news helicopters hovered close overhead, four black youths hauled Denny out of his truck and battered him with a five-pound piece of medical equipment and a claw hammer. A former star high school athlete called Damian "Football" Williams hurled a slab of concrete at the head of the defenseless man and then for the crew and cameras of the Los Angeles News Service chopper flashed some signs of his gang, the Eight Tray Gangster Crips. He laughed and pointed at the unconscious truck driver and then performed a ghastly dance, like some gridiron showboat who had just scored a touchdown.

Against that backdrop, the political and governmental network C-SPAN prepared to cover a celebrity roast of Texas governor Ann Richards in Port Arthur. The Texas native and CBS anchor Dan Rather had promised to emcee the roast, but the explosive events in California obliged him to cancel. That afternoon at the Beaumont–Port Arthur airport, Ann announced at a press conference that she was endorsing her friend Bill Clinton in his bid for the presidency. From the White House, President George H. W. Bush was calling for decency and calm in a speech to the nation. And at the request of the networks and the Democratic National Committee, Clinton, the putative front-runner, had been asked to add a short speech after the president spoke.

The roast had become a major source of revenue for civic and charitable projects since Ann had appeared at the one honoring football coach Bum Phillips in 1989, and she had come back each year since. To accommodate the networks, Clinton and his wife, Hillary, had to leave the event early. Rather's substitute emcee, a jocular county judge, set aside a pastor's invocation so the young governor could say his piece. Clinton offered a joke in reference to Phillips and the Golden Triangle's veteran congressman Jack Brooks: "Brooks brought Bum to Washington last month. Somebody from Texas said, 'Hey, Bum!' And three hundred congressmen turned around." He said Ann and Lena Guerrero were "the Thelma and Louise of Texas politics." (It left to the audience's imagination the movie's closing scene, in which the runaway women drive their convertible off a cliff.)

Molly Ivins was then writing nationally syndicated columns for the *Fort Worth Star-Telegram*, many of which were collected in a series of best-selling books. Clinton turned to Molly, who was seated at the speakers' table, and made fun of himself and his up-and-down campaign, which had nearly been sunk by a parade of women alleging that he was given to lascivious extramarital behavior. "You know what Molly does, don't you? She's in the business of trying to make politicians look silly. I've devoted my campaign to trying to eliminate the middleman." But he changed the tone then and with considerable eloquence echoed Ann's call at the airport that day for a renewal of bonds of common humanity, in light of the horrors in Southern California.

On videotape, Rather delivered a herky-jerky and heavily scripted performance of himself parodying Clinton's aspirations for the presidency in 1992. Bum Phillips then took his turn. Bum had been the most popular man in Houston when the Oilers' owner, Bud Adams, fired him twelve years earlier, and though his next coaching stint, with the New Orleans Saints, had turned out just so-so—at one point, a disaffected fan in the stands dumped a cup of beer on his head—he commanded an affection among Texans that the Cowboys' owner, Jerry Jones, and the team's coach, Jimmy Johnson, who were in the audience, could never match, despite their march to two winning Super Bowls. Bum said, "Godamighty, I'm gonna tell you one thing, we're gonna slow it down a little bit. All these people going 'yap, yap, yap, yap.'" He paused, then said, "It's hell to get old, you know? Everything that works, hurts. And everything that don't hurt, don't work." The crowd laughed at the mild sexual innuendo. He went on: "So far, I haven't said anything bad about the governor, so if I say something that offends you, I am damn proud of it. When I was young, I wanted to be the governor. . . . I had all the qualifications—I drank, I gambled, I chased women. . . . But then my mom made me go to school, and I was overqualified. . . . We have got a woman governor now and they tell me next thing we are going to have is women playing football. But I don't believe that, because I don't believe you could ever get forty-five women to go out in front of 125,000 people dressed just alike."

Ann, in a lavender dress and pearl necklace, was seated next to the podium. Her cackle carried through the microphone like the sound of someone having a fine time. Phillips spoke about the repetitive corniness of the roast phenomenon, and his great love of Texas, and then he said, "I'm damn glad Ann Richards is my governor. And I wanted to tell her so."

Then the county judge introduced Molly with a joke that fell flat, and he mangled the title of her book. "Gosh, thank you, Judge," she said wryly. "Of all the introductions I've ever had, that one was the most . . . recent." As it happened, Molly also wore lavender—a suit coat over a white sweater with a string of pearls. Molly was a prepossessing woman. She looked almost as tall and broad-shouldered as Bum Phillips. After some good-natured gibes at other speakers, she said, "Of course we're here to salute Ann Richards. I've known Ann Richards since Ann and Exxon were still Humble." Ann hooted and rocked forward in her chair.

"Sometimes people ask me what she was like in the old days. Just like she is now. I remember several years ago there was a political do at the Scholz beer garden in Austin, Texas, and everybody in political Texas was just meetin' and drinkin' at a furious pace. And about halfway through it, a few of us got a little tired of meetin' and went to lean our butts against a table in the Scholz beer garden, kinda like birds in a row: Bob Bullock, who was then the state comptroller; myself; and a black guy named Charlie Myles, who was then the head of Bob's personnel department—the reason Bob had such a good record of minority hiring; and Miz Ann Richards, then utterly obscure, a mere county commissioner.

"Bullock having spent thirty years in Texas politics knew every no-good son of a bitch in the entire state. And some dreadful racist judge from East Texas came up and said, 'Bob, my boy, how you?' And they commenced to slap each other on the back and have a big greeting. Bullock said, 'Judge, I want you to meet my friends. This is Molly Ivins with the *Texas Observer*.' The judge peered up at me and said, 'How you, little lady?' Bob said, 'And this is Charlie Myles, the head of my personnel office.' Charlie put out his hand, and the judge got an expression on his face like he had just stepped in a fresh cow pie. It took a good long minute before the judge reached out and touched Charlie's hand and said, 'How you, boy?' And then turned with great relief to Ann Richards and said, 'And who is this lovely lady?' And Ann Richards said, 'I'm Mrs. Myles.'"

The laughter was generous. Molly let it subside, muttering to herself and to Ann, who was seated just below her, "Great story. Great story." Then she launched into her second anecdote. "Along about that same era, as you know, Texas tends to be behind the cultural curves. And this was the early seventies, and the women's movement had not made it to the shores of our great state, and there was a dinner in West Lake Hills."

The mike carried a groan from Ann that had an undertone of displeasure; she realized what was coming. Molly gave her old friend a glance and continued, "And our friend Tony Korioth, who is a wonderful man but a terrible sexist, got to talking about how he was driving home from work that evening, and he passed this young lady on the street who had the most remarkable set of jugs Tony Korioth had ever witnessed in his long years of jug-watching. He described in great detail how they wiggled and jiggled and bounced and jounced, and how he drove around the block to see them again and now described once more how they jiggled and wiggled and bounced and jounced.

"You women well remember that in those days we had a wonderful social skill when men introduced topics like that into the conversation: we would gaze off

338 into the middle distance, pretending not to be there. And all the women were gazing off into the middle distance, pretending not to be there, when suddenly Ann Richards said in a clarion voice, 'Well, girls, have you seen any good dicks lately?'"

The governor was leaning over toward her bouquet of flowers, dabbing at what may have been a tear in her eye. Those stories told in the company of Mad Dog, Inc., were one thing, but Ann was preparing to speak about all the appointments she had made in Port Arthur, Beaumont, Orange, and Vidor. *Texas Monthly's* Mimi Swartz would soon be writing a cover story in which she branded all-white Vidor as "Hate City," a stronghold of the Klan. The Golden Triangle was full of industrial workers and union members who were conditioned to vote in large numbers for Democrats, but the region was also Deep South in its history and orientation. Here one still could hear the word "miscegenation." Ann could not have been pleased to hear her old canoeing friend and political ally Tony Korioth mocked in public in this way. And it was preserved for all time on C-SPAN. It was mid-1992, and already there was a lot of GOP talk about a strong challenge coming her way from George W. Bush. In a state still controlled by conservative white males, Ann was gearing up to run for reelection!

"Molly, Molly, Molly, Molly," Ann said when she got up to make her comic speech about her first experience hunting wild turkeys out in the bush with good old boys. "The Goodwill [Industries] fashion statement. I knew this was an important event to Molly when I walked in and saw she had combed her hair."

She was none too pleased to have had Molly's little dagger of humor poked in her. She often grumbled to her staff, "Friends. They're the ones who'll do it to you every time."

During that spring of 1992, *Texas Monthly's* young art director, DJ Stout, noticed a newspaper story that quoted Ann as saying she wanted to get a motorcycle license by the time she turned sixty. That birthday was coming up in September 1993. At the Port Arthur roast, a local dealer had given her a specially tailored Harley jacket, to her delight. Someone in the Harley-Davidson plant and home office saw the story also and sent her one of its rather small models, which she duly reported as another gift. And in an isolated parking lot, she learned to ride it on weekends with the help of a coach. DJ hatched the idea of putting her on a cover in boots and white leather with fringed sleeves, riding a white Harley. The governor's publicists expressed some interest, but DJ was disappointed on inspecting the one she had. He envisioned her on a great big Harley hog, the kind he had grown up seeing before the Hell's Angels came and went and before the

American company set out to change its image in the face of stern European and Japanese competition. Word came back to DJ that Ann liked the idea, but her schedule was so hectic that no time for the photo shoot could be nailed down—she was off to New York to chair the Democratic National Convention.

One of her aides talked to DJ, though, and said that the governor had liked a cover that came out during the 1990 campaign in which, with new and still difficult digital magic—not yet perfected by Photoshop—the magazine had placed a stock shot of her and a grinning, Stetson-wearing Clayton Williams on the bodies of a two-stepping couple, and then run it with the caption "Dirty Dancing: Stepping Out With Ann and Claytie as They Stomp Across Texas—and Each Other!" Ann told or sent word to DJ she had gotten a kick out of that, and suggested that they just fake it again. He went to work with a photographer in Dallas and a Smithville, Texas, fashion designer who specialized in leather apparel, and the July 1992 issue hit newsstands with the governor looking straight at the camera, somewhat sternly, while astride a large Harley with the gas tank painted gleaming white. This caption was "White Hot Mama: Ann Richards Is Riding High, Can She Be the First Woman President?" Ann thanked DJ profusely for matching her face with a model that had such a "sexy body." She remarked to Dorothy that she hadn't had thighs like that in thirty years.

In early July, Ann left for New York with an entourage of about forty people, plus a contingent of Department of Public Safety troopers and a makeup artist. Wary of GOP sniping and any possible ethics backlash, employees of the Governor's Office made sure they had enough vacation time accumulated to cover the time off. The entourage included Ann's family members Ellen Richards, Cecile Richards, and Kirk Adams; her political advisers Jane Hickie and Jack Martin; her old friends Liz Smith, Bob Armstrong, and Chula Reynolds; senior staffers John Hannah, Bill Ramsey, Chuck McDonald, Joy Anderson, Carl Richie, Marlene Saritzky, Rebecca Lightsey, and Richard Moya; Mark McKinnon and Matthew Dowd, who would later play prominent roles in the politics and administration of the second President Bush; and junior staffers, including the publicist Margaret Justus, the travel aide Chris Hughes, and Shawn Morris. Shawn spotted Bianca Jagger, Michael J. Fox, Timothy Hutton, and Oliver Stone in a Madison Square Garden full of celebrities. This show was the Clintons', but as the convention chair, Ann had booked interviews with Jesse Jackson on CNN, Mario Cuomo on *Face the Nation*, Dan Rather on CBS, Maria Shriver on NBC, Jim Lehrer and Robert MacNeil on PBS, and one of the governor's self-proclaimed heartthrobs, Peter Jennings on ABC.

When David Gergen analyzed her opening speech, he dwelled on the *Texas Monthly* cover with the likeness of Ann on the motorcycle. Wayne Slater, the *Dallas Morning News* reporter who had been standing in the wings and had gotten the first comment from Ann after her career-driving keynote speech in Atlanta four years earlier, filed his story under the headline: "Richards' Popularity Puts Her in the Limelight Dawn to Dusk":

> Ms. Richards is bound for the network's sky-booth to appear on *Face the Nation* with correspondent Bob Schieffer, who greets her in a hallway cluttered with computer terminals, portable tables and miles of television cable.
>
> They chat briefly, but not about politics. Mr. Schieffer wants to know about the Harley-Davidson motorcycle that she straddled, dressed in white leather, on the July cover of *Texas Monthly*. The headline: "White Hot Mama."
>
> . . . Lena Guerrero, the Texas Railroad Commissioner, arrives in a black Cadillac limo. By the time Hillary Clinton, wife of the presumed Democratic nominee Bill Clinton, pulls up in a multi-car caravan, the place has the frenetic look of a Hollywood opening. . . . The chorus line does appear, people keep talking, and under the club's deep-blue ceiling and gold sconces, in the jostle and swirl of the crowd, Ms. Richards is surrounded by a crush of well-wishers well into the night.
>
> It is enough, Ms. Richards concedes, to make her think about next week, when she will be on vacation.
>
> "I'm going to Switzerland," she says. "Nobody knows me there."

CHAPTER 26

Heartaches by the Number

UNBEKNOWNST TO ANN at the time, her fortress harbored a Trojan horse, one in the shape of that black Cadillac limo that came rolling to a halt in the bright lights outside Madison Square Garden.

With eerie foresight, Bud Shrake had faxed her a letter in mid-June that she might well have taken to heart, even if the old rounder was sounding a bit preachy.

> Dear Guv:
> While you were playing croquet in Wonderland I have been deeply involved in *real life* . . .
> I've been reading *March of Folly* by Barbara Tuchman. Her definition of folly is: "Wooden-headed attraction to a goal or course of action that is against your best interest, deprived of powerful warnings and feasible alternatives."
> Do you know how *hard* the Trojans had to *work* to get that big wooden horse inside their walls?
> Which reminds me that Susan [Walker] wants the Punzars to appear at [Jerry Jeff's] next Paramount birthday show—on national cable TV.
> This ain't folly, because I have no attraction to it. But stupid?
> Love, Bud

He did not accompany her to the Democratic National Convention in July. A Manhattan full of drunk and bellicose politicians and Democratic Party groupies was not Bud's idea of a good time.

Amid campaign supporters and television newsmen, Austin State Representative Lena Guerrero beckons to her friend and mentor Ann Richards during the 1990 campaign for governor. Governor Richards was wounded by Guerrero's false academic claims in 1992.

Stupidity would be a cruel way to describe the governor's handling of her first political debacle of 1992, but she effectively threw herself under her own bus. Eight days after her inauguration, she had appointed Lena Guerrero to fill a vacancy in a statewide elected office, officially making her one of the stars of her New Texas. Guerrero had been elected to the Texas House of Representatives in 1984, when she was just twenty-six. By all accounts, she was an energetic and able legislator. Reviews of her performance in the 1990 campaign were mixed, but she added to her reputation as a tough customer in a reported chest-to-chest argument with Mattox at a gathering of Mexican American Democrats in Corpus Christi. When Ann appointed her to the Railroad Commission in its one-hundredth year, every previous commissioner had been a white male. At one of her early hearings, a boorish trucker insulted her. "I have just one question—what's your bra size?"

"Not big enough," she fired back. The guffaws signaled that she had won admission to the club.

By the early 1990s, railroads had almost nothing to do with the job Ann handed her. Railroad commissioners dealt in the intricacies of regulating oil and gas production, mapping old wells, pipeline permitting and safety, trucking regulations, coal and uranium mining, and consumer use of propane, compressed natural gas, and liquefied natural gas. And the office is a trampoline for politicians seeking higher office.

When Guerrero's limo arrived at Madison Square Garden that summer night in 1992, she was on a USA Today list of who might be the first female president. At the Democratic National Convention that nominated Bill Clinton and Al Gore, Governor Ann Richards, as chair, made sure that Guerrero got to deliver her up-from-the-barrio speech in a prime-time slot. Guerrero was never accused of any malfeasance in her years of public service. She just got tangled up in the handiwork of creating her own myth.

According to speculation, Ann expected a Bush landslide in 1992, regardless of the Democrats' nominee, and she hoped that a dynamic Hispanic woman on the state ballot might awaken a dormant voting bloc in Texas, one that the governor constantly courted, and erect a firewall for Democratic legislators. Guerrero had expected to run against Carole Keeton McClellan Rylander (not yet Strayhorn), a former Austin mayor and onetime local ally of Ann who had switched to the Republican Party. But "one tough grandma," as the former mayor styled herself, lost the GOP primary to Barry Williamson, an attorney who directed the Minerals Management Service in Bush's Department of the Interior. Williamson's campaign consultant, Karl Rove, was then forty-two. After starting a profitable consulting firm in Austin, he had guided Rick Perry and Kay Bailey Hutchison to their winning races in 1990, but those were down-ballot offices, whatever the future importance of the occupants. Rove's only reputation outside Texas was as a collegiate dirty trickster that the elder George Bush had to caution on what his life would be like if the FBI got hold of him. During the 1992 campaign, he provided direct-mail and fund-raising service for Dick Thornburgh, a former Pennsylvania governor and an attorney general under presidents Ronald Reagan and George H. W. Bush who ran for the U.S. Senate in his home state and was upset by Harris Wofford. Rove later sued Thornburgh for lack of payment and won an award of $310,000 in a settlement. That battle is detailed in *Bush's Brain: How Karl Rove Made George W. Bush Presidential*, by Wayne Slater and James Moore.

The Williamson campaign launched assaults that cast Guerrero as for gays and lesbians, against gun rights, and for abortion. Nothing was working until the husband of Austin's ex-mayor, Carole Keeton McClellan Rylander, saw a University of Texas release that said Guerrero was going to be honored as an outstanding alumna. The man tipped Rove that his alumni group could find no record that she had graduated from the University of Texas. But she claimed to have a communications degree in broadcasting from the university—and to have been Phi Beta Kappa. (Dan Rather had mentioned her degree in his videotape for the Ann Richards roast in Port Arthur.)

Transcripts of students at state-supported colleges are supposed to be privileged, but Rove soon knew that her academic record was dotted with Cs, Fs, and incompletes. At the start of that summer, Guerrero addressed a graduation ceremony at Texas A&M and began, "I remember well my own commencement. . . ." Rove waited a few weeks, until she had made the ride in the limo and enjoyed her big night in New York City. He delayed his ambush until his candidate got to make his speech about the president's energy policy at the Republican National Convention. Then he passed on the tip about Guerrero's academic claims to a *Dallas Morning News* reporter. At first she lost her composure, raising her intimidating telephone voice and warning the reporter that if the paper went anywhere near that story, she was going to sue the *Morning News*. That was like tossing a glass of gasoline on a charcoal fire.

She then tried to stall, saying that it had to be a clerical error and that she would check with the university. Then she changed her story again. It turned out that Guerrero was nineteen credits short of her degree, not the four she claimed. She had failed a course on the Texas legislature, which an adroit team might have spun into a comic positive, given her glowing record there. But the Austin-based political journalist Lou Dubose wrote about an Austin political consultant who said, "Karl had Lena's transcript. He held it until the right moment. The perfect moment. And then he screwed her."

Ann had warned Guerrero when she gave her the job, "They're going to pick through your innards when you run." One of the consultants who worked with Ann stretched his mouth in disdain at the mention of the former legislator and commissioner. "Lena Guerrero was a bully," he told me, "and she was the most unfit public official I've ever seen." That overstated the case, but she did prove incapable of preparing for rigorous opposition research—a requisite of anyone with great political ambition. In their book *Bush's Brain*, Wayne Slater and James Moore related a telling story of the Guerrero campaign's demise. Chuck McDonald, a press aide for Richards, told them that Mark McKinnon, the media consultant, had lined up an advertising shoot that went on as planned in a simulated Texas oil field: "Lena has $2 million dollars in the bank, so we're going to run this unbelievable bioepic—the poor, humble girl who is now running Texas. McKinnon's got this crane. Lena's walking—she's got on a dress, the wind blowing. Then we go to the Governor's Mansion for shots on the porch and patio. We're just out there shooting this while the world's falling apart."

Later the same day, the commissioner held a press conference. Accompanied by her husband, her four-year-old son, and her mother, she claimed the graduation claim was a memory lapse, and the Phi Beta Kappa thing had gone out in some press release she failed to catch.

McDonald told the governor, "Nobody's going to believe this story."

Guerrero went on, "I now realize that I have been in a hurry all my life. In my haste, I was reckless. I made mistakes. I allowed misperceptions, embellishments, and errors of fact about my academic record to go uncorrected. I didn't admit to the truth of those facts when questioned about them. And I betrayed the trust placed in me by the people of this state and a woman I admire dearly, Governor Ann Richards."

Guerrero said that she would resign her office as railroad commissioner, but that she would not withdraw her name from the ballot. She would try to win an election in which, she pleaded, both candidates were now challengers. Ann issued a supportive statement in response to her mea culpa and pledge to fight on. Guerrero sent the governor a letter whose postscript read, "Please allow me to clarify one last lingering misperception: When asked why there were misrepresentations on my resumé, I said it was something I wanted to be true so badly I began to believe it myself, and it wasn't until I was called by a reporter from the *Dallas Morning News* and asked about my college career that I realized the misrepresentation was over." Which of the layered versions was hardest to believe?

With McKinnon acting as her campaign manager, Guerrero launched her "Get Up" campaign with a charge that her deception was less serious than Williamson's activities on behalf of his family's oil business while running for an office that would make him an oil business regulator. "I made a serious mistake," she said in her new ad. "I misled people about my academic record. I've resigned my position as railroad commissioner to show you how sorry I am. But I'm staying in the race because I'm the only candidate without a conflict of interest. The only candidate whose family doesn't make money from oil or the decisions I make. I hope you can forgive me. Growing up in Texas, I've learned it's not how often you fall that matters, but how often you get up."

Ann hosted a fund-raiser for Guerrero at the Governor's Mansion that was roundly jeered by the Republican Party. "The Lena Guerrero that I know has worked all her life for the good of the little guy, or the underdog and for those who have had a bumpy ride on the road of life," Ann said. "Now that her road has developed a bump or two, I'm here to help smooth the way for her—just as she has done time and time again for others during her tenure in the House and at the Railroad Commission. I make no apologies for standing by a friend as she has stood by me—and many of you in the audience tonight. Lena is a lot of things, but one thing she is not, is a quitter. She has never dodged a fight in her life. Last week, she stood before a packed House chamber and did the right thing. . . . She told the people of this state that she would atone for her mistakes and make a break with the past by resigning her seat on the Railroad Commission and as chair of the High Speed Rail Authority. In turn, she asked the voters to give her a second look. A fresh look."

One more major bump in the road came when the *Austin American-Statesman*'s Bruce Hight consulted the governor's ethics adviser, Barbara Jordan. The interview contained an emphatic nonendorsement, in Jordan's rococo style.

Jordan: The Lena Guerrero situation has been a very, very unfortunate occurrence for Lena Guerrero personally, for the governor's commitment to ethics, and for the whole ethical atmosphere, which has been a staple inclusion of the administration of Ann Richards. It is regrettable that it took Lena Guerrero as long as it did to simply resign the seat, but she finally did, but her name remains on the ballot because she wants to be elected. And my problem with that is that a person who is a public official, a public servant, must adhere to the highest ethical standard conceivable to the minds of the people who live and work in this state and Lena Guerrero did not do that, and that is a very sad situation.

Hight: If elected, should she resign her seat?

Jordan: In my opinion, if Lena Guerrero is elected Railroad Commissioner, the high ethical ground position would be for Lena Guerrero to resign that seat and allow the governor to have a new appointment.

Hight: But in reality that probably won't happen . . . do you think that Lena Guerrero is of the highest moral character?

Jordan [dodging the question]: I have not seen any indication that we may anticipate a resignation post-election, if election does occur.

Hight: Have you expressed your concerns to Ms. Guerrero or to the governor?

Jordan: I have not expressed anything to Lena Guerrero because I was not asked my opinion by her at all. The governor did not ask for my advice in this matter, and as a special counsel on ethics, you give advice when it is asked.

Hight: Do you think she should've asked, considering you are the ethics advisor?

Jordan: I believe that is the governor's call, not mine.

Guerrero could only respond: "I am very surprised that Barbara Jordan would make these kinds of remarks without talking to me or the governor. I have great respect for Barbara Jordan. But I believe that since I have already resigned my seat on the Railroad Commission, I have placed this matter before the people of Texas."

Mark McKinnon deep-sixed the oil field bio-epic, and the "Get Up" campaign sank faster than the *Titanic*. In a year when Bill Clinton swept into the presidency and pinned down George H. W. Bush so badly he had to pour millions of dollars into Texas to avoid losing his home state—he came within 3.5 percentage points of doing that—Guerrero lost to Williamson by 13 points and 845,000 votes. The farce had a deep etching of tragedy. Although Guerrero was young when she dug herself that hole, she must have realized her political career was over. The timing of her resignation cost her lifelong coverage by the state's medical insurance plan, and she needed it badly. She went on to start a lobbying firm and represent some high-paying clients, but an inoperable brain tumor claimed her when she was just fifty.

At the time it seemed like a pyrrhic victory for the Republicans. Just twenty months after President Bush, the decisive world leader, had assembled a broad international coalition and chased Saddam Hussein's Iraqi army out of Kuwait, the humbled man carried only eighteen states and 37.4 percent of the popular vote. He lost by nearly six million votes. His family and team were particularly bitter about Perot, who nursed a grudge against the president—they believed that a majority of Perot's nineteen million votes would have gone to Bush. One Bush ally said with contempt that anything was possible in politics those days: "A B-Teamer just got elected president of the United States." There was joy at the Governor's Mansion, and Democrats frolicked in the streets of downtown Austin. But Chuck McDonald told Karl Rove's biographers Wayne Slater and James Moore, "I think that was the beginning of the end for Ann Richards, when they blew up Lena Guerrero."

Ann's term as Texas's governor can be charted as a nearly perfect parabola—two years up and two years down. Except for the local furor over Gary Bradley's tip on how to get the Treasury lights to turn themselves off at night, she had rigorously avoided abuse-of-office accusations during her sixteen years as an elected official. But trouble brewed for Ann the ethicist throughout 1992.

The governor is the titular commander of the Texas National Guard. It is a quasi chain of command, relevant mostly when the reservists are called out to help in the wake of natural disasters. The full-time and noncommissioned

348   officers directing sprawling Camp Mabry on Austin's west side wear uniforms of the army and the air force, and the president is really their commander in chief. In late September that year, Carl Richie, a member of the governor's Policy Council, alerted Ann that a federal grand jury was investigating the National Guard. Ann wrote to the U.S. attorney in San Antonio that she did not know what the grand jury was looking for, but she had ordered everyone in her administration to cooperate fully.

A week later, the adjutant general of the Air National Guard wrote the governor that Colonel Richard Brito had been indicted for perjury after the arrest and trial of his brother for trafficking illegal drugs in Grimes County. In 1987, a drug bust on a landing strip near the small town of Navasota had resulted in the capture of a private plane loaded with Mexican marijuana. Two brothers of Colonel Brito were arrested. The colonel posted bail for the suspected smugglers, and two years later, he became head of the Texas Guard's drug-interdiction operations. In 1990, his brother Mario was found guilty and sentenced to ninety-nine years. He became a fugitive, probably fleeing to Mexico with his brother Billy, the plane's pilot, who had not yet been tried.

In December 1990, the adjutant general briefed outgoing governor Bill Clements on this unusual convergence of charges and relations. A Department of Public Safety official told the *Corpus Christi Caller-Times* he believed the 1992 federal investigation began because Colonel Brito had used a house in Brownsville as collateral when posting the suspects' bond, and he had worn his army uniform when demanding what evidence the Grimes County prosecutors had against his brothers. Brito was never indicted by the federal grand jury, but in March 1992 the army suspended his security clearance. Although reassigned from the drug-interdiction program, he received a promotion in August, and was allowed continued access to classified military information. A month later, a Grimes County grand jury indicted him on five counts of perjury. Brito wrote to Hispanic civil rights activists that he was a victim of bigotry among Texas Guard officers.

It was a sorry mess, and Brito was placed on administrative leave without pay. That October, the G.I. Forum filed discrimination complaints against the Guard on behalf of six soldiers, including Brito. Governor Richards met with members of the House Hispanic Caucus and asked for a list of people who could help her select an independent arbitrator. A lieutenant colonel and spokesman for the Guard called this proposed new investigation unwarranted: "We would prefer obviously to look to see if there are any problems ourselves. Military people ought to look at what military people are doing."

A real commander in chief would have called that insubordination. But for Ann, the messiest revelations were that Colonel Danny Kohler, the Guard's chief of staff, and two other officers had known about the army's suspension of Brito's security clearance and his continued access to classified material, but still allowed his promotion to go forward. A story about the scandal in the *Corpus Christi Caller-Times* included a photograph of Kohler. The alleged crimes occurred under Bill Clements's watch, but Colonel Kohler and the other officer cited in the *Caller-Times* story had to go.

The Brito scandal was particularly painful to Ann and her staff because Danny Kohler, an affable part-time rancher, was the husband of Ann's longtime soul mate and ace scheduler Nancy. For nearly fifteen years, drunk or sober, they had known each other about as well as two very funny and popular women could. Some members of Ann's staff believed Kohler obfuscated throughout his summons during his interview at the governor's office, but Bill Cryer, for one, claimed that Danny was guilty of nothing more than having his picture in the paper. The episode was a crushing blow for Nancy, who left the staff not long before being diagnosed with the cancer that claimed her. Ann's handling of that inner-office dynamic did not win the admiration of some of her aides. "Ann could have at least gone up to Nancy and given her a hug," said one. "She never did."

While the Guerrero and Brito sagas were unfolding, one of my closest friends made a mistake that cost him more than a trip to the governor's woodshed. Selden Hale suspected that Josh Allen, one of his fellow members on the Texas Board of Criminal Justice, had an ongoing, questionable business relationship with Mark Stiles, a former legislator from Beaumont who supplied much of the concrete used in the construction of the Mark Stiles State Prison. Based just on that repeated name, there was a glaring conflict of interest surrounding the construction of the prison, but the name was "Mark Stiles," not "Josh Allen." Selden loved having a badge he could flash to get buzzed inside prison gates. And instead of passing on his suspicions and any evidence to appropriate law enforcement officers, he ordered prison system officials to investigate Allen. Word of this reached Ann at precisely the time when Lena Guerrero was resigning her office and a Grimes County grand jury was indicting Colonel Brito for perjury regarding his brothers' drug smuggling.

In no mood for more foolishness, Ann made a speech one night in Gatesville at the women's drug-treatment unit. Because of my wife's involvement in that program, she saw the speech. She said that afterward, Ann sat in a chair on

350   the stage with her legs crossed, leaning toward Selden and doing all the talking. Selden went back to Amarillo and wrote her the resignation letter she demanded. Their exchange of letters mentioned only the settlement of the *Ruiz* case, the women and members of ethnic minorities they had brought to leadership roles in a prison system staff that had largely been all-male and all-white, their launch of the country's most ambitious drug and alcohol treatment program for convicts, and, on Ann's part, gratitude for the service to the state of Selden Hale. The "no comments" on reasons for the resignation raised GOP howls that they were stonewalling. Kent Adams, an unsuccessful Republican candidate for state representative from Beaumont, issued a press release that read in part: "In the wake of the Lena Guerrero scandal, the resignation of the state's Prison Board chairman, Selden Hale, raises serious questions about how Governor Richards is running Texas and how our state prison system is doing business. . . . What did Hale find? Why hasn't the Governor released the results of the investigation?"

I thought Ann overreacted to Selden's imprudence, that she was feeling intense pressure from the Guerrero and Brito embarrassments. She did put out the fire of that potential scandal before it got started. But the image of Ann publicly chewing out a silver-haired white guy who wore cowboy boots and had been one of her most loyal supporters for years stuck in the minds of white males in the prison system, and they made sure word of that got spread around.

CHAPTER 27

Troubles by the Score

ANN'S BIGGEST HUMILIATION in 1993 came about not because of anything she did or did not do. It happened because her friend President Bill Clinton named Texas senator Lloyd Bentsen his Treasury secretary.

One would think that with all the proclaimed Democratic talent in Texas that Ann personified, it would have been a pleasant and rewarding chore to appoint one of her peers to fill Bentsen's Senate seat. She must have wanted to yank her hair out on finding out that was not to be the case. The first choice was the handsome and charismatic former mayor of San Antonio. George Shipley had introduced Ann to Henry Cisneros, and the rapport they established that day won her his active support in the 1990 campaign. George now arranged for them to meet again. "Henry was trying to patch things up with his wife," he told me. "He had just told her about his affair and the mistress and the money he'd been giving her. He bared his soul to Ann, too, really opened up. Told her all about it." Ann was blunt with Cisneros, Shipley said. She was there on an important political errand; she was not there to be his confessor. George said she told him, "When Republicans see something they want, things can get kind of nasty. What are you gonna do when they get to this other woman and give her half a million dollars? Are you gonna be able to handle that?"

Henry said he thought he would, hoped he could.

"Well, let me know," Ann said, and she and George headed back to Austin. Cisneros was a perfect choice in so many ways—a Texas A&M and Harvard graduate who was then just forty-five years old. He was a superb orator and had star

Ann as seen from behind at one of the birthday parties in major urban centers that launched her 1994 campaign for reelection.

quality. When he was San Antonio's mayor, the U.S. Jaycees had honored him as one of the ten outstanding young men of America. He had been short-listed for a vice presidential nomination. In 1991, VISTA magazine had named him the Hispanic man of the year. The Republicans would have had a hard time fielding a candidate who could beat Cisneros in the 1993 special election, regardless of the deceit and turmoil in his married life.

"Unknown to us," George Shipley told me, "all of this was kind of a catalyst of reconciliation between Henry and his wife. Meanwhile I flew up to Washington and set about getting senators on board. We set a date, a Sunday, for Henry to arrive and get the grand tour. [West Virginia senator] Jay Rockefeller was going to introduce him around. 'Here, take a seat, this is the very chair where Daniel Webster sat,' things like that. Then Henry called and said he couldn't make our meeting on Sunday. You know, a fair amount of work had gone into arranging it, and I said, 'Do you mind telling me why not?' He said, 'On the way up I stopped in Little Rock.'

"In a hall of George's office was an enlarged photo of Ann and the mayor in their happier days. George beat his feet on his carpet and leaned over his desk in a burst of laughter. 'Henry said, "I told Governor Clinton the same things I told you, and he said, 'You did the right thing, giving that woman the money.'"

Clinton nominated Cisneros as secretary of Housing and Urban Development, and he sailed through his Senate hearing and was confirmed unanimously. But later he attracted the attention of one of the special prosecutors who were so numerous in those years. He wound up pleading guilty to lying under oath while being questioned by a federal official. It was a misdemeanor, but still a criminal act, and an admission of shameful behavior. He resigned before the end of Clinton's first term to go into the Hispanic cable-television business. I saw him once amid a group of people who asked why he had let a personal failing like that destroy a career of great promise. "No, no," he said. "You don't know how people look at me. You don't see them staring in the airports." Politics had damaged that man, for sure.

With her strongest candidate picked off by Bill Clinton, Ann looked anew at her options for filling the Senate seat. Though it would have been the pragmatic and Machiavellian move, appointing Jim Mattox was out of the question—their attacks on each other had been too brutal, too recent. Jim Hightower and Garry Mauro were too scarred by the FBI investigations and damning news stories; they could never win confirmation by the Senate. Ann moved from the class of 1982 to the Democrats' down-ballot comers of 1990—attorney general Dan Morales and comptroller John Sharp. "Morales didn't like her," George Shipley told me. "They did not get on." In any case, Morales would soon wind up in prison for trying to use his power and office to deal a crony into a lawyer's share of a huge settlement Texas won in a class-action lawsuit against big tobacco companies. But what disqualified Morales was his opposition to abortion. In contrast, Ann got along very well with John Sharp, but he was raised a Catholic, and as a state senator from Victoria, he had once tried to sneak an amendment onto a bill that would have undercut *Roe v. Wade*. Since then, his positions on that question had been elusive. To many of Ann's aides, advisers, and friends, Sharp had proclaimed himself pro-choice much too soon after the vacant Senate seat materialized. Both Morales and Sharp told the press that the governor had approached them and that they had turned her down. They were entitled to spin their own stories.

As time passed and she didn't offer a nomination, Ann looked hapless; at one point, she considered her sometime nemesis on the ethics front, Travis County district attorney Ronnie Earle. A *Texas Monthly* profile of Earle that I wrote in 2005, when House majority leader Tom DeLay had been indicted for money laundering, contains this scene: "At their home in western Travis County, Twila Earle was reading the paper about the impasse one morning and told Ronnie he was as

354   qualified and as formidable a candidate as any of those being considered. 'By the time I got out of the shower,' Ronnie told me, 'I was feeling positively senatorial.'"

In the end, Ann had to face the fact that the vaunted Democrats had no bench. With such ambivalence that it must have made her dizzy, she turned to a man who had yearned and prepared for years to serve in the United States Senate—the intelligent, decent, fiscally conservative, unexciting Bob Krueger. He had a doctorate in English literature from Oxford, and in his academic career he had attained a prestigious rank, the dean of arts and sciences at Duke University (where he had earned his MA). Returning to his hometown of New Braunfels, he was part of the Watergate class of new members of Congress in 1974, and after the first of his two terms, he was voted "most effective" by his colleagues, largely because of his mastery of energy issues.

In Krueger's 1978 Senate race against John Tower, the election returns ticked over at two in the morning and he lost a heartbreaker by three-tenths of a percent. Six years later, with Tower retired and Phil Gramm representing the GOP, the favored centrist found himself squeezed out of the Democratic primary by Kent Hance on the right and Lloyd Doggett on the left. Once more, the twist of the knife came at two in the morning.

Between those failed campaigns, President Carter had appointed him ambassador at large to Mexico and United States coordinator of Mexican affairs. And in a 1990 comeback little noted amid the furor of the governor's race between Ann and Clayton Williams, Bob had run for a Railroad Commission seat, smashed an Austin liberal in the Democratic primary, and led all candidates on the general election ballot, crushing his GOP opponent by a sixteen-point margin. The great irony in early 1993, given the contempt in which several of Ann's associates held him, was that no man could have been more aligned with the governor on issues that mattered most to her. One of his position papers offered eloquent support of *Roe v. Wade* and stem cell research: "When I imagine my daughters grown and making their own reproductive decisions, I want them to be able to embrace life as they define it and as they define what makes it fulfilling. I cannot side with people who would bind my daughters and their generation to back-alley solutions or coerced births, nor can I join in repressing medical research that could yield dignity and enrichment for millions of people."

But Ann couldn't have been more disingenuous or blasé in her announcement of his appointment: "I had many, many good people from which to choose. Many of them also happen to be good friends. But Bob Krueger is a man who will need no on-the-job training. He can hit the ground running in Washington." One note that stood out in those remarks, and may have been unintended, was that she did not appear to count him as one of her friends. Bob realized his dream of serving in the United States Senate, but his tour there lasted just less than five months. It had been fifteen years since he had run his best race. The theme song for his prospects in the special election could have been B. B. King's "The Thrill Is Gone."

The special election was another one of those ninety-day horse races, with six candidates of note heading out of the starting gate. The state treasurer, Kay Bailey Hutchison, outspent and outperformed two GOP congressmen, Joe Barton and Jack Fields, while Krueger fended off the challenges of a Dallas businessman, Richard Fisher, and José Angel Gutiérrez, who had formerly been aligned with the breakaway party La Raza Unida. Hutchison led Krueger by 99 votes, with both candidates gaining just over 593,000. The next round would be a complicated affair for Ann because she genuinely liked Hutchison. But in the interest of Clinton's young presidency and her prospects for reelection, she had to hope Krueger could hold the Senate seat for the Democrats. She assigned her son-in-law Kirk Adams to get the party strongly behind him.

Hutchison veered to the right as time wore on in her career, but in that pivotal race, she held her ideological cards close to her chest. Her bumper stickers in 1993 were a jaunty bright red and simply read "Kay!" In the Democratic camp, a glum feeling arose that it had really been no dead heat. An incumbent Democrat should have gotten better than 29 percent. Krueger was a very dignified man. His idea of sport was an impromptu recitation of Shakespeare amid Texans who had last given any thought to the bard when required to read a play or two in junior high school. But flash polls showed him twenty points down against Hutchison, and like many other Democrats, he put stock in the brainstorms of Roy Spence, who, with Garry Mauro, had guided him in 1974. The ad man talked him into putting on a Hollywood biker jacket and wraparound shades for his campaign commercial and mimicking Arnold Schwarzenegger's line from *Terminator 2*, "Hasta la vista, baby!"

The attempt to give Krueger some public flair and illumine his self-deprecating sense of humor was worse than lame. The ads were likened to a Hail Mary pass at the end of a football game; the *New York Times* described them as "zany." Hutchison put him to rout by a 2–1 margin. It was the worst defeat a challenger had ever inflicted on an incumbent U.S. senator. Krueger had irked Clinton by voting against his first budget—and its tax increase—on the grounds that the government needed to be audited for waste first. But he had excellent diplomatic experience, and the president wanted to do something for a man whose electoral

356 days were over. Jane Hickie had a fine time describing the ambassador's appointment in an interview by Brian McCall for his book *The Power of the Texas Governor*. "Do you remember the movie *Dave*?" McCall quoted her. "They sent the vice president to Burundi. They had to send him away. Which is why Krueger went to Burundi: The people in the White House saw the movie *Dave*. You think I'm kidding, but no, I'm not. I was at the Governor's Mansion when they called. There was an encyclopedia at the Mansion, and Ann said, 'See if you can find out where Burundi is.' We got the book, and oh, we were just dying laughing."

If true, the anecdote doesn't reflect well on Ann Richards, her team, or the Clinton administration. Burundi was one of the ten poorest countries in the world; only four countries from the developed world bothered to have embassies there. The preceding year, the country's first democratically elected president, a member of the Hutu ethnic majority, had been assassinated by repeated bayonet thrusts of soldiers' rifles, and the vice president and leaders of the assembly had also been killed. A retaliatory massacre of ethnic Tutsis ensued, and about 700,000 people fled the country.

In mid-1994, Bob Krueger took his wife and young daughters to the small mountainous country in central Africa. During that time, ethnic genocide in neighboring Rwanda took about 800,000 lives of Tutsis and moderate Hutus in a three-month period, and more than three million refugees and avenging militias spilled into neighboring Uganda, Zaire (now the Democratic Republic of the Congo), Tanzania, and Burundi. Almost alone among Clinton's diplomats, Krueger helped protect people from the slaughter. When he challenged Tutsi marauders, two newspapers called for his assassination, and an ambush was soon attempted, leaving Bob unhurt but two people dead and eight more wounded. One day his wife, Kathleen, faced down a dozen African soldiers who were intent on killing one of their household workers. The Kruegers' bravery and subsequent award-winning book, *From Bloodshed to Hope in Burundi*, won praise from South Africa's Nobel Peace laureate Desmond Tutu, President Jimmy Carter, and the renowned Ethiopia-born American author and physician Abraham Verghese.

Kay Bailey Hutchison's landslide win was immediately hailed as a novel convergence of feminism and conservatism. But according to an investigative story published by the *Houston Press* at the end of the saga, four days after Hutchison's June 1993 victory, a Treasury employee approached the office of the Travis County district attorney and in a purge of guilt said he had taped Hutchison ordering subordinates to destroy possibly incriminating state records. The Public Integrity Unit under Ronnie Earle had been monitoring rumors of Hutchison abusing her staff, but the investigation had not been considered hot. But with that information, the prosecutors moved fast, serving initial subpoenas for fifteen Hutchison aides as well as telephone, computer, and personnel records. The newly elected senator hotly denied the accusations and initially said she would refuse to testify before a grand jury. But according to the *Press* account, thirty-three witnesses testified, including twenty-six employees of the state Treasury. "Hutchison clearly perceived Austin was brimming with political enemies," according to a second deputy treasurer, Michael Barron. She was "constantly almost in a state of paranoia," Barron testified. "From day one, she announced to us that Paul Williams [the governor's executive assistant] was out to get her; that [Comptroller] John Sharp was out to get her; that everybody in the legislature was out to get her."

Stories leaked out of the Treasury and grand jury that were not incriminating, but still shocking—the one that most tantalized Austin political junkies had Hutchison whacking John Connally's daughter with a notebook because she wasn't doing something fast enough. Her purse boys, characterized by the *Press* as "taxpayer-subsidized butlers," were ordered to do things like put her nail polish in the refrigerator. One Treasury aide said she refused their repeated advice to open a political office and would not part with campaign funds to hire a political travel aide. The initial whistleblower—or snitch, in the GOP's view—carried his evidence to the grand jury in a pizza box.

The *Houston Press*, an alternative newspaper, did not disclose how it obtained such detailed information from the sealed records of a grand jury, but the *New York Times*' Sam Howe Verhovek confirmed that "one person who worked in the treasurer's office, speaking on condition of anonymity, says the files include handwritten memorandums by Ms. Hutchison suggesting that she was aware of political activities, like fund raising and scheduling of political events, that went on in her office, and that she gave orders to destroy the evidence once it became apparent that it could constitute a legal problem."

On one point, all parties agreed: just four months after her historic election, Hutchison was indicted on three counts of official misconduct, two of which were second-degree felonies, one a misdemeanor. The most sobering one carried a possible penalty of up to twenty years in prison and a fine of up to $100,000. Specifically, she was accused of misusing state workers and equipment for political advancement and trying to destroy evidence once an investigation was underway. Michael Barron and Hutchison's planning director, David Criss, were also indicted.

Furious, Hutchison claimed the indictment—she spoke only of her own—was "merely another chapter in the sleazy campaign tactics employed by Democrats during the U.S. Senate campaign this year." Bentsen would have been up for reelection in 1994. This meant that she would not only have to run again just eighteen months after winning the office, but also have to campaign with a cloud of serious criminal charges over her head. Why, the GOP's arguments went, Ann was known to bully her top staff! She had travel aides who were expected to hang on to her purse! The Republican Party charged that the indictments were a cynical ploy designed to lure Henry Cisneros back from Washington and into the Senate race for the Democrats. And one month after the indictments were handed down, the *Orlando Sentinel* reported, "Rejecting an intense lobbying effort by Texas Democrats, U.S. Housing and Urban Development Secretary Henry Cisneros said Wednesday night that he does not want to run for the Senate next year: 'I don't want to lead anybody on.'"

Ronnie Earle's prosecution and conviction of an incumbent treasurer for misuse of his office had launched Ann Richards's career in statewide office. His wife and daughter had worked for Ann, and Republicans knew that Earle had offered himself for the appointment that went to Krueger. The Republicans were justified in contending the odor was not perfume.

The state GOP chairman, Fred Meyer, launched a counterattack with considerable help from Karen Hughes. It didn't take long for them to learn that nine of the twelve members of the grand jury had voted in Democratic primaries, none in those of the GOP, and that Governor Richards had thirteen telephone lines in her office. In her memoir *Ten Minutes from Normal,* Hughes later wrote, "That was the first time in my career I remember feeling as if I was going to war every morning." In press releases, she branded the prosecution as a "witch hunt" and "vicious partisan politics orchestrated by a Democrat district attorney and a stacked Democrat grand jury." Meyer claimed, "Texas Governor Ann Richards and her staff apparently run a massive political operation by telephone from the state governor's office, using more private telephone lines in the taxpayer-funded state office than the entire Republican Party [has for] its state administrative offices."

The counterattack's drift, of course, was that whatever Hutchison might have done at the Treasury, Democrats in statewide office were just as guilty. Over in Bob Bullock's office, members of his inner circle smiled at the amateurishness of that facet of the governor's operation; one told me that the lieutenant governor had just a single telephone line of that nature, and its use was tightly controlled. Mary Beth Rogers had left Ann's staff to write and teach at the LBJ School; an able hand from Mark White's administration, John Fainter, was now the governor's chief of staff. The Republican siege via open-records requests, along with disapproving newspaper stories about telephone calls, forced an admission from him that some telephone records had been destroyed in the course of removing mundane clutter, and Fainter had to write a memo to Governor's Office personnel that read:

> The purpose of this memo is to remind all employees that state telephones are to be used for official state purposes only.
>
> Prohibited use of state phones includes: personal business calls, personal social calls and political calls of any kind. In other words, every phone call you make on a state phone should be related to your official work as an employee of the Governor's Office . . .
>
> We must remember that office telephones are not "Our" phones—they belong to the people of the State of Texas, and must be used to serve *them*, not ourselves.

How degrading, the Bullock team's observer said, that Fainter had to take the public fall for that. Nothing about the prosecution of Texas's junior senator boded well for its governor. The first set of indictments had to be thrown out because a member of the grand jury had been charged with theft in 1988. Another grand jury indicted the three defendants again. A retired appellate judge named John Onion, Jr., presided over the trial. Dick DeGuerin, a Democrat and one of the most gifted trial lawyers in the state, assumed the lead of Hutchison's defense team. Onion granted a change of venue to Fort Worth and told the prosecutors that some of the charges against Hutchison were so vaguely worded she could not defend herself against them. He gave them ten days to clarify the wording of the charges. Momentum swung back and forth: David Criss, the indicted planning director, told the *Houston Chronicle* that he was ready to cooperate with Earle. "I won't be the scapegoat anymore," he said. "Kay Hutchison lied when she said she didn't know what I was doing."

The trial at last began in February 1994. Shortly after the senator pleaded not guilty, a bomb threat emptied the courthouse. It turned out that the threat concerned a simultaneous trial of antiabortion protestors. When they were able to proceed, DeGuerin told me, Judge Onion said he wanted and intended to see the governor's phone records—a chilling demand, to some Democrats. The judge began the often-tedious task of considering pretrial motions. Then, in a move that baffled many seasoned courtroom observers, Ronnie Earle asked the judge for a pretrial ruling to approve certain evidence in bulk. Onion declined, saying he would rule on each piece of evidence as it was presented. Earle said he would have to drop the charges. Onion told him to proceed with the trial, and Earle refused. The judge angrily swore in another jury and ordered them to acquit the senator. They did, and under the constitutional protection against double jeopardy, she could never be tried on those charges again.

I was having an after-work drink at the Texas Chili Parlor when this thunderous news blew through Austin. An attorney at our table said, "You don't take it to nuclear war and then *fold*!" Earle shared some of the disallowed evidence with the press and threatened to make all the grand jury testimony public. But the prosecutors' tempers cooled, and charges against Barron and Criss were dropped. Some observers speculated that Earle had thought he could get another set of indictments from another grand jury and make his evidentiary case before another judge. Onion said afterward that he probably would have approved the evidence if Earle had agreed to do it his way. After losing the big cases against Mattox and Hutchison, Earle's reputation as a courtroom lawyer was forever besmirched.

But the Republicans never did get rid of him or his Public Integrity Unit. Eleven years later, Earle attained an indictment of U.S. House majority leader Tom DeLay for money laundering. Ronnie had retired by the time DeLay's case finally went to trial in November 2010, and his team of prosecutors won a conviction in an upset of Dick DeGuerin. The judge listened to DeLay's indignant speech in the punishment phase of the trial and, unimpressed, gave him three years. Even if an appeals court of elected Republicans overturned the verdict and he never served a day, as expected, the much-feared Hammer, as he was known in Congress, was reduced to being a pundit and a cha-cha-ing contestant on *Dancing with the Stars*.

Ann told *Texas Monthly*'s Paul Burka, "The minute I heard about Kay's indictment, I said, 'This is the worst thing for everybody.' I knew how it was going to play out. We're both women. We both held the same office. I knew that her guys—and I don't think it was Kay—were going to come after me."

Burka, who had a law degree, could make no sense of the way the senator's trial ended. He told Ann that "everybody in Texas" believed she had persuaded Ronnie to tank his reputation to benefit her. "Absolutely not," she responded. "And, no, everybody doesn't. I never talked to him about the case or anything else while it was going on.

"I like Ronnie, but we're not close. I tried to cut his budget when I was county commissioner."

For Ann, what must have resonated from Hutchison's trial was her former friend's taunt when she consented to appear before the grand jury: "They know that if I have a sixty percent margin in 1994, the entire Democratic power structure in this state is finished."

Attempting a comeback after his bitter loss to Ann, Jim Mattox ran in the Democratic primary for the Senate against a Dallas businessman, Richard Fisher, the same man whom Krueger had defeated and whom Mattox accused of being a closet Republican. Fisher dealt him another hurtful wound, winning with 54 percent. In that fall's general election, Kay Bailey Hutchison defended her seat with flair, bashing Fisher by 955,000 votes.

Her margin of victory: 60.7 percent.

Ann takes aim from thirty feet at a target on an FBI *firing range for handguns, 1993 or 1994.*

CHAPTER 28

Sass

THE APEX OF ANN'S POLITICAL CAREER had come about in a period full of events that were almost too unexpected to comprehend. Riots had erupted in the Soviet Union's satellites in 1986, when she was winning her second term as treasurer, and in late 1989 the riots escalated into a full-blown rebellion that eventually cost the Soviet Union control of those "republics" it had claimed and held by resolute force. (What was one to make of these vast new Asian countries called Kazakhstan, Kyrgyzstan, Tajikistan, Turkmenistan, and Uzbekistan?) Further hastening the end of the Cold War, the Berlin Wall fell in November 1989. After the seven-month Gulf War against Iraq ended in February 1991, George H. W. Bush enjoyed the greatest stature of any man on earth. Certainly, he had the power. And once the Soviet Union collapsed completely in December 1991, amid claims that Ronald Reagan had bankrupted and brought down what he called the "Evil Empire," one would have thought his successor would just have to bask in the glory. Yet just twenty-two months after his wartime triumph, he lost badly in his bid for reelection.

George W. Bush could not bring himself to believe that Bill Clinton had actually defeated his father. In his view, Clinton was the beneficiary of conservative infighting, not a real victor. Pat Buchanan's guerilla challenge in the primaries and the image he projected of Republicans as the party of nativist anger had sown the seeds of defeat. "Never shoulda happened," the younger Bush said. The time I heard him make that claim, he didn't mention the night his dad looked at his watch during the debate with Clinton and Perot as if he had more important things to do. That was when I thought, "He is really going to lose."

Clinton prevailed, many Democrats thought, because so many A-list candidates, such as New York governor Mario Cuomo and Texas senator Lloyd Bentsen, thought Bush couldn't be defeated and sat it out. From the outset, Ann had a warm relationship with the young president who had shocked the GOP. Once when President Clinton needed to do some business with the Texas governor, he tracked her down to an appointment with Gail Hewitt, her longtime hair stylist. Gail handed the governor the telephone and they spoke quickly, resolving the matter. Then Ann shifted to her easygoing voice and told him a joke. "Bill? If two people get married in Arkansas and move to Texas, what do you call them?" On the other end, he chuckled or sighed and waited for the punch line. She drawled, "Cousins."

But her familiarity and friendship with the president did not mean they would always agree. The Superconducting Super Collider was being gouged under one-time tallgrass prairie, now mostly sun-baked farmland, near Waxahachie, a short drive south of Dallas. Lobbying the Clinton administration and Congress to keep those grandiose projects alive was a top priority of Jane Hickie, who now directed the Office of State-Federal Relations. And the governor enlisted additional help in Washington from a sort of lobbyist without portfolio, the lawyer Shelton Smith. As a University of Texas student, Shelton had gotten hooked on politics and government while working for Governor Preston Smith (no relation). He had made a great deal of money in a hurry as a plaintiff's lawyer in Houston, and he had a beautiful Hill Country retreat with several guest homes along the banks of the Blanco River, southwest of Austin. Ann and her staff at the Treasury had used Shelton's ranch for working retreats, and during her first gubernatorial campaign, Shelton had been a generous contributor. "I've got a deal for you," she told him in late 1992. "I want you to move to Washington for a year and a half and make sure this Supercollider thing stays on track. And I can't pay you. You have to do this on your own nickel." What a deal! But Shelton agreed to do it.

The secret of why matter has mass is believed to reside in a particle called the Higgs boson, also known as the "God particle." This theoretical particle has never been observed in experiments. Theorists' calculations project that it exists in detectable amounts at incredibly high temperatures and pressures—such as were present at the Big Bang, which created the universe, most scientists believe. To subject it to empirical research, the federal Department of Energy set out to create the most powerful particle accelerator in the world. It would slam particles together with more force than anything known to mankind, producing a beam of protons and antiprotons that superconducting magnets would control by bending the beam around an oval-shaped tunnel fifty-four miles long and two hundred feet underground. More than half the states vied for this megalaboratory, but in 1987, with Governor Bill Clements's promise of state funding of $1 billion, a site in Ellis County was chosen. Digging began in 1991, using a tunneling bore that was fifteen feet in diameter. Labs were going to be built aboveground to produce the superconducting magnets. The simulated Big Bang beneath the sandstone and limestone bedrock was going to be under the direction of a physicist with the University of Texas and Harvard. (As this book was going to press, teams of scientists working at the Large Hadron Collider, near Geneva, Switzerland, claimed to be close to detecting the Higgs boson. But in almost the same breath, scientists at the press conference said it would be many months before they could offer any proof.)

Like the race to catch up with *Sputnik*, and the invention of the missiles and satellites that eventually put American astronauts on the moon, the Super Collider intrigued the Reagan and Bush administrations in part because of its possible military applications and its potential to create unearthly amounts of energy. And they did not want the Soviets to do it first. But in 1992 there was no Soviet Union. And in addition to the sudden end of the Cold War, by 1993 the projected cost of completing the Super Collider had ballooned to $8.25 billion. Congress was having a severe case of buyer's remorse with the Super Collider, and the Clinton administration's passion for it was tepid, at best.

As the grand experiment's fate became more apparent, Shelton Smith's mission in Washington evolved into reclaiming the initial $150 million that Texas had invested. (According to the *Houston Chronicle*, Texas's bond expenditures on the project totaled $400 million.) Clinton and his Energy Department bureaucrats weren't too hot on refunding the money. The disagreement escalated to the point where Shelton found himself seated in the White House with Ann and the president. As the bargaining grew more intense, Shelton got increasingly nervous. "She said to President Clinton, 'I want you to understand something, pal. You owe me a lot of money, and if you don't pay it back, I'm gonna sue you.' Then she turned and pointed at me and said, 'And this is the guy who's gonna do it.'"

Shelton continued to describe the moment: "Clinton's a big guy. He had turned beet red. He sat there glaring at me, both hands on his thighs, and said, 'How much are you gonna sue me for?'"

"I said, 'I don't know for certain, Mr. President, but it's probably gonna be four or five billion.'

"'Do you think you can win it?'

"'Yes, sir, I do.'

"He turned and stared at Ann a while longer, then he got a huge grin on his face, and he said, 'Well, Governor, I guess we'd better get you your money.'"

Another series of meetings ensued with officials at the Department of Energy. Taking charge of the transaction was an undersecretary named Bill White, later a popular Democratic mayor of Houston and an unsuccessful candidate for governor. In the final meeting, Shelton said, "They handed me an envelope with three checks totaling one hundred fifty million dollars. I thought it was going to be a wire transfer! So I'm going out of there with these checks in my briefcase. I called Ann and said, 'What am I gonna do?'

"She said, 'Well, you idiot, get on a plane back down here and let's put it in the bank!'

"So I jumped on the first flight, and after I was back in Austin and the checks were deposited we went to the Four Seasons Hotel lounge. She saw I was acting kind of twitchy, and she said, 'Oh, go ahead, have a drink. I don't care.'"

———

IN APRIL 1993, another crisis arose for Ann involving the federal government. A federal judge in West Texas and officials of the U.S. Fish and Wildlife Service indicated that several aquatic species that lived only in the San Marcos Springs of the Edwards Aquifer qualified for protection under the Endangered Species Act. One species imperiled with extinction was a blind salamander. San Antonio and smaller towns relied entirely on the aquifer for their drinking water, and large-scale irrigated agriculture in Central and West Texas pumped from the aquifer to meet its needs. A rebellious uproar ensued over the court's power and that blind lizard-like amphibian. The Endangered Species Act, which had been signed into law by Richard Nixon, was cast as the ominous villain.

Gib Lewis, the House Speaker from Fort Worth, had run afoul of the Travis County district attorney's Public Integrity Unit by accepting and failing to report several gifts. He pleaded guilty to two misdemeanors, resigned as Speaker, and did not seek reelection in 1993. The Democrats, who still had a healthy majority in the House, chose a well-liked Panhandle farmer, Pete Laney, as the new Speaker. Trying to head off a political firestorm, Susan Rieff, John Hall, and Bob Armstrong, whom Clinton had made an assistant secretary of the interior, composed a letter to Interior secretary Bruce Babbitt, the former governor of Arizona, with copies to Bullock and Laney. It explained how the state had devised a plan that would keep the San Marcos Springs flowing even during a drought, thereby protecting the species. And they asked Babbitt for a very specific letter outlining the consequences if the state just ignored the Endangered Species Act. On her copy of the memo, Ann bracketed the latter part with a star of emphasis and the notation "Important to get done."

Babbitt obliged with a somber explanation that the state's failure could cause federal funds for highways, military bases, and crop subsidies to be withdrawn. Texas then got lucky, because rains broke the drought and increased the springs' flow, reducing the danger that the fragile species would become extinct.

In the 1993 legislative session, Gary Bradley, Ann's old friend and onetime major contributor, got the legislature to pass a bill that proposed to overturn and countermand any City of Austin attempt to enforce the strictures on developers laid out by the activist group Save Our Springs. Out-of-town legislators had a history of indulging in the capital's pleasures while spiting the city however they could. Without hesitation, Ann vetoed her old friend's anti-sos bill. She thought that should signal reasonable environmentalists of her goodwill. And for some, it did. But in the other camp, a number of legislators' animosity toward Ann's environmental team and their policies festered to the point that a senator who had been adding an amendment to a bill looked up at the gallery and shot Susan Rieff the finger.

Then the U.S. Fish and Wildlife Service released yet another study, this one designating thirty-three Texas counties as critical habitat of endangered black-capped vireos and golden-cheeked warblers. It raised the possibility of listing jaguars as an endangered species, even though not one of the big spotted cats had been seen in Texas in many years; the last one killed was in Mills County in 1903. Organizations calling themselves Farmers and Ranchers for Property Rights and Take Back Texas rose up. The leader of the latter organization was a man named Marshall Kuykendall, whose former wife, Karen, was Ann's friend, and their son had worked for Ann during the 1990 campaign.

Ross Ramsey, then with the *Houston Chronicle*, wrote, "Richards initially supported efforts to win federal 'outstanding national water resource' protection for four areas of the state. She later backed off, saying the state should find someone other than 'ham-handed' federal regulators to act as steward." The state Republican Party, for this purpose calling itself Associated Republicans of Texas, issued a press release accusing Ann of more flip-flopping.

Ann had increasingly less time to spend with Bud, but they managed to work things out. Even when they couldn't align their schedules, the correspondence never stopped. In the summer of 1992, he still had some hooks in the water in Hollywood, and then he planned to join her on vacation in Switzerland.

Dear Guv:

My plane tickets to Gstaad arrived today. I suppose I am really going to climb down out of my tree and go over there.

By the time you get this note I'll be in L.A. playing Hollywood—don't cry for me, Limo-zina—but I want you to know I'm thinking about you. If that sounds too sinister, you're in my heart.

Love always, Bud

He accompanied her on a trip to Los Angeles in which she courted CEOs, raised money from celebrities, and lobbied for more movies shot in Texas. He elected to go home early.

Dear Guv:

Sorry I couldn't hang around L.A. for a few extra days, but I had to hurry home to my blind dog and my grouchy cat.

Call me when you get a breather.

It's only 74 months until the next century. I guess I've got to hurry to get things tidy in time for the end of the world.

Love, Bud

Another time he sent her a great photo taken when he was a younger man with a broad smile, holding a long fly rod and a very big salmon.

Dear Guv:

I'm sure you never doubted my story about catching a 35-pound salmon on a two-handed fly rod in the Alta River in Norway, thus earning membership in the X Kilo Club—but we know how people are about fish stories.

I still have the boots and slicker in my hall closet. I gave all my fishing tackle (except for one light spinning rod) to my oldest grandson.

We had the fish canned and ate it.

The fly I used was called "Thunder and Lightning."

I wasn't kidding about the swarms of stinging flies, either.

Love, Bud

But for every one of those welcome messages, it seemed now there were three broadsides from the Republican Party and Karen Hughes. The former television journalist was like a machine gun of press releases, in which she often quoted herself.

Republicans Stand Up for Taxpayers, School Children;
Governor Ann Richards Acting Like a Playground Bully

Austin—"Republicans in the Texas House of Representatives today stood up
for taxpayers and school children in Texas in rejecting a $4 billion tax increase
and redistribute-the-wealth plan which Governor Ann Richards stubbornly
tried to shove down the throats of reluctant legislators," Texas GOP executive
director Karen Hughes said today.

"Despite Governor Richards' playground bully tactics, the House Republicans did what they were elected to do and stood up for the best interests of the
taxpayers and the school children of Texas . . .

"Governor Richards has acted irresponsibly in attempting to threaten and
intimidate Republicans into accepting an unacceptable plan. We are proud of
our Republican elected officials, of their integrity, and of their willingness to
do the right thing in the face of irresponsible threats and criticism from the
governor."

Ann's Policy Council aides and Bill Cryer were able to refute most of the Republicans' charges, or at least tell their side of the story, but it was a constant, time-
consuming task. Cryer was pleased to issue a release when an Austin district judge
ruled that the Governor's Office had complied with Open Records Act requests
by releasing more than 35,000 pages of records to the Republican Party. A staffer
named Don Temples spent almost all his time faxing documents demanded by
the GOP's requests. It was harassment and logjamming, plain and simple, and the
strategy was working: Ann and her team were constantly on the defensive.

In September 1991, a man named George Hennard rammed his pickup into a
Luby's Cafeteria in the Central Texas army town of Killeen, and then used two
handguns to murder twenty-seven trapped people and wound twenty more before killing himself. At the time, it was the worst mass murder in American history. A chiropractor named Suzanna Gratia Hupp watched her father and mother
executed by Hennard—her dad had tried to tackle the man. Hupp was haunted
by her belief that if she hadn't left her .38 revolver in the car, she could have shot
the maniac and saved them. She later ran for the legislature on that single issue
and won, becoming a heroine for a growing number of Texans. Ann was troubled
by the slaughter in Killeen and by a grieving daughter's proposal that every man
and woman should be free to go armed and take the law into their own hands.
But the tragedy in Killeen sent Ann down a road to a stand of principle she would

370   not back away from, and it put her in direct opposition to the forces personified by Representative Hupp.

The wrangles related to crime-fighting policies were not wholly devoid of humor. Ann took a strong hand in ordering the Texas Rangers to remove obstacles that kept women from qualifying for the elite law enforcement group. The storied Ranger Joaquin Jackson got fed up and retired, partly over that episode and her bossy manner. She was, of course, the boss. Joaquin and a novelist, David Marion Wilkinson, wrote *One Ranger*, an excellent book about his hair-raising and sometimes hilarious experiences. Third- or fourth-hand versions of what happened next sounded like material for Cormac McCarthy's *No Country for Old Men*. I asked Joaquin to elaborate on his rumored feud with the governor. He wrote back:

> Reference Miss Ann, Shelton Smith is a good friend of mine, and he was a lead attorney for the governor. Well, David Wilkinson and I were at Shelton's place on the Blanco right after we had finished the manuscript of *One Ranger*. Shelton told me that I needed a woman to write a blurb for the book. I asked him who he had in mind, and he said Ann Richards. I said, "Shit, Shelton, she's one of the reasons I left the Rangers."
>
> But he sent her the manuscript. He said she called him and did not say, "This is Ann" or "This is the governor." She just said, "Shelton, you tell that old bastard that I will write him a blurb for his book, but I will tell you I know he rode his horse from Amarillo to Austin to turn in his Ranger badge, and I damn sure don't appreciate it."
>
> Shelton replied, "No, Ann, I know what he did was to ride his horse from Alpine to Austin."
>
> Of course I did not ride a horse from Alpine to Austin, but I drove the sorriest vehicle I ever drove for the State, a Jeep Cherokee. Now you know the rest of the story.

Episodes like that only added to her lore as a colorful leader, and Ann was hardly indifferent to the issue of violent crime. Following the horrifying spree of the serial murderer Kenneth McDuff, in March 1993 she announced the formation of the "Fugitive Squad," an apprehension program targeted at capturing the most violent parole violators. "I want to do whatever it takes to make sure that any Kenneth McDuff, or any potential Kenneth McDuff, is brought in before he can hurt innocent people," she said. "The Fugitive Squad consists of five law enforcement officers from the Department of Public Safety, the Texas Department of Criminal Justice and the head of Texas Crime Stoppers. They will work closely with local law enforcement agencies, the Pardons and Paroles Division, and Texas Crime Stoppers. Their job will be to go through the files of Pardons and Paroles searching for parolees who fit the profile of a repeat violent offender. The team will then establish a Ten Most Wanted list of violent parolees. We are going to turn the heat up on these guys." The squad included a Texas Ranger, Stan Oldham, and at the end of the first year, Ann was able to announce the apprehension and arrest of the first fifteen ex-cons who wound up on that list. But the success was underreported because of what happened on the rolling hills a few miles east of her hometown, just before she announced the formation of her Fugitive Squad.

On February 28, 1993, Ann was traveling in Brenham when she received a call from staffers informing her that a surreal and savage drama had erupted inside a compound called Mount Carmel, where a religious cult called the Branch Davidians had been drawing increasing scrutiny and suspicion by law enforcement for some time. The Davidians were a rebellious offshoot of the Seventh-day Adventists. In 1988, the cult's leader, a sometime rock guitarist who changed his name to "David Koresh," was involved in a gunfight with a cult rival named George Roden. Koresh was acquitted at trial, while Roden went to prison. In late 1991, activities inside the compound had begun to alarm caseworkers at the state's Child Protective Services agency, and reports of automatic weapons and explosives being stockpiled at the compound got the attention of local law enforcement officials and agents of the federal Bureau of Alcohol, Tobacco, and Firearms (ATF).

John Fainter, the governor's chief of staff, compiled a riveting diary of the unfolding tragedy at Mount Carmel. In early December 1992, ATF agents approached the Richards administration with requests to borrow state aerial-reconnaissance equipment. The governor is titular commander of the Texas Air National Guard; the ATF could also have gotten what it wanted through military channels, which it did. In January and February 1993, aerial photos and infrared videos allegedly conveyed a "hot spot" image that the agents interpreted as an illegal weapons cache.

Ann and her chief legal counsel, David Talbot, contended that the National Guard could participate in arrest missions only if illegal drugs were involved. The ATF responded with accusations, never proved, that the Branch Davidians were manufacturing methamphetamines inside their compound. The morning of February 28, though the agents knew that the cult members had been tipped off and that the element of surprise was lost, heavily armed ATF officers tried to serve warrants at the compound for firearms violations, with support from eight National Guard helicopters and crews. In a vicious gunfight, four ATF agents and at least six residents of the compound were killed. One of the slain was the two-year-old daughter of David Koresh.

The next morning at the Capitol, Ann had planned to wax nostalgic about her high school and college years in concert with "Waco Day," but the bloodshed and standoff changed the subject. Ann told a crowd of reporters, "The sad part about a situation like this is that you're trying to make sense out of a senseless event. I'm worried about those children in the compound. I want them to get those kids out. If the adults make a choice that they want to be there, then they have to live with the consequences. But kids don't have a choice."

Answering a reporter's question, Ann said that she would take "a serious look" at legislation to ban assault weapons in Texas.

The standoff grew more tense and more bizarre every day. The FBI listened for hours as Koresh ranted about his interpretation of Scripture. Under cover of darkness, the Branch Davidians hung a huge banner on the roof that read: "God Help Us, We Want Press." Bumper stickers appeared in the area that read: "*Nothing* Happened in Waco!" Ann learned that the foray by the National Guard had resulted in three shot-up helicopters and state expenditures of $300,000. "The thing that frightens me," she said as the siege wore on, "is that everyone wearies of it. I think eventually we can reach a peaceful solution, but I'm going to respect the decisions that are made by the FBI. I think they're all sort of tired of listening to the evangelizing on the telephone, and I can't say I blame them."

Koresh's mother contacted the Houston defense attorney Dick DeGuerin, and he gained admission to the compound. He later said that when he walked up to the front door, the crunching and crackling under his boots was not gravel, but rather an amazing number of spent cartridges. He told me that Koresh had been wounded in the gunfight and smelled strongly of raw garlic, which he believed was a natural antibiotic. DeGuerin believed he could negotiate a deal for the Davidians' surrender, but Ann watched in anguish as Koresh backed out, saying that God was giving him this chance to reveal the mystery of the seven seals in the Book of Revelation. He demanded and got a live broadcast on a Christian radio station.

The FBI blasted the besieged cultists at night with deafening recordings of chanting Tibetan monks, the whine of a dentist's drill, shrieks of rabbits being slaughtered. An FBI tank destroyed Koresh's prized Camaro. Then at five thirty on the morning of the fifty-first day of the standoff, the National Guard informed

Ann's office that the FBI was going in, using tear gas. The outcome stamped on the nation's consciousness a uniquely Texas image of explosions and inferno. Ann was snookered and used by federal agents who wanted to go in like a platoon of military commandos. The ATF got their wish, they got the hell shot out of them, and it led to that horrifying image of the compound ablaze with women and children inside. And to an extent, the tragedy had Ann Richards's name on it.

Clinton's attorney general, Janet Reno, had recently come down to tour with Ann and some staff members, who included my wife, the drug-treatment prison in Kyle, south of Austin. Among the paranoid and conspiracy-minded element of Americans who perceived black helicopters roaming the country at night—a group that included the Oklahoma City bomber, Timothy McVeigh—word spread that the purpose of Reno's tour of Kyle was a masquerade so that she and Ann could plot the attack on the Branch Davidians.

That fateful April, as the ashes and bones of Mount Carmel were still being collected and sifted by forensic experts, the legislature signaled that it would send a bill to allow private citizens to carry concealed handguns. Its Senate champion was a Houston-area Republican legislator, Jerry Patterson, who would later win multiple terms as land commissioner. Ann promised she would veto it, proclaiming: "The people of this state do not need to be reminded that weapons of violence produce death to innocent children and adults. I am an avid hunter and believe strongly in the rights of individuals to own guns. That is not the question here. This legislation will only increase the level of violence on our streets. I have not talked to one law enforcement officer who supports this bill, and I cannot in good conscience ask them to patrol the streets of this state and face additional hazards that this bill will encourage. Frankly, the only outcome of the passage of this bill will be more people killed by gunfire."

Reporters mobbed her in the Capitol over the issue, and one of them asked what Bullock thought of this bill and her veto threat. My friend John P. Moore, a senior aide of Bullock since his days as comptroller, told me what happened next: "Ann said, 'I don't know. Let's go ask him.' And here they came barging into his office, the governor and a crowd of reporters, TV cameras and lights and all. I think that's when the relationship of Ann and Bullock was ripped for good."

In response to her standoff with the legislature, she heightened her rhetoric: "The move by sponsors to report out a stripped-down version of the concealed gun bill is nothing more than game-playing by a few legislators who appear intent on embarrassing this great state as a place where gun-toting vigilantes roam the streets."

At a press conference to announce her veto of a bill allowing private citizens to carry concealed handguns, Governor Ann Richards is joined, from left, by State Representative Elliott Naishtat, Senator Royce West, State Representative Sherri Greenberg, and two uniformed policemen confined to wheelchairs by gunfire.

The legislature passed the bill, and she vetoed it as promised. In a speech she turned to police chiefs, county sheriffs, and constables who supported her veto; her voice rang with withering contempt for her adversaries: "I especially want to thank you for choosing to stand by me on this day when we say no to the amateur gunslingers who think they will be braver and smarter with gun in hand."

With her reelection in mind, she had started appearing at town-hall-like meetings around the state. People in the audiences kept raising the question. On remarks by the bill's sponsors that women wanted to be able to carry guns in their purses, she quipped that she didn't know a woman who could *find* a gun in her purse in an emergency. She must have gotten tired of hearing about pistol-packing Texans, and one night on the trail she lost her patience—some would say her discipline—in characteristic fashion. She wouldn't mind so much, she said, if these trained shooters were required to hook their pistols to chains around their necks. That way, others could say, "Look out, that one's got a gun!" She wasn't just parting company with the people who disagreed with her. She ridiculed them.

CHAPTER 29

Collision Course

WITH ITS GLAMOUR AND TRAGEDY and the mythos of Camelot, the Kennedy clan usually gets first mention as America's modern political dynasty. In one generation, three of its men accounted for a president and three U.S. senators. But over a span of three successive generations, four Bushes accounted for two presidents, a vice president, a senator, and two governors. Ann Richards was too good a politician to take an electoral challenge from that family lightly.

The patriarch, Prescott Bush, was a World War I army officer in artillery and intelligence and then a Wall Street banker who directed a firm tied to a German coal and steel corporation that helped finance the rise of Hitler and utilized slave labor from Auschwitz. Overcoming poor publicity and a lawsuit by Auschwitz survivors, Prescott Bush was elected to the Senate from Connecticut in 1952 and served until 1963, a key moderate ally of President Eisenhower.

During World War II, Prescott's son, George Herbert Walker Bush, was not quite nineteen when he was commissioned an ensign in the navy, where he trained first as a photographic officer keeping a record of the destruction wrought by bombs falling from the bays of B-24s and B-29s. Then he retrained as a pilot of a light bomber called a TBM Avenger. He joined an aircraft-carrier-based squadron as U.S. forces closed in on Japan. In the intense air battle over the Mariana Islands, he sank a cargo ship but also had to ditch a plane. Everyone in his crew survived that splash in July 1944.

Three months later, twenty-year-old Lieutenant (junior grade) Bush and a radioman and gunner flew off a carrier toward one of the Bonin Islands, 600 miles

Ann enjoys a rousing welcome from students of Tyler Junior College who have come over to Athens for a campaign rally in 1994.

from Japan, that was called Chichi Jima. The small mountainous island bristled with antiaircraft gun placements. The target was a long-range radio station that had been intercepting American transmissions and warning the Japanese mainland of impending air strikes. From an approach at 8,000 feet, Bush aimed the nose down in the steep-glide bombing pattern, the third of four planes going in over the sides of the mountains. Black puffs of smoke and flak blew up all around them, and Bush felt the plane jump when one of those explosions ripped shrapnel into the engine in the Avenger's nose.

He wrestled the plane onward and dropped four 500-pound bombs on the enemy station's buildings and its antenna, then veered off to sea. The cockpit filled with smoke, and he could see flames in the crooks of the wings. He got the plane high enough and far enough over the water that he bailed out, and his parachute opened. One of his crew, he never knew which one, tried to parachute as well, but the tail's stabilizer blasted into him and he was killed. The other crewman went down with the plane and died in the crash. One of the victims released the life raft, which inflated, and after a desperate swim, Bush clambered in, puking and crying like the boy he was. Downed fliers in the Pacific were often torn to shreds by sharks. The beasts idly rubbed their backs against the bottoms of the lifeboats, like a horse scratching an itch on a gatepost, and then suddenly one would lunge and leap out of the water, trying to snatch and pull a man out of the raft. Great white sharks looked like an onrushing train with a gaping maw and teeth the size of bayonets. Bush didn't mention that dread in his reports, but all the fliers in his squadron had heard horrid rumors about Americans who had been captured and held on Chichi Jima—beheadings and even cannibalization by one Japanese who thought he could destroy a man's eternal spirit by eating his liver. Bush saw a Japanese craft headed his way, but protective fighter pilots chased it away. A submarine called the *Finback* eventually surfaced and rescued George Bush. He was awarded the Distinguished Flying Cross for that combat mission, one of the fifty-eight he flew.

After the war, George Bush married Barbara Pierce and attended Yale, where he became a father for the first of six times and played first base for the Bulldogs in the first two College World Series. He got to shake the hand of Babe Ruth. He raised family eyebrows by taking his young family to the desert oil town of Midland, Texas, where he had extraordinary luck drilling for and finding oil in the Permian Basin, as he later did in the Gulf of Mexico. In 1958, he moved the oil-company headquarters and his family to Houston, where he started his political career by winning two terms in Congress. This was the man that *Newsweek* put on a 1987 cover with an unflattering photograph and the caption "Fighting the Wimp Factor."

On his father's political team, George W. Bush screened all reporters requesting an interview with his dad. "Give me one good reason why I should let you talk to George Bush," he would say. He shrugged off journalists' complaints: "Just doing my job, protecting the old man." Some reporters disliked him, and the feeling was mutual. He had vetted the *Newsweek* reporter, Margaret Warner, and he let her know what he thought of the "wimp" story. "I was red-hot," he wrote in his book *Decision Points*. "She muttered something about the editors being responsible for the cover. I did not mutter. I railed about her editors and hung up. From then on, I was suspicious about political journalists and their unseen editors."

Then a year later that woman from Austin was on national television claiming his dad was born with a silver foot in his mouth. And for years she insulted him again and again. It is true that Ann's disdain was ongoing. When I was drafting her environmental position papers during the 1990 campaign, I knew that President Bush had taken actions to protect wetlands and was a staunch defender of the Clean Air Act. I wrote something to the effect that as governor she would look forward to working with the president on those and other issues. She wrote in the margin: "I don't think so."

Born in 1947, George W. Bush went to grade school and junior high in Midland. He spent enough of his adolescence in Houston's posh River Oaks enclave that he and Molly Ivins, a future nemesis who gave him the nickname "Shrub," ran in somewhat the same private-school crowd. But like his dad (and David Richards), he went on to attend the prestigious Phillips Academy in Andover, Massachusetts. His grades at the prep school were good, and the legacy of his grandfather and father guaranteed him admission to Yale and its famous secret society, Skull and Bones. He was a child of the sixties, but like his contemporary Karl Rove, he recoiled from what was becoming youthful fashion. His dad had been a Phi Beta Kappa. George W. chased tail with the guys and just got by with his grades. During a visit home after graduation, George W. veered drunkenly into his parents' driveway, overran the garbage cans, then offered his disgusted father a fistfight, "*mano a mano*." Great numbers of American families have experienced something like that.

His hell-raising years coincided with the height of the war in Vietnam. Without question, some political calls were made for him, one to the Democrat Ben Barnes, then the lieutenant governor. Those calls scooted George W. to the head of the waiting list to join the Texas Air National Guard, which enabled him to avoid the draft. He was commissioned a second lieutenant and learned to fly F-102 fighter jets. George W. Bush obtained an MBA from Harvard, and then, like his dad, he drove out to Midland to make it as a wildcatter. He raised $2 million for his company, Bush Exploration, and lost it drilling dry holes. After two years out there, he ran for Congress because Jimmy Carter was trying to regulate natural gas and, he said, had the nation "headed toward European-style socialism." The Democratic state senator from Lubbock, Kent Hance, whipped him handily in 1978, casting him as a beer-drinking party boy who needed to grow up.

On the good side of the ledger, George W. had met and married a public school librarian, Laura Welch, who had moved back to her hometown after enjoying her own fun-loving years in Austin. He woke up with a crushing hangover after his fortieth-birthday celebration in Colorado Springs and abruptly quit drinking. Another defining thing that happened for him in those years was that he became a fervent born-again Christian. He attributed it to a long conversation with Billy Graham at his parents' retreat in Kennebunkport, Maine, and in men's Bible-study classes he attended in Midland. Still, in apparent fear of what George might blurt, his mother had him seated at the far end of the table during a formal dinner for Queen Elizabeth and Prince Philip. Barbara fondly remarked to the queen that he was the black sheep of the family.

A succession of fortunate mergers gave him the chance to run a Cincinnati-based company, Spectrum 7, and for three years, he was president of a company with dozens of producing wells. Then the eighties oil bust almost took Spectrum under. A merger with a company called Harken Energy staved off that calamity, and because of his dad's power and stature, George W.'s role drew scrutiny when Harken outbid much bigger Amoco for exclusive rights to drill offshore in the Persian Gulf for Bahrain.

Having failed to replicate his dad's success as a West Texas oilman, he moved his family to Dallas. In 1998, a month before the old man, that alleged wimp, demolished Michael Dukakis, George W. learned that a Bush family friend wanted to sell the Texas Rangers baseball team. He helped arrange a syndicate that bought the then-mediocre team for $89 million. George W. borrowed $500,000 to obtain a small stake in the franchise and the title of managing general partner. One highlight of his role was when the Rangers were able to sign Nolan Ryan away from the Houston Astros, and it turned out the old fireballing pitcher still had plenty of gas in his tank.

In the run-up to the 1990 elections, before the emergence of Clayton Williams, there was a bit of talk about George W. as a gubernatorial candidate. But the family's hopes for another star politician were reportedly focused more then on his younger brother Jeb in Florida. And the launch of a political career was feasible for neither of them as long as the old man was president. George W.'s principal job was, once again, to put his good name to use, this time by lobbying for a new, publicly funded, $191 million stadium for the Rangers. The referendum passed by a 2–1 margin. Local legislators crafted and pushed a bill to create the Arlington Sports Facilities Development Authority; they needed the quasi-governmental body in order to use the power of eminent domain. In one of the choice ironies in both their lives, Governor Ann Richards had signed that bill into law in 1991.

The authority condemned thirteen acres of private property—two owners sued, unsuccessfully trying to stop construction of The Ballpark in Arlington. Bush then owned 1.8 percent of the franchise, plus a 10 percent bonus if it was sold again and the original owners recovered their investment, plus interest. That occurred in 1998. Bush had invested $606,302 of his own money in the team; his profits from the Rangers' sale earned him $14.3 million. Ann Richards helped make him a very rich man.

George W. had a friend in Dallas named Bob Beaudine. In his habit of awarding his friends and acquaintances nicknames, he called him Bobby Boy. Beaudine was a corporate headhunter and later a motivational speaker and author who developed a profitable sideline in matching college coaches with schools that were making a change; that bloomed into relationships with the PGA Tour and the front offices of the National Basketball Association, the Arena Football League, and Major League Baseball. *Sports Illustrated* lauded him as "the most influential man in sports you never heard of." In 1992, an owner of the Atlanta Braves made him head of a search committee for the next baseball commissioner, who would succeed Fay Vincent. "George asked me to come over to his office one day," Beaudine told me. "We talked baseball for a while, then some politics. He got serious and said, 'Bobby Boy, you might as well get me the commissioner's job because these people have got me running for governor, and I don't think I can beat Ann Richards.'"

If he felt that way, why was he being pulled toward a race that might offer nothing more than a respectable loss and the chance to run again and win against a lesser Democratic opponent in 1998? And who besides Karl Rove were "they"? Bush told several people that he was motivated by scorn for what he perceived as her ineptitude, especially on issues of public education. Robert Draper, the author of the incisive *Dead Certain: The Presidency of George W. Bush*, told me flatly that while the family-vengeance motive might provide a neat narrative arc, he believed that the silver-spoon line and other insults were most likely about number thirty on George W. Bush's list of reasons why he entered the race in 1994. But Bush's rationale and behavior must be viewed in part through the prism of his subsequent history. When questioned during his presidency about his decision to take the country into war in Iraq, he pointed out that Saddam Hussein had tried to have his dad assassinated after the war over Kuwait. Certainly, that would be a matter of personal honor for any decent and loving son. But it does underscore that "looking out for the old man"—as the younger George Bush described his role in turning away most interview requests and being the one who told John Sununu he was fired as chief of staff during his father's presidency—was a prominent aspect of his psychological makeup.

Ann officially announced her campaign for reelection on her sixtieth birthday, September 1, 1993. A large crowd of supporters packed into a midsize Austin convention hall. Dorothy and I were there. As he had at the kickoff for her first governor's race, the singer Jimmie Dale Gilmore performed in a voice and style that was part Jimmie Rodgers, part Buddy Holly, and Ann followed with a fiery, fist-pumping speech. She followed with birthday parties and kickoffs in Houston, San Antonio, and Dallas—to a roaring crowd in the last city, the comedian Robin Williams performed in her behalf. But that first event felt odd to me. It didn't have a pulse.

Mary Beth Rogers had been at a distance for a while, writing and teaching at the LBJ School, but she again came back to manage Ann's campaign. Kirk Adams, Ann's trusted son-in-law, had also come back. "Kirk and Cathy Bonner were trying to hold things together," Mary Beth said. "It was a different experience, a totally different experience."

"How so?" I asked her.

"Just the atmosphere. There were way too many people on the staff, and they were too set in their ways. Ann had kept a political office open the whole time, and there were eight or nine people on staff. There was just a different feel to it. Ann was not the same candidate. We were less clear about message, about focus, about what Ann wanted to do. We knew from the polling data that people were sick of negative stuff."

Yet plenty of negative stuff was flying their way. Carole Keeton McClellan Rylander Strayhorn, who had been a friend when she was Austin's mayor and Ann was a county commissioner, had recast her lot with the Republicans. Ann wasn't too surprised when Strayhorn called her "an honorary lesbian." Among the gay women close to Ann, Jane Hickie was the one her political enemies disliked the most. Hickie's attachment to Ann was clearly profound. They had been friends since 1972, and you don't subject yourself to the emotional and psychological torment of initiating an intervention for addiction with someone you care little about. The attack dogs' innuendo about Ann's alleged involvement in a bisexual affair almost always posited Jane as the other lover. And Hickie's personality often just rubbed people the wrong way—including people who were politically on the same side. In January 1989, when Ann was basking in the glow of celebrity that followed the keynote, the *Dallas Morning News* had run a short piece about the contributors included in a campaign finance statement.

Ms. Richards' latest report, filed last week, is replete with famous names—actor James Garner, feminist poet Maya Angelou, and the eminent sage of the New York public library system, Vartan Gregorian. "And we got several thousand dollars from this guy whose name is Don Henley," said fund-raiser Jane Hickie. "He said, 'You won't know who I am, but ask your children.'"

Henley was a lead singer for the superstar rock band the Eagles, and a native of northeast Texas's Piney Woods; he generously contributed to environmental causes, especially the protection of Caddo Lake. The Dallas news item reached him, and he fired off a letter to Hickie.

> I do not appreciate being referred to as "this guy whose name is Don Henley." While I am well aware that campaign donations are a matter of public record, I also don't appreciate the reference to "several thousand dollars." No amount was mentioned in connection with the other famous names. In fact, I think your entire statement is extremely tacky and unprofessional. I have contributed to Ann Richards because I believe in her and what she stands for, not because I wanted some amateurish publicity blurb in the *Dallas Morning News*. "This guy" thinks Hickie is quite an appropriate name for you.

That dustup of course came to the attention of Ann, and Hickie had to write him a prompt letter of contrition.

> Dear Mr. Henley—
> I certainly understand your anger at the quote attributed to me in the Dallas paper. I did not however talk with any member of the press about any of our contributors, and cannot, at this point, figure out where they got their story.
> I have laughed about the fact that you thought Ann would not know who you were and that you suggested that she ask her children—but have never been derogatory of you, your reputation, or your generosity to Ann.
> I hope you will accept my apology for whatever I did to contribute to the writer's attribution to me of something I have no memory of having said and giving it a tone that is not one I have ever felt.
> Mr. Henley, I wouldn't have insulted you for any reason. I thought your letter was genuine and funny—reflecting the fact that we have a candidate who reaches across generations—even to a generation whose icons she doesn't (or didn't previously) know.

Then had come her angry and impulsive bolt from the 1990 campaign when Ann hired Glenn Smith as campaign manager and did not make him subordinate to her. Then the months when she and Ann were not on speaking terms. When the campaign was in disarray over the drug issue, she marched back to the rescue, and she pushed for the television ad that may have salvaged the race and certainly infuriated Mark White. Young campaign staffers said that without a word of explanation, she started barking orders; some, who were recent hires or volunteers, didn't know who *she* was.

She had served Ann faithfully and well in the race against Clayton Williams and in the early months of the term, recommending and vetting her appointments. Then she and Chula Reynolds, her partner of some years, broke up. She was ready for a change, and she easily won approval from the Senate when Ann appointed her director of the Office of Federal-State Relations. In addition to lobbying the White House and Congress for Texas on the future of NASA and the Super Collider, she directed a staff of thirty-seven people. Her salary, $82,500, was in line with that of peers employed by New York and California. But the contention about her was sufficient that a file in Ann's political archive was headed "The Jane Hickie Problem."

In a confusing report, a legislative audit found that she obeyed the law in billing the state for additional "per diem travel expenses on days she never left town ... in addition to hundreds of dollars in per diem payments on days she didn't work at all." Taking exception to the audit's conclusions, the *Houston Post*'s Lynn Ashby blistered Hickie and her boss in a long run of editorials that he wrote and cartoons that he published on the editorial page.

Hickie's Hokum: Washington Lobbyist Should Quit—or Be Fired

What will it take for Gov. Ann Richards to see that the case against Jane Hickie is not about politics?

When will she realize that the high-spending ways and arrogance of the state's chief lobbyist in Washington do not sit well with most Texans?

When will she summon the courage to dismiss Hickie? Better yet, when will Hickie have the decency to repay the money she has pocketed without earning it and go quietly away into the political night? . . .

All this comes on top of earlier revelations that Hickie had racked up a $10,000 airline tab for traveling in the state—when her job is in Washington, not Texas—and that her office had destroyed its records after the *Post* began investigating.

Richards insults our intelligence by insisting questions about Hickie amount to nothing more than "a political game." Indeed, Richards' Republican opponent, George W. Bush, was too mild in his assessment of Hickie's actions as "ethical lapses." They were much more than that.

The governor should abandon her silly claim that Hickie has brought some $5 billion to Texas from Washington. That old dog not only won't hunt, it won't even bark.

Ann was catching grief from Bush and his team, from the Republican Party, and from the press, and in subtle ways she was being lobbied by friends who pulled out all the stops in calling on her loyalty. Molly Ivins now received nearly as much daily mail as the governor. One time a fan in Kansas sent her just a photocopy of a short news item in the *Wichita Eagle-Beacon* that read: "Man Arrested for Sodomy with a Duck." And then there were the hate letters, such as one from a frequent reader of her columns. They clearly got him all revved up.

> Molly Ivins,
> You pea-brained, idiotic, stupid liberal, stop writing about senators being weasels. The Clintons and the Jesse Jacksons, your partners in ludicrous and hypocritical thinking, are the enemies of this country. Clinton, weak character that he is, and his masculine wife are tearing this country to pieces. You—not partisan?—I hate your columns. You are the scum of the earth. Grow up will you?
> Try God—be good.
> You are mean spirited. Satan!!

Well, she would plead guilty to one of those charges. She was an unapologetically partisan Democrat. And as her own fame and the controversy surrounding her grew, she was more charitable to her old friend the governor. In January 1994, she wrote Ann a letter of thanks for an invitation to a party. It was nostalgic, sentimental, but it also contained an inspired bit of lobbying. She invoked Ann's father, Cecil; Maury Maverick, Jr.; Congressman Henry B. González; and Tony Korioth, whom she had pilloried for his sexism, in what she thought was a sweet-spirited way, at the roast of the governor in Port Arthur.

> Dear Ann,
> A thousand times thanks to you for a wonderful evening. That was awfully close to magic. [A guest of the party named Janet] is perhaps the most perfect example I've ever met of how much easier it is in the world to just be your own self, or how you should.
> T. Korioth's contribution will not be forgotten.

I had intended to tell you that among my favorite memories is the sight of you dancing with your daddy. At Cecile's wedding and on three or four other occasions that I recall. My, he was such a stylish dancer, and you two looked so good dancing together. I wish I could give you a video of those dances so you could have those memories too. I guess you do, but yours are from close up.

Love, Molly Ivins

P.S. I also forgot to tell you that Maury Maverick called the other day, and allowed as how he understands how there's yet another big push to repeal the Texas Homestead Act and that if Ann was to support such a thing he, Maury, would pretty much have to go out in his backyard and put a bullet through his brain. Which he might actually do, on account of he keeps grumblin' about bein' 73 and not feelin' all that well.

If I were you, I would not appreciate a friend layin' that kind of pressure on me. On the other hand, if I had a bunch of real sharp lawyers in real nice suits with three-color charts comin' in [I would] explain to 'em that while I understood and agreed with their every point, such a move would cause Maury to kill hisself and Henry B. to have a heart attack, and that I was not, just at this present moment, prepared to accept responsibility for that much bloodshed; and that they will just have to wait until both of those gentlemen die natural. By which time, with any luck, it will be someone else's problem.

Another one of their old friends, Bob Bullock, no longer had any use for Ann, but was he trying to undercut her in the race against Bush? Some Democrats thought that was the case. Facing only a feeble GOP opponent that year, he had plenty of time for mischief. The subsequent emergence of Mark McKinnon and Matthew Dowd as top members of Bush's political team framed liberal suspicions in this way: they had worked for Jack Martin, who directed them to an affiliation with Bullock, and the next stop on the climb up the opportunistic ladder was George W. Bush. Did even Martin turn on Ann? When did the defections begin? Were they all covert operatives for Bush in the 1994 campaign?

"I don't believe any of that," said Chuck Bailey, the attorney and chief of staff who had been with Bullock since his early days as comptroller. Bailey added that he had accompanied the lieutenant governor to a meeting with Mary Beth Rogers and John Fainter in early 1994: "He pressed them on how serious she was about running, and after that he said to me, 'All right, she's in. She'll be up to it.' He sounded satisfied to me. And Ann's team had all the polling information that Bullock's had. I don't know what he could have actively done to damage her."

But Bullock had a way of playing perverse mind games with people. For example, Ann wanted to appoint Max Sherman, the former Panhandle senator and dean of the LBJ School, as her chair of the board of the Department of Health and Human Services. Sherman said he would be pleased to serve, but he doubted his nomination could ever get past Bullock, who bore a grudge more than twenty years old. Ann told Bailey that she wanted to make the appointment and that Sherman would be calling the lieutenant governor. Sherman described the conversation to Dave McNeely:

> I picked up the phone, and here are the first words from Bullock: "Senator, the worst thing that can happen to a man is not to be confirmed by the Texas Senate." I then held the phone a couple of inches from my ear for several minutes as he leaned in on me. He said, "I want you to know that I remember you were one of the senators who voted to bust my appointment to the insurance board in '72, and I want you to know that that was one of the worst things that ever happened to me in my life—to be busted by the Senate of Texas. I went home and cried like a baby. No man should have to go through what I went through. And because of that, I will support your nomination."

Bullock held the same grudge against Barbara Jordan. As a state senator, she too had opposed his appointment in that two-decade-old vote. Sherman was spooked by the conversation with the lieutenant governor, but he took the job on an interim basis for several months as a favor to Ann. A cancer diagnosis gave him a reason to pull out before Bullock got to lead the Senate in officially taking up his nomination and watch him twist in the wind.

And then there was Bullock's complete turnabout on the subject of a personal income tax. Texas was one of only nine states that did not have one. Ann had let *him* twist in the wind over his brash insistence that an income tax was fair and inevitable. Then she created a task force that ended up agreeing with Bullock. Yet in 1993, Bullock declared that Texas would get an income tax when a Russian submarine sailed up the Houston Ship Channel. He engineered a constitutional amendment that barred the legislature from imposing an income tax unless voters approved it in a referendum. Some critics said he made enactment of an income tax impossible. Defenders said he left the door open, since only a simple majority of both houses was required to call a referendum. Whatever his intention, he got the income tax monkey off his back. Almost 70 percent of the voters approved his amendment. Ann's pollster meanwhile told her that 43 percent of the voters believed she wanted an income tax.

In the governor's race, there was a persistent story, perhaps apocryphal, that a charm offensive began as soon as the former president's son went to meet Bullock. In that tale, Bush said in his friendly way, "You know, Governor, you and me, we're both just a couple of old drunks."

George Shipley, "Dr. Dirt," was Bullock's neighbor and good friend. He blamed Ann for the failure to heal the animus with her old drinking partner: "Ann was awfully well liked in this state. When it started out, she had a twenty-point advantage on Bush. But too much of her attention was on being a national celebrity. Bullock had been taking care of business in the '93 session. He was an old-school guy. All Ann had to have done was go to him and say, 'Bob, you're a man, and you know so much about this business, you've been doing this for twenty-five years, and I really need your help.' He would have just melted."

George gave his desk a resounding slap with the flat of his hand. "Just like that—Mary Beth Rogers beat her hand on her desk and said, 'No! We're not going to reward bad behavior!'"

He stared out his office window at the Capitol and went on: "Ann had a lot of promise, but she had this coterie of women around her—Jane Hickie, Mary Beth, Cathy Bonner, Susan Rieff, Marlene Saritzky. Jane Hickie had the worst political judgment of any of them. She got it in her mind once that Ann was going to bring in Roy Spence and get rid of Jack Martin. She said, 'You're not a leader, Jack.' Roy was going to be the guy."

Cooler heads prevailed on that idea. But George offered more recollections of how Ann's 1994 race shaped up: "She raised a lot of money, but most of it was going to salaries of campaign staff. When the time came that she really needed it, she didn't have the money to compete with Bush on TV. I really disagreed with their insistence that they couldn't go negative against George. There was plenty to go with. And we were all naïve. We forgot to remember who we were up against. Hell, those guys who were doing 'security' for George worked for the old man when he was running the CIA."

Election night, governor's race, 1994: George W. Bush celebrates his victory over Ann Richards with Karl Rove. One of Bush's nicknames for the GOP strategist was "Boy Genius."

CHAPTER 30

Queen Bee

ANN WAS WORN OUT PHYSICALLY, and she looked it. In addition to waging a hard-fought campaign, she was determined to do her job as governor—she continued to take those bulging files of work home with her at night. Looking young and fresh, always in good shape, George W. Bush did not have that problem. Still, Ann was the popular governor with the aura of gravitas and glamour. In June 1993 John Connally died, and the political elite came to his funeral in Austin's First Methodist Church. People in the gallery gasped when Richard Nixon walked in and took a seat beside Ann. Their heads tilted and they spoke briefly. The former president told her, "You're very good on television."

Veteran members of the press liked her even as they illuminated her faults and failures. Wayne Slater of the *Dallas Morning News* related how she was once in Washington for a meeting of the National Governors Association. He knew he wasn't going to get much of a story because the important events were closed. Ann told Slater to come to the Democratic governors' closed meeting, pretending to be a member of her staff. He couldn't take notes, just observe. He readily agreed. When they were inside and she was talking to her peers, she said, "Wayne, would you go get me a cup of coffee?" He asked if she wanted cream and sugar, got her the coffee, and carried it back to her. She looked at him, then dismissed him with an imperial flip of her wrist.

But for all the laughs, the open-records requests cascaded into the Governor's Office from the press, not just from state Republican headquarters. The *Houston Chronicle*'s R. G. Ratcliffe, who was as unrelenting in filing those requests as any reporter, offered a sober note in a story he filed in mid-June:

390   Twenty-eight death threats against Gov. Ann Richards and 181 "security risks"
to her safety are currently under investigation, the head of the Texas Department of Public Safety revealed today.

Col. James Wilson cited those figures in explaining to a state district court why he opposes an Open Records request by the Texas Republican Party for Richards' past detailed daily schedules.

The strain and growing doubt were showing in the Governor's Office, not just over at the campaign. Joe Holley, who had written the State of the State speech with Suzanne Coleman's help at the start of Ann's term, told me about the unease he felt: "I ended up writing more speeches, never as many as Suzanne, but I worked on position papers, press releases—I was observing more, really, than participating. And it was a time when our people were in power. That was the first thing I realized when I started working for Ann. I walked into the governor's meeting room, with all of her people sitting in chairs. And what interested me over the next months and years was that all of us who had been writing, pushing, lobbying for things to happen in the state of Texas, finally we had the opportunity to make those things happen.

"We were trying to avoid the same mistakes that we had criticized the opposition for making. And I'm not sure that we did. I was at this one meeting where Mary Beth Rogers was in charge. People like Susan Rieff and Pat Cole and Deece Eckstein all had their areas, and everybody was pushing to make sure that Ann was aware of the vital work that they were doing. And of course she thought it was vital, too. But as I listened to it, I began to realize that Ann had to communicate better with the people of Texas, who were suspicious of her anyway. What she really ought to do was figure out three or four ideas that she would focus on. I got the feeling that it had gotten too complicated, with too much stuff swirling about. The other thing I found interesting is that we were all liberals, high-minded, we had the people's interests at heart, but we were susceptible to the same kind of personality quirks and shortcomings as those people that we'd been criticizing.

"I would watch it sort of like a beehive, with a queen, and everybody maneuvering. The third thing I noticed when the race really began: there was a real strange sense that she almost didn't want to win. The prospect of another term wasn't something she really pushed for. Her defeat was almost a self-fulfilling wish."

Karl Rove was then all but unknown in national politics. He had prospered and
shown he had talent grooming Texas candidates to win victories in down-ballot
races. But in George W. Bush he saw a thoroughbred, a Seabiscuit that he could
ride all the way to the top, and that was just what he did.

"Bush stumbled in the beginning," Mary Beth Rogers told me. "They took him
off the road for about two weeks. They had him going to small towns in East
Texas, and when he came back he was a different candidate. And in the meantime
the stealth campaign was going on: all the antigay stuff; Ann's gonna take your
guns away; Ann's gonna take your land away. Karen Hughes was very good. They
besieged us with Open Records requests, wore poor Don Temples down at the
copy machine. They were effective. Joe Allbaugh was very skillful running that
ship. Karl Rove kept George on message. We had a democracy, they had a dicta-
torship. We had way too many people making decisions."

When Bush came back, he was more disciplined than Ann, and under Rove's
direction, the only issues he talked about were education, juvenile crime, and tort
reform (code words for putting plaintiffs' lawyers who bankrolled Democrats out
of business). Over and over and over.

Any criticism about Ann's record on crime and prison policy got her riled. In
February, she addressed the National Conference on Drugs and Crime in Dallas.
In an indirect but barbed way, she addressed Bush's perceived slights of her reliance on Alcoholics Anonymous; he boasted that he had quit his drinking simply
through his faith and strength of character.

Sam Houston was president of the Texas Republic and he later served as senator
and governor. One of his staunchest opponents was Mirabeau B. Lamar. And
one of the most popular sayings of their day held that "Sam Houston drunk in a
ditch is worth ten Mirabeau B. Lamars."

She then launched into spirited defense of the crime-fighting policies she had
pushed through to heal the damage of the shell games played by Bill Clements.

We doubled the time that violent offenders must stay in prison, and required
that the most violent—those convicted of capital offenses—serve no fewer
than 40 years.
We cut the parole rate by two-thirds.
And we undertook the most ambitious prison-building program in the history of Texas.

We have authorized the construction of 75,300 new spaces—enough to double the capacity of the system Texas had when I took office.

When I finish we will have a prison system that will probably be one of the largest in the world—with space for 140,000 inmates.

This year, we will have 39,000 spaces coming on line.

Generally, I agree with the idea that we can never build our way out of the crime problem. But in Texas, we were playing catch-up, and we had little choice.... Here in Dallas last year, crime was down almost 15 percent and violent crime decreased by more than 16 percent.

Who would have ever dreamed that Ann Richards would end up framing her legacy not as one of social justice and women's rights, but of a vastly expensive prison-building spree that doubled the number of people in Texas prisons?

No program initiated by Ann was more important to her than the one administered by my wife, Dorothy. As prison construction raced to keep up with the number of convicts sentenced by the courts, and as longer sentences were imposed and paroles denied, the program struggled to keep the drug and alcohol treatment programs growing apace. The expert at projections on the sheer numbers was Dorothy's friend Tony Fabelo. Born in Cuba and raised in Puerto Rico, he was a very funny man—when he got going, he sounded like Ricky Ricardo on *I Love Lucy*. Tony was the executive director of his own agency, the Criminal Justice Policy Council. One day in mid-1994, he remarked in public that the prison system was not going to need all the 14,000 new beds that had been projected for the drug and alcohol abuse programs.

"It was the only time I ever got the treatment from Ann," Dorothy said. "She called me up and yelled, 'Darthy! Do you want me to lose this election?' She kept on yelling. 'Did you know Tony Fabelo was going to do this? You get him on the phone, and you two get over here, right now.' And when Tony and I got to her office, she just went on and on like that. We were in a room with all these white guys and her. I kept thinking, it doesn't do any good to say, 'Ann, it's the truth.'"

On the issue of capital punishment, this governor was never going to strut past photographs of executed men as Mark White had done in the 1990 campaign. But nineteen prisoners had been executed during White's four years as governor. Under Ann, the number reached forty-eight. The liberal reforming governor James Allred, a former district attorney, had instituted the pardon system in the 1930s in response to bribes-for-freedom allegations under Pa and Ma Ferguson. On capital-offense convictions, the governor's options were limited to

pardoning the offender, commuting the sentence to life imprisonment, or granting a thirty-day reprieve. The real decisions were placed in the hands of a Board of
Pardons and Paroles, whose members no longer even met to talk about the cases;
by Ann's time, they voted by fax. Aides swore she agonized over every one of the
executions. But her only acts of clemency were in granting two thirty-day stays.
One in 1992 went to Johnny Frank Garrett, who was seventeen at the time of the
murder he was convicted of committing, and was, according to Amnesty International, "extremely mentally impaired, chronically psychotic, and brain-damaged
as the result of several severe head injuries he sustained as a child." He had been
defended by my friend Selden Hale, and was especially loathed in Amarillo as
"the nun killer." In Cuba, Leoncio Perez Rueda said he was the one who had raped
and killed the seventy-six-year-old woman. (Perez Rueda was later convicted of
raping and killing another elderly Amarillo woman four months before Garrett
was alleged to have killed the nun.) But the execution went ahead. Garrett's last
words were: "I'd like to thank my family for loving me and taking care of me. And
the rest of the world can kiss my ever-loving ass, because I'm innocent."

In 1993, Ann allowed the executions of two foreign nationals to go forward
in two days. She refused to meet with the Dominican Republic's ambassador to
the United States and former U.S. attorney general Ramsey Clark, who together
pleaded for the life of Carlos Santana, who admitted taking part in a robbery in
Houston, but another man involved in the holdup did the killing. Then Ramón
Montoya became the first Mexican citizen executed in the United States in fifty-
one years, despite pleas from Mexico's president and the Vatican. Three thousand
people gathered to receive his body on the Rio Grande bridge at Reynosa. These
were matters of conscience and policy, but also of politics. At one campaign
meeting on criminal justice, George Shipley said, "Dorothy, I don't want to hear
one more word about capital punishment!"

In her book *Ten Minutes from Normal*, Karen Hughes claimed that Bush later told
her that he decided to run for governor when he attended Senator Kay Bailey
Hutchison's victory rally in June 1993. On the ballot that day was the constitutional amendment to enable a school-finance law that Ann supported, and it failed.
He told Hughes that on television he saw Richards "wringing her hands" and saying she was out of ideas. He said he thought, "I know what to do," and made up
his mind to take her on.

Bush's ideas on curriculum would lead, on the national stage, to the controversial No Child Left Behind Act, with its overriding emphasis on reading and

394 math, standardized testing, and holding schools accountable for results through funding; the law left teachers saying they were required to spend all their time "teaching the test." On how to pay for his proposed reforms, he campaigned for governor on a platform of increasing the state's share of public school funding in order to limit increases in local property taxes. The outcome was a shell game: he was able to claim $1.4 billion in tax cuts, but at the expense of depleting a $1 billion budget surplus, and nearly two-thirds of the cuts went to businesses and their affluent shareholders, the rest to homeowners. And property taxes in the state still rose.

It may be true that Bush decided to run on the basis of his commitment to public education and how to fund it, but the day before he attended Senator Hutchison's victory rally, Governor Richards carried out her promise to veto the concealed-weapons bill. The state was in an uproar over gang violence and drive-by shootings. Especially in Houston, people feared thugs, most of them young blacks, who, in the murderous fashion of the moment, were jerking drivers out of BMWS and Mercedes-Benzes and, not content with the carjackings, were popping rounds into old white guys' heads before dumping them on the asphalt and racing off. And the National Rifle Association was mindful of Ann's stated interest in a ban of assault rifles. Bush didn't have to make guns one of his stated issues. He just quietly let it be known that he would sign a concealed-weapons bill. Ann had her heels dug in, and she was doing nothing to defuse the emotions that aroused.

In April 1994, she spoke to a crowd of supportive police chiefs about her battle with the legislature. She began by thanking Plano's chief, Bruce Glasscock.

> His advice was helpful to me when I was considering the conceal-to-carry bill.
> But I have got to tell you that when you all asked me to veto that bill, it was not a hard decision to make.
> It is a mystery to me how anyone can think we make Texas safe by encouraging every Tom, Dick, and Henrietta to arm themselves to the teeth.
> No one is more secure when every driver stuck in rush hour traffic and every customer at McDonald's is legally packing heat.
> So I was proud to veto that bill and I am ready to do it again.

Political reporters were not lying down for Ann, any more than they had in 1990. As the 1994 race warmed up, R. G. Ratcliffe summarized her term in the *Houston Chronicle*.

She is, according to polls, the most popular Texas governor in 30 years.... But
the record also shows that Richards signed a $2.7 billion tax increase during
her first year in office, after making a campaign promise that it wouldn't be
necessary to raise taxes, and has overseen a 30 percent increase in the state
budget. Her tenure has occasionally been marked by tentativeness and failure:
She briefly favored a statewide property tax for schools, but quickly withdrew
her support in the face of opposition from school superintendents and school
boards, and she backed a constitutional amendment for school finance that was
soundly rejected by voters. And she failed to follow through on a promise to
bring teachers' pay to the national average. During her 1990 campaign, Richards pledged to regulate health insurance and lower other insurance rates. But
health insurance remains largely unregulated in Texas and homeowner and
auto insurance rates have risen.

With reporters, she continued to give as good as she got. One time, as part of a
"Smart Jobs" economic development initiative, she led the Capitol press corps to
an East Texas factory where laid-off workers were being retrained as welders. A
stifling day was made hotter by the welding torches. At the press event that followed, a television reporter named James Moore, who seldom let up on any politician, cracked, "If welding is a smart job, what's a dumb one?" She let him go on
sweating under his boom mike for a moment, and then smiled. "You know, Jim,
it don't look to me like it takes a whole lot of smart to be a microphone holder."
Yet on receiving a letter from Moore's young daughter, Ann carried on a warm
correspondence with the girl that lasted through her college years.

George Shipley was disgusted by the results of her courting all those CEOs she had
enlisted as economic advisers. In June 1994, she found herself assailed over her
support for Garry Mauro's compressed-natural-gas initiatives by executives of
Southern Union Gas, Texaco, and Shell, and a lobbying firm representing refiners in Houston, El Paso, and the Golden Triangle. They wanted a product called
reformulated gasoline to be certified as a clean fuel under Texas law. The worst
backstab came in a letter from a man who had praised her warmly as a friend of
the business community.

> Dear Gov. Richards:
> The Greater Houston Partnership is the primary advocate for the Houston busi-
> ness community and has more than two thousand members with over 500,000

employees who are affected by Texas environmental regulation. As Chairman of the Board of Directors for the partnership, I am writing at the Board's direction to express their concern over the Texas Natural Resource Conservation Commission's proposed rules regarding the Texas Alternative Fuel Fleet (TAFF) Program because, as now proposed, the rule will exclude fuels [such as reformulated gasoline] that do not meet the federal Clean Air Act standards . . .

As the heart of the nation's energy production, Texas should be especially sensitive to providing an equitable competitive climate for both innovation and prosperity for that important sector of our economy. The TAFF, as proposed, will seriously undermine the Houston region's innovation, competition, and cost-effective air quality improvement. We ask that you encourage the commission to make the TAFF fuel-neutral.

That tacit declaration of war by the energy industry was delivered by her good friend Ken Lay, the later convicted chairman of Enron. (Still, ever loyal, when that house of cards crashed down, she somehow defended Lay, saying he had always treated her right.)

Ann cautioned aides and volunteers not to take Bush lightly. In fact, they all thought he was a hothead who would blow up under pressure. But Ann was the one with overheated rhetoric. In April 1994 at the Democratic State Convention in Fort Worth, a video of highlights of her term preceded her speech. One of the images that raised roars from the crowd was the march down Congress Avenue before her inauguration.

Looking at that video, seeing that march again, it seems impossible that it has been almost three and a half years since we met on the bridge down by the IBEW hall, gathered ourselves up, and set off on this great adventure.

It was an incredible, emotional day.

I remember looking up at the buildings and seeing people leaning out of the windows—smiling and waving—a lot of them with little American and Texas flags.

If we did not know it before that day, I think we all realized at that moment that we had done something truly remarkable, truly extraordinary. We took back this state for the people of Texas . . .

But here's the part I like the best. What simply mystifies me is why we suddenly hear from people at election time who have actually filed to run for statewide office when we have never heard an idea about government from them before.

People who never seemed to have the slightest interest in what the people care about—who were never there when there was a piece of legislation discussed or debated, who were never there for a public hearing, who never wrote a letter asking for a position on any vote on anything that we have done in government—and suddenly pop out of a P.R. back room claiming to have a better way of doing everything.

It's just like your brother-in-law who was supposed to help with the moving, and then shows up after it's all done and tells you the furniture isn't in the right place.

All we have to say is: Where were you when we were doing the heavy lifting?

These *Johnny-come-latelies* . . . let me tell you, serving in public office is not some sort of beauty contest. You have to go through a lot of living. You have got to have some experience with people. You have got to serve at the local level to understand the impact of what is happening with state policy and state laws when they are passed down to the local level.

You have to have someone who understands the impact of the power of what transpires in state government. You can't wake up one morning and stand there shaving, looking in the mirror, and say, "Mmmmm, mmmmm, mmmmm, I think you're so cute you ought to run for governor."

It was a partisan event, and it was her job to get the juices flowing. But it wasn't funny, and lacking in her rhetoric down the stretch was Lily and the Baptist pallet—the passion for what she might yet accomplish, not just the bristling defense of what she was proud to have done.

The internal polling by Harrison Hickman showed that 59 percent of respondents felt Ann had "new ideas to improve government," 78 percent believed she was "out front on important issues," 75 percent felt she presented "a good image of Texas to the rest of the country." In March, Kirk Adams had written to supporters with advance word of a poll by the *Houston Chronicle* and *Dallas Morning News*: "The poll results will show Governor Richards with a 50 to 40 lead over George W. Bush among decided voters and a 52–42 lead if leaners are included."

But that summer, Chuck McDonald wrote to Ann's supporters and contributors: "The Texas Poll reveals what most of you have known for a long time: This is going to be a *real* race. The Bush campaign has closed the gap to 4 points—the results of a nearly $2 million TV buy they put up during the two weeks the poll was in the field. Bush ran an attack crime ad playing to voters' fears about crime and got this bump as a result. . . . The good news for this campaign is that Ann Richards still has a 47–43 lead in this race. There's more good news in the governor's fave/unfave ratings. She is still at 63 in personal favorabilities. *You should brace yourself for more scary crime ads from Bush*" (emphasis in the original).

That summer the governor was personally wounded by a gay-bashing incident in northeast Texas. Ann liked and had worked closely with the Mount Pleasant senator Bill Ratliff on education issues. A regional coordinator of Bush's campaign, Ratliff suddenly appeared at a press conference and blasted Ann for hiring gays and lesbians and giving them "hundreds of administrative positions." He went on, "It elevates the lifestyle. . . . I don't agree with appointing avowed homosexual activists."

Bush then got to say, "That's not an issue with me." And in his heart and in his face-to-face encounters with people, no doubt it wasn't. But Karl Rove had earned his reputation as a youthful dirty trickster and the best friend of the elder George Bush's attack dog, Lee Atwater, and again, one cannot ignore the perspective provided by subsequent events. When George W. Bush's 2000 presidential campaign wobbled on the brink of defeat by John McCain, a campaign run by Rove benefited from vicious, barely whispered attacks in the South Carolina primary: the Arizona senator was mentally unstable because of his torture at the hands of North Vietnamese captors, and he had won favor from those same captors because he had fathered a bastard Vietnamese child, but on the other hand, he was really gay, and his adopted daughter from Bangladesh was really a love child with a mother who was an American black woman. Democrats were baffled by Ratliff's turning so contemptuously on a woman he had always treated with great courtesy and cooperativeness on some of their mutual legislative priorities. Rove strenuously denied the accusations. But Ann's aides and politicos grew ever more convinced, though they could offer no proof, that the lesbian smear against Ann happened because a campaign manager and a candidate countenanced those kinds of tactics as long as they could claim their own hands were clean.

Compared with Ann's brawls with Jim Mattox, Mark White, and Clayton Williams, the 1994 race was remarkably short on fireworks. Ann's team tried to make an issue of Bush claiming to be a Major League Baseball executive while owning just 2 percent of the Texas Ranger franchise. That was just lame. But one story was circulating that could have hurt Bush—his record as an Air National Guard officer during the Vietnam War. It was fairly well known by then that Ben Barnes, when he was Speaker of the House, had made some calls that helped bump Bush up a long waiting list and remove the danger of his being drafted. No one who remembered the home-front politics of that war could have been surprised by that; it was just more evidence of Bush's lifetime of privilege. But the more damning part of that story was that he had skipped several of his monthly meetings while volunteering on a campaign in Alabama during 1972 and 1973. That was the one sure way a reservist or member of the National Guard could get called up to active duty and sent to Vietnam; and it was all the more outrageous that Bush could have gotten away with that as an officer.

The governor and her challenger had just one debate, in Dallas, in the 1994 race. In Karl Rove's memoir, *Courage and Consequence: My Life as a Conservative in the Fight*, he wrote that Bush was coming down out of an elevator and was surprised when the doors opened, and Ann and her security detail stepped in. In his *Dallas Morning News* column, Wayne Slater later offered this quote from Rove's book: "They all stepped aboard. Bush said, 'Governor,' and tilted his head to greet her. She said nothing. Then, as the elevator reached the ground floor, Richards turned to Bush and said, sotto voce, 'This is going to be tough on you, boy.'"

Slater continued: "None of those with Richards that night recall such an encounter. Not only was there no such exchange, they said, the candidates were never in the same elevator together. For one thing, the governor's security typically holds an elevator so that doors on various floors don't open, making such an encounter unlikely."

Whatever the truth or falsehood of Rove's allegation, the Dallas debate was a tipping point in the race. Starting that night, Bush developed a habit of holding his own, contrary to expectations, against an experienced and highly rated debater. Truthfully enough, he laid out his premise, "I'm the conservative candidate and she's the liberal."

Again according to Slater, Ann lapsed into sarcasm in scoring one point. Bush had been criticizing wasteful free-lunch programs in the schools. "Perhaps he means the free-lunch programs that I heard Kay Bailey Hutchison saying how proud she was to provide."

She conceded, "He means well," but went on, "This is not a joke. We're talking about who is going to run the State of Texas."

When she discredited his spotty record in the private sector, he countered, "This business of trying to diminish my personality based upon my business career is, frankly, astounding to me. We ought to be discussing welfare reform, juvenile justice, ways to make Texas a better place for our children."

400   That retort was the best and most telling line in the debate.

Though it was nothing like the gantlet that Ann had to run over the drug question four years earlier, several reporters were eager to press Bush on how he got in the Air National Guard in the first place and then how he got away with effectively going AWOL during his months in Alabama.

Asked about his military record by one of the moderators, he looked hurt and pointed out that he was flying an F-102 fighter. "It was a thrill, but it also wasn't trying to avoid duty. Had that engine failed, I could have been killed."

Ann dismissed the matter as irrelevant with a flip of her wrist. Bush looked at her and said, "Thank you, Governor."

She gave him a pass, doubtless to George Shipley's chagrin. She waved off the one advantage she might have had with independent and conservative-minded white men. A prominent theory was that the issue was taken off the table because a son of Lloyd Bentsen had gotten in the Guard the same way. After that debate the issue evaporated in the campaign.

A columnist named Bill Thompson assessed the outcome thus: "When asked who won the debate, a *Star-Telegram* citizens panel gave Richards the edge by a ratio of 4–3 because, one panel member said, the governor had more 'stage presence.' As it happens, Texans won't be voting on stage presence when they go to the polls November 8. They won't be selecting a raconteur and song-and-dance artist, or a Secretary of Snide Remarks."

Bill Cryer told me that the Richards campaign was terrified that the press and the Bush campaign were going to spring a story that would hand the Republicans the equivalent of the Willie Horton bogeyman that had sunk the Dukakis presidential campaign in 1988. The reporter who had the story was R. G. Ratcliffe of the *Houston Chronicle*. "The criminal was a guy named Howard Pharr," R. G. e-mailed me the story years later. "He's dead now. But he went to school with Ann and Dave. He had a fairly successful middle class life, and then suddenly one Christmas he cracked up and robbed some banks.... Some very prominent Austin folks testified as character witnesses trying to get him probation, but the judge gave him a prison sentence because a gun was involved.

"Then the family started trying to get him paroled. They talked to Ann on the phone and in person at the Governor's Office. Pharr had a parole [consideration] date set for about a year away.... If my memory is correct they met with Ann in early December 1992. Then I think the parole board chairman told Ann no early release was possible. But in January 1993, I think, suddenly the prison system cuts Howard loose. The signature on the release form is impossible to read. Howard had heard from another inmate about a couple near Houston who had an oil well on their farm and didn't trust banks, so thousands of dollars were stuffed in their mattresses. So a couple of days after getting out of prison, Howard goes down there and tortures and kills this elderly couple. He ends up getting convicted of capital murder with a life sentence.

"Pharr's son told me he had no idea whether Ann was involved in his father's release. He told me he couldn't see how it could have happened without her intervening. But there was no smoking gun.

"I talked to an editor and had mixed feelings. It was a damn good story. But it was only weeks before the election, and was it fair to do it that close to the voting? The line editor I was talking to thought the story needed to be presented to higher-ups. She told me to go ahead and get a comment from the Richards campaign. That's when I called Bill [Cryer]. And all hell broke loose.

"The Richards people started calling every Republican in the prison system or parole board to accuse them of leaking the story. . . . By ten that night, I was getting calls from Republicans wanting to know what the story was. I couldn't tell them, and besides, I knew at that point that upper *Chronicle* management had decided to hold the story because of the timing issue. . . . Republicans got talk radio stations in Houston to allude to it, saying the *Chronicle* was sitting on a story that would blow Ann out of the water. At the Bush-Richards debate, a high-ranking Republican consultant accused me of sitting on the story to protect Richards . . .

"My only regret is that the story did not run after the election. So much pressure had been put on the *Chronicle* editors that they thought if the story ran it would look like we sat on it to protect Ann, when it really was a question of the fairness of timing."

So Ann and her campaign dodged the worst October surprise they could have imagined. Mary Beth Rogers told me, "Polls were always fairly close. I went back and looked at all the succession of polls after it was over. I realized I didn't see the trends as they were developing. And our pollster, Harrison Hickman, was afraid to tell us the truth. Ann's likeability was always high. But when the question was, 'Who are you going to vote for?' Ann never got over 47 percent. Now she was leading Bush with that; it wasn't like he was getting 49 percent. There was a Libertarian in the race, who we thought would pull 2 or 3 percent, hurting George.

Governor Ann Richards makes her speech of concession to George W. Bush that was the conclusion of the 1994 governor's race and the end of her career in electoral politics. Watching Ann are family members (from left) David Adams, Dan Richards, Linda Richards, Lily Adams, Ellen Richards, Hannah Adams, Clark Richards, and Sharon Zeugin.

But it didn't happen. The last ten days, when we weren't moving up and he was, we knew what was coming. We got a little bump when Ross Perot endorsed her, but it probably didn't last more than a day."

The race wasn't decided when Bush performed well in the debate, Mary Beth said. "Ann knew the die was cast before that. Karl Rove has since said there was one point when he knew Ann was out of control, and they had a real shot at winning it. This had occurred during the summer. We knew we had to take the high road. We had planned a full day where she was hitting cities all over the state, and she was going to end with a rally in Texarkana. The day had been perfect. Bill was calling me from the road all day long. About 10:30 that night, Ann called me at home and said, 'I've just done a horrible thing. I want you to know it from me. I just don't know what happened to me.'

"That was when she made the remark about 'some jerk' running against her. About thirty minutes after that, Bill called again. 'This is the story,' he said. 'It's not the great day we had.' *Some jerk.* That shook Ann's confidence in herself. It was a turning point for me too. It was when I thought this was really going to be hard to win. Because in effect, Ann had done what Clayton Williams did. Which was to let that resentment build and run away about someone having the audacity to challenge her."

Whatever her relationship with Ann might have become, Molly Ivins described the endgame of the race in a way that was wholly loyal to her old friend, yet not entirely hostile to George W. Bush—whom she had nicknamed "Shrub," since he lived in his father's shadow. One of her strongest statements about the race came in November, just days before voters went to the polls.

> I still don't see anything particularly wrong with him. He's nice. He's not dumb. He works real hard at making people like him. True, he is awfully . . . privileged, but that's not his fault. It's a little creepy to hear him say that schools are his top priority when you know that he went to prep school and his kids go to prep school. It's fine for him to say he's going to clean up welfare . . . do you think he's ever actually known anyone who's stuck on welfare? . . .
>
> The problem is not Shrub Bush; it's the comparison with Ann Richards. . . . Anyone who has seen Ann Richards with a bunch of school kids knows the magic of a great teacher. I'll never forget Richards with a group of forty or so Anglo, black, and brown kids from Dallas visiting the Capitol. She uses the Socratic method: She asks the questions; they figure out the answers. "Who owns this building?" she asked. It took several steps for the kids to realize they're taxpayers, too, and finally shout with delight "*We* own it. It's *ours.*"
>
> . . . It's not that there's much wrong with Bush; it's the comparison to Richards that makes one want to refer to him as "little," "young" (as though forty-eight were young), "callow," and, frankly, sort of a jerk. When you compare the two of them in wisdom, life experience, understanding and liking of people, and knowing how to get things done for Texas, he *is* a shallow little twerp who's too dumb to realize how much he doesn't know.
>
> He may well beat her. It's up to you.

Though the Texas news organizations were saying it was a dead heat, and several national observers predicted Ann would pull it out, her Austin supporters seemed to brace themselves for what was coming. You could see it on the faces of the crowd that greeted the plane when she came home the night before the election.

Ann's first gubernatorial campaign manager, Glenn Smith, spoke often of young women in Texas for whom the governor was a hero. These expressions of young supporters capture a ride coming to a bittersweet end. Austin, election night, 1994.

Harold Cook is a political consultant and witty and well-read blogger who hadn't been in the game too long in 1994. After the polls closed the next evening, the governor, her family, and the extended team gathered to watch and analyze the returns. "Kirk Adams knew we'd lost," Harold told me, "but everyone was getting assignments—there were closure issues. We were waiting on returns from Dallas County, where she had run very well in 1990. It was getting on toward 9:30, and everybody was keeping an eye on Dallas County. It fell to *me* to break the news to her. I said, 'Well, Governor, here's what happened. Dallas is just coming in. It's just not gonna be your night.'

"She was not happy at all, hearing that, and I was not happy being the one standing there in front of her. Then one of her grandchildren started pulling on her skirt. There was just this reflex of hurt or embarrassment or rejection, then she looked down at that child, and the expression on her face completely changed. She leaned over and had this moment with that little girl, then she looked at me and said, 'Well, all right then, what do I do now?'

"I said, 'Well, Governor, you know we took the precaution of drafting two speeches for you.'

"She said, 'All right, let me see it,' and it was like this burden had been lifted."

Ann got 91,258 more votes than she had in 1990. But she lost by 334,066—the new governor was proud of citing that number in weeks to come. He got 53.5 percent of the vote to her 45.8 percent. It was a rout.

The Texas governor's race in 1994 did not occur in a vacuum, of course. Hillary Clinton's imperious mismanagement of the universal health care bill in Washington had been a disaster. Newt Gingrich and his fellow ideologues swept the Democrats out of power in the House of Representatives. Mario Cuomo, the eloquent orator whom Democrats had once longed for as a presidential candidate, was booted just as rudely from the governor's office in New York as Ann was in Texas. Later that night, Bill Clinton called his friend in Austin to console her, and he told her it was his fault. That was also the verdict of the startled press in Washington and New York.

But I have never believed that. The outcome was not preordained. Ann blew that election all on her own, and a man who was a decent sort and a very good politician was propelled toward occupying the White House; fourteen years later, he would leave office as discredited as Jimmy Carter, as Herbert Hoover.

There were so many what-ifs surrounding the Texas race in 1994. What if Bush had gotten the job as the commissioner of Major League Baseball? What if he had listened to his doubts and decided not to run? What if Ann hadn't run? What if she had won?

On election night George H. W. Bush was both delighted and sad. George W. had won, but Jeb lost his race for governor of Florida. A citizen had asked him during the campaign what he was going to do to help the black community, and he replied, "I'm going to answer your question by saying, 'Probably nothing.'" He went on, "I think what we ought to do is to have a society where you go out and pursue your dreams and you're not punished." But the two-word sound bite marked him as a bonehead, and the resulting Democratic turnout, especially among blacks, sank him like a stone.

In 2010, Wayne Slater devoted one of his newspaper columns to Karl Rove's memoir *Courage and Consequence*. In it, he retold Rove's account of a poignant moment from election night in 1994: "The same night that Bush won as governor, brother Jeb lost his race for governor of Florida. Jeb was the brother seen as most likely to rise politically, not George. And so when his parents called, they were so anguished they barely acknowledged Bush's extraordinary upset of Richards. 'Bush listened to his father's distress over his brother's defeat; when the conversation finished, he shrugged his shoulders and went back into a room awash in joy and excitement.'"

Was there an element of getting even in the Texas race? You bet there was. In December 2004, the elder George Bush would say to the *Washington Post*'s Hugh Sidey, who was writing an article for *Time*: "Remember when Ann Richards said George Bush was born with a silver foot in his mouth. And then when George beat her in his first run for governor, I must say I felt a certain sense of joy that he finally had kind of taken her down. I could go around saying, 'We showed her what she could do with that silver foot, where she could stick that now!'"

The day after the election, a woman in the GOP stronghold of Midland wrote Ann a letter on school notebook paper. She said she wanted to tell her before she left office how appreciated she was for the work she had done for some Texas families. Three years earlier, her oldest son had gone to prison at the Eastham Unit. Deep in the East Texas woods, Eastham was state's first maximum-security prison. Clyde Barrow had helped engineer one of the few successful jailbreaks out of there, in 1934, and a guard was killed. It was known as one of the most brutal prisons in the country, and in 1972 one of its inmates had been the writ writer David Ruiz. The Eastham Unit personified the conditions that compelled a federal court to rule in 1979 that imprisonment in Texas amounted to cruel and unusual punishment. The woman's letter continued:

It was a very sad day for our family. We thought all the doors were shut forever. He came from a good family. We were a farming family, we work hard, raised five boys. Raised our boys to believe in God, Country, and family. We didn't have much money. But we had lots of love, place to live, food to eat, clothes—I thought we had it made.

We came to Midland from Plainview. We left farming and went into the oilfield. Our oldest son was in the Army. He came here in '82 and started to get in trouble. I asked many questions as to why—no answers. No one knew what to do and if I had lots of money I could have found help . . .

I thought are the minor drinking and drugs my son was doing that minor? When he was sent to prison this time my world fell apart. I had just buried my 23 year old son and now my oldest son was gone. After he was at Eastham Unit time was coming around for his release. He called and said he was being sent to Kyle [the model unit for Ann's drug and alcohol treatment programs]. I could not understand why the State was doing this to us. I knew nothing about Kyle, no one knew. Little did I know it was the first step in my son getting his life back.

It is one year later, and now we have our son back. If it had not been for Kyle and your program I might have lost him forever.

This last Thanksgiving was the best. We have so much to be thankful for. You will be remembered in our prayers. There are no words I can say—what do you say for a child's life? You have touched our family life and made it better.

As the transition proceeded, a forlorn news story circulated that the Richards campaign was auctioning off mementos to help retire her $50,000 campaign debt. "She didn't have a job, she didn't have a car, she didn't have a place to live," Bud Shrake told me. "She didn't know what the future held for her at all. Then one day this guy called her up for Frito-Lay and said they had an idea for her and Mario Cuomo to make a commercial for Doritos chips that would run during the Super Bowl. With nothing else to do, she and Cuomo were going to sit around with doleful expressions, poking Doritos in some dip and watching the game. She said, 'Oh, I don't know. It sounds all right. Does Mario want to do that?' The man said Mario was game. Then there was this pause, and he said, 'And . . . we'll pay you a million dollars.'"

"That thing was a real production," Marlene Saritzky told me. "They flew her out to LA, and I was with her the last three days she was governor. It was like a full-blown movie set. She had a nice trailer, and she kept rewriting lines of the script. It happened that they were winding up the day Bush was inaugurated. He took the oath at noon, just like she had. It was ten o'clock in the morning in California. The state trooper who was out there with her, Mike Escalante, came to me and said he was going to go tell her good-bye. I was pretty worried about her. We had made plans to go to a movie later that day. Ann said, 'Please don't take this personally, but I'd like to be alone for a while.' She came back after an hour or so, and that was that. She was off into another life, and we went to the movie."

Ann with some of her grandchildren: from left, David Adams, Lily Adams,
Hannah Adams, and Jennifer Richards.

Passages

THE YEAR THAT ANN TURNED SEVENTY, she sat for an interview one day with a young political scientist at the University of Texas named Jim Henson. She was in a relaxed and reflective mood. "I got involved in politics as a very young woman," she told him. "I was nineteen years old when I married a man who was interested in politics. We did it like other couples, you know, go bowling, joined dance clubs, we joined the Young Democrats at the University of Texas, and we participated in political campaigns, we rabble-roused, carried picket signs, and we had a ball at it—what you call the grass roots. If there was a protest, we were participants. And these were the days of the Civil Rights marches, the protests against a government that repressed African-Americans in this country, and it was a great time to be a part of politics."

But she also spoke of the growing disaffection she came to feel with the role she inherited as a wife and mother—as a woman. "No one ever told me when I was in college or in graduate school that I might be preparing myself for life. My whole goal was to be married, have fun, be with the man I love, get away from my folks, but still have them support me for a while, and I was going to do all the things that the slick magazines said I ought to do. You know, I was going to have a family. I was going to have this lovely house. I wasn't going to have to worry about anything, and I was going to have a bunch of kids named Dick and Jane and we'd have Puff and Spot. And pretty much, that's what I did. And it just bored the living hell out of me. I was so bored, cooking and sewing and—you know, there were days when I spent the entire day ironing shirts."

Henson asked her whether she was satisfied with the progress made by American women in her time. "Oh, I am hardly satisfied," she replied. "I am outraged most of the time at how progress seems to stall—how difficult it is for young people to realize that their very freedoms are in jeopardy if they are not willing to fight for them. But you also have to look back and accept and be pleased that things *have* changed. My grandmother, during a period of her life, didn't have the right to vote. The law in Texas was that idiots, imbeciles, the insane, and women could not vote. And, less than one generation later, I was the governor of Texas. Now that'll tell you that we have progressed."

———

ANN LIVED IN A SERIES OF NICE condominiums in Austin, and it seems now that we saw her fairly often. Sometimes it was just at the grocery store, or she would be shooting up and over the hills of Fifteenth Street in her tidy Chrysler. But we were aware, too, that she was gone, living someplace else. First, for three years, it was Washington.

A few days before Christmas 1997, in her *New York Times* column, Maureen Dowd blistered Ann and some of her big-name colleagues for the depths to which they had sunk. "While cashing in has become a national calling," she wrote, "their Faustian bargain with Big Tobacco has left many here speechless." A firm formed by Harry McPherson (a former aide to Lyndon Johnson), Ann, George Mitchell (the distinguished former senator from Maine), and Howard Baker (the former Tennessee senator and a voice of conscience during the Watergate hearings) had billed its tobacco clients for $5 million in the past year, Dowd claimed. She said of her targets:

> Cigarettes are a particular scourge of women, minorities, and the poor. Yet here is Ann Richards, a heroine of women, minorities, and the poor, twisting arms to help a murderous industry that preys on the downtrodden she once championed. Hawking Doritos with Mario Cuomo was just tacky. Hawking tobacco—especially given the fact that the former Texas Governor speaks movingly about being a recovering alcoholic who understands the iron trap of addiction—is reprehensible.
>
> How can George Mitchell be both a statesman working against death in Northern Ireland and a shill for death in America?
>
> We proudly remember Howard Baker for asking, at a pivotal moment during Watergate, "What did the President know, and when did he know it?" Well, shouldn't he be asking the same question of his new clients? It was grim to

watch the former Senate majority leader, whose first wife died of lung cancer, relinquish his spot as chairman of the board of trustees of the Mayo Clinic because his tobacco work nauseated his doctor friends.

Had Ann, her good friends, and those former Senate majority leaders sold out? Newspaper editors schedule columns more often than the columnists do, but Dowd's Christmas gift to Ann, Mitchell, and Baker in the *New York Times* made no attempt to underscore the complexity of the tobacco settlement story, much less to explore whether there might be another side to it. The only point of view that counted was hers, and she loaded up her presentation with remarkably harsh rhetoric: "scourge of women . . . reprehensible . . . shill for death . . . nauseated his doctor friends."

None of the people under Dowd's attack had the resumés of thieves and scoundrels. They had served in government ably and well for decades. But even in the best of lights, Ann hadn't waited long to slip through the revolving door she had decried during her 1990 campaign and her term as governor—this particular door just happened to go around in Washington, not Austin. In fact, she had made up her mind to do it while technically still governor.

The man who offered Ann an as-counsel position with the law firm of Verner, Liipfert, Bernhard, McPherson and Hand was a man whose friendship went back to the days when he and David Richards were enrolled in the University of Texas Law School and Ann was getting a teaching certificate. Harry McPherson and his wife, Clay, were their closest friends when they went to Washington in 1962 in hopes the New Frontier was real, and then they welcomed them back with the fond dinner party that made Senator Ralph Yarborough throw a paranoid fit and send them limping back to Dallas after David's employment of just one day. As a senior adviser to Lyndon Johnson, McPherson tried to talk the president out of escalating the war in Vietnam, and he helped design and build the War on Poverty. He has been credited with persuading LBJ to call out the National Guard to protect the civil rights marchers in Selma, Alabama, in 1965. Former Senate heavyweights and failed presidential candidates Lloyd Bentsen and Bob Dole also had positions at Verner, Liipfert, though they were not registered as active lobbyists. George Mitchell brought more stature and knowledge to the lineup of the Democratic-leaning establishment firm, as did McPherson's longtime friend Ann Richards. McPherson said of their association with the country's major tobacco corporations: "This is a chance to work on an issue that if it is completed successfully would make a very large contribution to the public health of the country."

Verner, Liipfert and its star politicians were not alone in that noble or ignoble quest. Howard Baker committed his law and lobbying firm to representing the interests of tobacco company clients, as did Haley Barbour, the former chairman of the Republican Party and a future governor of Mississippi. According to Public Citizen, a nonprofit organization of integrity-in-government advocates, Big Tobacco besieged the Capitol and the Clinton administration with 208 lobbyists in 1997, dishing out $35.5 million to them in that year alone. The top four of Big Tobacco were Philip Morris USA, R. J. Reynolds Tobacco Company, Brown and Williamson Tobacco Corp., and Lorillard Tobacco Company. Ann's new employer represented all those corporations plus a smokeless tobacco producer, UST, Inc., to the tune of $10.3 million in its 1997 billings. Haley Barbour's firm registered a distant second with $1.7 million.

As far back as 1950, the *British Medical Journal* had published an article linking smoking to lung cancer and heart disease. According to *USA Today*, the Justice Department claimed to have evidence that in a private meeting at the Plaza Hotel in New York in 1953, executives of Big Tobacco spawned a scheme to lie about the dangers of smoking, load tobacco with higher-than-natural nicotine levels to increase addiction, and target the youth market. Hundreds of private suits by ailing and dying smokers against the tobacco companies were filed in state courts, but only two plaintiffs prevailed, and those decisions were reversed on appeal. By the nineties, state governments were in an uproar over the smoking-related costs being paid by Medicaid and other public health programs, but Big Tobacco moved to ward off any sort of coordinated assault, petitioning Congress for a "global resolution." The tobacco industry's power and leverage in Washington ensured that Congress was never going to act.

Seeing no progress at the federal level, forty state attorneys general—including Texas's Dan Morales—sued the four biggest tobacco corporations, which became legally known as the "Original Participating Manufacturers." In 1997, the parties reached a "Master Settlement Agreement," in which the four companies agreed to pay $368.5 billion to settle smoke-related lawsuits filed by the states and finance antismoking campaigns—Texas was to receive $17.3 billion. In addition, the companies would restrict the marketing of cigarettes, permit the federal regulation of tobacco, and pay fines if tobacco use by minors did not recede. That sounded good, but there was a big catch: in the words of Public Citizen, the proposed settlement would "almost completely immunize the tobacco industry from past and future legal responsibility for the harm caused by their deadly products," and it would cap jury awards and eliminate punitive damages.

But to enforce this, Congress had to approve the settlement, which led to the   413
scramble and swarm of lobbyists in 1997. Charles Lewis, the director of the non-
partisan Center for Public Integrity, told the *New York Times*: "This is probably the
most expensive and formidable array of talent ever hired by a single industry.
What's troubling is to see so many politicians aligning themselves to lobby for an
industry that has been responsible for so much death."

Those politicians included Ann Richards, George Mitchell, Howard Baker,
and Haley Barbour.

Trial lawyers, not the attorneys general and their staffs, performed most of the
litigating and negotiating, and their individual shares of the settlement proceeds
totaled hundreds of millions of dollars—fees for the team of lawyers in Texas
came to $3.3 billion altogether. Dan Morales abruptly dropped out of a race for
reelection as attorney general in 1998 and later, after pleading guilty in 2003 to
charges of mail fraud and tax evasion, went to prison. The charges stemmed from
his efforts to help Mark Murr, a Houston attorney, obtain more than $200 million
in fees for working on the tobacco negotiations; other attorneys who worked on
the case claimed Murr had contributed little or nothing to the effort. And complaints were soon raised that Big Tobacco was passing off the billions of dollars
in liabilities to smokers by hiking the price of cigarettes.

What was in it for Ann? According to "Shattered Icon," an *Austin Chronicle*
article by the author and journalist Robert Bryce, she was billing clients roughly
$385 an hour while employed by Verner, Liipfert. Those clients, he reported, were
not just Big Tobacco; they included the City of Austin, Motorola, the Texas Association for Homecare, NBC, the often-fined military contractors Lockheed Martin
and McDonnell Douglas, and a developer of vast shopping malls called the Mills
Corporation. One of its proposed projects targeted 206 acres of wetlands along
the Hackensack River near East Rutherford, New Jersey. Mills offered to refurbish
380 acres of nearby wetlands in exchange for a permit to dump enough material
to fill a domed football stadium on the Hackensack's acres of fragile marshes.
One of the opponents of the development was the ubiquitous environmentalist
Robert Kennedy, Jr. Still, a taxicab dispatcher and self-proclaimed Hackensack
River keeper seethed, "Our regulators, the paid stewards for our resources, are
going to be cowed into granting permits that are not in the public interest because a high-powered ex-politician from Texas has gotten involved in something
she knows nothing about."

Bryce wrote that he cornered Ann when she returned to Austin to make a
speech at the University of Texas in August 1997. "Richards refused to say whether

or not the project was good for the environment. However, Richards did confirm that she has met with [Bill Clinton's] Environmental Protection Agency chief Carol Browner. 'I have talked to Carol Browner, not about the specific project, but about whether or not they are going to get their SAMP [Special Area Management Plan],' said Richards. 'Frankly, I don't know when that's going to happen. All of that is under the aegis of the Corps of Engineers. So what the Mills Corporation wants—and what they frankly deserve—is for the governmental entities to decide what they are going to do with the property. And if the property is going to be commercially developed, they want the opportunity to do that.'"

As a sidebar to his article, Bryce noted that Ann's "environmental agenda for the new Texas" in 1990 criticized the revolving door at the Texas Water Commission: "Questions have been raised about the influence of lawyers and lobbyists over the environmental protection role of the Commission." One of the illustrations was a page from that twenty-four-page document. It read:

Richards' Environmental SWAT Team
Target High Priority Cases
  • Protect Water Supplies
  • Prevent Destruction of Wetlands
  • Prosecute Illegal Dumping
  • Investigate Toxic Discharges

It was strange to see that document again in that context. Those were words I once wrote for the next governor.

Along with her friend Jane Hickie, Ann found work she seemed to like better with Public Strategies, the expanding firm of Jack Martin. Jane opened the office in Seattle, while Ann worked in the one in New York. Ann had a great apartment a short walk from Lincoln Center. Liz Smith and Lily Tomlin were two of her closest pals. This is not to say that Bud Shrake ever faded from her life. His diabetes had slowed down his walking, even if not his writing books. He could be seen hobbling after her on Manhattan's streets, unable to quite keep up. She was so exhilarated by the wonder of living in that city; when people hollered her name and taxi drivers honked, she was usually looking up. One time while doing that in 2002, she walked right off into a sidewalk construction pit, and she hurt herself. Her diagnosis of no broken bones told her she was doing something right about her early stage of osteoporosis. So she came out with another book, in 2004, this

one about confronting that health problem with diet and exercise. *I'm Not Slow-*   415
ing Down was written with a clinical obstetrician and gynecologist at Columbia
Medical School, Richard U. Levine.

Because she could afford it, and so loved it, she traveled to as much of the
world as she could reach. One time she came back through Austin and regaled us
about a cruise to Antarctica. Her firstborn child, Cecile, was still her boon travel
companion. "Whether it was the gardening phase, or getting in the peace movement, or seeing the world later in life," Cecile told me with a laugh, "she was never
the stay-at-home-and-bake-cookies kind of mom. She was very clear about that.
She never fit into that traditional mode. But she and I saw the world together. Of
course, that was the best for her, that she could have a trip sharing it with her children. We went everywhere—once to Siberia. That was one of my favorite trips,
where we got off the plane and we're going to go with these women leaders. We
wind up in this place called Tong Duurai. It had been like a four-hour trip from
St. Petersburg, and in the middle of nowhere we get off the plane, and someone
says, 'Is this your first time in Siberia?'" Cecile guffawed. "It's like someone's going
to make the return trip?"

Days after Ann lost the 1994 race—and she never considered making another
one—her literary agent at ICM told her she would be hearing from the woman
who directed the agency's speaker's bureau. Apart from the public relations work
she did for Public Strategies, and hamming it up whenever she was asked as one
of the favorite guests of Larry King, her profession was traveling the country to
make speeches. She talked about women's rights, the right to choose, and engagement in politics. A couple of times, in the unexpected ways that lives recon-
nect, she was driven around Colorado by Shawn Morris, who had been Dorothy's
assistant at the governor's office and one of the most dedicated volunteers in the
1994 campaign. As they drove toward the prairie town of Pueblo, Shawn mentioned that she had some inclination to run for office, except she was so busy
being a mom. As Morris recalled, "She said, 'Oh, Shawn, you've got to run for
county commissioner. You must. It's a place where you can really make a difference in people's lives.'

"When we got to Pueblo, she was speaking on behalf of the National Democratic Party in the 2004 election at the Colorado State Convention. She had to get
ready in the Grand Hall at the State Fairground—in the women's restroom. Because she always wore black slacks and shirts, this was a matter of changing jackets and touching up her always-perfect makeup and hair. She did have some parts
of the big do that needed some tending to, so I helped with the back. I thought

hair picks had been outlawed since the 1970s, but she had one to match most of her outfits.

"The place was completely asleep before she walked up to the stage ramp. Fan after fan gathered to get a snapshot with her. She was quite comfortable with her fame and her boundaries. Her speech was the usual hilarious and fiery fare, and they were suddenly inspired. To think a Texan would bring such inspiration to this very local crowd. As she got off the stage, I pointed out one of the guys running for the Senate [Ken Salazar, who was a future senator and then Barack Obama's Stetson-wearing secretary of the interior]. She said, 'What's with the hat?' She met him, and we watched a little bit of his speech. When we got back to the car I said, 'I think they need some coffee in here.' To which she replied, 'They need more than that, they need crack!'"

Another one of the youngsters, Mark Strama, was the recently graduated Ivy Leaguer who in 1990 coined the strange metaphor of Clayton Williams as a fraudulent honking goose. "Fourteen years later," he said, "I decided to run for the Texas House of Representatives, and I knew she was the first phone call that I had to make. Even though she held no office, she was the most powerful Democrat in Texas. At thirty-six years of age, I was still terrified of her! I told her I wanted to run and she said, 'Mark, why are you running?' So I go into this long, drawn-out explanation that was basically a stump speech, a lengthy soliloquy. She said in the most compassionate voice that I've ever heard her use—it was just so dear. 'Awww, sweetie. That may be the dumbest thing I've ever heard. The only reason you should run is because you can win.'

"I sent her my campaign plan, and she called me back out of nowhere and she said, 'You can ask one favor, and that's it. I don't want you to put my name on everything.' You could tell that others had done that and she was probably burned by it. So I told her, 'I'd like for you to help me put on a fund-raiser in New York.' She was in New York half the time then. I was thinking she could put together something and a few Texans might show. Next thing I know, I'm in this sweet loft in Tribeca! Ann gave a really nice speech, and if it was insincere, nobody knew it. She was the master at fund-raising, and of course there were more checks written as people left than when they came in. You know her big line—'If your shoes cost more than what it cost to get in here, you need to give more!' There were people like Lisa Ling and a bunch of MTV folks. I couldn't believe it."

Ann's mantra about winning being everything came from a politician whose won-loss record, counting local contests and primaries, was a modest 7 and 1. Of course, she got started pretty late. Her son Clark told me, "You know, years and years went by, and Mom was still quite stung by that loss to Bush. It would come up and she'd say, 'Oh, a woman trying to win in Texas, that's impossible—damn place run by all these men.' I thought she carried that hurt around with her for an awfully long time.'"

After she was out of the game in Texas, I never heard her speeches, except what she might be saying on CNN. The best parting one I know about came in June 1994, when she probably knew she was losing her reelection race. She spoke to the Southern Conference on Women's History.

> Women in Texas don't mind their place on earth being thought of as the habitat of the good ol' boy. You all know what I'm talking about.
>
> These are the guys whose preferred method of transportation is a pickup with a bad clutch, a gun rack that's not for show, and a bumper sticker that reads "I Don't Brake for Liberals."
>
> The women in this audience know these guys well. When they are still in the dating stage, they show respect for women by hanging an air freshener on the rear-view mirror. We've all seen the deep blue of a starlit night and the orange glow of the campfire, and around it another group of good ol' boys, doing what real he-men do—drinking beer and staring at nothing in particular.
>
> Now, you look at that image and the historical concepts that go with it, and you might begin to think that Texas is not the kind of place where change is readily accepted. But here I am as governor—so you know something is going on.
>
> In an incredibly short time, we have moved from watching the parade to joining the end of the procession, and now we move, with our brothers, to the head of the procession. We ask only that our perspective as women be valued. Not because it's better—but because it's different—and it's been missing.

Dorothy works in the Texas House of Representatives now, the chief of staff for Elliott Naishtat, who grew up in Queens, New York, came to Texas as a volunteer with the Great Society organization VISTA, went to law school, and rode Ann's 1990 coattails to victory in a liberal, central Austin district—a fine man and a good legislator. One day in March 2006, Dorothy answered the telephone there, and a familiar voice said, "Darthy, I've got a young woman here who doesn't know what she wants to do with her life." Ann never killed time getting started on a conversation. She said she had served with the young woman's father on "the car wash board" and wondered whether Dorothy might help her find an internship at the Capitol. Recalling how her own involvement in government began, Dorothy said she would gladly try. The young woman eventually came to work in Elliott's office.

Dorothy then asked her mentor, "How are you doing, Ann?"

There was a pause, then she said, "Not so good." It was one of the few times Dorothy ever heard her voice sound small. Ann said that the day before, she had been diagnosed with esophageal cancer. Her beloved father had died that way in 1994. Ann sounded frightened. Who wouldn't be?

And yet the first thing she had done on the second morning of this terrifying turn in her life was to make a call on behalf of a young woman she didn't know.

Ann quickly decided on a course of treatment at M. D. Anderson, the renowned cancer hospital in Houston. As word of her illness raced around the country that spring, the flood of correspondence began to arrive. New York senator Hillary Clinton sent a nice note in her rather stiff prose style: "Dear Ann: With news of your diagnosis, what first came to mind was sadness, but what immediately followed was the strength and courage with which you have confronted every other challenge that life has put before you. My thoughts and prayers are with you and positive thoughts for a complete and uneventful recovery. With blessings, dear friend, I remain, Sincerely yours, Hillary. (I hope to see you while in Texas next week.)"

From the much more self-assured writer and first-term Illinois senator Barack Obama: "Dear Ann—I want you to know that I'm thinking of you, praying for you, and expect that a tough gal like you won't let this stuff get you down. Love ya—Barack."

Ann replied: "Dear Barack Obama, What a treat to have your good wishes. I feel ready for this cancer challenge. Thanks for thinking of me and giving me your prayers. Fondly, Ann."

Handwritten from the president: "Laura and I have read about your battle with cancer. We wish you all the best and pray for your strength and comfort. Knowing your strength and courage, all will be well. George Bush."

A note from Katie Couric at CBS: "Wanting to talk soon about everything: You, career, Asshole sexists, adorable Feminists like you."

Ann's longtime assistant Barbara Chapman came down to Houston to help with all that. Early on, Ann wrote some letters that were quite personal. To her late mother's sister, who had entertained her during girlhood summers in the little town of Hico: "Dear Aunt Oleta, The Doctor at M.D. Anderson Hospital actually used the word 'cure' in my case. The treatment is long, but I can deal with it. Thank heaven for Ellen. She has been a godsend and has everyone organized to take care of me. I will be doing chemo once a week for two months and then radiation following that. I'm not sure whether surgery will be called for or not. Please know that I love you and am so happy to have your prayers. Love to your kids, Ann."

To former secretary of state Madeleine Albright, an update that went out to many of the correspondents, but with a handwritten note at the bottom: "Hi Toots—this cancer is no worse than a right wing opponent. I am doing fine. Minimal pain—dealing with chemo well. Loved hearing from you. A."

Anita Perry, the First Lady of Texas, wrote with consideration and a delicate touch: "Dear Governor Richards, I was saddened to hear about your latest challenge. Please know that I would never interfere with your privacy, but am always 'on call' for *whatever* you need. Please do not hesitate. I am thinking of you and sending you my best. Anita."

The same day brought a somewhat odd note from the governor, Rick Perry, who with great ambition and growing ideological fervor had succeeded George W. Bush. He was clearly trying to cheer her up, but did he think she gave much of a hoot right then that he had enlisted his old Aggie roommate and buddy, John Sharp, as a bipartisan adviser on taxes? "Gov—Anita and I have you in our prayers as you deal with this thing. . . . Sharp and I talked about you today (in a very good way, I might add!). Some think the second coming is just around the corner with the hurricanes, fires & me and Sharp getting back together! We love you and look forward to a total Recovery . . . Rick."

It was so hard for people to know what to say, and harder still for Ann. As her strength waned, most of her replies were form letters drafted by Barbara and approved by Ann. A stock one read in part: "Patience has never been my strong suit, but I am learning. Treatment started last week and I am taking one day at a time. The M. D. Anderson Hospital is fabulous. It is a whole lot like 'Star Wars' with more interesting machines than Buck Rogers ever imagined."

But then a letter came from Dave Richards.

Dear Ann—I should have written sooner—didn't quite know how to express my concern—I've stayed abreast of developments through the kids—am delighted to know that you have withstood the chemo treatments in good shape—they can be quite debilitating—you are often in my thoughts—as always you seem to be handling this unexpected blow with courage and determination—continue to be strong—and let me know if there is anything I could do to be of aid—Dave.

420   The reply to this was one Ann had to write. Her words sounded moved and mystified by the two of them, as ever.

> Dear David, I am about to embark on cutting edge rocket science at M. D. Anderson and I feel fortunate to be able to afford it and have it available to me. Cancer is no piece of cake and the treatment itself is challenging, but I refuse to lead a "sickness" life. . . . I should be coming out of this tunnel by the end of the year and look forward to a return of my energy and opportunities. My goal right now is to recover from the radiation enough to take the boys fishing in Alaska in July. Something to look forward to. Thanks for the letter. A.

Bud spoke to Ann and e-mailed her almost daily, but he told Dorothy that despite Austin's proximity to Houston, he never went down to see her. I suspect it wasn't just that he feared to see her so ill; he didn't want to make the ordeal that much worse for her. "One time we brought her home," Clark Richards told me. "But she got so sick that she had to go right back to Houston in an ambulance.

"The chemo and the radiation were brutal," Clark said. "The doctors said that killed the tumor, but it also destroyed her esophagus. She was on a feeding tube, couldn't eat. There was no way she could withstand the surgery, which was supposed to be next. She was just too weak." Six months after the diagnosis, in the midst of her family, she died on September 13, 2006, twelve days past her seventy-third birthday.

Her flag-draped coffin lay in state in the rotunda of the Capitol. Bill Clinton came that night and held Ellen Richards in his arms as she wept and thanked him for how much he had brought to their mother's life. At the public ceremony in the Erwin Center the next day, September 18, 2006, Hillary Clinton was funny, telling how Ann would look at her, shake her head, and say she was just never going to figure out this problem of hair: "She said, 'You know, really, you gotta make up your mind. You either just have to do something people forget about and pay no attention to, or you gotta make a statement.'" Senator Clinton observed that right after September 11, when so many Americans were inclined to put distance between themselves and New York, Ann chose to live in Manhattan.

Ann was in New York on the day of the attacks. On the street, she found a young woman from another country wandering, not knowing where to go, or how or whom to ask. Ann took her under her wing and made sure she was not lost and out of her wits with fear in the best city in America.

Lily Adams, the "nearly perfect grandchild" whom Ann introduced to the na-
tion in the 1988 keynote in Atlanta, stood before Austin's audience of thousands,
a confident young woman now, sharing memories of the woman she called
"Mammy." Outside, I saw my tall friend John Hall, for whom I had written during
her term as governor. He put his hand on my shoulder and said, "Maybe our time
will come around again."

In the Texas State Cemetery, early that morning there had been a private farewell
under a tent as a light morning fog cleared away. I found a chair next to Ann's
friend and onetime lawyer Shelton Smith. Seated next to Shelton was his friend
Bob Kerrey, the former governor and U.S. senator from Nebraska. Since leaving politics, he had been the president of the New School, a university in New
York City, and was a thoughtful and influential member of the 9/11 Commission.
I shook his hand on Shelton's introduction and uttered something I had never
been able to say before: "I supported you for president." With a modest smile, he
nodded and said, "Thank you."

    Also seated near us was Ann's friend and frequent critic Molly Ivins. She had
been battling recurring cancer for several years. She wore a scarf on her head
and looked thin and frail; she would lose her last battle with the disease just four
months after Ann. There were so many reasons that morning to have tears in
your eyes, but she still wore that great big grin that said she was glad to see you.

    At a time when she might have thought, "Oh, the hell with it," sometime back
she had withstood the trauma and strain of giving up booze. She did it, she said,
because she didn't want to be remembered as a drunk. She had long wanted to
run the Colorado River in the Grand Canyon, and she had just returned from that
arduous trek in the wilderness. Dave and Sandy Richards, along with Brady Coleman, a jovial Austin lawyer turned actor and musician, had fulfilled a promise to
take Molly on the trip. Her friend Ellen Sweets would write a book titled *Stirring It
Up with Molly Ivins: A Memoir with Recipes*. Dave and Sandy recounted to her what a
brave and determined adventure that had been.

    Although Molly mainly hung out at the river's edge while others went on hikes,
she also helped out in the kitchen, chopping ingredients and telling stories about
her early years as a reporter. True to Molly form, she organized a sing-along and
talent show. As sick as she was, she still had the energy to invigorate others.

    For all that, getting her in and out of the raft was a major undertaking, but,
typically, she insisted on doing everything on her own. As Dave Richards put

it, "We for damn sure weren't going to let anything happen to her, not on our watch. For the most part it was pretty quiet water except for a few places like Rattlesnake Rapids. Molly, being Molly, insisted on sitting up front, where you take the brunt of the shocks when you hit the rapids. You really have to hold on. Well, Molly lost her grip and went airborne. Somehow she came down partially straddling the boat. I got hold of her and we're still in the middle of the goddamn rapids. Brady held on to one leg and I held on to her until we got to calm water. I think that chastened her for the time being, but it sure as hell scared the shit out of me." . . .

"Molly seemed to get stronger as we went along," [Sandy] said. "In the end it was the right thing to do and she was a wonderful companion. Much of the trip was hiking trails, so either Dave or I stayed with her while the others went on the walks. We talked, and of course we sang. We were ten days on the river, and at the end Molly insisted on taking everyone to dinner. I was so glad she had made the trip and enjoyed it so much. I don't remember anything anybody ate. I just remember there were some people on the trip that we didn't know and by the time we parted company Molly had them all singing along."

All these friendships, all this loss. In remembrance of Ann, Lily Tomlin related a very funny tale about how she and a group of friends had hatched plans to take over a Manhattan building and, without regard either for leases that had held firm for generations or for the city's daunting policies of rent control, they would just buy the building and make it a guarded salon of artistes and intellectuals—their playground. Ann listened to the plan and, in that voice of absolute knowing, said, "Bad idea, Lily."

The most eloquent words of loss were written and delivered by Bud Shrake.

For the last seventeen years Ann has been the anchor of my life.

We don't know what life really is, or where life comes from, or where life goes, or what to do with it while we have got it.

But we know life is far grander than just chemistry. We are beings of spirit.

And even across the divide of death, Ann's spirit remains an echo in our hearts this morning.

Father Taliaferro says hell is being in heaven and not liking it.

I think that is Ann's message to us.

Put a smile on your face, and a good thought in your heart, and try to do the right thing—and you will find Ann standing beside you with a fresh bag of popcorn.

Thank you, Ann. I love you.
Ah-men. And Ah-women. And Ah-Ann.

Bob Bullock did some inexplicable things at the end of his life, one of them point-
less and cruel. Garry Mauro couldn't stand to watch the Democrats just stand
aside, offering no opponent, as George W. Bush ran for the 1998 reelection that
was the first lap of his presidential campaign. Garry threw a bunch of well-made
ads at Governor Bush early in the summer. The polls didn't budge, and after
that, the outcome was a foregone conclusion. Near the end, Bullock decided to
endorse Bush over his protégé. They had been through intimidation by the FBI
together. Bullock was the godfather of two of Garry's children. His announcement left Garry's friends speechless. When Bullock was dying, he made amends
with Garry and other people he had hurt in his turbulent life. He predicted on his
deathbed that Bush would be president and the Texas House would keep going
Republican—"there wasn't any saving it." As soon as he was gone, his beloved
Senate went Republican, too.

The Texas State Cemetery was Bob Bullock's abiding wish for a thing of beauty,
and when it is not crowded with mourners and sorrow for someone you know
who is being buried, you see what a fruition of his dream it is. On a hot June day, I
wandered through it, pausing a moment before the monument of one, Stephen F.
Austin, the father of Texas, who went out into a dangerous frontier, willing to
make his way as a colonist and an immigrant to Mexico. John Connally's celebration of self is much overdone, bearing a life-size sculpture of some bearded wise
man holding an open book in one hand and a board in the other. A board?

Tom Landry's stone sports an engraving of the iconic fedora that symbolized
his coaching tenure with the Dallas Cowboys. Tom Lea's gravestone is as exquisite as his paintings and prose. The writers Walter Prescott Webb and Fred Gip-
son lie side by side; I wonder whether they were friends. I stop for a moment on
seeing the chiseled name of Charlie Wilson, that great East Texas rascal—some
say scoundrel—who took it upon himself to arm the mujahideen against the Soviet might in Afghanistan.

I am not sure how to find what I am looking for. I do come across the grave of
Bill Kugle, who shocked his friend Ann once by inquiring whether she would be
pleased to go to bed with him. Kugle's service in the legislature was short, but the
epigraph on his tombstone is a classic: "He never voted for Republicans and had
little to do with them." I see some teenage kids who have also been looking about
with interest and have retreated to park benches in the shade of a blooming crepe
myrtle. I stop and ask them whether they have seen the grave of Ann Richards.

424 Most look away from whatever this old man with a cane presents to them. A couple of them ask me to say the name again. They look at each other and dismiss me with a sort of giggle. My God, I realize, they have never heard of her.

But over in the southwest part of the city there is an innovative middle school that bears her name and has won acclaim as a leadership school. During her time in New York, Ann came across such a school in a tough part of the city. A wealthy old man in Dallas told Ann that she ought to take the lead in bringing those schools to every city in the state. All the students at the Ann Richards School for Young Women Leaders are girls. Getting in is very competitive, and for reasons I don't quite fathom, the concept seems to work educationally. Ellen Richards has given its board the organizational talent her mother described, and Jeanne Goka, a friend, neighbor, veteran principal, and wife of my colleague Lou Dubose, has brought it from concept to thriving classrooms. Many of the students come from disadvantaged backgrounds; about 60 percent of them qualify for free or reduced-price meals. A Japanese American, Jeanne knows a great deal about overcoming hardship in this country; her parents were sent to internment camps in California during World War II. She says, "I tell the teachers we are going to get this girl into college, she's going to come back and take her siblings through, and they're going to lift this whole family out of poverty."

Dan and Clark Richards are practicing law in downtown Austin with their father, which has been a treat for all three of them. Dan is a lifelong hot-rodder, and he goes zooming off with Sam, the older of his two half siblings. Sam's sister, Hallie, is a former star softball pitcher and a college student, as tall, confident, and pretty as her mother, Sandy. Clark has a passion for playing some kind of big drum in a troupe, and he and his brother are collaborating on a mystery novel featuring two brothers practicing law and fishing on South Padre Island. And how proud Ann would be of Cecile, the president of the Planned Parenthood Federation of America, carrying on one of the fights for hearts and minds that was so important to her mother.

The subtext of birth control is abortion, and no one can think that the most wrenching political disagreement in American life is going away. But on *Good Morning America* on May 10, 2010, Cecile said, "The invention of the birth control pill revolutionized life for women in America. It's completely changed women's options." It was the fiftieth anniversary of the pill's invention. Cecile and Kirk live in New York now. Not long before I took my walk through the State Cemetery, *Time* proclaimed Cecile one of the twenty most influential people in the world. Dorothy and I looked at each other and said, "The world?"

Our friend Bud Shrake made it through life only a couple of years longer than Ann did. He died in May 2009. He went out with a blaze of creativity, finishing a novel and a play before lung cancer brought him to an end. After being told what ailed him, he remarked with annoyance that he hadn't smoked in twenty years. In an e-mail interview Bud granted not long before he died, Brant Bingamon asked whether he thought people with drinking in their past are more prone to cancer. Bud wrote, "I have no idea if drinking and cancer are linked in any way. However there's not as many old drunks as it seems there used to be."

The admirer continued, "What's it like to not have a wife in your old age? Do you have a girlfriend?"

Bud replied that he loved both his wives, Joyce and Doatsy. "I've been divorced since 1980 but always had a girlfriend and for seventeen years until she died my girlfriend was Guv Ann Richards. Ann and I planned to get married eventually, talked about it a lot but never got around to it. I don't know if I miss having a wife or not. I certainly do miss Ann."

Some mutual friends were driving in the hills west of Austin not long after he died. They laughed so hard they had to pull over on the shoulder of the road after seeing the pink granite tombstone jouncing in the bed of a pickup. "Edwin 'Bud' Shrake, Jr.," the tombstone read, and below that the carefree motto that sustained him, "So Far So Bueno."

I find them finally. Anyone who believes theirs wasn't a genuine love affair needs to see them side by side. They arranged it that way—he was as deserving a writer as others buried here, but former governors do have pull. Bob Bullock and his wife are buried three rows back. Bullock chose a plot that he said was sixteen paces from Stephen F. Austin. The chiseling on the back of Bullock's gravestone reads, "Only death will end my love affair with Texas." I grin on seeing that to his front and to his rear there is no more than a horseshoe toss to the graves of two women who irked him to no end, Ann Richards and Barbara Jordan. I like to think that late at night, you can almost hear them scaring up an argument.

Some people don't care for Ann's abstract marker of white marble. The lines of it flow all right for me. A couple of political buttons have been left on a small shelf of the marble. I lean close enough to read them. One says, "Pass the E.R.A."; the other, "Hillary 2012." Engraved on the other side of Ann's tombstone is a graceful line that I couldn't hear when the helicopter was circling the Capitol that day of her inauguration, all those years ago: "Today we have a vision of a Texas where opportunity knows no race, no gender, no color—a glimpse of what can

426 happen in government if we simply open the doors and let people in."

Ann belongs here beside Bud in the shade of an old and majestic live oak tree. But what a wonder she became for the whole country. I see her in New York, strapping her purse over her shoulder—having no harried male aides to lug it around, as she did when she was governor—and barging up those sidewalks grinning, proud of her good heart and thrilled by the journey.

Notes

MY PATH TO WRITING THIS BIOGRAPHY began with a November 2006 *Texas Monthly* essay on her passing, "Ann: An Appreciation." That led to another essay, "The Case for Ann Richards," in the anthology *A Legacy of Leadership: Governors in American History*, edited by Clayton McClure Brooks (Philadelphia: Univ. of Pennsylvania Press, 2008).

Much as I admired Ann and was indebted to her in my personal and professional life, I would never have attempted to write this book if I had not, in researching the second essay, discovered the wealth of materials and knowledge in the Ann W. Richards Papers in the Dolph Briscoe Center for American History at the University of Texas in Austin (hereafter cited as Richards Papers). The index alone runs to 700 single-spaced pages. Early on, I saw that important sections bore a proviso that authorization by the governor would be required. Since she had passed away two years earlier, I asked the lead archivist, Evan Hocker, what that now meant. A day or two later, he reported happily that only capital punishment and personnel files remained confidential and closed. She had stipulated that a year and a half after her death, she wanted scholars and interested citizens to have access to whatever they might find and learn. That transparency is very rare among politicians today. My job was to be thorough and fair.

David Richards and his children, Cecile, Dan, Clark, and Ellen, contributed to this undertaking from the outset. We had no formal agreement that it would be an "authorized biography"; they just trusted me to do my best to tell Ann's story right. Bud Shrake's sons, Ben and Alan Shrake; the Wittliff Collections at Texas State University in San Marcos; and the archivist Joel Minor contributed correspondence and an insightful interview of Bud by Brant Bingamon. Bud fell ill before we had the long conversations about the book that we planned, and I did not want to intrude on the medical difficulty that he fended off with bravery and creativity in his last months. But in the course of our friendship, he had already told me a great deal.

My wife, Dorothy Browne, was a friend of Ann and David Richards before she became a senior aide of Ann for almost a decade. She was also my knowing critic here. Her administrative assistant in the Governor's Office, Shawn Morris, in turn was my helpful research assistant. So I knew many of Ann's associates before I began. Still, I was startled by the response of professional colleagues who made generous time for interviews. The same was true of her political advisers. In addition to the archival work, I conducted over one hundred interviews over a three-year period.

Some important figures, such as Jane Hickie, politely declined to be interviewed. Ann's speechwriter Suzanne Coleman did not respond to my calls and e-mails about the book. She had been our good friend since Dorothy went to work at the Treasury, and I knew that in addition to her work and whatever she felt in retrospect about her long creative partnership with Ann, she had a loved one to care for, and I did not want to intrude on their privacy. For one reason or another, there were a few others whom I did not get to interview, but their roles and words were abundantly documented in the archives.

Ann Richards's memoir *Straight from the Heart: My Life in Politics and Other Places*, written with Peter Knobler (New York: Simon and Schuster, 1989), and David Richards's *Once Upon a Time in Texas: A Liberal in the Lone Star State* (Austin: Univ. of Texas Press, 2002) are secondary sources, but read together, I found they became something more than that, for they offer different perspectives, sometimes disagreements, on many experiences that were richly shared.

Other books I consulted were *Land of the Permanent Wave: An Edwin "Bud" Shrake Reader*, edited by Steven L. Davis (Austin: Univ. of Texas Press, 2008), and Davis's *Texas Literary Outlaws: Six Writers in the Sixties and Beyond* (Fort Worth: TCU Press, 2004); Gary Cartwright's *HeartWiseGuy: How to Live the Good Life after a Heart Attack* (New York: St. Martin's, 1998) and *Turn Out the Lights: Chronicles of Texas during the 80s and 90s* (Austin: Univ. of Texas Press, 2000); and Molly Ivins's *Molly Ivins Can't Say That, Can She?* (New York: Random House, 1991) and *Who Let the Dogs In? Incredible Political Animals I Have Known* (New York: Random House, 2004).

On politics and government, I learned much from *Bob Bullock: God Bless Texas*, by Dave McNeely and Jim Henderson (Austin: Univ. of Texas Press, 2008); Brian McCall's *The Power of the Texas Governor: Connally to Bush* (Austin: Univ. of Texas Press, 2009); *From Bloodshed to Hope in Burundi*, by Robert Krueger and Kathleen Tobin Krueger (Austin: Univ. of Texas Press, 2009); George W. Bush's *Decision Points* (New York: Broadway, 2011); Robert Draper's *Dead Certain: The Presidency of George W. Bush* (New York: Free Press, 2008); Mike Cochran's *Claytie: The Roller-Coaster Life of a Texas Wildcatter* (College Station: Texas A&M Univ. Press, 2007); Karen Hughes's *Ten Minutes from Normal* (New York: Viking, 2004); Wayne Slater and James Moore's *Bush's Brain: How Karl Rove Made George W. Bush Presidential* (New York: Wiley, 2003); and Karl Rove, *Courage and Consequence: My Life as a Conservative in the Fight* (New York: Threshold Editions, 2010).

To refresh my memory and double-check sources, I also revisited *Beaches, Bureaucrats, and Big Oil* by Garry Mauro (Austin: Look Away, 1997), a book that I helped edit, and *Boy*

Genius: Karl Rove, the Brains Behind the Remarkable Political Triumph of George W. Bush (New
York: Public Affairs, 2003), on which I collaborated with Lou Dubose, Carl M. Cannon,
and, in an important unsigned chapter, John Ratliff.

———

Prologue: Glimpses. I first described the "gonzo bridge" party in Austin where I met Ann
Richards in the previously mentioned *Texas Monthly* essay "Ann." For the intervention,
see *Straight from The Heart*, 202–212. I conducted interviews with David Richards and Dan
Richards, and Michael and Sue Sharlot, who took part in the intervention.

For Ann's work for Sarah Weddington, see *Straight from the Heart*, 137–145, and for the
keynote address, the same book, 11–32. In interviews, Mary Beth Rogers and Bill Cryer
described the pressured speechwriting sessions in Atlanta. Dan Richards told me about
watching his mother deliver the speech from the stage wings. The *Dallas Morning News's*
Wayne Slater recalled her remark to him on finishing the speech in a KLRU-TV interview
by Paul Stekler. The faxed letter of congratulation from Bud Shrake is in the Richards Papers. Copies of the exchanged notes between Ann and President George H. W. Bush are
there as well. The summary of her accomplishments and shortcomings is mine alone.

Chapter 1: Waco. Ann Richards's Waco High School yearbooks, mementos, and photographs are in her personal effects in the Richards Papers. David Richards spoke of her
father, mother, and uncle in conversations with the author. For the effect on Texas of the
Civil War and Reconstruction, see T. R. Fehrenbach, *Lone Star: A History of Texas and the
Texans* (New York: MacMillan, 1968), 393–432. The postwar constitutions are described
thoroughly and well in *The Handbook of Texas Online*, published in multiple editions by the
Texas State Historical Association, Austin. The *Handbook* also relates the story of William Cowper Brann, "the Iconoclast." The colorful tale of the invention of the soft drink
Dr Pepper is related in papers and articles at the Dr Pepper Museum in Waco, as well as
on the museum's website.

For Ann's descriptions of her parents' origins, her birth, her childhood in Lakeview,
her adolescent years in San Diego, and her move to Waco, see *Straight from the Heart*, 33–
57. David Richards described his parents' arrival in Waco in several conversations with
the author. He confirmed and added to the story of his father's participation in the navy
in both world wars and his coaching career at Clemson University, which I had gleaned
from histories of that school's athletic programs; he likewise confirmed his mother's indignation at the provincialism of Waco and Baylor University. Ann reminisced about her
high school romance with David and her introduction to the sophistication of his family
in *Straight from the Heart*, 69–81. On the fascination that the story of Robin Hood held for
David and Ann, see *Straight from the Heart*, 74, and *Once Upon a Time*, 7. In conversations
with the author, David described the nights of dancing and music on Waco's segregated
black east side.

For their brief drifting apart and Ann's conversion in response to a sermon by Billy
Graham, see *Straight from the Heart*, 74–78, and *Once Upon a Time*, 8–9. Their involvement
in the Young Democrats' liberal politics is recounted in *Straight from the Heart*, 83–88, and

430   *Once Upon a Time*, 8–13. Ann's year of teaching history in junior high and her return to Waco to give birth to their first child, Cecile, is recounted in *Straight from the Heart*, 89–91, and in David's conversations with the author.

Chapter 2: New Frontiers. Ann's isolation as a young mother in Dallas, David's bewildering plunge into labor law, and the oppressive atmosphere of Dallas in the 1950s are conveyed in *Once Upon a Time*, 16–19, and *Straight from the Heart*, 90–97. I learned more about the Dallas years in conversations and interviews with David, Cecile, and Dan Richards and Gary Cartwright. For the effects of the 1960 presidential election on Texas, see *The Handbook of Texas Online*. For the experience of Ann and David in Washington, see *Straight from the Heart*, 96–110, and *Once Upon a Time*, 20–26. Both books describe the effects on them of LBJ's tirade at a private party.

Chapter 3: Lovers Lane. In *Once Upon a Time*, 16–21, and in several conversations with the author, David Richards related his high regard for labor union members as leaders of the progressive political movement. For the race to fill Lyndon Johnson's Senate seat in 1961 and the election of John Connally as governor, see *The Handbook of Texas Online*. For Ann's involvement in the North Dallas Democratic Women, see *Straight from the Heart*, 110–118. Interviews by Ruthe Winegarten are archived in the Richards Papers. Numerous copies of the irreverent Christmas cards of Ann Richards and Betty McKool are there also. The summary of the cashiering of General Edwin Walker and his near assassination by Lee Harvey Oswald is drawn from Dallas newspaper accounts and the report of the Warren Commission. David Richards described the near mob scene at a Dallas appearance by U.N. Ambassador Adlai Stevenson in *Once Upon a Time*, 32, and in conversations with the author. David told me about his alarm at seeing the motorcade of President John F. Kennedy with so little apparent security. Ann wrote about waiting at the luncheon where Kennedy was scheduled to speak and then the mass fright in *Straight from the Heart*, 120–122. Cecile Richards told me about hearing the news that the president was dead over an intercom at a school where older students cheered. David recalled the chaotic aftermath of the assassination, his desperation to have his family all together, and the shock of Jack Ruby's murder of Lee Harvey Oswald on live television in *Once Upon a Time*, 33–34. Lynn Whitten told me about the families' frigid escape to a camping ground north of Dallas.

For the troubled pregnancy and two grand mal seizures Ann suffered, see *Straight from the Heart*, 123–125. They were described in more detail in conversations with David Richards and Lynn Whitten, whose mother, Virginia, was in the car Ann was driving during one of those episodes. Ann's diagnosis of epilepsy followed her in medical records, and her prescribed use of the drug Dilantin is confirmed in the Richards Papers. In interviews, Cecile Richards and Lynn Whitten relayed memories of the elaborate parties for children and their mothers' political engagement in boycotts of nonunion produce. David told me about their friendship with Stan Alexander, a North Texas State University professor of English and sponsor of a storied folk music club in Denton, and the night Alexander brought to a Lovers Lane party Eddie Wilson, who later was a figure of great importance in Austin's burgeoning music scene and remained a close friend of both Ann and David. David told me about his brief term as a Democratic precinct chairman and his friendship with Shel Hershorn, a neighbor and noted freelance photographer whose papers and images are in the Dolph Briscoe Center for American History. I learned more about Ann's talent and vaudeville-style showmanship in an interview with, and images taken by, the photographer Tad Hershorn.

In correspondence archived in the Richards Papers and through my conversations with David, I learned details of their early friendship in Dallas with Bud Shrake and Gary "Jap" Cartwright. I learned about Bud Shrake's early life from conversations with Gary Cartwright and in compiling Bud's obituary in the *Austin American-Statesman*. For the madcap gymnastic act the Flying Punzars, see Cartwright's *HeartWiseGuy*, 25–26, and for their frequent encounters with Jack Ruby and Shrake's affair with one of Ruby's strippers, see *HeartWiseGuy*, 16–20. David recounted John Connally's urging of his ouster as a Democratic precinct chairman in *Once Upon a Time*, 35, and in conversations with the author. I learned about the many whitewater expeditions and campouts in conversations with David, Dorothy Browne, Sue Sharlot, and in *Once Upon a Time*, 188–195, and *Straight from the Heart*, 126–129. For David's brief employment by Senator Ralph Yarborough, see *Once Upon a Time*, 56–58.

For the *Dallas Notes* lawsuit and Supreme Court argument, see *Once Upon a Time*, 65–73, and *Straight from the Heart*, 136–137. For the farmworkers' march to Austin, see *Once Upon a Time*, 48–49.

Chapter 4: Mad Dogs and First Fridays. For the Richardses' move to Austin and early months there, see *Straight from the Heart*, 134–137, and *Once Upon a Time*, 77–84. David, Cecile, Dan, and Clark Richards, and Eddie Wilson, told me about their arrival in West Lake Hills. Cecile, Dan, and Clark told me in detail about their parents' changes in lifestyle in liberal Austin. Lynn Whitten told me about the roaring arguments that their fathers would engage in for sport. David remembered the march to protest the Kent State killings in 1970 as a pivotal moment in the politics of Austin. For the Richardses' involvement in First Fridays, Mad Dog, Inc., and the Armadillo World Headquarters, see *Straight from the Heart*, 196–201, and *Once Upon a Time*, 173–187. Conversations with David, Eddie Wilson, and Gary Cartwright added more details about this period. Also see Steven L. Davis, *Texas Literary Outlaws*, 228–238, and his *Land of the Permanent Wave*, 175–185.

The columns of *New York Times* editor Abe Rosenthal about Ann and the parties on Red Bud Trail are in the Richards Papers; also see *Once Upon a Time*, 77. In many conversations, David, Gary Cartwright, Doatsy Shrake, and Mike and Sue Sharlot shared memories of their lives in Austin in the early 1970s. Cecile, Dan, and Clark Richards added their perspectives in interviews. David, Cartwright, and Doatsy Shrake recounted the night when the Flying Punzars showed up on the Richardses' deck hours past midnight, voicing hopes that Ann's Santa Claus costume from an earlier party would enable them to obtain prescription drugs from a pharmacist at that hour.

Members of the Richards family, Gary Cartwright, Sue Sharlot, and other friends told me about her alcoholism and affection for marijuana in the 1970s. A conversation with David led me to the literature of the National Center for Biotechnological Information and stark accounts of the side effects of Dilantin; see also *Once Upon a Time*, 215–216.

Chapter 5: The Hanukkah Chicken. Ann's accounts of the canoeing armadas in the canyons of the Rio Grande and the campout at Sam Rayburn Lake are in *Straight from the Heart* and in the Richards Papers. David, Gary Cartwright, and Sue Sharlot added details about these episodes in our conversations. I attended the wedding of Gary and Phyllis Cartwright in the back room of an Austin bar called the Texas Chili Parlor. During this time, I came to know Bud Shrake and his wife Doatsy. For Ann's battles with the schools of West Lake Hills, see *Straight from the Heart*, 147–151. In interviews, Cecile, Dan, and Clark Richards described their experience in those public schools and at the private St. Stephen's Academy. Dan told me about a comic performance that Ann, Molly Ivins, and Maury Maverick, Jr., staged around the Richardses' swimming pool, reading from transcripts of the Watergate hearings. Sue Sharlot told me about what a beautiful and generous person Ann was in those wild days. Ann's collected letters concerning her family's trip to England and France in 1973 are in the Richards Papers.

Chapter 6: Problem Lady. For the institutional contempt that Ann felt for the Democratic Party because of its treatment of women, see *Straight from the Heart*, 111–112 and 136. Garry Mauro told me about how his friendship with Bill and Hillary Clinton began when they were campaign workers for George McGovern in 1972. Don Roth, who taught history at St. Stephen's, told me about Ann guiding him in his role as their Democratic precinct chairman in the camp of McGovern. See *The Handbook of Texas Online* for a summary of the Sharpstown scandal of 1972. For Ann's experience as Sarah Weddington's campaign manager, see *Straight from the Heart*, 137–145. The chastening and telling letter from Maury Maverick, Jr., concerning his support of that year's lieutenant-governor candidate, Bill Hobby, is in the Richards Papers.

In recounting the history of birth control in the United States, I relied on multiple online accounts of the lives and careers of Margaret Sanger, the physiologist Gregory Pincus, the gynecologist John Rock, and the Polish émigré and inventor Carl Djerassi. Particularly useful as an overview is David Allyn, *Make Love, Not War: The Sexual Revolution: An Unfettered History* (Boston: Little, Brown, 2000). The landmark legal cases are examined in *History Blog: Scholarship News and New Ideas in Legal History* (www.legalhistory blogspot.com). Though the subtitle incorrectly slights the role of Linda Coffee, Sarah Weddington's memoir of the legal battle is balanced and incisive: *A Question of Choice: By the Lawyer Who Won "Roe v. Wade"* (New York: Penguin, 1993). For Cecile Richards's stature as an adult, see Jill Lepore's "Birthright: What's Next for Planned Parenthood?" in the *New Yorker*, November 14, 2011.

In an interview, Richard Moya told me how Ann and Claire Korioth raised money for his race for the Travis County Commissioners' Court and the legislative race of Gonzalo Barrientos. For Ann's description of her experience when asked to serve as Weddington's legislative chief of staff, see *Straight from the Heart*, 144–145. Doug Zabel granted me access to the priceless correspondence he carried on with Ann when they were legislative aides.

Chapter 7: Landslides. For Ann's recruitment to run as a Travis County commissioner and the campaign, see *Straight from the Heart*, 152–161, and *Once Upon a Time*, 151–153. In conversations, Gary Cartwright and Carlton Carl contributed their perspectives about that race. The how-to workbook published by the National Women's Education Fund is in the Richards Papers. For how David's federal court-shopping and Bob Bullock's testimony enabled the student voting that helped Ann's campaign, see *Once Upon a Time*, 154–160, and Dave McNeely and Jim Henderson, *Bob Bullock*, 68–69. Clark Richards told me about the last day of his mother's winning campaign. Ann's note of thanks to Bud Shrake for a contribution is in the Richards Papers.

For Ann's story about the resentful road crew and how she broke the ice by asking about their ugly dog, see *Straight from the Heart*, 163–165. Jan Jarboe Russell wrote about Ann's change in apparel and style on being elected commissioner in "Ann's Plans," *Texas Monthly*, July 1992. Jane Hickie's descriptions of the early days of working for Ann at the county are in the Richards Papers. Gary Cartwright wrote about the pitched battle between Austin developers and environmentalists in "High Noon at the Circle C," *Texas Monthly*, May 1984. The most reliable information on the construction of the Percy Pennybacker Bridge on Austin's Loop 360 is found in the archives of the U.S. Department of Transportation, Federal Highway Administration. The bridge won the Excellence in Highway Design award in the first year of competition. Evelyn Wanda Jackson's work with Ann on the bridge project was noted in her *Austin American-Statesman* obituary in December 2011.

Chapter 8: Raw Deals. In an interview, Mary Beth Rogers told me about the National Women's Conference. For Ann's perspective on that conference, her enlistment in President Jimmy Carter's Advisory Committee for Women, and her unpleasant experience with Carter over the Equal Rights Amendment, see *Straight from the Heart*, 174–185. A concise and valuable chronology of the history of the ERA is on the National Organization for Women's website (www.now.org/issues/economic/cea/history.html).

David and other sources told me about Ann's affection for marijuana. David told me about the Chattooga River expedition and his growing alarm about Ann's drinking; also see *Once Upon a Time*, 215–216. Ann's letter to Bud Shrake about David's possible appointment to a federal appeals court is in the Shrake Papers, the Wittliff Collections. For the Richardses' reflections on their troubled marriage, see *Straight from the Heart*, 183–184, and *Once Upon a Time*, 213–216. Documents related to the Women in Texas History project and her correspondence at the commissioners' court are in the Richards Papers. The elaborate profile "Ann Richards: Laughing All the Way to the Bank: A Personal Account" was written by Roberta Starr for *Third Coast*, February 1984.

McNeely and Henderson's *Bob Bullock* is a well-researched biography and good portrayal of the mercurial career and personality of the comptroller and lieutenant governor. I also learned much about him from his former aides Chuck Bailey and John P. Moore and from stories relayed by David Richards. For the Richardses' very different experiences with Frank Erwin, see *Once Upon a Time*, 125–136, and *Straight from the Heart*, 202.

Chapter 9: Capsized. Dan Richards told me about Jane Hickie's insistence that Ann's drinking had reached a point requiring intervention, and Sue and Mike Sharlot added their perspectives. The Sharlots and David Richards allowed me to read painful

434   narratives that participants in the intervention had to compose and read aloud to her; also see *Straight from the Heart*, 203–211. Sue Sharlot shared Ann's fearful letter from Minnesota. Clark Richards told me that the "Family Week" at the hospital was torturous for him, as well. Dave McNeely, a participant, told me about the Richardses' last canoeing expedition through canyons of the Rio Grande. Ann's unsparing notes about her alcoholism for a speech are in the Richards Papers. Clark Richards told me about his then-troubled relationship with his mother and the "rage attacks" when she was drunk and he was a child.

Chapter 10: *The Class of '82*. I learned a great deal about the Democrats' surprising sweep of the elections in 1982 while working for land commissioner Garry Mauro. For a summary of George W. Bush's losing congressional race to Kent Hance, see Dubose, Reid, and Cannon, *Boy Genius*, 14–17. Bill Cryer, who worked in Bill Clements's campaign with Karl Rove, conveyed the shock of the GOP on losing every statewide office. For Bob Bullock's conduct as secretary of state and comptroller, and his eventual enrollment in "Drunk School," see McNeely and Henderson, *Bob Bullock*, 134–149. For the call from Bob Armstrong urging Ann Richards to run for treasurer and the ensuing scramble, see *Straight from the Heart*, 213–217. Dan Richards told me about his experience as her travel aide in that campaign. In the Richards Papers, campaign documents and in-house interviews of Jane Hickie at the Treasury describe the campaign and the surreal transition to the agency and office held by Warren G. Harding. A memo from Hickie detailing the financial contributions that enabled Ann's first statewide race is in the Richards Papers. The colorful history of the Treasury, including its eventual demise, is told in *The Handbook of Texas Online*.

Chapter 11: *Raise Money and Wait*. Nadine Eckhardt shared her correspondence with Ann about projections of her long-range political future. Ann's letter to Gary Cartwright is in the Richards Papers. A *Dallas Morning News* story related Ann's performance at a Dallas fund-raiser for Congressman Jim Mattox. Several staffers at the attorney general's office told me about David Richards's role when Mattox was fending off an indictment for commercial bribery; also see *Once Upon a Time*, 227–241. Bill Cryer's memo about Ann's prospects for higher office is in the Richards Papers. Ann's moving eulogy of Sam Whitten is in the Richards Papers.

Chapter 12: *Cheap Help*. Mary Beth Rogers told me about the extent of the staff's ignorance of finance when Ann won the election. Jane Hickie was the force behind in-house interviews conducted by both Lynn Whitten, a graduate student and intern at the Treasury, and the historian Ruthe Winegarten. *Third Coast* published several articles about Ann—in one, she shrugged off being known as an Austin liberal and professed to be serene about her separation and pending divorce from David. But Rogers told me about the weeping, screaming outburst in their adjoining offices when Ann learned David had filed the papers, which were withdrawn that time.

Interviews by the *Houston Chronicle*'s Barbara Karkabi and Ruthe Winegarten are in the Richards Papers. One interview, conducted by Winegarten as Ann was preparing to move out of her house on Red Bud Trail, relates her wariness toward the press, her exasperation with Walter Mondale and other Democratic presidential contenders in 1984, and her dismissal of press suggestions that she might be a vice presidential nominee that year. The letter that Ann wrote to her divorce lawyer is in the Richards Papers.

Chapter 13: Poker Faces. For Governor Mark White's explanation of his loss in the 1986 rematch with Bill Clements, see Brian McCall, *The Power of the Texas Governor*, 81–83. Dave McNeely, then a reporter for the *Austin American-Statesman*, told me about Clements's embarrassing involvement in the SMU football scandal. Having started writing speeches for Garry Mauro, I gained an unexpected outlook on the practices of the FBI and the fear that investigation struck even in the heart of Bob Bullock; I contributed these conversations and impressions to *Boy Genius*, 38–41. Mary Beth Rogers and Bill Cryer shared their differing views of Ann's plans for the election of 1990. Steve Hall told me the story and shared his diary entry of the day Jim Mattox had reason to believe he had bluffed Bill Hobby out of the governor's race. Bob Bullock's friendly note of advice to Ann is in the Richards Papers.

Chapter 14: The Speech. Ann's correspondence with Bud Shrake about her periodontal surgery and his growing fondness for her is in the Richards Papers. Bill Cryer told me about the call from Ann that she had been invited to deliver the keynote speech at the Democratic National Convention in 1988; also see *Straight from the Heart*, 11–32. Cryer and Mary Beth Rogers told me about the marathon speech-writing sessions in Atlanta. The shifting drafts of the speech, the encouraging notes from Bud Shrake, the critique of the speech and recommendations on delivery by Kirk Adams, the rave in the *New Yorker*, Erma Bombeck's column, Patricia Kilday Hart's *Texas Monthly* story about Ann's heightened gubernatorial prospects, Adam Perlman's *Boston Globe* profile of Donna Alexander, and Ann's letter to Shrake at the end of the Dukakis campaign are all in the Richards Papers.

Chapter 15: Dispatches. Doatsy Shrake told me about the end of her marriage to Bud. For details of Shrake's near-fatal health breakdown and the necessity of ending his alcohol and drug abuse, see Davis, *Land of the Permanent Wave*, 258–259. More revealing is the interview that Shrake granted Brant Bingamon and his direction to a passage in his novel *Custer's Brother's Horse*, 259–260. Ann and Bud's lively correspondence, Ann's speech at the roast of Bum Phillips, Suzanne Coleman's unsigned memo when she feared Ann was losing heart for what lay ahead, and the vicious anonymous letter to Baptist ministers and newspaper editors are in the Richards Papers. George Shipley told me about Ann's meeting with Henry Cisneros before she decided to run for governor.

Chapter 16: Backyard Brawl. Her campaign manager, Glenn Smith, contributed an extensive and insightful interview concerning the 1990 Democratic primary. Monte Williams, Dorothy Browne, and I took part in the boat trip that launched Ann's campaign for governor. The correspondence between Ann and Bud Shrake, Ellen Richards's letter to a disenchanted supporter, and Mark McKinnon's memo on capital punishment are in the Richards Papers.

Chapter 17: Answer the Question. In interviews, Glenn Smith, Dan Richards, Mary Beth Rogers, and Chris Hughes offered perspectives on the brutal turn in the 1990 campaign.

Jane Hickie's proprietary claim and Mark White's protest about the controversial television ad about pockets being lined are in McCall, *The Power of the Texas Governor*, 96. Newspaper clippings about the race's outcome are in the Richards Papers. For David Richards's retrospective on Mattox, "Junkyard Jim," see the *Texas Observer*, December 12, 2009.

Chapter 18: Bustin' Rocks. Clayton Williams offered the biographical sketch in announcing his campaign. For information on his family, see *Handbook of Texas Online*. Gary Cartwright's article on his ranching success, "The Last Roundup," appeared in *Texas Monthly*, July 1986. Extensive newspaper clippings about his GOP primary race and gaffes in the general election are in the Richards Papers. Jan Jarboe's campaign profile, "Clayton Williams: Onward to the Past," was published in *Texas Monthly*, October 1990. Sources for the passages about Kay Bailey Hutchison and Rick Perry are their official websites and the extensive collection of newspaper clippings in the Richards Papers. George W. Bush's fund-raising letter in behalf of Williams is in the Richards Papers.

Chapter 19: The Rodeo. Continued correspondence with Bud Shrake that lifted Ann's spirits in the long-shot comeback is in the Richards Papers. In interviews, Glenn Smith, Mary Beth Rogers, and George Shipley described the transition of campaign managers, opposition research into Williams's business record, and the "fraudulent honking goose" episode. Ann's recollections about being inspired by the old woman in La Joya, news stories and correspondence related to the downfall of Jim Hightower, and the excited correspondence between Ann and Bud at the end of the race are in the Richards Papers. Also see Molly Ivins, "How Ann Richards Got to Be Governor of Texas," in *Molly Ivins Can't Say That, Can She?*, 275–284.

Chapter 20: The New Texas. Warm correspondence between Ann and Bud Shrake continued after the election. In interviews, Mary Beth Rogers described the sessions on South Padre Island, where the inner circle turned their attention from campaigning to governing. I took part in the march down Congress Avenue the morning of her inaugural speech and witnessed the encounter between the new gubernatorial staff of Ann and the departing one of Bill Clements. Abundant newspaper clippings and Bud Shrake's remarks on his nervousness about waltzing bolstered my observations of the inaugural balls.

Chapter 21: Fast Start. In one of our conversations, David Richards reflected on the unlikely nature of Ann's election. Richard Moya, Joy Anderson, and Joe Holley told me how they became members the governor's staff. I witnessed Ann's appointments of Ellen Halbert, Selden Hale, Josh Allen, and John Hall; Hale told me about taking Ann on a tour of Amarillo's prison. Joe Holley's *A Blueprint for the New Texas* and the State of the State address he crafted with Suzanne Coleman are in the Richards Papers, as are the resignation letter of James Saxton and details of Ann's order of a moratorium on new hazardous-waste permits.

Chapter 22: Ethicists. Paul Burka's rhapsodic "Ann of a Hundred Days" ran in *Texas Monthly*, May 1991. Newspaper clippings on the rejected nomination of Karl Rove and Ann's appointment of Terry Hershey to the board of the Texas Parks and Wildlife Department are in the Richards Papers, as are the different views of Ann, District Attorney Ronnie Earle, and Barbara Jordan on the worth of the ethics bill of 1991. Also in the Richards Papers is Ann's speech at the Waco reunion of the Texas Rangers.

Chapter 23: Odd Couples. Correspondence between Ann and Bud Shrake on movies, laughs, and love are in the Richards Papers. The reception for Queen Elizabeth and Prince Philip and the seating arrangements at the formal dinner are detailed at length in the Richards Papers. On the income tax proposal and the uproar that followed, see McNeely and Henderson, *Bob Bullock,* 174–175 and 184–185. On the consolidation of environmental agencies and the initiatives regarding clean air and natural gas, see the Richards Papers. Also, I was much involved in these matters while writing speeches and research papers for Garry Mauro and John Hall, and I have continued to follow the evolution of these areas. On the lieutenant governor's bullying of Andy Sansom, see *Bob Bullock,* 228–229; I also interviewed Sansom about that and his relationship with the governor. For the lieutenant governor's near fistfight with Dan Morales over redistricting, see *Bob Bullock,* 213–214. For the exasperation of his chief of staff, see *Bob Bullock,* 206–207 and 224–225. In interviews, Mary Beth Rogers and Chuck Bailey told me about the breakdown in relations between the governor and lieutenant governor. Chuck Bailey and Dave McNeely told me about the meeting with Bullock that Ann left in furious tears.

Chapter 24: Favorables. A video clip of Morley Safer's October 1991 *60 Minutes* profile of Ann is in the Richards Papers, along with the poll conducted by Harrison Hickman and interpreted by Matthew Dowd and Mary Beth Rogers. Molly Ivins's admiration of Ann's former husband is conveyed in "David Richards," in *Who Let the Dogs In?,* 163–165. Extensive files full of details on prison policy and the *Ruiz* lawsuit are in the Richards Papers, along with details of the murderous rampage of Kenneth McDuff. In addition to material found in the Richards Papers, Dorothy Browne briefed me extensively and shared documents on the launch of the most ambitious drug and alcohol treatment program in the nation's prisons. Ann's "Texas Facts" and "Texas Commitment" drives to bring new industries and jobs to Texas and prevent the closing of a General Motors plant, the stated approval of her probusiness outlook by Ken Lay, and her speech in support of NAFTA are in the Richards Papers. Mike Sharlot told me about the vacation at the Pacific retreat of Mexican president Carlos Salinas de Gortari.

Chapter 25: White Hot. In an interview, Marlene Saritzky told me about meeting Ann and taking her to meet helpful people in Hollywood before she had become a national figure, and about Ann's subsequent hiring of her as the Texas film commissioner. The Ann Richards roast in Port Arthur may be viewed in the C-SPAN Video Library, December 29, 1991. In the Richards Papers are details of Bud Shrake's commitment to write *Harvey Penick's Little Red Book* and newspaper clippings about Ann's barbed joke about President George H. W. Bush at the Washington Gridiron Show. Files in the Richards Papers tell the story of DJ Stout's brainstorm to put Ann on the July 1992 cover of *Texas Monthly* in white leather, riding a Harley-Davidson, and the star treatment Ann received in New York at the Democratic National Convention that nominated Bill Clinton and Al Gore. David Gergen's mention of the *Texas Monthly* cover and Wayne Slater's *Dallas Morning News* story about her arrival at Madison Square Garden are in the Richards Papers.

Chapter 26: Heartaches by the Number. Bud Shrake's letter to Ann about folly and the Trojan horse, along with details of the downfall of Lena Guerrero, are in the Richards Papers; especially vivid are the description of the incident by Chuck McDonald, as told to

438   Karl Rove biographers Wayne Slater and James Moore in *Bush's Brain: How Karl Rove Made George W. Bush Presidential* (New York: Wiley, 2004), and Barbara Jordan's stern criticism of Guerrero's ethical behavior in an interview by the *Austin American-Statesman*. Also in the Richards Papers are files on the scandal involving National Guard colonels Richard Brito and Danny Kohler. Dorothy Browne witnessed Ann's demand that Selden Hale resign for ordering prison system employees to investigate another board member's possible ethics conflict.

    Chapter 27: Troubles by the Score. In an interview, George Shipley told me about Ann's ill-fated attempt to appoint Henry Cisneros to fill the U.S. Senate seat of Lloyd Bentsen, whom Bill Clinton had appointed his secretary of the treasury. Details related to her eventual appointment of former congressman Bob Krueger and his eloquent memorandum of support for her positions on women's choice and stem-cell research are in the Richards Papers. For the *New York Times* coverage of Kay Bailey Hutchison's rout of Krueger in the ensuing special election and Jane Hickie's amusement about Krueger's appointment as ambassador to Burundi, see McCall, *The Power of the Texas Governor*, 108–109. For his brave and vindicating performance as U.S. ambassador during the genocide in central Africa, see Krueger and Krueger, *From Bloodshed to Hope in Burundi*, 87–174.

    The *Houston Press* and the *New York Times* detailed charges against Senator Hutchison in the indictment for official misconduct in February 1994. For Ann's response to the indictment, see Paul Burka, "Sadder But Wiser," *Texas Monthly*, April 1994. A GOP counterattack orchestrated by Karen Hughes resulted in an embarrassing memo about the improper use of telephones to Governor's Office employees by the chief of staff, John Fainter, which is in the Richards Papers. Dick DeGuerin shared some details about his defense of Senator Hutchison. Also there are numerous press clippings that relate District Attorney Ronnie Earle's apparent missteps that led to the ordered verdict of acquittal by the trial judge.

    Chapter 28: Sass. I heard the newly elected governor George W. Bush blame Patrick Buchanan for his father's defeat in a 1994 meeting with reporters. In an interview, attorney Shelton Smith told me about his lobbying in Washington for Ann in behalf of the Superconducting Super Collider and the meeting with President Clinton in which she threatened to sue him if Texas's investment in the project was not returned. Ann's difficulties with environmentalists, property-rights activists, and the federal Department of the Interior are detailed at length in the Richards Papers.

    The governor and Bud Shrake kept their romance alive throughout these governmental difficulties, as demonstrated by letters in the Richards Papers. The GOP barrage of open-records requests and press releases written by Karen Hughes are in the Richards Papers. Former Texas Ranger Joaquin Jackson e-mailed me about his amusing dustup with Governor Richards. Chief of Staff John Fainter kept an unsigned diary of the Branch Davidian standoff and tragedies. Also, Dick DeGuerin, who met with David Koresh and tried to negotiate a peaceful settlement, shared his perspective on the tragedy with me, as did an FBI agent who took part in the siege and assault. John P. Moore told me of his belief that the relationship of Ann and Bullock was damaged beyond repair when she led an invasion of reporters into his office to demand his position on the concealed-weapons bill.

Chapter 29: Collision Course. I learned details of the combat career of the young bomber pilot George H.W. Bush in official records of the U.S. Navy. George W. Bush wrote about his fury over a *Newsweek* cover depicting his father as a reputed "wimp" in *Decision Points,* 43–44. The Richards Papers contain abundant files on George W. Bush's career as an oilman. In an interview, Bob Beaudine told me about Bush's uncertainty about challenging Ann and his request to help him win the job as commissioner of Major League Baseball; also see Beaudine, *The Power of Who* (New York: Center Street, 2009), 6–9. Mary Beth Rogers told me about the totally different feel of the campaign and the performance of the candidate in 1994. The Richards Papers include a file labeled "The Jane Hickie Problem," which includes her apology to rock star Don Henley in 1989, as well as *Houston Post* editorials alleging misconduct and calling for her resignation as director of the Office of State-Federal Relations. Samples of the correspondence Molly Ivins received, along with an undated, affectionate letter she wrote to Ann, are in the Molly Ivins Papers, in the Dolph Briscoe Center for American History. In an interview, Chuck Bailey discounted conjecture that Bullock helped Bush in his campaign against Ann. For Bullock's long-held grudge against Barbara Jordan, see *Bob Bullock,* 85–88, and for his grudge against Max Sherman for the same reason, see *Bob Bullock,* 249–250. In an interview, George Shipley criticized Ann's coterie of feminists, blaming them for failing to court Bullock's favor, but said they were all at fault for underestimating the Bushes' CIA-related skill in running a negative campaign.

Chapter 30: Queen Bee. In interviews, Mary Beth Rogers told me about George W. Bush's early stumbles, and Joe Holley related his discomfort with how Ann's inner circle operated and her apparent lack of fervor about winning another term. Ann's increasingly defensive speeches are in the Richards Papers, along with details of her record on capital punishment. The letter of rebuke from Enron's Ken Lay and the internal memos about Bill Ratliff's denunciation of the appointment of "homosexual activists" are in the Richards Papers; John Ratliff's unsigned summary of Bush and Rove's campaign tactics in the 2000 presidential race is in Dubose, Reid, and Cannon, *Boy Genius,* 133–143. The progression of the polls and reports on the debate between Ann and George W. Bush are in the Richards Papers. R. G. Ratcliffe e-mailed me about the story he didn't get to file about Howard Pharr. Details of Karl Rove's allegations, along with verified highlights of the Bush-Richards debate, can be found in Wayne Slater's online columns for the *Dallas Morning News.* In interviews, Mary Beth Rogers told me that she and Ann knew the race was likely lost when Ann called Bush "a jerk" in Texarkana; Karl Rove shared their opinion. Molly Ivins wrote about the incident and Ann's prospects in a column reprinted as "Ann Richards vs. Shrub II," in *Who Let the Dogs In?,* 171–173. Harold Cook told me about having to bring her the news she had lost. Slater attributes the poignant telephone conversation between the Bushes to Karl Rove in an online *Dallas Morning News* column.

In an article for *Time,* Hugh Sidey recorded George H. W. Bush's exultation about his son's payback for that insult about the silver spoon. Dorothy Browne shared the letter from the woman in Midland who wrote thanking Ann for the prison alcohol and drug abuse program that saved her son's life. Bud Shrake told me about Frito-Lay's offer of a million dollars to be in the Super Bowl commercial with Mario Cuomo, and Marlene

440   Saritzky told me about accompanying Ann on the Doritos video shoot in California and being with Ann on her last day as governor.

Epilogue: Passages. Jim Henson shared the transcript of his incisive interview with Ann when she was seventy. I located Maureen Dowd's Christmas Eve 1997 column excoriating Ann and former senators George Mitchell and Howard Baker for accepting high-dollar fees from tobacco companies. My examination of Ann's lobbying activities is drawn from extensive, multisource research of the tobacco suit and its settlement; see especially the *New York Times*, December 15, 1997, and Public Citizen, "Burning Down the Houses: Big Tobacco's 1997 Congressional Lobbying," March 1998, http://www.citizen.org/congress/article_redirect.cfm?ID=908. Robert Bryce detailed the New Jersey wetlands-development dispute and lobbying in "Shattered Icon," *Austin Chronicle*, October 24, 1997. Cecile Richards told me about the joy Ann experienced in traveling the world with her children. Shawn Morris told me about accompanying Ann to a speech to Democrats in Pueblo, Colorado, and Texas House representative Mark Strama wrote to Morris about Ann's arrangement of a fund-raiser for him in New York. In the Richards Papers, I found Ann's 1994 speech to the Southern Conference on Women's History.

Dorothy Browne told me about Ann's heart-rending call seeking an internship for a young woman she didn't know the morning after she was diagnosed with esophageal cancer. The letters of consolation and encouragement from Senators Hillary Clinton and Barack Obama, President George W. Bush, Governor Rick Perry and First Lady Anita Perry, and Katie Couric are in the Richards Papers, as are her note to former secretary of state Madeleine Albright and her correspondence with her first love and husband of twenty-nine years, David Richards. Clark Richards told me about how her strength and resistance failed in six months in spite of her hope and the skill and treatment of doctors at M.D. Anderson.

I attended the memorial ceremonies in Austin, where Bill Clinton consoled Ann's children and I met former senator Bob Kerrey and spoke with Molly Ivins. An account of her wilderness experience in the Grand Canyon with David and Sandy Richards and Brady Coleman is in Ellen Sweets, *Stirring It Up with Molly Ivins: A Memoir with Recipes* (Austin: Univ. of Texas Press, 2011), 239–240. I heard the humorous tales of Hillary Clinton and Lily Tomlin and the self-assured eulogy of Ann's granddaughter Lily Adams. Archivists of the Shrake Papers at the Wittliff Collections found the eloquent farewell Bud Shrake read at the grave site that morning; they also shared with me Shrake's e-mail interview by Brant Bingamon. Jeanne Goka described the mission of the Ann Richards School for Young Women Leaders in Julie Tereshchuk's "Jeanne Goka, In a Class All Her Own" in *Austin Woman*, August 2010. On a hot summer day, I visited the Texas State Cemetery, which Bob Bullock had made once again a place of beauty, and I stood alone for some moments before the graves of Bud and Ann, side by side in the shade of a live oak tree.

Photo Credits

101 Photo by Tad Hershorn.

107 Photo by David Stark.

110 Photo by Tad Hershorn.

120 Photo by Tad Hershorn.

135 Richards (Ann W.) Papers, di_07711, DBCAH.

136 Richards (Ann W.) Papers, CN# 10702, DBCAH.

138 Richards (Ann W.) Papers, di_07792, DBCAH.

145 Richards (Ann W.) Papers, di_07778, DBCAH.

154 Photo by Scott Newton, arranged by Doug Zabel.

157 Photo by Tad Hershorn.

162 Photo by Scott Newton.

164 Photo by Senate Media Services. Richards (Ann W.) Papers, di_07768, DBCAH.

174 Richards (Ann W.) Papers, di_07847, DBCAH.

183 Richards (Ann W.) Papers, di_07777, DBCAH.

192 Photo courtesy of Gary Cartwright.

202 Photo by Ave Bonar.

208 Photo by Lisa Davis, Associated Press. Richards (Ann W.) Papers, di_07774, DBCAH.

217 Photo by Ave Bonar. Richards (Ann W.) Papers, di_07739, DBCAH.

220 Photo by Tad Hershorn.

225 Photo by Tad Hershorn.

234 Photo by Ave Bonar. Richards (Ann W.) Papers, di_07736, DBCAH.

247 Photo by Alan Pogue.

253 Photo by Ave Bonar. Richards (Ann W.) Papers, di_00737, DBCAH.

256 Photo by Phillip Hamilton. Used with permission of *Plainview Daily-Herald*, Plainview, Texas.

259 Photo by Ave Bonar.

260 Richards (Ann W.) Papers, di_00753, DBCAH.

264 Photo by Tad Hershorn.

270 Photo by John Makely, *Houston Post*. Richards (Ann W.) Papers, di_07756, DBCAH.

272 Richards (Ann W.) Papers, di_07714, DBCAH.

277 Photo by Ave Bonar. Richards (Ann W.) Papers, di_07795, DBCAH.

286 Richards (Ann W.) Papers, di_07843, DBCAH.

289 Richards (Ann W.) Papers, di_07745, DBCAH.

296 Richards (Ann W.) Papers, di_07759, DBCAH.

312 Richards (Ann W.) Papers, di_07760, DBCAH.

323 Richards (Ann W.) Papers, di_07731, DBCAH.

328 Richards (Ann W.) Papers, di_07744, DBCAH.

334 Richards (Ann W.) Papers, di_07763, DBCAH.

342 Photo by Ave Bonar.

352 Photo by Shane Bowen. Richards (Ann W.) Papers, di_07721, DBCAH.

362 Richards (Ann W.) Papers, di_07772, DBCAH.

Index